SAGE was founded in 1965 by Sara Miller McCune to support the dissemination of usable knowledge by publishing innovative and high-quality research and teaching content. Today, we publish over 900 journals, including those of more than 400 learned societies, more than 800 new books per year, and a growing range of library products including archives, data, case studies, reports, and video. SAGE remains majority-owned by our founder, and after Sara's lifetime will become owned by a charitable trust that secures our continued independence.

Los Angeles | London | New Delhi | Singapore | Washington DC | Melbourne

PLANNING
AND
ECONOMICS
OF CITIES

PLANNING AND ECONOMICS OF CITIES

Shaping India's Form and Future

PRASANNA K. MOHANTY

Los Angeles | London | New Delhi
Singapore | Washington DC | Melbourne

First published in 2019 by

SAGE Publications India Pvt Ltd
B1/I-1 Mohan Cooperative Industrial Area
Mathura Road, New Delhi 110 044, India
www.sagepub.in

SAGE Publications Inc
2455 Teller Road
Thousand Oaks, California 91320, USA

SAGE Publications Ltd
1 Oliver's Yard, 55 City Road
London EC1Y 1SP, United Kingdom

SAGE Publications Asia-Pacific Pte Ltd
18 Cross Street #10-10/11/12
China Square Central
Singapore 048423

Published by Vivek Mehra for SAGE Publications India Pvt Ltd, typeset in 10.5/13 pts Bembo by Zaza Eunice, Hosur, Tamil Nadu, India and printed at Chaman Enterprises, New Delhi.

Library of Congress Cataloging-in-Publication Data

Name: Mohanty, P. K. (Prasanna Kumar), author.
Title: Planning and economics of cities: shaping India's form and future/
    by Prasanna K. Mohanty.
Description: New Delhi, India; Thousand Oaks, California: SAGE Publications
    India, 2019. | Includes bibliographical references and index.
Identifiers: LCCN 2018037967 | ISBN 9789352808687 (hbk) | ISBN 9789352808694
    (e-pub 2.0) | ISBN 9789352808700 (e-book)
Subjects: LCSH: City planning—India. | Regional planning—India. | Urban
    policy—India. | Urban economics.
Classification: LCC HT169.I5 M64 2019 | DDC 307.1/2160954—dc23 LC record available at https://
lccn.loc.gov/2018037967

ISBN: 978-93-528-0868-7 (HB)

SAGE Team: Rajesh Dey, Alekha Chandra Jena, Madhurima Thapa and Ritu Chopra

To

Smita, my wife

Thank you for choosing a SAGE product!
If you have any comment, observation or feedback,
I would like to personally hear from you.

Please write to me at **contactceo@sagepub.in**

Vivek Mehra, Managing Director and CEO, SAGE India.

Contents

List of Tables

List of Figures

List of Boxes

List of Abbreviations

4 Ts	transport, transaction, tariff and time
ALS	Area Licensing Scheme
AMRUT	Atal Mission for Rejuvenation and Urban Transformation
ANPR	Automated Number Plate Recognition
AONBs	Areas of Outstanding Natural Beauty
APCRDA	Andhra Pradesh Capital Region Development Authority
ARV	annual rental value
ASCI	Administrative Staff College of India
AUDA	Ahmedabad Urban Development Authority
BBMP	Bruhat Bengaluru Mahanagara Palike
BCR	benefit–cost ratio
BDA	Bengaluru Development Authority
BMR	Bengaluru Metropolitan Rail
BMRCL	Bengaluru Metro Rail Corporation Ltd
BoP	bottom of the pyramid
BRT	bus rapid transit
BRTS	Bus Rapid Transit System
BSUP	Basic Services to the Urban Poor
BWSSB	Bangalore Water Supply and Sewerage Board
CAGR	compounded annual growth rate
CBD	central business district
CC	congestion charging
CDP	city development plan
CEPAC	Certificate of Potential Additional Construction
CGG	Centre for Good Governance
CIP	capital improvement plan
CPWD	Central Public Works Department
CSP	community service personnel

CVM	*Comisao de Valores Mobiliarios*
DCRs	development control regulations
DDA	Delhi Development Authority
DE	development entity
DIFs	development impact fees
DMRC	Delhi Metro Rail Corporation
DP	development plan
DPC	District Planning Committee
DPRs	Detailed Project Reports
DRC	Development Right Certificate
DT&CP	Director of Town and Country Planning
DTP	Director of Town Planning
ECS	equivalent car space
EDC	external development charges
ERP	electronic road pricing
EUS	Employment and Unemployment Surveys
EWS	economically weaker sections
FAR	Floor Area Ratio
FDI	foreign direct investment
FSI	Floor Space Index
FUNDURB	*Fundo de Desenvolvimento Urbano*
GDA	Ghaziabad Development Authority
GDP	gross domestic product
GFN	group forming network
GHG	greenhouse gas
GHMC	Greater Hyderabad Municipal Corporation
GIS	geographic information system
GNCTD	Government of National Capital Territory of Delhi
GNI	gross national income
GoAP	Government of Andhra Pradesh
GoI	Government of India
GoUK	Government of the United Kingdom
GSDP	gross state domestic product
GST	goods and services tax
GTPUDA	Gujarat Town Planning and Urban Development Act
HDRUAA	Haryana Development and Regulation of Urban Areas Act

HGT	Henry George Theorem
HIG	high-income group
HMDA	Hyderabad Metropolitan Development Authority
HPEC	High Powered Expert Committee
HSR	high-speed rail
HTF	Highway Trust Fund
HUDA	Haryana Urban Development Authority
IBM	International Business Machines
ICT	information and communication technology
IDC	infrastructure development charge
IDP	inclusive development plan
IH	inclusionary housing
IHSDP	Integrated Housing and Slum Development Programme
ILO	International Labour Office
IQ	intelligence quotient
IZ	inclusionary zoning
JAY	Jan Awas Yojana
JDM	joint development mechanism
JJ	jhuggi jhopri
JNNURM	Jawaharlal Nehru National Urban Renewal Mission
KMC	Karnataka municipal corporations
LA	land acquisition
LAC	Land Acquisition Collector
LAP	local area planning
LBT	local body tax
LDDs	local development documents
LGT	land gains tax
LIG	low-income groups
lpcpd	litres per capita per day
LPP	land pooling policy
LPS	land pooling scheme
LVC	land value capture
LVIT	land value increment tax
LVT	land value tax
MCGM	Municipal Corporation of Greater Mumbai
MDGs	Millennium Development Goals

MGNREGA	Mahatma Gandhi National Rural Employment Guarantee Act
MHRD	Ministry of Human Resource Development
MHT	Mohring–Harwitz Theorem
MIG	middle-income group
MIS	management information system
MIZ	Mandatory Inclusionary Zoning
MMRDA	Mumbai Metropolitan Region Development Authority
MoF	Ministry of Finance
MoH	Ministry of Health
MOHUPA	Ministry of Housing & Urban Poverty Alleviation
MoRTH	Ministry of Road Transport & Highways
MoSPI	Ministry of Statistics and Programme Implementation
MoUD	Ministry of Urban Development
MPD	Master Plan of Delhi
MRT	mass rapid transit
MRTS	Mass Rapid Transit System
MTA	mass transit account
NDMA	National Disaster Management Authority
NEG	new economic geography
NGT	new growth theory
NIUM	National Institute of Urban Management
NMT	non-motorized transport
NOIDA	New Okhla Industrial Development Authority
NSS	National Sample Survey
NSSO	National Sample Survey Office
NUHHP	National Urban Housing and Habitat Policy
NUTP	National Urban Transport Policy
OECD	Organisation for Economic Co-operation and Development
O&M	operation and maintenance
OODC	*Outorga Onerosa do Direito de Construir*
OP	original plot
PDE	*Plano Diretor Estrategico*
PFSI	premium FSI

phpdt	per hour per direction traffic
PPP	public–private partnership
PT	public transport
PTC	private trip cost
R-AH	residential affordable housing
RDP	road development plan
R + P	rail plus property
RRTS	Rapid Rail Transit System
R&R	rehabilitation and resettlement
RSS	regional spatial strategies
SAS	self-assessment scheme
SCGE	spatial computable general equilibrium
SDGs	Sustainable Development Goals
SEBI	Securities Exchange Board of India
SEWS	socially and economically weaker sections
SIA	social impact assessment
SMC	Surat Municipal Corporation
SRA	Slum Rehabilitation Authority
SRS	Slum Rehabilitation Scheme
SSSIs	Sites of Special Scientific Interests
STC	social trip cost
SVR	site value rating
SWOT	strengths, weaknesses, opportunities and threats
TCPO	Town and Country Planning Organisation
TDM	transport demand management
TDR	transferable development right
TFP	total factor productivity
TIF	tax increment financing
TND	traditional neighbourhood design
TOD	transit-oriented development
TPO	Town Planning Officer
TPS	town planning scheme
TSM	transportation system management
UA	urban agglomeration
UAM	unit area method
UAV	unit area value

UDPFI	Urban Development Plans Formulation and Implementation
UIDSSMT	Urban Infrastructure Development Scheme for Small and Medium Towns
UIG	Urban Infrastructure and Governance
ULBs	urban local bodies
ULCRA	Urban Land (Ceiling & Regulation) Act
UNEP	United Nations Environment Programme
UOs	Urban Operations
URDPFI	Urban and Regional Development Plans Formulation and Implementation
USEPA	United States Environmental Protection Agency
UT	urban transport
VCF	value capture financing
VIF	value increment financing
VLT	vacant land tax
VoIP	Voice over Internet Protocol
WEB	wider economic benefits
WIEGO	Women in Informal Employment: Globalizing and Organizing
YEIDA	Yamuna Expressway Industrial Development Authority
ZDP	zonal development plan
ZQA	Zoning for Quality and Affordability

Preface

Planned urban development will be a vehicle for India's transformation to a developed nation. Economically efficient, socially inclusive, environmentally sustainable and financially viable cities will drive the country to prosperity. Agglomeration and network externalities of urban areas will present cost-effective ways to accelerate growth and reduce poverty. India needs to invest in planning and development of cities to speed up structural, spatial and socio-economic transformation processes. The country must harness the synergy between land, transport and urban economics and spatial planning to avail the opportunities unleashed by the Urban Revolution. Dense, diverse and networked cities, distinguished by their land use intensities, transportation and communication grids and economic growth drivers will shape India's form and future.

The Government of India has launched the Smart Cities Mission with the objective to promote sustainable and inclusive urban development. Smart cities will provide infrastructure that uses 'smart' solutions to improve civic services. They will create models for replication by other cities. Effective planning and management of urban land and transport will be critical for the success of smart cities. These strategies will be the keys to make serviced land and floor space available in tune with the demands of economic growth. Land is essential for workplaces, housing, recreation and infrastructure facilities such as highways, rail-based transit, water supply, sewerage, storm water drainage, parks and playgrounds. It is also critical for accommodating the poor, who are driven out of the formal urban land market as well as the urban planning system. Transportation is the single-most important factor to service land and enhance the working efficiency of cities. Transport–land use integration is the principal instrument available with planners to avoid the unplanned development of cities that results in sprawl, uneconomic extension of infrastructure, slums, environmental degradation and segregation between the rich and the poor. However, Indian cities have not benefitted from such integration due to the inadequacies of 'master planning' and neglect of investment in urban public transport for long. The issues are closely connected with the abysmal state of urban finance and governance. The country must adopt 'smart' ways of planning, financing and governing cities.

This book draws lessons from theory and practice to suggest reforms in master planning in India—by cities, in general, and smart cities, in particular. Our objective is not to present generalizations based on a limited analysis of data gathered from a handful of cities. We refer to known principles and practices that have worked in India and elsewhere. The book calls for incorporating the economics of cities into the urban planning model. It is meant to assist students, teachers and researchers in urban economics, regional and urban planning, land economics, transport economics and related fields, and officials of urban local bodies, urban development authorities and other government agencies in analysing the key urban issues of contemporary significance. It is also meant to guide policymakers at the local, state and national levels in the design of urban planning and policy.

The present volume would not have been possible without the contribution from many practitioners and scholars. I have tried to combine my research with my own experience as the Municipal Commissioner of Visakhapatnam and Hyderabad cities, Vice-Chairman of Hyderabad Urban Development Authority, Director of Urban Development and Mission Director of Jawaharlal Nehru National Urban Renewal Mission in the Government of India. I recall the deliberations of a national workshop on 'Master Plan Approach: Its Efficacy and Alternatives', organized by the Ministry of Urban Development, Government of India, in 1995 with the support of the Town and Country Planning Organisation (TCPO). Based on the recommendations of the workshop, the 'Urban Development Plans Formulation and Implementation (UDPFI) Guidelines' were framed by TCPO in 1996. Taking subsequent developments into account, the Government of India has issued 'Urban and Regional Development Plans Formulation and Implementation (URDPFI) Guidelines 2014'. Although the new guidelines are laudable, it is felt that the incorporation of the economics of cities would significantly improve the efficacy of urban planning as an instrument to promote efficient, equitable, sustainable and financially viable cities. This is the primary motivation behind the book.

I am grateful to Professor Jeffrey Williamson of Harvard University, Professor Jerry Rothenberg of the Massachusetts Institute of Technology and Professors John Harris, Kevin Lang and Michael Riordan of Boston University who taught me the fundamentals of urban economics. I thank Dr Isher Judge Ahluwalia, Professors O. P. Mathur, Abhay Pethe, Chetan Vaidya, Jagan Shah, S. K. Kulshrestha, Sivanand Swamy, Darshini Mahadevia and Neelima Risbud, and Shri S. Viswanath, D. S. Meshram and J. B. Kshirsagar for contributing to my understanding of the key issues of urban planning and development in India. I also thank Dr Alok Kumar Mishra, who teaches Urban Economics and Transport Economics along with me at the University of Hyderabad, for valuable suggestions. I acknowledge the support provided by Mr Shabbeer Sheikh, Director, Urban Management Group at the Centre for Good Governance (CGG), Hyderabad; Bhaskara, Ravi Rohan, Gowthami, Vinay and Kiran at the National Institute of Urban Management (NIUM), Hyderabad; and Namrata, Shibani, Prerna, Saloni and Tulika at the School of Economics, University of Hyderabad, in data compilation and analytical support.

I hope the book will contribute in bridging the divide between urban planning and economics to accord a rightful place to the city in India's structural transformation process and transition to a developed country.

Prasanna K. Mohanty

1

Planning and Economics of Cities
An Overview

India must harness the opportunity ushered in by the Urban Revolution. Nothing else will bring so much benefit to people as urbanization. Dense, diverse, networked and dynamic cities will shape India's form and future. The country must integrate the planning and economics of cities to harness urbanization as a national resource.

India's urban population, estimated at 410 million in 2014, is projected to reach 814 million by 2050. The country will have three times as much population in cities and towns in the next 75 years. With about 860 million residing in villages in 2014, projected to reduce only marginally to 810 million by 2050, India will urbanize in the presence of huge problems of development in rural areas (United Nations 2015). Rural–urban migration, annexation of rural areas to existing urban boundaries and in-situ transformation of villages into towns will be amongst the key factors fuelling urban growth. Providing land, housing, workplace, infrastructure and services to the large numbers in cities and towns, existing and to be added, is a daunting task for policymakers and planners in India. In particular, affordable housing, transport and basic amenities to the urban poor, including slum-dwellers, accounting for more than a quarter of urban residents, pose major challenges. The issues are critical as cities are the engines of economic growth, providers of employment to millions in formal and informal sectors and generators of public finance for socio-economic development, including rural and urban poverty reduction. The number at the bottom of the urban pyramid is so large that even a small improvement in their productivity due to public policy would make a big difference to gross domestic product (GDP) and national welfare.

Cities and towns in India, containing about 3 per cent of the country's geographical area, contributed 62–63 per cent of GDP in 2007. This contribution is projected to rise to 75 per cent by 2021 (Planning Commission 2008). Cities will create 70 per cent of all new jobs over the next two decades. They will generate 80–85 per cent of tax revenues of governments. However, the country will need ₹9.74 million crores for investment in affordable housing and infrastructure over a period of 20 years to sustain the contribution of cities (McKinsey Global Institute 2010). Cities cannot discharge their fundamental role as drivers of economic and social transformation, unless they are firmly in position to meet the 'backlog', 'current' and 'growth' needs of firms and households for land, floor space and public services. Regional and urban planning, infrastructure development, energy security, environmental sustainability, social equity and housing affordability are amongst the key issues in India's urban transition. These are particularly important for 'smart' cities, which are expected to act as 'lighthouses' and present replicable models to guide other cities.

The Smart Cities Mission in India aims at robust models of urban development based on smart plans, projects, processes and solutions. The Government of India (GoI) will invest ₹100 crores annually in each of the 100 smart cities for five years; states and urban local bodies (ULBs) will mobilize an equivalent amount or more. These sums are expected to catalyze further funding from internal and external sources of cities to implement 'area-based' and 'pan-city' programmes. Area-based models include city improvement or retrofitting, city renewal or redevelopment and city extension or green field development. Pan-city models include projects having citywide implications. Procuring land for planned urban development, integrating transportation and land use, creating floor space in tune with the demands of economic growth, leveraging central and state funds with local revenues and market borrowings to finance infrastructure, especially transportation, and making urban development equitable and sustainable are amongst the key challenges of smart cities. Electronic networking and software solutions alone will not lead to enduring outcomes. They must be accompanied by hard-core reforms in the systems of urban planning, financing and governance. These reforms call for understanding the economics of cities and the reasons why economic activities continue to localize in spite of globalization and revolution in information and communication technology (ICT).

Contrary to the belief of scholars like Thomas Friedman (2006) that a globalizing and electronically networked world is decreasing the role of geography, the spatial concentration of economic activity in city regions continues to be overwhelming—in both developed and developing countries. Urban areas contribute more than 80 per cent of the GDP in South Asia and worldwide (World Bank 2015). The top 750 cities of the world contribute 57 per cent of the global GDP, and their share would rise to 61 per cent by 2030 (Oxford Economics 2017). The largest 123 metropolitan areas account for 8 per cent of global population, but more than one-third of economic output (Brookings Institution 2015). The trends in localization of growth suggest that new technology is strengthening the forces of agglomeration in cities rather than weakening them. It is enhancing the returns to face-to-face contact and collaboration. This is particularly so in developing countries like India where cities are the centres of human capital accumulation, nurseries of new ideas, hubs of innovation and platforms for application of new technology. The economic significance of cities derives from their agglomeration and network externalities.

Economic activities collocate and network. Agglomeration economies, occurring on the supply side, arise from the clustering of firms, households and institutions in cities. They manifest in the benefits of higher productivity and lower transaction costs. They reduce the costs of moving goods, people, information, ideas and knowledge. Network economies arising on the demand side are linked to the use, integration and merger of networks, including transportation, communication and knowledge. Agglomeration and network externalities lead to economies of learning, sharing and matching (Duranton and Puga 2004). Small market towns generate scale economies in marketing and distribution of agricultural inputs and outputs. Medium-sized cities catalyze localization economies of manufacturing and specialization, acting as technological enclaves. Large cities offer urbanization economies associated with market size, diversity and innovation. Metropolitan city regions combine the benefits of specialization, diversity, competition and networking. They attract a large variety of skilled activities and act as breeding grounds of new ideas, practices and products. The economies of cities are closely connected with land use, density, and backward and forward linkages between economic activities. Urban land, with its horizontal and vertical dimensions, lies at the core of agglomeration; transportation is the key to networking. A good system of regional and urban transportation enhances 'accessibility' to the economic mass and catalyzes 'wider economic benefits (WEB)'.

Spatial transformation accompanies structural transformation. Cities propel growth as an economy specializes in secondary and tertiary production. For these activities, not only scale but also location matters. In particular, high-tech manufacturing and knowledge-based services locate in city regions to gain from the processes of generation, transmission and diffusion of knowledge. The externalities of cities create multipliers for growth through direct, indirect and induced effects. They enable firms to benefit at a stage of development when the scarcity of physical and human capital favours the spatial concentration of economic growth. They also facilitate the mobilization of public finance for development by taxing 'agglomeration rents'. The externalities of cities are, however, not without limits. When the concentration of economic activities in a node or carrying capacity of a network exceeds a threshold, congestion externalities creep in. Diseconomies of agglomeration manifest in overcrowding, sprawl, deterioration in public services, wastage of resources, traffic congestion, pollution, slums, poverty, crime, social unrest, vulnerability to disasters and the like. Density also leads to public health hazards, including spread of communicable diseases. Globally, cities account for 75 per cent of the consumption of natural resources, 80 per cent of energy supply and 75 per cent of carbon emissions (United Nations Environment Programme [UNEP] 2015; UN-Habitat 2016).

Urban land occupies a central place in the socio-economic transformation of a developing country. It is an input, an output and also a resource to finance urban development. Serviced land is essential to address the needs of an ever-expanding urban population. It provides a platform for economic growth to occur. It is instrumental in avoiding the unplanned expansion of cities. It is the key to inclusive urbanization and addressing the needs of the urban poor, including slum-dwellers. Transport plays a pivotal role in servicing land, unifying labour markets and matching jobs and skills. It extends product markets, increases competition, expands labour market choices, balances employment and housing, enables the formation of economic agglomerations and enhances the tax bases of governments. Transportation grids and land use densities define the morphology of a city. Transportation and land use integration has been the principal instrument adopted by developed countries during their urban transition to enhance the positive effects of urbanization and mitigate its negative consequences. However, Indian cities have not been able to exploit the benefits of such integration due to their fragmented approach to land use and transportation planning.

Cities in India face constraints of serviced land and floor space due to ill-functioning land and housing markets, faulty model of urban planning to address market failure and irrational restrictions on land use and floor space index (FSI) or floor area ratio (FAR), defined as permissible built-up area divided by plot area. The problems are compounded by increasing demand for land, fuelled by localization of growth, speculation in land market and lack of investment in infrastructure, especially transportation. Exorbitant pressure on urban land prices is making housing unaffordable to not only the poor and low-income segments but also the middle-income group (MIG). Excessive pressure on congested central locations is resulting in haphazard development. Unwarranted expansion of cities is leading to suboptimal land use, resulting in wasteful commuting, traffic congestion and severe strains on civic services. If unchecked, these trends will lead to serious environmental consequences for both urban and rural areas. They will result in unsustainable use of land, air, water and energy resources. Production of food grains will also suffer due to indiscriminate conversion of fertile agricultural land to urban use. Mounting pressure on the environment, linked to greenhouse gas (GHG) emissions will have global repercussions. A major negative social impact of unplanned urban development is segregation of the poor from the rich. This breeds social unrest and crime.

Many of the observed urban problems in India are rooted in the present models of urban planning, land management and infrastructure financing. Indian cities are under-planned, under-funded, under-managed and over-regulated. They lack plans to guide economic development. They are obsessed with physical control of land markets rather than enabling them to work for inclusive growth and sustainable development. They are plagued by the outdated 'master planning' model, which treats transportation as a 'residual' rather than a 'leading' force. Cities also suffer from gross under-investment in transportation infrastructure due to the failure of urban planning to present a coherent strategy of plan financing. Master planning has resulted in an utter scarcity of serviced land and floor space for value-creating activities, including affordable housing. The paradigm based on the Town and Country Planning Act, 1947, in the United Kingdom, is not suitable to Indian conditions. Ironically, the model has undergone several critical changes in the United Kingdom in response to evolving needs of the economy and the society, but remains largely unchanged in India.

Master planning, as practised in India, has three major flaws. First, it aims at artificially confining the city to a predetermined, rigid and utopian built form. It pays scant attention to what the great urbanist Jane Jacobs calls the 'organized complexity' of cities, making them inherently dynamic. This results from 'dealing simultaneously with a sizable number of factors which are interrelated into an organic hole' (Jacobs 1992 [1961], 432). Master plans adopt a physical view of the city, disregarding its economic fundamentals. They fail to integrate the economics of land, transport and cities with spatial planning. They neglect the determinants of 'location', including scale economies, transport costs, agglomeration externalities and factors such as market access, backward and forward linkages, costs, prices, rents, amenities, technology access and learning opportunities. Second, while the majority in Indian cities belongs to the poor and low-income groups (LIGs), master plans, with dictatorial connotations, rely on the space norms of the average middle-class household in the city. These plans are not in sync with the population composition and income distribution structure in urban areas. As a result, they have squeezed the urban poor out of formal land markets. The informal economies of cities which engage the bulk of their residents do not find a place in the formal urban plans.

Master plans have 'mastered' over the poor. While the essence of cities is about people living, working and learning together to benefit from collocation, master plans are neither people-centric, nor people-driven. Third, master planning, by neglecting the externalities of cities that capitalize into tax bases of governments, fails to incorporate the principles of benefit taxation, congestion charging (CC) and value capture financing (VCF) into the strategy of planned urban development.

Transportation is the backbone of a city. It connects households to opportunities, and firms to prosperity. Along with land use, it shapes city form and functions. A successful urban form is one in which the negative consequences of urbanization are outweighed by its positive effects due to factors such as spatial planning, 'just-in-time' investment in infrastructure and land management. Transport infrastructure, including arterial and radial roads, public transit system and commuter rail networks, influences economic growth by facilitating external economies and investment multipliers. However, it is expensive. In particular, mass rapid transit (MRT) and high-speed rail (HSR) are very costly. Paradoxically, the ambitious master plans in India have neglected the planning and financing of public transport (PT) for long. The land use planner's vision, the transportation planner's strategy and the urban economist's perspective are not integrated. This is conspicuous in India's metropolitan city regions, which are the powerhouses of economic growth. These regions suffer from an utter lack of connectivity infrastructure, resulting in their inability to exploit the benefits of accessibility, density and networking. They are facing premature suburbanization, much before they could harness their agglomeration potential.

Great cities of the world are products of not only market forces but also policies and actions by governments that magnified the beneficial effects of externalities while minimizing their negative consequences. The enduring contribution of these cities to the development of their nations can be traced to the innovations adopted by governments at crucial stages of urban transition. For example, the 1667 Building Code of London after the Great Fire, the renovation of Paris from 1853 to 1870 by Baron Haussmann, the 1811 'Grid Plan' of Manhattan, the 1916 Comprehensive Zoning Ordinance of New York City and the Standard State Zoning Enabling Act issued by the United States Department of Commerce in 1922 laid solid foundations for orderly development of cities spanning over a long period of time. During the nineteenth century, the built-up area of Manhattan increased sevenfold along the 1811 Grid Plan. This plan, along with major transportation investments, enabled New York City to rise to commanding heights. Spatial planning and timely development of infrastructure were key instruments that shaped the structure and functions of world's great cities. In particular, transport–land use integration created a congenial environment for creative entrepreneurs and skilled workers to engage in value-generating activities. It reduced the cost of connecting, interacting, networking, organizing, producing, transacting, transporting, consuming, learning and innovating.

This book is about addressing the issues of land, transport and urban planning in India's transition to a developed country. It is concerned with policies and instruments to make serviced land and floor space available in tune with the demands of inclusive growth and sustainable development. The driving force behind this book is the belief that India will be at the forefront of the Urban Revolution sweeping across the developing world in the twenty-first century. Urban planning and economics, with their implications for density, accessibility, scale, agglomeration and networking economies, will be the key factors driving India's socio-economic transformation. If enabled, cities will act as powerful drivers of economic growth and generators of public finance for development. If neglected, they will lead to disastrous consequences for the environment, including climate change. The largest metropolitan cities of India are already subjected to serious forms of environmental degradation. Pollution in Delhi is reaching life-threatening levels, culminating in the 'odd–even' scheme. Bengaluru is no longer a 'garden city' as once called. Devastating floods of Hyderabad in August 2000, Chennai in November 2015, Bengaluru in July 2016 and Mumbai in July 2005 and August 2017 demonstrate how fragile Indian cities are. They reveal that not only regional and urban planning but also infrastructure systems have failed to keep pace with urbanization. These issues are deeply rooted in the paradigm of master planning that neglects the key principles of land, transport and urban economics.

Good urban economics is good urban planning and vice versa. If growth is India's prime concern, 'where' growth occurs needs to be a key consideration for policymakers. Urban planners and economists must work together, combining physical planning and economic instruments, to assist cities in discharging their fundamental role as engines of spatial and structural transformation. The speed of economic development depends on how these two fundamental processes supplement and reinforce each other. Unless efforts are made in time to augment agglomeration economies and mitigate congestion diseconomies as cities evolve, the positive impacts of clustering and networking on economic growth will be offset by their negative effects on environment and quality of life. With this perspective, the present book refers to theoretical and empirical research in land, transport and urban economics, new economic geography (NEG), network science, regional and urban planning and management to address the shortcomings in India's present models of master planning and city development. Our emphasis is on both theory and practice. Theory is important as it contributes to conceptual clarity, consistency and coherence in policymaking. Practice matters as it conveys which policies work and which do not.

Chapter 2 attempts to clear the myth that ICT is making location irrelevant and reducing the importance of cities. We refer to Friedman's influential hypothesis of a 'flat' world in which innovation can take place 'anywhere'. Referring to urban economics and network theories, we argue that the increasingly globalizing and networked world is also becoming increasingly local. Economic activity, innovation and growth localize. The agglomeration and network externalities of cities lead to increasing returns. These returns are shaped by circular and cumulative causation processes in the spatial economy and power laws of networks. Cities attract skill- and knowledge-intensive activities as structural transformation progresses. The creative class, which benefits the most from networking, chooses to locate in cities to gain from 'skill premium', access to a variety of amenities and services, and opportunities for learning. Cities also facilitate innovative business strategies such as the 'long tail' and the 'bottom of the pyramid' (BoP). Such strategies are not economically viable in markets with low demand density and high transport cost. Further, cities are uniquely placed to benefit from the 'platform revolution' due to their networking properties. The ease of experimenting and propagating innovation in products, processes and strategies adds reason as to why cities will remain important in the new knowledge economy. We identify integrated spatial planning and timely investment in core urban infrastructures, especially public transport, as the key instruments to internalize the externalities of cities.

Chapter 3 analyses the trends, patterns and prospects of urbanization in India, including spatial concentration of urban population, state of slums, housing, poverty, civic services, infrastructure and municipal finance. It identifies key urban issues and their implications for land and transport policies. We highlight five major policy challenges in India's spatial transformation: making serviced land and floor space available for productive activities in tune with the demands of growth; integrating transportation planning and land use planning; land assembly without relying on compulsory acquisition of land; incorporating the space needs of the poor for living, working and vending in urban planning; and rooting the strategy of financing urban and regional infrastructure in the paradigm of planned urban development that leads to windfall benefits to many. These challenges warrant a restructuring of the present models of urban planning and development. The new approach needs to take into account the economics of cities, including interplay between market forces and public policies in shaping spatial and economic outcomes.

Chapter 4 deals with urban land markets, with focus on the impacts of land use planning. It refers to the peculiar characteristics of urban land and development rights, including horizontal and vertical dimensions, access to infrastructure and services, and linkage to externalities. It also refers to land and urban economics to examine the operation of land markets and efficacy of government interventions to address market failure. We highlight five major factors influencing the supply of and demand for serviced land in cities: agglomeration economies due to clustering and networking of economic activities; location choices by firms, households and developers based on appraisal of benefits and costs; building technology and FSI that permit developers to substitute capital for land; transport technology that expands labour market choices; and government policies that influence location, land use, construction, infrastructure, services, taxation and growth. These factors imply that urbanization in India will be propelled by market forces and public policies, not by spatial planning alone. They also suggest that making urban land markets work for all without adverse social and environmental consequences ought to be a key objective of urban policy. We trace the severe constraints on supply of serviced land and floor space in Indian cities to the command and control approach of master planning. We highlight the shortcomings of the model in the light of difficulties in compulsory acquisition of land to implement master plans. We refer to issues in India's new Land Acquisition Act, 2013, and constraints of outdated regulations, including FSI and rent control. Finally, the chapter calls for shift from a prescriptive and rigid planning regime to a responsive and flexibly regulated paradigm that considers density and accessibility as key resources for planned urbanization.

Chapter 5 looks at urban planning through the lens of transport economics. While transportation makes or mars a city, master planning in India has accorded a subsidiary role to transport, with primary importance given to land use. Referring to the two-way relationship between land use and transport, we counter the view of physical planners that transportation should follow land use rather than guide spatial structure. We stress the crucial role of major urban transport (UT) projects in leading development by creating externality-induced benefits to locations and the economy as a whole. These phenomena significantly raise the benefit–cost ratio (BCR) of such projects that would otherwise receive a low ranking under the conventional appraisal methods. The impacts of transport on conservation of the environment, expansion of labour markets, mobility of the poor and increase in land values that could be captured to finance infrastructure constitute other reasons why PT should receive utmost attention from policymakers. Referring to India's urban transport policy, we present arguments as to why PT investments in cities in anticipation of growth, including MRT and HSR, are necessary to achieve the long-term goals of efficient, inclusive and sustainable cities. We argue for a public transport-led and transit-oriented development (TOD) strategy to harnesses the benefits of accessibility, density, networking, mixed land use and VCF. The key guiding principles are: access to public transport within 15 minutes of walk, and a commuting time of 1 hour to work. We argue for converting the national and state highways passing through large cities to mass transit corridors by developing bypasses and regional ring roads, and to promote transit-oriented development.

Chapter 6 focuses on land assembly to make serviced land and floor space available in tune with the demands of urbanization and economic growth. It recognizes that the model of compulsory acquisition of land for planned urban development is not going to be smooth under the new land acquisition (LA) law. Moreover, one cannot justify why the farmers' contributing land for value creation in cities should not be partners in the city development process. Recognizing the need to liberalize FSI and other land use planning norms, the chapter calls for exploring a combination of options for land assembly: strategic densification of growth nodes, renewal of derelict areas and infill development guided by TOD; planned urban expansion based on land pooling; development of ring towns and satellite towns connected to large cities by limited access expressways, regional transit and HSR taken up in phases; and promotion of new towns on emerging industrial growth corridors with fast connectivity to regional cities and incentive for industrial location. We suggest that urban land assembly in India be guided by: overriding priority to conservation and transportation; public transport-led and transit-oriented development; inclusionary zoning (IZ) and inclusionary housing (IH); pricing of development rights; and value increment partnerships. We refer to some best practices for replication: town planning scheme (TPS) in Gujarat, land pooling scheme (LPS) in Amaravati in Andhra Pradesh, Uppal Bhagath, Hyderabad in Telangana and Magarpatta city, Pune in Maharashtra; removal of FSI restrictions and incentive-based road-widening scheme in Hyderabad; and integrated transportation–land use planning in Copenhagen and Curitiba. We also suggest the auctioning of development rights in urban nodes with high economic potential following the transparent model of Certificate of Potential Additional Construction (CEPAC) in Brazil.

Chapter 7 is focused on the needs of the urban poor for land and transport. The master planning model in India is exclusionary. It is not based on the income distribution pattern in cities. It also ignores the informal economy which engages the bulk of the urban poor. These segments suffer from an acute scarcity of space for living, working and vending. In a bid to be close to work, they seek shelter in slums. A quarter of the urban population in India is deprived of 'legal space'. Not only markets but also governments have failed the urban poor, depriving them of the 'right to the city'. A fundamental role of cities is to create employment. This role cannot be effectively discharged without incorporating the needs of the urban poor and LIGs for wage employment and self-employment, including home-based work and street vending. The severe constraints on land and housing markets in India due to unrealistic space norms and stringent development control regulations (DCRs) have led to artificial scarcities of floor space, not only for the lower income groups but also the middle class. These constraints need to be relaxed with strategic densification and decongestion programmes along with investment in PT rooted in a value capture framework. Cities must also explore the instruments of IZ and IH adopted by the developed countries and Gujarat. This suggestion is based on the principle that growth must mitigate its impacts, including the need for affordable housing. Further, it is the poor who make cities work. Recognizing this, we argue for the allocation of land to lower income groups in the planning process itself, as in the TPS in Gujarat. We also advocate the location of high-density residential developments for these groups around public transit nodes and corridors. TOD provides a unique opportunity for reengineering cities and reconnecting the poor to economic opportunities.

Chapter 8 focuses on financing urban development plans (DPs). It regards borrowing as the most appropriate method to finance lumpy infrastructure projects whose benefits spread over generations and jurisdictions. However, the debt incurred for projects, whether executed by the government directly or on a public–private partnership (PPP) mode, will have to be repaid. In this connection, a tax increment financing (TIF) approach is worth adopting. This approach aims at escrowing future revenue increments due to projects and supporting policies to repay the debt incurred to finance them. Land, transport and urban economics highlight the importance of benefit taxation and congestion pricing. They emphasize that spatial planning and infrastructure development, in conjunction with the externalities of cities, provide significant opportunities to mobilize resources based on 'users pay', 'beneficiaries pay', 'congesters pay', 'exacerbaters pay' and 'growth pays' instruments. In particular, land value tax (LVT) constitutes an ideal source to finance urban infrastructure, which capitalizes into land value due to enhanced accessibility and increased intensity of development, often facilitated by favourable changes in land use and building regulations called 'up-zoning'. We argue for value-creating partnerships between local, state and central government authorities to finance major urban development projects in the spirit of cooperative federalism. The repayment of debt for these projects may be linked to land taxation, impact fee, betterment levy, congestion charges and dedicated funds based on the benefit principle. The sources of dedicated funds may include instruments such as fuel tax in the United States, transport tax in France and 'earmarked' transfers from higher levels of government. A city share in the Goods and Services Tax (GST) will be desirable for sustained funding of bus rapid transit (BRT), MRT, HSR and other major projects in metropolitan city regions.

Chapter 9 combines lessons from the previous chapters to suggest directions for reforms in urban planning in India. It refers to the economic approach to cities that emphasizes people-centric, rather than place-centric design of cities. It acknowledges that cities evolve due to actions, interactions, initiatives and enterprise of numerous firms, households and developers–builders. They choose locations and make operational decisions based on appraisal of benefits and costs. Dense, diverse and dynamic cities lead to productivity benefits and reduce costs. They act as catalysts of innovation and economic growth. Urban planning can play a key role in maximizing the positive effects of density while minimizing the negative consequences of overcrowding and congestion. With this perspective, the chapter reviews the Urban and Regional Development Plans Formulation and Implementation (URDPFI) Guidelines 2014, issued by the GoI. It calls for incorporating the principles of land, transport and urban economics into urban planning. It argues for shifting from a prescriptive, technocratic, rigid and land use-based master planning approach to a responsive, people-centric, flexible, transport-led and strategic planning paradigm. The overriding considerations of environmental sustainability and social equity suggest that urban planning in India must adopt a public transportation-led and transit-oriented development strategy. We advocate a two-tier approach: regional plans in the form of structural plans focused on conservation and transportation, and local area plans aimed at transport–land use integration, social inclusion and using planning and infrastructure development as resource. We suggest reforms in urban public finance to facilitate investment in MRT and HSR; a liberalized FSI and land use regime; strategic densification of city centres and sub-centres; land assembly with farmers as partners based on land pooling; new townships combining TOD and incentives for industrial location; inclusionary zoning; and a mix of benefit taxation, congestion pricing and value-increment financing partnerships to raise resources.

The crucial importance of cities in developing countries like India derives from their central role in two fundamental processes of economic development, namely structural and spatial transformation. These processes, when facilitated by urban planning and infrastructure, reinforce each other, creating conditions for accelerated economic growth and resource generation for development. However, economic development planning and spatial planning in India have been pursued in isolation, without tapping the synergy between the two. Even the Planning Commission of India did not have a spatial planning division during the long period of its existence. This book suggests that socio-economic planners and physical planners need to work together, understanding each other's perspective on urban issues. Both are confronted with the same problem: how to accord a rightful place to the city in the socio-economic transformation of the nation. Urbanization offers a unique opportunity, which needs to be harnessed. Well-functioning cities will present the clearest path to India's prosperity. Policymakers, planners and administrators in India must remember the profound observation by the great urbanist Jane Jacobs.

Whenever and wherever societies have flourished and prospered rather than stagnated and decayed, creative and workable cities have been at the core of the phenomenon. Decaying cities, declining economies, and mounting social troubles travel together. The combination is not coincidental. (Jacobs 1992 [1961], xvii–xviii)

2

The World Is Not Flat
Agglomeration, Networking and Cities

A SPIKY WORLD OF CITIES

The lack of understanding of land, transport and urban economics is a key factor behind the poor design of urban planning in developing countries. This is associated with the view that the globalizing and electronically networked world is making geography and location redundant. Some researchers believe that information and communication technology (ICT) and globalization, facilitated by it, mark 'the end of geography' (O' Brien 1992), 'the death of distance' (Cairncross 1997), 'a borderless world' (Ohmae 1990, 1995) and 'supra-territorialization' (Scholte 2000). Friedman (2006) refers to the global playing field 'being levelled' and a 'flat world' in which 'you can innovate without having to emigrate'. These narratives link cyberspace, including Internet routers, global fibre optic superhighways, virtual communities, telecommuting, web surfing, cloud computing and the like with physical space. They underestimate the importance of face-to-face interaction, collaboration and learning in cities. However, the theory of a 'flat world' is not supported by hard evidence. In fact, the increasingly globalizing world is also becoming increasingly localized in a limited number of spiky cities and mega-regions. Location matters and significantly so in developing countries.

Friedman (2006) identifies 10 'flatteners' that have enabled more people from more different corners of the planet to compete and collaborate in real time with more other people on more different kinds of work on a more equal footing (Box 2.1). He argues that these forces are

Box 2.1 *Friedman: The 10 Forces That Flattened the World*

1. The New Age of Creativity (the Berlin Wall falling in November 1989; Windows 3.0 coming into operation in May 1990)
   This force 'tipped the balance of power across the world towards those advocating, democratic, consensual, free-market-oriented governance, and away from those advocating authoritarian rule with centrally planned economies' and led to 'a single market, a single ecosystem, and a single community'. It is linked to the information technology revolution created by the diffusion of a critical mass of IBM personal computers and Windows operating system that 'vastly improved horizontal communication—to the detriment of the exclusively top-down form that communism was based upon'.

2. The New Age of Connectivity (shift from personal computer-based platform to an Internet-based platform)
   This factor 'enabled more people to communicate and interact with more other people anywhere on the planet than ever before'.

3. Workflow Software (efficient global collaboration using a shared medium)
   This tool 'enabled more people in more places to design, display, manage, and collaborate on business data previously handled manually', resulting in more work flowing 'between companies and continents faster than ever'.

4. Uploading (open online collaboration and communities)
   This force brought 'newfound power [to] individuals and communities to send up, out, and around their own products and ideas, often for free, rather than just passively downloading them from commercial enterprises or traditional hierarchies', thereby 'reshaping the flow of creativity, innovation, political mobilization, and information gathering and dissemination'.

5. Outsourcing (sub-contacting to third parties to cut costs or increase efficiency)
   This factor resulted in 'taking some specific, but limited, function that your company is doing in-house ... and having another company perform that exact same function for you and then reintegrating their work back into your overall operation'.

(Continued)

Box 2.1 *(Continued)*

6. Offshoring (moving a company's processes to a foreign land to save costs)
   This force enabled manufacturing 'the very same product in the very same way, only with cheaper labour, lower taxes, subsidized energy, and lower health-care costs' in another country, 'then integrating it into [your] global supply chains'.

7. Supply Chaining (increasing connection between suppliers, retailers and consumers)
   This factor permitted '[horizontal collaboration]—among suppliers, retailers, and customers—to create value', resulting in 'the adoption of common standards between companies' and more efficient 'global collaboration'.

8. In-sourcing (performing services for other companies)
   This force implied that 'small companies could suddenly see around the world' and sell their products and services globally, while large companies could 'act really small' and 'customize products at the last minute'.

9. In-forming (ability to gather information about many things and many people)
   This factor gave 'all the world's knowledge, or even just a big chunk of it ... to anyone and everyone, anytime, anywhere', enabling in 'becoming your own self-directed and self-empowered researcher, editor, and selector of entertainment, without having to go to the library or the movie theatre or through network television'.

10. The Steroids (digital, mobile, personal and virtual gadgets, including Voice over Internet Protocol (VoIP), wireless, mobile phones, iPods, personal digital assistants, instant messaging, file sharing, videoconferencing, peer-to-peer networking, etc.)
    This force, powered by specific technologies, supercharged all other flatteners, amplifying the effects of outsourcing, offshoring, uploading, supply chaining, in-sourcing and in-forming. It meant that 'engines can now talk to computers, people can talk to people, computers can talk to computers, and people can talk to computers farther, faster, more cheaply, and more easily than ever before'.

Source: Friedman (2006).

converging into a new global, web-enabled and creative platform that connects users 'anywhere' irrespective of their location. This platform 'now operates without regard to geography, distance, time, and in the near future, even language' (Friedman 2006, 205).

Friedman (2006) refers to the role of globalization and ICT in powering the drivers of the new knowledge economy: competition, collaboration and convergence. However, it does not provide an empirical assessment of the impacts of these forces on the location of economic growth. Nor does it present a coherent theory to explain why electronic networking should reduce the importance of the clustering of firms, households and institutions in cities. It also does not examine 'where' economic activities that benefit the most from global integration and ICT locate. Ironically, the technology giant IBM, which promoted 'remote work' for decades with the slogan of 'the anytime, anywhere workforce', has reportedly decided to bring employees back into office. This is based on the logic that such a move will accelerate the pace of workplace learning and collaboration, a view articulated by urban economics for long. Both empirical evidence and economic theory suggest that globalization, powered by urban, transportation and ICT revolutions, is localizing growth in cities. This is particularly so in developing countries where city regions are gateways to the knowledge economy. These regions act as laboratories for application of new knowledge to products, processes and business strategies. They are the chosen locations for firms and households due to their agglomeration and network externalities. The paradigm: 'location, location, location' rules.

This chapter refers to the externalities of cities and their interactions with new technology and globalization in strengthening the forces of localization. Agglomeration externalities are powered by circular and cumulative causation forces; network externalities are subject to power laws. These externalities reinforce each other. In particular, transportation networks play a key role in agglomeration by enhancing access to the 'economic mass' and connecting centres of gravity in the spatial economy. Cities attract skill- and knowledge-intensive activities. The creative class which benefits the most from electronic networking chooses to locate in cities to gain from 'skill premium', access to modern amenities and opportunity for learning. Further, cities facilitate the application of innovative business strategies such as the 'long tail' and the 'bottom of the pyramid (BoP)'. Such strategies are not economically viable in markets characterized by low demand density and high transportation cost. Cities are also uniquely placed to benefit from the 'platform revolution' due to their networking properties. Keeping these considerations in view, this chapter is focused on agglomeration externalities; power laws of networks; the phenomena of 'long tail', 'BoP' and 'platform revolution'; and role of cities in catalyzing innovation that lies at the heart of growth. It argues that the future of developing countries like India depends on how they position their cities as engines of agglomeration-driven, network-powered and knowledge-led growth. It calls for policymakers and planners to understand the economics of the 'spiky' and 'paved' world of cities, distinguished by their land use densities, transportation networks and drivers of local economic growth.

GLOBALIZATION AND LOCALIZATION

Localization forces remain strong in spite of globalization and ICT revolution. The level of integration in the global economy is still very small. More than 90 per cent of all telephone calls and web traffic is local. Foreign direct investment (FDI) accounts for only about 10 per cent of total capital investment globally. The overwhelming majority of interactions, including investment, trade, commerce, tourism and migration occur within—not between—nations (Ghemawat 2007; Ghemawat and Altman 2014). Recent data on 'Global Connectedness Index' also reveal a decrease in the overall 'breadth' of such connectedness. This conclusion is based on a metric that captures the number of different nations a particular country is interacting with, and the distances over which such interactions take place, among other things (Fox 2014).

Friedman's hypothesis of a 'flat world' is not supported by empirical findings. Studies in both developed and developing countries suggest that economic activities and innovations localize in mega-regions. These regions comprise of a 'series of cities physically separated but functionally networked, clustered around one or more larger central cities and are connected with dense flows of people and information using important transport infrastructures' (Hall 2009). As Richard Florida documents:

The world's ten largest mega-regions in terms of economic activity, which house approximately 416 million people or 6.5 percent of the world's population, account for 43 percent of economic activity, 57 percent of patented innovations, and 53 percent of the most-cited scientists.

The top twenty mega-regions in terms of economic activity account for 10 percent of population, 57 percent of economic activity, 76 percent of patented innovations, and 76 percent of most-cited scientists.

The top forty mega-regions in economic activity, which make up about 18 percent of the world's population, produce 66 percent of economic activity, 86 percent of patented innovations, and house 84 percent of most-cited scientists. (Florida 2011, p. 289)

Brookings Institution (2015) reveals that 300 largest metropolitan economies of the world, containing only 20 per cent of global population, accounted for 50 per cent of global output in 2014. A third of them were 'pockets of growth', outpacing their national economies in annualized growth rate of employment and real GDP per capita. Further, metropolitan economies with the fastest rates of growth in 2014 belong to developing regions (Brookings Institution 2015). The contribution of urban areas to GDP in India increased from 29 per cent in 1950–1951 to 47 per cent in 1981, 55 per cent in 1991 and 60 per cent in 2001. In 2007, cities and towns, with 30 per cent of population, contributed about 62–63 per cent of the country's GDP. This contribution is expected to rise to 75 per cent by 2021 (Planning Commission 2008). The globalizing and increasingly networked world is thus not flat. It is distinguished by spiky and paved cities.

Harvard economist Edward Glaeser calls cities 'our species' greatest invention', making us richer, smarter, greener, healthier and happier. He argues that cities generate the benefits of living, working, producing, consuming, recreating, collaborating, learning and thinking together. They transmit knowledge, act as nurseries of new ideas, spur innovation, attract talent and sharpen it through competition. They nurture entrepreneurship and allow for socio-economic mobility. The greatest ability of mankind is to learn from people around. Cities facilitate that. They enable fertile minds to meet as scale economies, greater market access and lower transport costs make a finer division of labour possible. Cities magnify the strength of humanity. 'Consumer cities' attract people with a variety of goods and services, high levels of amenities and broad avenues for socialization. Denser agglomerations reduce sprawl, car-dependent transportation and carbon emission. In developing countries, cities remain the best hopes for millions in urban and rural areas to escape abject poverty.

Cities represent a mass of connected economic activities. They link people to opportunity, and firms to prosperity. Entrepreneurs and skilled workers are the prime beneficiaries of networking, including that facilitated by ICT. They locate in cities to gain from face-to-face contact that breeds trust, generosity and cooperation. They benefit disproportionately from employer–worker matching, returns to skilling and opportunities for learning. Electronic communication acts as a complement to face-to-face interaction, not a substitute. This is particularly so in developing countries where knowledge is scarce and is localized in the routines of firms and households in cities due to historic, economic and other reasons. Glaeser rightly observes:

> For over a century, pundits have been predicting that new forms of communication would make urban life irrelevant. One hundred years ago, the telephones were supposed to make cities unnecessary. That didn't happen. More recently faxes, e-mail and videoconferencing were all supposed to eliminate the need for face-to-face meetings, yet business travel has soared over last twenty years. To defeat the human need for face-to-face contact, our technological marvels would need to defeat million years of human evolution that has made us into machines for learning from the people next to us. (2011, 36–37)

CITIES AND THEIR EXTERNALITIES

The economic significance of cities is rooted in their externalities, leading to productivity benefits and cost savings. Agglomeration externalities, occurring on the supply side, arise from the collocation of firms, households and institutions. Cities reduce the cost of moving goods, people and knowledge. They manifest in gains from learning, sharing and matching (Brueckner 2011; Cheshire, Nathan and Overman 2014; Combes et al. 2012; Duranton and Puga 2004; Duranton, Henderson and Strange 2015; Fujita 1989; Fujita and Thisse 2002; Henderson 1974; Puga 2010; Rosenthal and Strange 2004). Network externalities, arising on the demand side, lead to benefits from increased use, integration and merger of networks, including transportation, communication, knowledge and social networks. The interplay between agglomeration and network externalities facilitates the exchange of ideas and information between diverse actors in cities, catalyzing human capital accumulation, innovation and economic growth.

Cross-country studies find a near perfect correlation between urbanization and economic development. As the level of urbanization of a country goes up by 10 per cent, its per capita output rises by 30 per cent. Per capita incomes are four times higher in countries with the majority of population in cities compared to those in which the majority reside in rural areas. A city in a developed country twice the size of another has a productivity premium higher by 1–5 per cent. Within the United States, workers in metropolitan areas containing large cities earn 30 per cent more than workers in non-metro areas. Persons in a metropolitan region with population exceeding one million are, on an average, more than 50 per cent productive than those in smaller metro areas. These relationships do not alter even after correcting for heterogeneity with regard to education, experience, intelligence quotient (IQ) and industry of workers (Glaeser 2011). The urban productivity–economic growth relationship appears to be much stronger in developing countries. The coefficient, when individual income is regressed on area density, is around 0.05 in the United States, 0.08 in India and 0.20 in China (Chauvin et al. 2016).

Spatial concentration of economic activities is a key phenomenon that Kuznets associated with modern economic growth (Kuznets 1966). The nature of such concentration changes with the stage of development; the benefits of dynamic agglomeration economies weigh against the costs of static congestion diseconomies. For example, the potential gains from human capital accumulation due to the collocation of economic activities and learning in cities may be large at lower levels of technological progress. Congestion diseconomies may assume greater significance at higher levels. Williamson's hypothesis suggests that agglomeration matters significantly at the lower stages of economic development; it provides a means to a developing country to address the resources constraints and overcome the 'development trap'. An inverted-U relationship is obtained between urban concentration and economic growth (Williamson 1965).

When infrastructure systems are underdeveloped and capital markets are shallow, efficiency gains can be harnessed by localizing production. The economy conserves on 'economic infrastructure'—physical infrastructure and management resources—by spatially concentrating economic activities. Such concentration also enhances information spillovers when the economy is 'information-deficient'. This facilitates the accumulation of knowledge, much needed for growth to occur. However, as a country develops, the rise of congestion externalities may favour a more dispersed pattern of economic geography. An important research using cross-country data for 105 countries spanning over the period 1960–2000 finds consistent evidence in support of Williamson's hypothesis that agglomeration boosts GDP growth up to a threshold of development. The level is around US$10,000 per capita in 2006 PPP prices (Brulhart and Sbergami 2009). India is way below this threshold and must not miss the opportunities presented by urbanization.

Agglomeration externalities on supply side and network externalities on demand side arise in the operation of market forces as well as public policies towards economic development. Networks that enhance 'access' to nodes of growth, transport and communication, in particular, magnify the importance of spatial concentration of economic activity. However, unlike agglomeration economies, research in economics has not devoted much attention to the nature and sources of network economies. The ICT literature, however, refers to the power laws of networks. These laws suggest that networks power themselves after reaching a 'critical crossover' point. They create 'circular and cumulative causation' forces, similar to those highlighted by research in new economic geography (NEG). These considerations are amongst the key factors that explain why city regions around the world act as the engines of innovation and economic growth. Metropolitan urban agglomerations (UAs) in developing countries like India, with their diverse economic activities, physical, economic and social networks and pools of skilled and creative people, are uniquely positioned to benefit from electronic networking.

SOURCES OF AGGLOMERATION

Urban economists suggest that cities form and grow to reap the external economies of agglomeration. The collocation of economic activities leads to benefits at four levels. Gains internal to individuals arise from wider choice for jobs, higher wage, larger scope for learning and greater access to retail facilities, public services and social, cultural and recreational opportunities. Economies internal to firms occur from sharing of fixed assets, inputs, markets and services, division of labour and specialization. Benefits internal to industry but external to firms, called localization economies, include technological spillovers, availability of intermediate inputs and access to markets for industry-specific skills. Economies external to industry, but internal to the city, arise from larger citywide and regional markets, greater diversity of economic activities, bigger pool of workers with cross-cutting skills, inter-industry knowledge spillovers and access to citywide, regional and national infrastructure networks.

As an economy moves away from agriculture to manufacturing and services, it enters a new arena of production where both scale and location matter. Economic activities subject to scale economies cluster to reduce transaction costs and benefit from backward and forward linkages. Being with a lot of other producers and consumers more than compensates for the costs of living and working in cities. Firms access common suppliers, service providers, financiers and customers. They share indivisibilities, including universities, research laboratories, airports, highways, public transit and other infrastructure facilities. The clustering of firms leads to the formation of 'unified' labour market. Cities match skills and jobs, firms and workers, buyers and sellers, and trainers and trainees; they improve the quality of matches too. They alleviate the 'hold-up' problem arising when a worker invests in human resource development, but cannot find a job matching the skills acquired. Cities enable learning on and off jobs. The strength of Silicon Valley and Bengaluru owes to exchanges of knowledge between creative people. Cities lead to benefits from specialization, diversity and competition.

The Specialization Hypothesis

Marshall (1890) refers to the external economies of industrial location. He argues that firms collocate in industrial districts to benefit from specialization.

> When an industry has thus chosen a locality for itself, it is likely to stay there long: so great are the advantages which people following the same skilled trade get from near neighbourhood to one another. The mysteries of the trade become no mysteries; but are as it were in the air, and children learn many of them unconsciously. Good work is rightly appreciated; inventions and improvements in machinery, in processes and the general organization of the business have their merits promptly discussed: if one man starts a new idea, it is taken up by others and combined with suggestions of their own; and thus it becomes the source of further new ideas. And presently subsidiary trades grow up in the neighbourhood, supplying it with implements and materials, organizing its traffic, and in many ways conducing to the economy of its material....
>
> ... a localized industry gains a great advantage from the fact that it offers a constant market for skill. Employers are apt to resort to any new place where they are likely to find a good choice of workers with special skill which they require; while men seeking employment naturally go to places where there are many employers who need such skills as theirs and where therefore it is likely to find a good market. (Marshall 1920, 224–225)

Marshallian externalities fall into three categories: knowledge, input and labour market. The clustering of firms in an industry facilitates the exchange of information; producers and workers gain from intra-industry knowledge spillovers. When firms collocate, they attract suppliers of non-traded inputs and ancillary services to locate in proximity. Producers purchase requirements more efficiently and save transportation costs. Localization of industry leads to gains from sharing of assets, intermediate inputs, markets, risks and public services. Further, the location of many firms in a single industry leads to specialized labour market pooling. Apart from positive externalities on production side, Marshall also refers to external benefits on consumption side such as comparison shopping:

... there is also the convenience of the customer to be considered. He will go to the nearest shop for a trifling purchase; but for an important purchase he will take the trouble of visiting any part of the town where he knows that there are specialty good shops for his purpose. Consequently shops which deal in expensive and choice objects tend to congregate together; and those which supply ordinary domestic needs do not. (Marshall 1920, 226)

The Diversity Hypothesis

The famous urbanist Jane Jacobs argues that it is the variety and diversity of geographically proximate economic activities, rather than single industry specialization that make urban externalities the drivers of innovation and growth (Jacobs 1969, 1984). According to her, important knowledge transfers occur between rather than within industries, leading to creativity and innovation. Jacobs calls innovation a process by which new work is added to old division of labour, leading to new ideas, processes and products, and prompting further division of labour. Innovation occurs through the application of economically useful knowledge cutting across industries, and flowing through the dense geography of cities. Jacobs observes:

... the urban environment yields a greater return on new economic knowledge and encourages innovation. (Jacobs 1969)

According to Jacobs, greater diversity in cities leads to faster and more meaningful exchange of information across firms and workers. Creative individuals combine their own ideas with the ideas of others. The exchange of complementary knowledge across diverse firms aids search and experimentation processes that lie at the root of innovation. Different people working on different things in different ways collaborate, cooperate and compete in unexpected ways as the dense environments of cities facilitate face-to-face interaction. While information and knowledge are direct inputs to industries such as publishing, journalism, biotechnology, media and financial services, they are of critical importance in many other sectors.

The Competition Hypothesis

Porter (1990) highlights the role of clustering in competitive advantage of regions and nations. A cluster is a geographic concentration of interconnected companies, specialized suppliers, service providers, firms in related industries and associated institutions (e.g., universities, standards agencies, chambers of business, etc.) in a particular field that compete, but also cooperate. Cities facilitate the clustering of firms with commonalities and complementarities. Physical proximity between firms leads to benefits of input sharing and access to management strategies of competitors. Competition encourages excellence in industry and drives firms to innovate or perish. Links with consumers also enable firms to get innovative ideas for designing new strategies and processes. Supplier and customer linkages in an industry are often traced out to specific UAs. Porter observes:

> Successful firms are frequently concentrated in particular cities or states within a nation. (Porter 1990, 29)

Porter refers to four stages in a nation's competitive development. The first stage is factor-driven, led by basic conditions of home factor markets such as low-cost labour and natural resources. The second stage is investment-driven, leading to improved efficiency in producing standardized commodities and services that become increasingly sophisticated. The third stage is innovation-driven. Propelled by developments in technologies, tools, processes and methods, it creates competitive strength based on low costs due to enhanced productivity rather than low factor prices. The fourth stage is wealth-driven, linked to past accumulation of wealth. The first three stages lead to successive upgrading of a nation's competitive advantage due to favourable demand, input quality and competitive pressures. In these stages, the concentration of leading industries in cities contributes to competitive advantage. A defined geographical cluster intensifies information flows, collaboration and competition between firms.

New Economic Geography and Cities

Krugman's NEG emphasizes the interactions between market access, scale economies, transport costs and externalities in the spatial concentration of economic activities. It refers to circular and cumulative causation processes operating on demand and supply sides. Firms locate near markets to reap the advantages of scale economies without incurring much transport costs. Low transport costs prompt them to produce centrally and export to far-off locations. But markets tend to be large where firms locate, as workers are customers. The clustering of firms also attracts the suppliers of intermediate inputs and services.

NEG models suggest that the rise of spatial agglomerations, including cities, reflects the interplay between centripetal and centrifugal forces. Key centripetal forces are: (a) market size: larger markets are preferred by producers due to consumers' preference for a variety of products (demand linkage); suppliers of intermediate inputs locally reduce the costs of other producers (cost linkage); (b) thick labour markets: the concentration of economic activities facilitates the emergence of markets for specialized skills; and (c) pure external economies such as those through knowledge spillovers leading to human capital externalities. Main centrifugal forces include: (a) transport costs; (b) immobile factors such as land and natural resources; (c) barriers to trade; (d) rise in rents due to overcrowding; and (e) pure external diseconomies such as congestion and pollution. Access to markets and immobile factors are dependent on distance and transportation costs. A larger concentration of economic activity puts pressure on land and housing, creates congestion and increases house and office rents. These factors discourage agglomeration. The relative strengths of centripetal and centrifugal forces shape the spatial concentration of economic activity, including that in cities.

NEG refers to the significance of 'home market effects'. Cities act as product and labour markets. They attract creative and consuming classes. The McKinsey Global Institute (2012) estimates that the size of the world's consuming class, defined to comprise of individuals with disposable income exceeding US$10 a day at constant 2005 PPP dollars, would more than triple between 1990 and 2025—to more than 4 billion people. About 2 billion of the new consumers would be from emerging market cities; 1 billion of these would join the ranks of the consuming class by 2025. The new consuming class would be responsible for rapid growth in demand for a wide variety of consumer goods and services. Urban households would create around US$20 trillion of additional spending up to 2025, with more than 70 per cent of it in the large cities of developing countries like India.

THE POWER LAWS OF NETWORKS

Economic activities not only agglomerate but also network. Network externalities pervade economic and social life. They influence firm and consumer behaviour. As the saying goes, 'the friend of my friend is also my friend'. Location in a network affects the reward to members who try to tilt the network in their favour. Networks connect, integrate and merge.

Network externalities arise when the benefit from a network or the use of a compatible product to a member is influenced by its use by others. They differ from scale effects, which arise from the expansion in a firm's scale of production. While scale economies occur on the supply side, network economies arise on the demand side. When network economies are present, the functional value of a network increases and the cost of its usage decreases as the number of users increase. Enquiry into the nature of such externalities has led to the formulation of power laws of networks in the ICT literature. These laws have influenced the way business in the new economy operates and also have important implications for economic growth in cities. They include Metcalfe's Law, Reed's Law, Odlyzko's law and Sarnoff's law (see Briscoe, Odlyzko and Tilly 2006 and Tongia and Willson 2011 for reviews).

Metcalfe's Law

Metcalfe's law—attributed to the coinventor of Ethernet, Robert Metcalfe—states that the power of a network scales with the square of the number of users. The basis of this law is that if there are n members in a network, each of them can make a connection with $n - 1$ other members. Assuming that all connections are equally valuable, the value of the network will then be proportional to $n(n - 1) = n^2 - n$. But the link from node A to node B is the same as that from B to A. Accordingly, the sum total of unique links will be $(n^2 - n)/2$. This approximates n^2 when n is sufficiently large. Examples of networks to which Metcalfe's law is applied include the Internet, the World Wide Web, cell phone and instant messaging.

Metcalfe believed that whereas the value of a communication network increases in quadratic terms, the cost of connecting at most grows linearly. His original intention was to emphasize the existence of a critical mass crossover value before which a network does not pay. This is illustrated in Figure 2.1.

Metcalfe's law suggests that when a network crosses the critical value, it begins to power itself. The more valuable a network is the more valuable it becomes. Further, while the value of a network increases with the addition of members, it can jump by interconnecting or merging with other networks. For example, if a network M of m members is interconnected with another network N of n members, the incremental values to the two networks due to interconnectivity can be approximated by:

$$\Delta V_m = m(m+n) - m^2 = mn \qquad (1)$$

$$\Delta V_n = n(m+n) - n^2 = mn \qquad (2)$$

Thus, each network gains by connecting to the other. An implication from the equations (1) and (2) is that the smaller network benefits relatively more by linking to the larger network. Further, when the

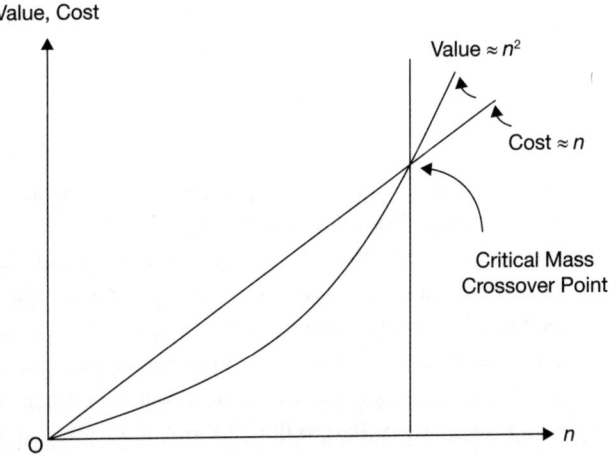

Figure 2.1 *Metcalfe's Law of Network: Crossover Value*

two networks merge, the incremental value generated by the combined network M+N is:

$$\Delta V_{m+n} = (m+n)(m+n) - m^2 - n^2 = 2\,mn = 2\Delta V_m = 2\Delta V_n \qquad (3)$$

This equation implies that a network may gain considerably by merging other networks and providing interconnecting services to members-users.

Reed's Law

David P. Reed's law recognizes that not only members in a network connect to each other as pairs, they also form groups to gain from group activities and synergies. The basis of this law is that if a network or set has n members, there will be 2^n possible subsets. The number of i member subsets is ^nC_i, $i = 1, 2, 3, 4, \ldots, n$. As the null set is also a subset, counted as $^nC_0$, the total number of subsets equals $^nC_0 + {}^nC_1 + {}^nC_2 + \cdots + {}^nC_n = (1+1)^n = 2^n$. But the null subset and the n singleton subsets are not relevant in a communication network. So the total number of groups in a group forming network (GFN) is $2^n - n - 1$, which approximates 2^n when n is large. This implies that the network effects generated by self-forming groups can scale up exponentially when the number of members increases. Reed's law does not apply to a telecommunication network in which one member communicates to another at a time. However, it makes sense for social networks, including Facebook and Twitter.

Odylzko's Law

Andrew Odylzko's law is based on the premise that the most valuable connections in a network are formed first, followed by less valuable ones. It questions the assumption of Metcalfe's law and Reed's law that all connections are equally valuable to members. It assumes that future connections will add positive value to a network but at a diminishing rate. In this regard, it refers to Zipf's law or the 'rank size rule' which states that the frequency of occurrence of an event, as a function of its rank, follows a power law or Pareto distribution. The rank size rule has been applied to the size distribution of cities in a broad cross-section of countries around the world, including the United States.

Drawing insights from the rank size rule, Odylzko's law postulates that the incremental value of adding one member to a network of size n is approximately the nth harmonic number. Thus, the value to a member will be proportional to the sum $1+1/2+1/3+1/4+\cdots+1/n-1$, which approaches logarithm of n with base 2 for large n. As there are n members who derive similar value from the network, the value to all n members thus increases as $n\log n$. Accordingly, Odylzko's law describes the power of a network of n members as $n\log n$. This law is applied to telephone networks.

Sarnoff's Law

David Sarnoff's law states that the value of a network varies linearly with the number of subscribers, that is, the power of a network of size n equals n. The basis of this law is that the larger the number of subscribers in a broadcasting network, for example, viewers or listeners, the greater will be the 'advertisement slot' revenues derived. Networks depicting this 'one-to-many' behaviour include newspapers, radio and televisions.

CITY REGIONS AND NETWORK LAWS

City regions are open economies characterized by seamless flows of goods, people, ideas, information and knowledge. They are driven by the activities of their inhabitants who choose location to optimize their objective functions. They are natural homes to network externalities and subject to power laws of networks. City regions catalyze and nurture diverse networks: transport, communication, water supply, sewerage, drainage, energy, labour contract, material supply, production, trade, logistic, distribution, retail, financing, health care, research and development (R&D) and the like. Metcalfe's law implies that when a city region crosses a threshold, its network externalities may be propelled by self-reinforcing forces. Further, as networks interconnect, integrate and merge, they generate values significantly higher than the combined value of the unconnected networks. Reed's law suggests that communicators are not simply groups of people; they are collaborators in enterprise, industry and innovation. Cities foster collaboration. Places that succeed in collaboration graduate to vibrant cities. With Reed's

law in action, city regions around the globe are promoting collaborative business models that involve research laboratories, universities,
industries, workers, financiers, traders and customers.

A city region acts as a super-network or network of networks,
spatially and functionally integrating activities in urban, suburban and
regional nodes that often include a metropolitan city. These nodes share
resources, infrastructure and services, leading to jointly generated and
mutually reinforcing external economies. With the concentration of
creative people, city regions are uniquely placed to benefit from networking. As clustering, networking and collaborating are crucial for a
business to remain competitive in the globalizing world, city regions
play a vital role in the economic growth of nations.

In practice, people do not connect to all members in a network. All
connections are not of equal value to an individual. Every connection
is also not used with the same intensity. In very large networks such as
the Internet, with millions of existing and prospective users, some connections are not used at all. Henry David Thoreau (1854), in his famous
work *Walden, or Life in the Woods*, aptly made the following remark
for the first large telecommunication network in the United States.

> We are in great haste to construct a magnetic telegraph from Maine
> to Texas; but Maine and Texas, it may be, have nothing important to
> communicate. (p. 54)

The aforementioned statement emphasizes that the utility of a network
depends on the activities or powers of the nodes it connects. A network
is valuable when its members are in a position to exploit the advantages
of connectivity. As is said of the Internet, creative people, rich content
and fast connectivity lead to great values. Similar is the case with cities
that network people, groups and activities. Connected and networked
cities succeed when they nurture creativity and collaboration.

GRAVITY MODEL AND TRANSPORT

Networks power nodes, and conversely. The paradigms 'connect,
connect and connect' and 'location, location, location' reinforce each

other. Transport networks play a crucial role in the location of economic activity as they link resources, people and opportunities. They expand input and output markets, enlarge labour market choices, catalyze agglomeration economies, facilitate cluster formation, enhance competition, accelerate knowledge transfer and generate wider economic impacts by enhancing access to the economic mass. Gravity models, popular in regional science, international trade, traffic engineering and transportation planning argue that transportation networks affect locations by influencing their economic potential. These impacts depend on the nature and volume of activities carried out in the nodes connected. The ongoing transport revolution in developing countries like India may thus be enhancing the importance of their cities. The same may also be true of the ICT revolution. The logic of the gravity models suggests that scale and network effects may reinforce each other (Box 2.2).

Apart from operating through interactions between market access, scale economies, transport costs and network effects, agglomeration and network externalities may also be powering cities for different reasons, not highlighted by the research literature. Cities, with their ICT networks, are also enabling the adoption of innovative business strategies by firms that would otherwise be economically unviable. Examples of such strategies include the 'long tail' and the 'BoP'. Cities are also uniquely positioned to benefit from technological innovations associated with the 'platform revolution'.

LONG TAIL OF URBAN SPACE

Chris Anderson, in his bestselling book *The Long Tail: Why the Future of Business Is Selling Less of More*, calls cities the 'long tail' of urban space in the same way the Internet is the 'long tail' of 'idea space' or 'cultural space' (Anderson 2006). He refers to how culture and economy are engineering the shift from a limited number of mass markets to millions of niches. Citing the experiences of online retailers such as Amazon, iTunes and Netflix, Anderson argues that digital technology and networking are rendering 'big hits' or 'blockbuster' products at the 'head' of the market demand curve less important than the rapidly growing

Box 2.2 *Gravity Model of Transportation Planning*

A gravity model portrays network effects as function of key characteristics of the connected nodes—origin and destination—such as
population, employment and gross output. The 'four step model'
of transportation planning, comprising of trip generation, trip
distribution, modal split and route choice, adopts the following
general formulation to estimate the traffic flows between places:

$$T_{ij} = A_i \, A_j \, T_i \, T_j \, f(C_{ij}) \qquad (1)$$

T_{ij} = Number of trips between origin i and destination j
T_i = Trips originating from origin i = 1, 2, 3,..., n
T_j = Trips attracted by destination j = 1, 2, 3,..., m
C_{ij} = Generalized cost of travel between origin i and destination
j (including money and time costs)
$f(C_{ij})$ = the impedance or distance-decay function
A_i, A_j = scale factors solved iteratively to ensure that the trip
production and trip attraction constraints are satisfied, that is,
$\sum_j T_{ij} = T_i$ and $\sum_i T_{ij} = T_j$
Usually, $f(C_{ij})$ is modelled as a negative function of the generalized cost of travel between origin i and destination j, proxied by
distance d_{ij}:

$$f(C_{ij}) = (d_{ij})^{-\lambda} \text{ where } \lambda > 0 \qquad (2)$$

T_i and T_j are often depicted as power functions and T_{ij} is specified
by the equation:

$$T_{ij} = A_i \, A_j \, T_i^{\alpha} \, T_j^{\beta} \, (d_{ij})^{-\lambda} \qquad (3)$$

Taking logarithms of both sides

$$\log T_{ij} = \log A_i + \log A_j + \alpha \log T_i + \beta \log T_j - \lambda \log (d_{ij}) \qquad (4)$$

Differentiating this with respect to d_{ij} yields $\lambda = -(d_{ij}/T_{ij})(\partial T_{ij}/\partial d_{ij})$,
which is similar to own price elasticity of demand in microeconom-
ics. This is a measure of own journey time elasticity of travel demand.
Empirical studies in developed countries find the value of this coefficient between 1 and 2 for intra-city travel and between 2 and 3 for
inter-city travel. These figures suggest that the percentage increase

in traffic flow between two nodes due to an improvement in transportation network exceeds the percentage decrease in journey times, indicating the presence of induced effects or externalities. Additional journeys between two nodes due to a reduction in travel time or cost are associated with not only newly generated traffic from the same route but also diverted traffic from other routes. Theoretical and empirical studies using gravity models of transportation planning and other disciplines suggest that scale economies associated with production and network effects linked to transportation improvements may lead to multiplier effects, magnifying the importance of location and agglomeration in cities.

Source: Ortuzar and Willumsen (2001) and Hensher and Button (2008).

variety of things demanded by smaller groups of people at the 'long tail' (Figure 2.2). As the costs of production and distribution plummet, especially online, and the consumers become more aware of obscure products through a word-of-mouth referral or state-of-the-art recommendation system, the potential aggregate size of many small markets may exceed that of popular products. In this context, Anderson turns to the genesis of the spiky world of cities.

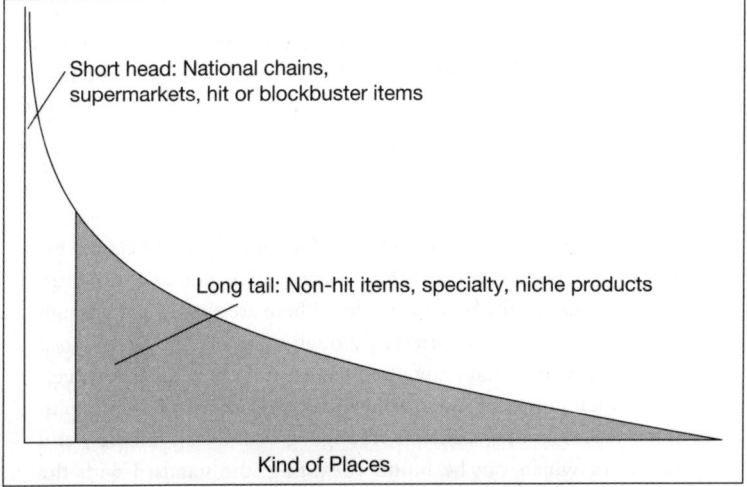

Figure 2.2 *The Long Tail of Urban Space*

These spikes—the great cities of the world—exist because the cultural and economic advantages of being around lots of other people more than compensate for the costs of urban living. One of those advantages, ironically enough, is massive variety in every possible niche. (Anderson 2006, 150)

Large cities offer more diverse markets that support greater varieties of business by catering to even a smaller subset of it, meaning that the longer will be the tail. The density of population ensures that the usually distributed demand for products becomes concentrated. In this context, Anderson (2006) quotes Steven Johnson.

A store selling nothing but buttons most likely won't be able to find a market in a town of 50,000 people, but in New York City, there's an entire button-store district. Subcultures thrive in big cities for this reason as well; if you have idiosyncratic tastes, you're much more likely to find someone who shares those tastes in a city of 9 million people.

Large and diversified cities like New York, London, Paris and Tokyo offer practically everything, starting from 'international food' to 'entertainment of every possible variety', 'services to cater to every need', and 'a bounty of products to rival even Amazon'.

Anderson echoes the views of Jane Jacobs who regards cities as natural homes to diversity. Jacobs aptly observes: 'Great cities are not like towns, only larger. They are not like suburbs, only denser' (1992 [1961], 30). She makes a distinction between cities and smaller settlements as follows:

Towns and suburbs ... are natural homes for huge supermarkets and for little else in the way of groceries, for standard movie houses or drive-ins and for little else in the way of theatre. There are simply not enough people to support further variety, although there may be people (too few of them) who would draw upon it were it there. Cities, however, are the natural homes of supermarkets and standard movie houses plus delicatessens, Viennese bakeries, foreign groceries, art movies, and so on, all of which can be found coexisting, the standard with the strange, the large with the small. Wherever lively and popular parts of cities are found, the small much outnumber the large. Like the small manufacturers, these small enterprises would not exist somewhere else, in the absence of cities. Without cities, they would not coexist.

The diversity, of whatever kind, that is generated by cities rests on the fact that in cities so many people are so close together and among them contain so many different tastes, skills, needs, supplies, and bees in their bonnets. (Jacobs 1992 [1961], 146–147)

BOTTOM OF THE PYRAMID IN CITIES

Like the long tail, the theory of the BoP introduced by Prahalad and Hart (2002) is based on the logic that millions of small sales can aggregate to large profits. Both the theories acknowledge that if the economic and physical bottlenecks in distribution can be removed, a previously neglected market can be accessed for profit. Prahalad's global bestseller *Fortune at the Bottom of Pyramid: Eradicating Poverty Through Profits* was concerned with how to sell products to the 4 billion poor people living on less than US$2 per day, constituting nearly two-thirds of the world's population for the benefit of buyers and sellers both (Prahalad 2005).

While the long tail is about nichification, the BoP is about commodification. The BoP is concerned with finding ways to make commodities cheaper or more attractive to the large un-served, under-served and emerging low-income markets. This is possible through new business models and customized approaches that provide products and services to the BoP segments at affordable prices while still maintaining margins. Such approaches are suitable to address the needs of the informal economy that accounts for between 30 and 60 per cent of total economic activity in many developing countries (de Soto 2000). Cities in India, with a quarter of population living in slums and squatter settlements, are eminently suitable for the application of the BoP strategy. The economic pyramid of the world as presented by Prahalad and Hart (2002) is shown in Figure 2.3.

PLATFORM REVOLUTION AND CITIES

Parker, Alstyne and Choudary (2016) refer to the 'platform revolution' and explain how networked markets are transforming the economy by

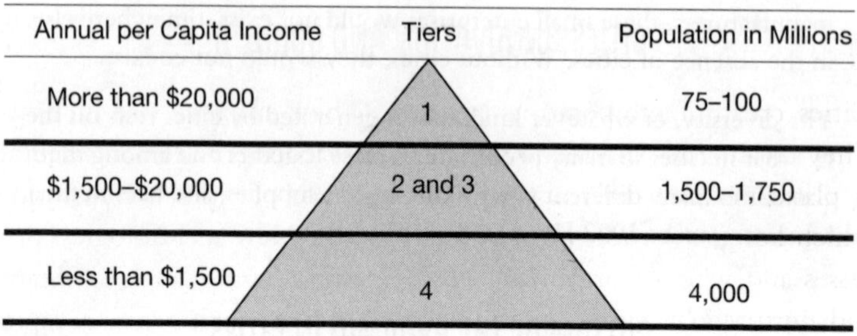

Annual per Capita Income	Tiers	Population in Millions
More than $20,000	1	75–100
$1,500–$20,000	2 and 3	1,500–1,750
Less than $1,500	4	4,000

Figure 2.3 *The World Economic Pyramid*
Source: Prahalad and Hart (2002).

promoting new business models. These models are using technology to connect people, organizations and resources in an interactive ecosystem that is creating and exchanging an enormous amount of value. The authors define a platform as 'a business based on enabling value-creating interactions between external producers and consumers.... The platform's overarching purpose: to consummate matches among users and facilitate the exchange of goods, services, or social currency, thereby enabling value creation for all participants' (p. 5). This definition implicitly refers to the role of network externalities which may be subject to power laws. Platform businesses include Amazon, Alibaba, Uber, Ola Cabs, Airbnb, TripAdvisor, eBay, Zomato, etc. While the emergence of giant firms in the industrial revolution era owed to economies of scale on the supply side, the current age of ICT revolution is leading to significant economies of scale on the demand side and fuelling mega businesses. Technology is facilitating the operation of two-sided markets that involve both producers and consumers in the creation of network effects.

Cities are in a unique position to benefit from the platform revolution due to their 'networking properties' highlighted by Jacobs. They specialize in information networks, creating, disseminating, sharing and applying information. Any industry which is information-intensive can be a candidate for benefitting from the platform revolution. Cities are natural places for such industries. They create density of demand, reduce transport costs and catalyze network externalities, making seemingly unviable business models commercially attractive.

CITIES, INNOVATION AND GROWTH

Cities create agglomeration benefits. They enhance productivity. They create mass and niche markets. They connect networks and act as platforms. But the most fundamental role of cities is innovation, which lies at the root of economic growth. New technologies, processes and ways of organizing business due to innovation facilitated and nurtured by cities, determine the efficiency with which capital and labour are combined in production. Ironically, inter-country and inter-regional differences in economic growth are explained, not by capital intensity but by total factor productivity (TFP). Innovation accounted for 70 per cent of long-term growth in the United Kingdom (Government of the United Kingdom [GoUK] 2014). Private return to R&D has been strongly positive over the past half-century, ranging from 20 per cent to 75 per cent (Hall, Mairesse and Mohnen 2009).

New knowledge has strong positive effects on the productivity of physical and human capital. Knowledge management thus lies at the core of the contemporary debate on economic growth. ICT, an ever-renewing technology, facilitates the efficient management of knowledge. Cities, with their ICT networks and skilled workers, shape economic growth through the ability to support the creation, diffusion and accumulation of knowledge. They serve as magnets for talented people, entrepreneurs and investors in the new knowledge economy. Cities produce new thinking and epitomize the progress of civilization. As Glaeser writes:

> Cities, the dense agglomerations that dot the globe, have been the engines of innovation since Plato and Socrates bickered in an Athenian market place. The streets of Florence gave us the Renaissance, and the streets of Birmingham gave us the Industrial Revolution. The great prosperity of contemporary London and Bangalore and Tokyo comes from their ability to produce new thinking. Wandering these cities— whether down cobblestone sidewalks or grid-cutting cross streets, around roundabouts or under freeways—is the study of nothing less than human progress. (Glaeser 2011, 1)

Glaeser refers to the power of cities in promoting 'collaborative brilliance'. He cautions that cities will remain viable as long as they are able to attract smart people and enable them to collaborate. They decline when they fail to provide employment to people, disconnecting them from economic opportunities.

The role of cities in facilitating inter-industry knowledge spillovers and innovation was eloquently stressed by Jane Jacobs. She recognized their ability to attract highly educated and enterprising people. This was aptly picked up by Lucas (1988) in his endogenous growth theory. Lucas argues that growth is conditioned by the formation of human capital, having non-decreasing marginal returns. He identifies two special attributes of human capital. First, it can be acquired without limit and when one has more of human capital, it does not take more effort to acquire the same. Second, when a person acquires more skill, not only his or her own productivity increases but also the average level of human capital in the economy goes up. This enhances the productivity of others, creating economies outside the market for earnings. The first feature permits an economy to grow without slowing. The second feature accords a crucial role to human capital externalities in economic growth. To support his theory of endogenous growth, Lucas searches for real-world example of such externalities. He realizes that 'the scope of such effects must have to do with the ways various groups of people interact' (Lucas 1988, 37). In this context, Lucas rediscovers 'Jane Jacobs' externalities' and links 'external human capital' to the interaction, exchange and learning processes in cities. Lucas observes:

> If we postulate only the usual list of economic forces, cities should fly apart. The theory of production contains nothing to hold a city together. A city is simply a collection of factors of production—capital, people and land—and land is always far cheaper outside cities than inside.... It seems to me that the 'force' we need to account for the central role of cities in economic life is of exactly the same character as the 'external human capital'.... What can people be paying Manhattan or downtown Chicago rents for, if not being near other people? (Lucas 1988, 38–39)

Romer, the leading exponent of New Growth Theory (NGT), considers knowledge as an intangible capital input in production with increasing marginal productivity. New knowledge or invention, once brought into existence, can be used in productive activities over and over again without being exhausted (Romer 1986). An important externality arises in the process as the creator of new knowledge can capture only a fraction of its benefits. Knowledge cannot be kept secret; it percolates to others without any compensation to the creator. It is the dense environments of cities that speed up knowledge spillovers. The clustering of entrepreneurs, producers, suppliers and workers facilitates a faster flow of ideas and information. Cities develop, incubate, nurture, deploy and disseminate new knowledge. Much of knowledge is tacit and embedded in the routines of firms, households and institutions in cities. It is not codified and leaves no paper trail to trace. The impacts of knowledge externalities on earnings and economic growth are strong in developing countries (Chauvin et al. 2016).

Richard Florida argues that to be successful in this creative age, regions must develop, create and attract talented people—'the creative class'—who put new ideas into practice, produce innovation and develop technology-intensive industries. The capacity of cities to develop, attract and retain talented people and enable them to innovate is critical to their success. Florida emphasizes the role of the dense environment in cities in fostering creativity.

> Ideas flow more freely, are honed more sharply, and can be put into practice more quickly when large numbers of innovators, implementers, and financial backers are in constant contact with one another, both in and out of the office. Creative people cluster not simply because they like to be around one another or they prefer cosmopolitan centres with lots of amenities, though both those things count. They and their companies also cluster because of the powerful productivity advantages, economies of scale, and knowledge spillovers such density brings. (Florida 2005, 50)

Florida reiterates the view of Jane Jacobs that creativity arises from combining thoughts and ideas of many actors, old and new, in the collaborative environments that cities offer. Cities with industrial diversity, educated workforce, skills and entrepreneurship innovate, invent, reinvent and flourish. Those focusing on a limited industrial specialization lose touch with the essential ingredients of urban innovation; they decay.

CITIES AND PUBLIC POLICY

The world is not flat. Globalization and ICT revolution are leading to a spiky world of cities. Skilled and creative people collocate in city regions to benefit from face-to-face interaction, networking and collaboration. New technology is also enhancing the importance of cities as fertile grounds for application of innovative business strategies such as the 'long tail' and the 'BoP'. It is also promoting 'two-sided markets' and enabling firms to benefit from the 'platform revolution'. The agglomeration and network externalities of cities accord them a unique place in the structural and spatial transformation of nations. Land use density is central to agglomeration externalities. Transportation is a key to network externalities. Transportation–land use integration is the single-most important instrument available with planners to assist cities in maximizing the gains from externalities while minimizing their negative consequences. India needs to invest in the planning of cities and just-in-time development of core urban infrastructure, especially transportation to catalyze the external drivers of economic growth, and benefit from new technology. The country must exploit the synergy between spatial planning and urban economics to accelerate socio-economic development and poverty reduction. Cities, distinguished by their land use densities, transportation networks and economic growth drivers will shape India's destiny.

While Jacobs, Lucas, Glaeser and Florida highlight the role of 'human capital' in shaping economic growth in cities, Kennedy (2011) refers to their 'physical shape' and 'design' in enhancing the efficiency of urban economies. He argues that the economics of cities and their 'infrastructure and urban planning' systems are closely intertwined. Together they create conditions for growth by impacting output, income and consumption. Smart Growth also provides impetus and ability to finance new infrastructure. Taking through a virtual tour of great cities of the world, from London to New York, Venice, Tokyo, Hong Kong, Dubai, Toronto and beyond, Kennedy concludes that cities which invested in spatial planning and transport in time, succeeded more than those which did not. He also cites the historical evidence presented by economic historian Norman Gras that a metropolis passes through three early phases—as a centre of commerce, a centre of industry and a hub of transportation—before graduating to a financial centre. The third phase of transportation infrastructure is crucial as it enables a city to connect to regional, national and global economies. Highlighting the importance of investment in transport infrastructure in the evolution of great cities, Kennedy observes:

> Such infrastructure has created new consumer markets, expanded existing markets, sparked agglomeration effects, supported suburbanization, provided a means of dominating hinterlands in cities' progression towards the status of financial centres, and constituted a fundamental part of the evolution of the new urban form. (Kennedy 2011)

The great cities of the world are products of market forces as well as government policies and programmes. Spatial planning, infrastructure development, land management and taxation were key instruments adopted by governments to address the externalities of cities and make serviced land and floor space available in tune with the demands of economic growth. They created long-lasting impacts, shaping the functionality, efficiency, equity, liveability and sustainability of cities. In particular, integrated transportation–land use planning channelized city development in desired directions, balanced employment and housing, magnified the beneficial effects of externalities and minimized their adverse consequences on the environment. By promoting accessibility to the economic mass, it facilitated knowledge transfer, learning and human capital accumulation. It created an enabling environment for entrepreneurs and skilled workers to pursue productive and innovative activities.

It is inconceivable that the phenomenal contribution that great cities of the world made to their nations could have been possible without the policies adopted by governments at crucial stages. For example, the 1667 Building Code of London after the Great Fire, the renovation of Paris from 1853 to 1870 by Baron Haussmann, the 1811 'Grid Plan' of Manhattan and the 1916 Comprehensive Zoning Ordinance of New York City laid solid foundation for the concerned cities. The 'Grid Plan' combined 'beauty, order and convenience' (Burrows and Wallace 1999). It provided a blank state for development, with accessible streets and adaptable blocks. It remains the single-most important document in the development of New York City (Augustyn and Cohen 1997). The built-up area of Manhattan expanded sevenfold along the 'grid' in the nineteenth century (Angel 2012). The visionary grid plan along with major transportation investments transformed New York City. Its growth was materially shaped by transport resources: the Erie Canal, protected harbour, shipping hub, connectivity to an extensive network of national railways, national highways and international airports and a comprehensive, well-used public transit system. The opening of the Erie Canal in 1825, connecting the Hudson River to Buffalo, linked New York to the Great Lakes Hinterland. Land use planning, transportation planning and timely investment in public transport (PT), interacting with economic forces, enabled New York to invent and reinvent itself to become the financial capital of the United States, and an economic colossus. London succeeded because of its port, railway networks and telegraph cables. The Saint Gotthard Tunnel in the Alps facilitated the emergence of Zurich and Milan as financial centres. Frankfurt benefitted significantly from its hub airport.

The importance accorded by developed countries to transport during urban transition can be symbolically gauged from the timely investments they made in metro rail to address not only the traffic issues but also guide development in desired directions. London started metro in 1863 (population 3.2 million), Paris in 1900 (population 4.2 million) and New York in 1904 (population 3.5 million; Table 2.1). The developed countries also invested in commuter rail to address congestion in large cities and to promote regional development. They invested in rail-based transit systems even when their income distribution structure did not yield the ridership numbers required to make them viable. They regarded transportation as a tool for responsive spatial planning, apart from catering to the mobility needs of people. However, cities in India, with population composition and densities favouring PT, are characterized by gross under-investment in mass transit and HSR, including commuter rail, thereby depriving them of wider economic benefits (WEBs). This is primarily due to the long neglect of urban infrastructure finance, which continues to be ad hoc.

Cities are critically important for India's future. The new knowledge economy in cities offers a massive opportunity for 'leapfrogged'

Table 2.1 *World: Details of Largest Metro Rail Transit Systems (2017)*

S. No.	City	Population* (Million)	Year of Opening	Network Length (km)	Daily Ridership (Million)	Length per Resident (mm)
1	Shanghai	15.0	1995	588.0	6.24	39.2
2	Beijing	11.1	1969	572.0	6.74	51.5
3	London	8.57	1863	402.0	3.21	46.9
4	New York	19.0	1904	380.2	4.53	20.0
5	Moscow	10.5	1935	346.2	6.55	33.1
6	Seoul	9.80	1974	326.5	6.90	33.3
7	Guangzhou	8.83	1999	306.8	5.00	34.7
8	Tokyo	35.7	1927	304.5	8.50	8.50
9	Madrid	5.57	1919	293.0	1.74	52.6
10	Shenzhen	7.58	2004	285.9	0.36	37.7
11	Delhi	15.9	2002	226.4	1.66	14.2
12	Paris	9.90	1900	219.9	4.18	22.2

Source: www.metrobits.org (accessed 16 December 2017).
Note: * Data pertain to 2010.

growth. The externalities of cities present a large, untapped resource to address the concerns of under-development and poverty. Cities remain the best hopes for millions of the marginalized in rural and urban areas to escape abject poverty and exclusion. The externalities of cities also create 'land rents' and 'agglomeration rents' that can finance their infrastructure needs. However, in spite of the phenomenal contribution of urban areas to GDP and public finance, policies to internalize the externalities of cities have not received much attention from policymakers. Thus, while spatial planning and just-in-time investment in transportation infrastructure had a strong influence on the rise of great cities of the world, these instruments have not been exploited by Indian cities. Many observed urban problems in India such as sprawl, haphazard development, shortage in affordable housing, workplaces and civic services, especially for the poor and LIGs, slums, insufficient land for public amenities, automobile-dependent urbanization, traffic congestion, pollution, vulnerability to disasters and unsustainable consumption of energy are rooted in the current models of city planning and development. They exhibit a lack of integration between land use, transportation, inclusion of the poor and plan financing. This is largely due to the master planning model followed by cities.

The master planning model adopts a top-down approach. It prescribes a 'grand', 'physical' view of the city. It focuses on detailed land use zoning and controlling development rather than promoting it. By artificially confining cities to rigid built forms, master planning has adversely affected the enterprise of households, firms and developers-builders in cities. The paradigm, with dictatorial connotations, also suffers from a lack of equity. Cities are about people collocating, connecting and collaborating to benefit from enhanced productivity. They attract people, including the rural poor in search of a better future, investing less and striving for more. However, while the majority in Indian cities belongs to the poor and LIGs, the master plans in the past designed cities based on the space norms of the middle class. This has led to exclusionary urbanization.

Infrastructure is the single-most important factor to make cities functional, efficient and inclusive. It encompasses water supply, sewerage, storm drainage, highways, public transit, HSR and ICT networks. It also includes buildings and facilities for employment, housing, education, health, recreation and the like. Infrastructure reduces costs to employers, workers and investors. It influences city form that has long-term implications for land use, economic development and environmental conservation. Infrastructure, along with spatial planning, is instrumental in augmenting the positive effects of externalities while mitigating their negative impacts. In particular, intra-city and inter-city highways, arterial and radial roads, transit networks and HSR catalyze economic growth through direct, indirect and induced effects. However, master planning in India has treated transportation as a 'residual', and not a 'leading' force in urban development. Divorced from the economics of cities, it has also neglected the financing of urban PT. As a result, Indian cities suffer from gross under-investment in transportation infrastructure, leading to inefficient and unsustainable patterns of land use, density and development. High Powered Expert Committee (HPEC; 2011) projects the investment requirement for roads, transport and traffic support infrastructure in India for the period 2012–2031 based on 2009–2010 prices at ₹2.3 million crores out of a total of ₹3.1 million crores needed for core urban infrastructure sectors. India must invest in urban PT, including MRT and HSR.

The official website of the then Ministry of Urban Development (MoUD), GoI, rightly observed: 'the growth story of India shall be written on the canvas of planned urban development'.[1] This statement implicitly recognizes the importance of cities in catalyzing the external drivers of economic growth. These drivers tend to be strong when an economy graduates to high-tech manufacturing and knowledge-intensive services, as is the case with India. However, the policy instruments available with governments to address the externalities of cities are limited. The most important tools are land use planning, transportation planning, transport–land use integration, land taxation, congestion charging and infrastructure development in anticipation of as well as in response to economic growth. India needs to make the best use of these instruments. This calls for revamping the current systems of urban planning, financing and governance. The fundamental forces that make cities grow or decline are largely economic. The design of India's urbanization strategy must incorporate the key principles of land, transport and urban economics. This warrants examining the trends, patterns and prospects of urbanization to derive policy implications, appreciating the role of land and transport economics in shaping the externalities of cities, and strategizing transportation–land use planning, land assembly, inclusion of the poor and investment in urban public transportation infrastructure to accelerate India's structural and spatial transformation processes.

---

[1] See moud.gov.in

3

India's Spatial Transformation
Trends, Challenges and Opportunities

INDIA'S SPATIAL TRANSFORMATION

The twenty-first century will witness an urban revolution. This will be far more important to developing countries than the agricultural and industrial revolutions in view of the scale of impact on the lives of people, especially the poor and the marginalized. It will enable millions in rural and urban areas to escape poverty. India, with a level of urbanization of 33 per cent at present, will be at the forefront of the Urban Revolution. This will provide a unique opportunity to the country to accelerate economic growth and reduce poverty by harnessing the synergy between spatial and structural transformation processes. The clustering of firms, workers, entrepreneurs and institutions in cities will offer the benefits of agglomeration and networking externalities. These forces will aid the generation, transmission and diffusion of knowledge, fuelling knowledge-led growth. Agglomeration in cities will also enable resource mobilization for development by augmenting the tax bases of governments. However, the externalities of cities are subject to limits; when they exceed a threshold, congestion diseconomies arise. Augmenting the beneficial effects of externalities and mitigating their negative consequences to support economic growth are amongst the principal challenges of India's spatial transformation.

Urbanization manifests in the densification of existing urban centres and conversion of rural areas to 'urban' by 'annexation' or 'in situ conversion'. It calls for changes in land use and provision of serviced land and floor space to meet the demands of economic growth—for workplaces, housing, infrastructure, recreation and other uses. The issues are closely connected with the management of urban land and transport. The magnitude of the spatial challenges of urbanization in India can be gauged from the McKinsey Global Institute (2010) and HPEC (2011). The McKinsey Global Institute report estimates that India needs 700–900 million sq. m of commercial and residential space each year till 2030. Connecting these spaces requires 2.5 billion sq. m of new roads and 7,400 km of new metros and subways, representing 20 times the infrastructure capacity that has been added in India since 1999. The availability of serviced land and infrastructure for productive activities in cities will be central to sustaining India's growth momentum. The considerations of efficient, equitable, inclusive, sustainable and financially viable cities call for long-term urban policy with focus on land and transport. In this context, policymakers and planners in India need to understand the trends, patterns, prospects and issues of urbanization and their implications for urban management.

This chapter aims at understanding the dimensions of India's spatial transformation challenges to derive implications for policy. It presents the trends in world's urbanization, an overview of India's urban scenario and projection of urban population to 2051. It highlights the quantitative and qualitative aspects of key urban issues facing India, including population concentration in large cities, slums and squatters, housing, infrastructure, basic services, poverty, informal sector, municipal finance and investment needs. The objective of this chapter is to understand India's urban challenges to convert them into opportunities for economic growth and poverty reduction.

WORLD URBANIZATION TRENDS

The world is urbanizing fast. The global urban population increased by 69.8 per cent over the period 1990–2014. For the first time in history, the share of urban population in global population exceeded 50 per cent in 2008, marking transition to 'the urban millennium'. The world's level of urbanization is projected to rise from 54 per cent in 2014 to 66 per cent by 2050. Urban population would go up from 3,880 million to 6,339 million over the same period. Asia, with 48 per cent urbanization and 2,060 million urban population in 2014, is expected to reach

64 per cent urbanization in 2050, with 3,310 million living in cities and towns. China and India each had a level of urbanization of 26 per cent in 1990. But China's urbanization has outpaced India's, reaching a level of 54 per cent in 2014; the level is expected to reach 76 per cent in China and 50 per cent in India by 2050. Table 3.1 presents the trends and prospects of urbanization in the world, high-income countries, India and China.

By international comparison, India's urbanization process has been rather slow. This is a cause of concern, as cities are the locomotives of growth. As the United Nations' data on 'percentage urban' for 2014 reveals, India, with 32 per cent of the population in cities and towns, is less urbanized than many developing countries of Asia and Africa— Malaysia (74), China (54), Indonesia (53), Thailand (49), the Philippines (44), South Africa (64), Ghana (53), Nigeria (47), Egypt (43) and Zambia (40). The share of urban population in total population was 48 per cent for Asia, while that for Africa, Europe, Northern America, Latin America and the Caribbean was 40 per cent, 73 per cent, 81 per cent and 80 per cent, respectively. In 1950, China was 11.8 per cent urban as against 17 per cent in India. However, China caught up by 1990 and overtook India thereafter (United Nations 2015).

Table 3.2 presents data on the largest UAs in the world in 2014 based on the definition adopted by the United Nations. Tokyo occupies

Table 3.1 *World Urbanization Trends and Prospects*

Population (in Million)	1990	2014	2050
World Total	5,421	7,244	9,551
Urban	2,285	3,880	6,339
Rural	3,036	3,364	3,212
Urbanization (%)			
World	43	54	66
High-income Countries	74	80	87
India	26	32	50
China	26	54	76

Source: United Nations (2015).

Table 3.2 *Largest Urban Agglomerations in the World (2014)*

UA	Rank	Population (in Million)
Tokyo	1st	37.8
Delhi	2nd	25.0
Mumbai	6th	20.7
Kolkata	13th	14.8
Bengaluru	31st	9.7
Chennai	32nd	9.6
Hyderabad	38th	8.7

Source: United Nations (2015).

the first rank globally, with 37.8 million population. In the 50 largest UAs, six are from India; Delhi ranks second with 25 million population and Mumbai sixth with 20.7 million.

INDIA'S URBANIZATION SCENARIO

The Census of India defines urban areas to include 'statutory towns' and 'census towns'. Statutory towns are places having a municipality, corporation, cantonment board or a notified town area committee, etc. Census towns are places satisfying the following three criteria simultaneously:

1. a minimum population of 5,000;
2. at least 75 per cent of the male working population engaged in non-agricultural pursuits and
3. a population density of at least 400 per sq. km.

The population of Urban India, comprising statutory and census towns, increased from 26 million in 1901 to 62 million in 1951, 286 million in 2001 and 377 million in 2011. The level of urbanization went up from 10.8 per cent in 1901 to 17 per cent in 1951, 28 per cent in 2001 and 31 per cent in 2011. Table 3.3 presents the trends in India's total, rural and urban population over the period 1901–2011.

Table 3.3 *India: Total, Rural and Urban Population (in Million) and Level of Urbanization (%; 1901–2011)*

Year	Total Population	Rural Population	Percentage Rural	No. of Cities/Towns	Urban Population	Percentage Urban
1901	238.4	212.5	89.2	1,916	25.9	10.8
1911	252.1	226.2	89.7	1,908	25.9	10.3
1921	251.3	223.2	88.8	2,048	28.1	11.2
1931	279.0	245.5	88.0	2,220	33.5	12.0
1941	318.7	274.5	86.1	2,427	44.2	13.9
1951	361.1	298.6	82.7	3,060	62.4	17.3
1961	439.2	360.3	82.0	2,700	78.9	18.0
1971	548.2	439.0	80.1	3,126	109.1	19.9
1981	683.3	523.9	76.7	4,029	159.5	23.3
1991	846.3	628.7	74.3	4,689	217.6	25.7
2001	1,028.7	742.5	72.2	5,161	286.1	27.8
2011	1,210.7	833.5	68.8	7,935	377.1	31.2

Source: Census of India for different years.

While the number of cities/towns in India increased by three times, urban population rose by 13 times between 1901 and 2011. This reflects the spatial concentration of urbanization, reflecting external economies of agglomeration in larger urban areas. In 2011, the number of UAs/towns in India was 7,935 as against 5,161 in 2001. While the number of statutory towns rose from 3,799 to 4,041 between 2001 and 2011, the number of census towns experienced a phenomenal jump over the same period—from 1,362 to 3,894. About 30 per cent of urban population growth in the last decade is accounted for by census towns. These trends reveal that considerable urbanization is occurring outside the statutory boundaries of municipalities. The census towns fall under rural jurisdictions that have little capacity for spatial planning. They are growing haphazardly. Without interventions for planned development, including provision of connectivity infrastructure, these towns would grow in a slum-like fashion.

As regards the sources of urban growth, natural increase and reclassification (population of new towns – population of declassified towns + increase in population due to annexation of villages to existing cities and towns) have been the dominant forces in India. Net migration contributed only about 20 per cent of urban population growth in India in the decades 1961–1971, 1971–1981, 1981–1991, 1991–2001 and 2001–2011 as may be seen from Table 3.4. Census 2011 reveals that net migration accounted for 21 per cent, reclassification 36 per cent

Table 3.4 Components of Urban Population Growth in India: 1961–1971 to 2001–2011 (%)

Component of Urban Growth	1961–1971	1971–1981	1981–1991	1991–2001	2001–2011
Natural Increase	64.6	51.3	61.3	59.4	43.8
Reclassification	16.7	29.0	17.0	19.2	35.6
Net Rural–Urban Migration	18.7	19.6	21.7	21.0	20.6

Sources: Census of India, Registrar General & Census Commissioner, India (1971, 1981, 1991, 2001, 2011) and Bhagat (2014).

and natural increase 44 per cent of urban population growth during 2001–2011 (Bhagat 2014; Census of India 2011). Apparently, cities and towns in India have not been able to create adequate employment opportunities for rural–urban migrants and commuters. This is partly due to the capital-intensive nature of urban production and weaknesses in the urban informal sector, which engages the bulk of the poor. However, as India moves to a higher growth trajectory, the importance of migration may go up.

Table 3.5 presents the distribution of population between size classes of towns in India. It reflects the top-heavy nature of urbanization structure, indicating the increasing concentration of urban population in large cities. The number of class I cities, with a population of 100,000 or more, increased from 24 in 1901 to 468 in 2011. The share of these cities in urban population went up from 26 per cent in 1901 to 69 per cent in 2001, and more than 70 per cent in 2011. Table 3.6 presents the trends in metropolitan population growth in India. The number of million-plus cities increased from one in 1901 to nine in 1971, 35 in 2001 and 53 in 2011. The share of these cities in urban population rose from 6 per cent in 1901 to 38 per cent in 2001, and 43 per cent in 2011. The largest five UAs in terms of population in India are: Greater Mumbai (18.4 million), Delhi (16.3 million), Kolkata (14.1 million), Chennai (8.7 million) and Bengaluru (8.5 million). The seven largest cities of the country accounted for 50 per cent of India's metropolitan population (Census of India 2011). The Ministry of Statistics and Programme Implementation (MoSPI; 2006) reveals that metropolitan regions in India, comprising of metro cities, their peripheries, satellite towns and suburban villages are witnessing a polarization of economic activity. But they are subject to premature industrial suburbanization (MoSPI 2006; World Bank 2013). Exorbitant land prices, traffic congestion, pollution and shortage in infrastructure are prompting manufacturing firms to move away from central areas to suburban locations even before they can exploit the full potential of agglomeration economies.

There are large interstate variations in the patterns of urbanization in India. Among the states, Delhi was the most urbanized in 2011, with 97.5 per cent urbanization, followed by Goa (62.2 per cent), Mizoram

Table 3.5 India: Number of Agglomerations/Towns and Percentage of Urban Population by Size Classes of Towns (1901–2011)

Census Year	Number of Agglomerations/Towns						Percentage of Urban Population					
	Class I	Class II	Class III	Class IV	Class V	Class VI	Class I	Class II	Class III	Class IV	Class V	Class VI
1901	24	43	130	391	744	479	26.00	11.29	15.64	20.83	20.14	6.10
1911	23	40	135	364	707	485	27.48	10.51	16.40	19.73	19.31	6.57
1921	29	45	145	370	734	571	29.70	10.39	15.92	18.29	18.67	7.03
1931	35	56	183	434	800	509	31.20	11.65	16.80	18.00	17.14	5.21
1941	49	74	242	498	920	407	38.23	11.42	16.35	15.78	15.08	3.14
1951	76	91	327	608	1124	569	44.63	9.96	15.72	13.63	12.97	3.09
1961	102	129	437	719	711	172	51.42	11.23	16.94	12.77	6.87	0.77
1971	148	173	558	827	623	147	57.24	10.92	16.01	10.94	4.45	0.44
1981	218	270	743	1,059	758	253	60.37	11.63	14.33	9.54	3.58	0.50
1991	300	345	947	1,167	740	197	65.20	10.95	13.19	7.77	2.60	0.29
2001	393	401	1,151	1,344	888	191	68.67	9.67	12.23	6.84	2.36	0.23
2011	468	474	1,373	1,686	1,748	424	70.15	8.54	11.11	6.39	3.36	0.45

Source: Census of India for different years.

Notes: Class I: 100,000 or more, Class II: 50,000–99,999, Class III: 20,000–49,999; Class IV: 10,000–19,999, Class V: 5,000–9,999 and Class VI: Below 5,000.

Each UA, comprising generally a number of cities, towns and outgrowths, is considered as one unit.

Table 3.6 India: Number of Metropolitan Cities and Their Share in Urban Population (1901–2011)

Census Year	Number	Population (in Million)	Population per City (in Million)	Percentage of Urban Population
1901	1	1.51	1.51	5.84
1911	2	2.76	1.38	10.65
1921	2	3.13	1.56	11.14
1931	2	3.41	1.70	10.18
1941	2	5.31	2.65	12.23
1951	5	11.75	2.35	18.81
1961	7	18.10	2.58	22.93
1971	9	27.83	3.09	25.51
1981	12	42.12	3.51	26.41
1991	23	70.66	3.07	32.54
2001	35	108.29	3.09	37.85
2011	53	160.70	3.03	42.61

Source: Census of India for different years.

(52.1 per cent) and Tamil Nadu (48.4 per cent). Table 3.7 presents the percentage of urban population in states and union territories in 1971, 1981, 1991 and 2011, and decadal annual exponential growth in urban population for 1971–1981, 1981–1991, 1991–2001 and 2001–2011.

URBAN CONSUMPTION PATTERNS

Urbanization has significant implications for changes in consumption patterns. As a country develops and urbanizes, the share of consumer expenditures on non-food items as a proportion of total consumption expenditure increases. Urban areas act as vibrant markets for non-food commodities. Periodic consumer expenditure surveys conducted by the National Sample Survey Office (NSSO) support this position as revealed by Table 3.8.

Table 3.7 *India: Level of Urbanization and Growth in Urban Population Across States and Union Territories (1971–2011)*

S. No.	States	Percentage of Urban Population					Annual Exponential Growth Rate			
		1971	1981	1991	2001	2011	1971–1981	1981–1991	1991–2001	2001–2011
1	Andhra Pradesh	19.3	23.3	26.8	27.3	33.4	3.9	3.6	1.4	3.04
2	Arunachal Pradesh	3.7	6.3	12.2	20.4	22.9	8.3	9.3	7.0	3.31
3	Assam	8.8	9.9	11.1	12.7	14.1	3.3	3.3	3.1	2.46
4	Bihar	10.0	12.5	13.2	10.5	11.3	4.3	2.7	2.6	3.03
5	Chhattisgarh	NA	NA	NA	20.1	23.2	NA	NA	3.1	3.49
6	Delhi	89.7	92.8	89.9	93.0	97.5	4.6	3.8	4.1	2.37
7	Goa	26.4	32.5	41.0	49.8	62.2	4.4	4.0	3.3	3.01
8	Gujarat	28.1	31.1	34.4	37.4	42.6	3.4	2.9	2.8	3.07
9	Haryana	17.7	22.0	24.8	29.0	34.9	4.7	3.6	4.1	3.68
10	Himachal Pradesh	7.0	7.7	8.7	9.8	10.0	3.0	3.1	2.8	1.45
11	Jammu & Kashmir	18.6	21.1	22.8	24.9	27.4	3.8	3.4	3.4	3.10
12	Jharkhand	NA	NA	NA	22.3	24.0	NA	NA	2.6	2.80
13	Karnataka	24.3	28.9	30.9	34.0	38.7	4.1	2.6	2.5	2.74
14	Kerala	16.2	18.8	26.4	26.0	47.7	3.2	4.8	0.7	6.56

(Continued)

Table 3.7 (Continued)

S. No.	States	Percentage of Urban Population				Annual Exponential Growth Rate			
		1971	1981	1991	2001	2011	1971–1981	1981–1991	1991–2001	2001–2011
15	Madhya Pradesh	16.3	20.3	23.2	26.7	27.6	4.5	3.7	2.7	2.28
16	Maharashtra	31.2	35.0	38.7	42.4	45.2	3.4	3.3	3.0	2.12
17	Manipur	13.2	26.4	27.7	23.9	32.5	9.7	3.0	1.2	3.70
18	Meghalaya	14.6	18.0	18.7	19.6	20.1	4.9	3.1	3.2	2.70
19	Mizoram	11.4	25.2	46.2	49.5	52.1	11.8	9.6	3.3	2.59
20	Nagaland	10.0	15.5	17.3	17.7	28.9	8.5	5.6	5.3	5.10
21	Odisha	8.4	11.8	13.4	15.0	16.7	5.2	3.1	2.6	2.38
22	Punjab	23.7	27.7	29.7	34.0	37.5	3.6	2.6	3.2	2.29
23	Rajasthan	17.6	20.9	22.9	23.4	24.9	4.5	3.3	2.7	2.54
24	Sikkim	9.4	16.2	9.1	11.1	25.2	9.6	-3.2	4.8	9.42
25	Tamil Nadu	30.3	33.0	34.2	43.9	48.4	2.5	1.8	3.6	2.39
26	Tripura	10.4	11.0	15.3	17.0	26.2	3.3	6.2	2.5	5.66
27	Uttar Pradesh	14.0	18.0	19.9	20.8	22.3	4.8	3.3	2.8	2.53
28	Uttaranchal	NA	NA	NA	25.6	30.2	NA	NA	2.8	3.36
29	West Bengal	24.8	26.5	27.4	28.0	31.9	2.8	2.5	1.8	2.60

Union Territories									
1	Andaman & Nicobar Islands	22.8	26.4	26.8	32.7	37.7	6.4	4.1	4.4	2.10
2	Chandigarh	90.6	93.6	89.7	89.8	97.3	5.9	3.1	3.4	2.38
3	Dadra & Nagar Haveli	0.0	6.7	8.5	22.9	46.7	—	5.3	14.6	11.57
4	Daman & Diu	—	—	46.9	36.3	75.2	—	4.9	1.9	11.59
5	Lakshadweep	0.0	46.3	56.3	44.5	78.1	—	4.5	-0.8	6.24
6	Pondicherry	42.0	52.3	64.1	66.6	68.3	4.7	4.9	2.3	2.73
	All India	20.2	23.7	25.7	27.8	31.2	3.8	3.1	2.7	2.76

Source: Census of India for different years.

Notes:

1. The figures for the states of Uttar Pradesh, Bihar and Madhya Pradesh for the 1970s and 1980s pertain to the undivided states as existed during that time. The figures for the 1990s are, however, for the new states and hence such figures are not temporally comparable.

2. In the absence of the Census data for total and urban population for the year 1981 in case of Assam, the urban and total population growth rates have been assumed to be constant during the 1970s and 1980s. The same has been assumed for the 1980s and 1990s for Jammu and Kashmir. The percentage of urban population has been arrived for Assam (1981) and Jammu and Kashmir (1991) based on these assumptions.

3. Goa in 1971 and 1981 corresponds to Goa, Daman and Diu.

Table 3.8 *Trends in Composition of Consumer Expenditure in Urban India: 1993–1994 to 2011–2012*

Item Group	Share in Total Consumer Expenditure (%)				
	1993–1994	1999–2000	2004–2005	2009–2010	2011–2012
Cereals	14.0	12.4	10.1	9.1	7.3
Gram	0.2	0.1	0.1	0.1	0.1
Cereal Substitutes	0.1	0.0	0.0	0.0	0.1
Pulses & Products	3.0	2.8	2.1	2.7	2.1
Milk & Products	9.8	8.7	7.9	7.8	7.8
Edible Oil	4.4	3.1	3.5	2.6	2.7
Egg, Fish & Meat	3.4	3.1	2.7	2.7	2.8
Vegetables	5.5	5.1	4.5	4.3	3.4
Fruits & Nuts	2.7	2.4	2.2	2.1	2.3
Sugar	2.4	1.6	1.5	1.5	1.2
Salt & Spices	2.0	2.2	1.7	1.5	1.7
Beverages, etc.	7.2	6.4	6.2	6.3	7.1
Food Total	54.7	48.1	42.5	40.7	38.5
Pan, Tobacco, Intoxicants	2.3	1.9	1.6	1.2	1.4
Fuel & Light	6.6	7.8	9.9	8.0	7.6
Clothing & Bedding	4.7	6.1	4.0	4.7	5.3
Footwear	0.9	1.2	0.7	0.9	1.2
Misc. Goods & Services	27.5	31.3	37.2	37.8	39.7
Durable Goods	3.3	3.6	4.1	6.7	6.3
Non-food Total	45.3	51.9	57.5	59.3	61.5
Total Expenditure	100	100	100	100	100

Source: National Sample Survey Office, Ministry of Statistics and Programme Implementation, GoI (2013).

PROJECTED URBAN POPULATION

Figure 3.1 shows the trends and projections of urban population till 2051. The urban population would more than double between 2011 and 2051. With an estimated rural population of 860 million in 2014, the country would still have 810 million in rural areas in 2050 (United Nations 2015). Thus, India would confront the dual challenges of urban and rural development for many decades. Ironically, it is the cities that have to shoulder the responsibility of mobilizing resources to address the concerns of rural development and poverty alleviation. Cities constitute the tax bases of all levels of government: central, state and local.

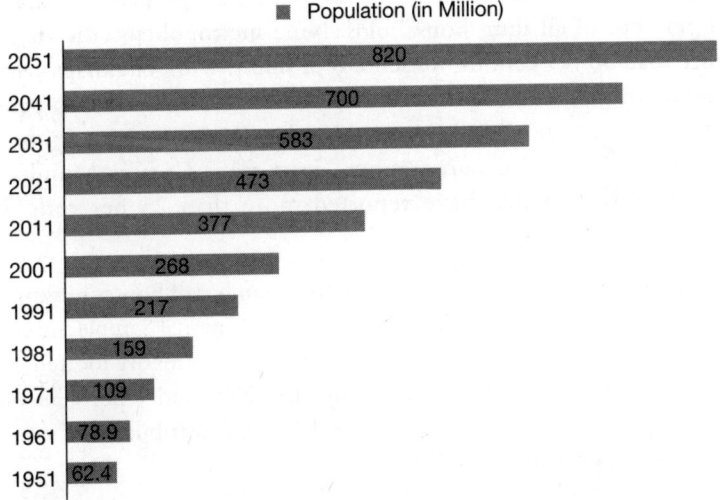

Figure 3.1 *Urban Population Trends and Projections in India (in Million)*

Source: Census of India for different years and projections.

SLUMS AND SQUATTERS

Census 2001 estimated the urban slum population in India at 42.6 million. It reported that 41.6 per cent of slum population in the country lived in metropolitan cities, with Mumbai having the largest number of slum-dwellers at 54 per cent of population. Census 2011 has placed the number of slum-dwellers in India at 65.5 million.

According to Census 2011, out of 4,041 statutory towns, 2,543 towns have reported slums. Among the major states, Tamil Nadu has the highest number of slum-reporting towns (504), followed by Madhya Pradesh (302), Uttar Pradesh (260), Karnataka (206) and Maharashtra (187). Andhra Pradesh has the highest proportion of urban households in slums at 35.7 per cent, followed by Chhattisgarh (31.9 per cent) and Madhya Pradesh (28.3 per cent). Kerala has the lowest percentage of urban households living in slums at 1.5 per cent. Census 2011 further reveals that 46 million-plus cities contain 38 per cent of all slum households. Nine metropolitan cities have more than 30 per cent of households in slums, with Visakhapatnam topping the list at 44.1 per cent, followed by Jabalpur Cantonment Board (43.1 per cent) and Greater Mumbai (41.3 per cent). Among the largest municipal corporations, apart from Greater Mumbai, Kolkata and Chennai have reported more than 25 per cent of households in slums.

Census 2011 reveals that out of the total number of houses in slums, 70 per cent are owned and 26 per cent rented. National Sample Survey (NSS) 2009 reports that nearly 40 per cent of the slums are located on lands belonging to ULBs, 39 per cent on private and 4 per cent on railway lands (NSSO 2010). Table 3.9 shows the distribution of slums by type of ownership of land.

Census 2011 defines 'slum' as a residential area with dwellings unfit for human habitation due to factors such as dilapidated condition, overcrowding, poor design of building, narrowness of streets, lack of ventilation, light or sanitation, or a combination of factors that are detrimental to public safety and health. It divides slums into

Table 3.9 *Percentage of Slums by Type of Ownership of Land in NSSs*

Year of Survey	Private	Public			Not Known
		Railway	Local Bodies	Others	
NSS 2002	35.3	4.9	41.2	17.5	1.1
NSS 2009	39.3	4.4	40.9	11.7	3.7

Source: National Buildings Organization: State of Slums in India: A Statistical Compendium 2013, Ministry of Housing and Urban Poverty Alleviation, Government of India, New Delhi.

'notified', 'recognized' and 'identified' categories. Notified slums are areas notified as 'slum' by state, UT administration or local government under any Act, including a 'Slum Act'. Recognized slums are those recognized as 'slum' by state, UT administration or local government, Housing and Slum Board, which may have not been formally notified as a slum under any Act. An identified slum is a compact area with at least 300 population or about 60–70 households living in poorly built, congested tenements and in unhygienic environment, usually with inadequate infrastructure, and lacking in proper sanitary and drinking water facilities. The slum population reported by Census 2011 is an underestimate as slums not notified, not recognized or not identified, and slums with less than 60 households are not enumerated by the Census. An official report estimated the slum population of India in 2011 at 93.05 million, representing 26.3 per cent of the urban population. This report adopts 20–25 households as one of the criteria to identify slum (Ministry of Housing & Urban Poverty Alleviation [MoHUPA] 2010).

Slums present islands of utter deprivation, subhuman living and poverty characterized by multiple vulnerabilities. They arise from the failure of both urban land market and urban planning system. Lack of security of tenure, precarious shelter, poor state of basic civic services, serious problems of health and vulnerability to disasters are amongst the key concerns in slum development and upgradation in India.

STATE OF URBAN HOUSING

Table 3.10 depicts the distribution of urban households by type of dwelling in 2011. More than 20 per cent live in temporary or semi-permanent structure. Table 3.11 shows the percentage of households by the number of dwelling rooms. About 50 per cent of slum-dwellers live in one room or less. Table 3.12 gives a picture of urban housing

Table 3.10 *State of Urban Housing in India (2011): Distribution of Households by Type of Dwelling Unit*

Type of Dwelling	% of Households	
	Urban	Slum
Permanent	84.3	77.7
Semi-permanent	11.6	16.0
Temporary	3.2	5.3
Any Other	0.9	1.0
Owned	69.2	70.2
Rented	27.5	26.3
Others	3.3	3.5

Source: Census of India (2011).

Table 3.11 *State of Urban Housing in India (2011): Distribution of Households by Number of Rooms*

No. of Rooms	% of Households	
	Urban	Slum
No Exclusive Room	3.1	4.4
One Room	32.1	44.8
Two Rooms	30.6	29.5
Three Rooms	18.4	12.3
Four Rooms	9.3	5.4
Five Rooms & Above	6.5	3.5

Source: Census of India (2011).

Table 3.12 *Distribution of Urban Housing Shortage in India (2012)*

| Category | Distribution of Housing Shortage | |
	Number (in Million)	Percentage (%)
EWSs	10.55	56.18
LIG	7.41	39.44
MIG and Above	0.82	4.38

Source: MOHUPA, GoI.

shortage in India in 2012, estimated at 18.78 million, 96 per cent of which pertains to economically weaker section (EWS) and LIG categories.

The shortage of housing in India covers homeless population and people living in congested, obsolescent and non-serviceable kutcha houses. Estimates based on Census 2011 data suggest that nearly 80 per cent of the housing shortage is due to congestion, another 12 per cent due to obsolescence and only 3 per cent households are homeless. The shortage of housing in India is so huge that only a multi-pronged approach, covering multiple alternatives to suit the varying needs and conditions on the ground such as rental housing, ownership housing, upgradation, security of tenure in slums, sites and services, etc., can make a dent on the problem. Paradoxically, the Census data reveals that 9 per cent of houses remained vacant in 2001 and the figure rose to 10.1 per cent in 2011 (Table 3.13). The vacant houses presumably belong to the high- and middle-income groups, including non-resident Indians. Outdated rent control regimes in states discourage homeowners to rent out their houses due to difficulty in evicting tenants when needed, and the fear of being dragged into prolonged litigation.

On the demand side, there are many urban residents who cannot or do not want to own a house, even if offered at a low price. Some poorer sections with non-fixed place of working prefer affordable houses on rent. Also, the large population of migrants, who are seasonal or who come to cities for specific purposes, require rental housing at

Table 3.13 *Urban India: Occupied and Vacant Census Houses (2001 and 2011)*

Use of Occupied Census Houses	2001 Census Houses	2001 % Share	2011 Census Houses	2011 % Share
Total No. of Census Houses	71,558,356	100.0	110,139,853	100.0
Occupied Census Houses	65,106,336	91.0	99,046,223	89.9
Vacant Census Houses	6,452,020	9.0	11,093,630	10.1

Source: Census of India.

affordable rates. Ironically, the rental housing stock in India has declined from 54 per cent in 1961, to 53 per cent in 1971, 47 per cent in 1981, 34 per cent in 1991, 29 per cent in 2001 and 27.4 per cent in 2011 (KPMG 2014).

STATE OF CIVIC SERVICES

Table 3.14 presents a picture of the state of access to civic services in India—in urban areas as a whole versus slums.

The shortages in basic services in cities owe to the chronic lack of investment in urban infrastructure. They are closely connected with the precarious state of municipal finance. Data from Census 2011 and recent studies present the following picture on the state of water supply, sewerage and sanitation, drainage, solid waste management and transport in India (Ahluwalia, Kanbur and Mohanty 2014; HPEC 2011; Mohanty 2014, 2016).

Water Supply

- Only 71 per cent of the urban population is covered with individual water connection in India compared to more than 91 per cent in China, 86 per cent in South Africa and 80 per cent in Brazil.

Table 3.14 *State of Civic Services in India (2011): Urban Areas Versus Slums*

Civic Service	% of Households	
	Urban	Slum
Access to Tap Water	70.6	74.0
Drinking Water Within Premises	71.2	56.7
Electricity as a Source of Lighting	92.7	90.5
Bathroom Facility	87.0	81.0
Access to Closed Drainage	44.5	36.9
Open Drainage	37.3	44.3
No Drainage	18.2	18.8
Latrine Within Premise	81.4	66.0
With Water Closet	72.6	57.7

Source: Census of India (2011).

- Duration of water supply in Indian cities ranges from 1 hour to 6 hours—as against 24 hours in China and Brazil, and 22 hours in Vietnam.
- Per capita water supply in Indian cities ranges from 37 litres per capita per day (lpcpd) to 298 lpcpd for a limited duration, while Paris supplies 150 lpcpd continuously and Mexico 171 lpcpd for 21 hours a day.
- Non-revenue water accounts for 50 per cent of water production, compared to 5 per cent in Singapore. System losses due to unaccounted for water in four large cities of Madhya Pradesh ranged from 33 per cent to 66 per cent.
- The average cost recovery in water supply is 67.2 per cent and collection efficiency 78.8 per cent.

Sewerage and Sanitation

- Ninety-four per cent of cities and towns do not even have a partial sewerage network. Almost 50 per cent of households in Bengaluru and Hyderabad have no sewerage connection.

- Thirteen per cent of urban households do not have access to any form of latrine facility; they defecate in the open.
- Only 21 per cent of wastewater generated is treated. Sewage treatment capacity is less than 40 per cent in cities with more than 100,000 population in 9 out of 11 states; it is less than 20 per cent in five states—Rajasthan (4 per cent), Odisha (8 per cent), Uttarakhand (10 per cent), Bihar (13 per cent) and Madhya Pradesh (15 per cent).

Drainage

- Of total urban households, 44.5 per cent have access to closed drainage; 37.3 per cent are faced with open drainage and 18.2 per cent have no drainage at all.
- Less than 20 per cent of the road network in the country is covered by storm water drainage.

Solid Waste Management

- Solid waste collection coverage ranges from 70 per cent to 90 per cent in major metropolitan cities and is less than 50 per cent in smaller cities and towns as against the benchmark of 100 per cent.
- Less than 30 per cent of solid waste generated is segregated; scientific disposal of waste is almost never practised.

Transport

- While urban areas accounted for only 7 per cent of the total road length of India in 2002, the number of motor vehicles in the 23 largest cities was 30 per cent of the total number registered in the country. The number of motor vehicles in 50 million-plus cities was 31.54 per cent of the total number registered in the country in 2015.
- Public transport (PT) accounts for only 27 per cent of urban transport in India compared to 49 per cent in the Philippines and Egypt, and 40 per cent in South Africa, South Korea and Brazil.

- The share of PT fleet in total number of registered vehicles has decreased from 11 per cent in 1951 to 1 per cent in 2015. In 2009, only 20 out of 85 Indian cities with a population of 0.5 million had bus service.
- The total vehicular population rose from mere 0.3 million in 1951 to 210 million in 2015. The share of two-wheelers, cars, jeeps and taxis has increased from 60.8 per cent to 87.1 per cent between the two years (Ministry of Road Transport & Highways [MoRTH], GoI, 2016).

DIMENSIONS OF URBAN POVERTY

A quarter of the urban population in India lives in poverty. An Expert Committee set up by the then Planning Commission under Dr C. Rangarajan has estimated the percentage of urban residents living below poverty line in 2011–2012 at 26.4 per cent, with the number of urban poor at 102.5 million (Table 3.15). According to the Committee, a person spending less that ₹1,407 per month or ₹47 a day was considered to be poor in urban areas. Whereas the number of rural poor has decreased by 65.4 million between 2009–2010 and 2011–2012, the number of urban poor has gone down by a much smaller figure of 26.2 million (Planning Commission 2014).

While expert committees in the past have defined poverty based on monetary criteria such as household expenditure or income, it is the non-monetary variables capturing multiple vulnerabilities having

Table 3.15 *India: Rural and Urban Poverty Estimates (2009–2010 and 2011–2012)*

Year	Poverty Ratio (%)			No. of Poor (in Million)		
	Rural	Urban	Total	Rural	Urban	Total
1. 2009–2010	39.6	35.1	38.2	325.9	128.7	454.6
2. 2011–2012	30.9	26.4	29.5	260.5	102.5	363.0
3. Reduction	8.7	8.7	8.7	65.4	26.2	91.6

Source: Planning Commission (2014).

residential, occupational and social dimensions that distinguish urban poverty from rural poverty. The urban poor, especially slum-dwellers, are subjected to the lack of access to affordable housing, decent workplace, clean water, sanitation, public transport, education, health and social security. According to National Family Health Survey (2007), the slum-dwellers are in a far worse condition than the rural poor on some key health indicators (Table 3.16). Further, the lack of security of tenure makes them vulnerable to eviction by municipal authorities in the name of master plan implementation and city modernization drives. Many slums, located in hazardous and eco-fragile areas such as river beds, tank beds, flood plains, banks of storm drains, hill slopes and the like are also prone to natural and man-made disasters, depriving the dwellers of the limited assets they possess from time to time.

THE URBAN INFORMAL SECTOR

The urban poor, including slum-dwellers, suffer from not only residential but also social and occupational vulnerabilities. Most of them engage in informal sector activities, characterized by poor working conditions—low wage, temporary nature of employment, absence of written contract, no job security, no paid leave and no social security. Employment and Unemployment Surveys (EUS) conducted by the NSSO define informal sector enterprises as units engaged in the production of goods or services for sale, wholly or partly, with the primary objective of generating employment and income of the persons concerned. These units typically operate at a low level of organization, with little or no division of labour and capital. They have the characteristic features of household enterprises. They consist of proprietary and partnership enterprises, besides those run by non-corporate entities such as self-help groups.

NSSO's EUS 2011–2012 provides the following picture about the urban informal economy in India (NSSO 2014).

- About 39 per cent of India's population was employed—40 per cent in rural areas and 36 per cent in urban areas.
- Fifty-five per cent of workers in India were engaged in non-agriculture and agricultural activities, excluding crop production,

Table 3.16 *State of Health of the Urban Poor in India (2005–2006)*

Indicator	Urban Poor	Urban Non-poor	Overall Urban	Rural	All India
Delivery in Health Facility (%)	44.0	78.5	67.4	28.9	38.6
Anaemia Among Women 15–49 Years (%)	58.8	48.5	50.9	57.4	55.3
Children Totally Immunized Before Completing 1 Year (%)	39.9	65.4	57.6	38.6	43.5
Children Stunted (%)	54.2	33.2	39.6	50.7	48.0
Children Less Than 3 Years Underweight (%)	47.1	26.2	32.7	45.6	42.5
Children with Anaemia (%)	71.4	59.0	63.0	71.5	69.5
Neonatal Mortality (Per 1,000)	34.9	25.5	28.7	42.5	39.0
Infant Mortality (Per 1,000)	54.6	35.5	41.7	62.1	57.0
Under-5 Mortality (Per 1,000)	72.7	41.8	51.9	81.9	74.3
Prevalence of Medically Treated Tuberculosis (Per 100,000)	461	258	307	469	418
Prevalence of HIV Among Adult Population (15–49 Years; %)	0.47	0.31	0.35	0.25	0.28
Children with Diarrhoea in Last Two Weeks (%)	8.9	8.9	8.9	9.0	9.0
Children with Acute Respiratory Infection in Last Two Weeks (%)	6.1	4.4	5.1	6.0	5.8
Women with at Least One Contact with Health Worker in Three Months (%)	10.1	5.8	6.8	14.2	11.8
Households Using a Sanitary Facility for Excreta Disposal (%)	47.2	95.9	83.2	26.0	44.7

Source: National Family Health Survey (2007).

plant propagation and non-specialized combined production of crop and animal—95 per cent in 2011–2012 in urban areas (94% in 2009–2010).

- Among the urban workers engaged in non-agriculture and agricultural activities, excluding crop production, plant propagation and non-specialized combined production of crop and animal, 98 per cent were working in the non-agriculture sector.

- Seventy-two per cent of all urban workers were employed in non-agriculture and agricultural activities, excluding crop production; 69 per cent of them worked in the informal sector in 2011–2012 (67% in 2009–2010).

- Among the informal sector workers in urban areas, the proportion of self-employed, regular wage/salaried employees and casual labourers were about 58 per cent, 27 per cent and 16 per cent, respectively.

- About 98 per cent of self-employed, 81 per cent of casual labourers and 40 per cent of regular wage or salaried employees in urban areas were engaged in informal activities.

- Manufacturing, construction, wholesale and retail trade, transportation and storage industries were the main providers of employment in the informal sector. Seventy-five per cent of informal sector workers in urban areas were employed in these industries (77 per cent for male and 66 per cent for females).

- Seventy per cent of informal sector workers in urban areas were employed in small enterprises (with less than six workers).

- Most informal sector workers were poor. The average daily earning of a regular wage/salaried employee in the informal sector was about ₹258 for urban males and ₹194 for urban females. The daily wage rate of a casual labourer in the informal sector was about ₹169 for urban males and ₹113 for urban females.

While total employment in the Indian economy rose from 457.9 million in 2004–2005 to 472.4 million in 2011–2012, employment in organized non-agriculture (employing 10 persons or more with the aid of power or 20 persons without the aid of power) increased from 28.8 million to 47.7 million. Employment in unorganized non-agriculture increased from 185.4 million in 2004–2005 to 209.6 million in 2011–2012. Thus, in absolute terms, the number of workers who joined the unorganized sector was more than those who joined the organized sector. The figures indicate that the informal sector in India is not only large but also growing. Cities present opportunities for informal activities by catalyzing agglomeration economies and supporting the formal sector in various ways, for example, providing logistics, catering and security services to IT and IT-enabled services.

EUS 2011–2012 reveals that among the workers in non-agriculture and agricultural activities, excluding crop production, 11 per cent of urban male workers and 4 per cent of urban female workers engaged in informal sector activities did not have a fixed workplace. They include mobile street vendors prominently. Seventy-two per cent of urban males in the informal sector worked in (a) employer enterprise/unit/office/shop, but outside employer's dwelling, (b) construction site, (c) own enterprise/unit/office/shop but away from own dwelling and (d) own dwelling unit. Seventy-three per cent of urban females working in the informal sector had workplace located in (a) own dwelling unit, (b) structure attached to own dwelling unit, (c) open area attached to own dwelling unit, (d) detached structure adjacent to own dwelling unit and (e) employer's enterprise/unit/office/shop but outside the employer's dwelling. These figures reveal the importance of organizing space for informal sector activities in cities. However, the formal master plans of cities in India, barring a few, did not recognize the presence of the informal sector. As a result, informal activities in cities are carried out in 'illegal' spaces, which do not conform to the zoning regulations. This is a key policy issue as the capacity of the formal sector in India to create employment is limited and most of the urban poor, including street vendors, waste pickers, home-based workers, domestic service providers, self-employed persons and casual labourers work in informal activities.

STATE OF MUNICIPAL FINANCES

While cities in India are plagued by problems of housing, infrastructure, basic services, slums, poverty, etc., municipalities are not financially equipped to address them. Municipal finances in India are characterized by non-buoyant tax base, lack of attention to user charges, ad hoc intergovernmental transfers, inefficient collection of taxes and lack of financial accountability in service delivery. Over the years there has been an erosion in municipal fiscal autonomy. The ratio of municipal revenues to combined central and state revenues has declined from 3.92 per cent in 2007–2008 to 3.62 per cent in 2012–2013. The ratio of municipal taxes to combined central and state taxes has gone down from 2.11 per cent to 1.79 per cent between the two years. The precarious state of municipal finances in India is reflected in the state of civic infrastructure and services. This is disturbing as urbanization is increasing, and so also the contribution of cities to GDP.

Table 3.17 presents data on revenues of municipalities by source in India in 2007–2008 and 2012–2013. In 2002–2003, 'own revenues' constituted 63 per cent of total municipal revenues. The share went down to 55.7 per cent in 2007–2008, and 51.6 per cent in 2012–2013. The share of tax revenues declined from 37.2 per cent to 32 per cent between 2007–2008 and 2012–2013. Non-tax revenues accounted for 18.5 per cent in 2007–2008 and 19.7 per cent in 2012–2013. The share of central transfers increased marginally from 9.1 per cent to 9.5 per cent. That from state government went up from 32.4 per cent to 34.5 per cent. All the key municipal fiscal autonomy ratios: own revenues–GDP, own taxes–GDP and property tax–GDP have declined between 2007–2008 and 2012–2013. Table 3.18 presents the distribution of municipal revenues by source in 18 states of India in 2012–2013. Except in Maharashtra and Punjab, the dependency of municipalities on intergovernmental transfers is substantial, exceeding 70 per cent in Himachal Pradesh, Jammu & Kashmir, Kerala, Bihar, Madhya Pradesh, Uttarakhand, Odisha and Karnataka. Maharashtra's figure is explained by the presence of Octroi in Mumbai and local body tax (LBT) in other municipalities. The LBT was subsequently abolished by the Government of Maharashtra based on demand by the business community. With Octroi being subsumed under the GST, it is no longer available to Mumbai. In Punjab, the municipalities had access to excise revenues.

While the municipalities have a narrow, inflexible and non-buoyant tax base, they also do not exploit the full potential of the revenue sources already assigned to them. Property tax, the single-most important municipal tax in India, is grossly under-exploited. A

Table 3.17 *Trends in Municipal Revenues in India by Source: From 2007–2008 to 2012–2013*

S. No.	Sources of Revenue	2007–2008		2012–2013	
		Total (₹ Crores)	% of Total Municipal Revenue	Total (₹ Crores)	% of Total Municipal Revenue
A. Own Sources					
1.	Total Taxes	18,366	37.20	30,912	32.00
	Property Tax	8,159	16.53	15,110	15.64
	Other Taxes	10,207	20.68	15,801	16.35
2	Non-taxes	9,134	18.50	19,002	19.70
	Total Own Source Revenues	27,501	55.70	49,913	51.60
B. Other Sources					
1	GoI Transfers	3,515	7.10	5,387	5.60
2	Central Finance Commission Transfers	986	2.00	3,760	3.90
3	State Assignment/ Devolution	9,342	18.90	18,537	19.20
4	State Grant-in-aid	6,653	13.50	14,809	15.30
5	Others	1,355	2.70	4,234	4.40
	Total Other Source Revenues	21,851	44.30	46,727	48.40
C. Total Revenues		49,351	100.00	96,640	100.00
GDP at Factor Cost in Current Prices		4,582,086		9,388,876	
Municipal Revenue as a % of GDP			1.08		1.03

Source: Administrative Staff College of India (ASCI; 2014) based on the data furnished by state governments to the Fourteenth Finance Commission of India; Indian Public Finance Statistics 2013–2014; Mohanty (2016).

Table 3.18 *Distribution of Municipal Revenues by Source in States in India (%): 2012–2013*

S. No.	State	Taxes	Non-taxes	Central Transfers*	State Transfers**	Others
1	Andhra Pradesh	33.5	24.3	7.5	34.7	–
2	Assam	14.9	14.7	11.9	23.3	35.2
3	Bihar	13.2	5.2	28.4	52.5	0.8
4	Gujarat	18.8	12.1	5.4	57.1	6.5
5	Haryana	18.5	24.3	14.9	37.6	4.9
6	Himachal Pradesh	–	–	55.8	44.2	–
7	Jammu & Kashmir	6.1	5.5	31.5	56.9	–
8	Karnataka	20.2	8.8	17.8	53.2	–
9	Kerala	9.8	5.9	39.1	45.1	–
10	Madhya Pradesh	10.0	8.6	8.8	69.2	3.4
11	Maharashtra	53.2	29.9	3.8	9.8	3.4
12	Odisha	10.2	9.2	41.4	33.7	5.5
13	Punjab	69.2	16.8	8.9	2.8	2.3
14	Rajasthan	7.0	32.1	12.0	47.7	1.3
15	Tamil Nadu	21.6	12.0	6.6	56.6	3.2
16	Uttar Pradesh	10.8	5.6	10.4	54.7	18.6
17	Uttarakhand	5.9	3.4	7.6	69.3	13.8
18	West Bengal	20.1	19.1	13.7	46.2	0.8
	All India	32.0	19.7	9.5	34.5	4.4

Source: ASCI (2014); Mohanty (2016).
Notes: * GoI transfer+Central Finance Commission transfer.
** Assigned revenues from state governments+devolution through State Finance Commission+state government grants-in-aid.

Reserve Bank of India study, using data for 35 metropolitan municipal corporations for the period 1999–2000 to 2003–2004 found that these corporations are subject to massive 'underspending' relative to normative requirements—varying between 94.43 per cent for Patna to 30.78 per cent for Pune. The average underspending was of the order of 76 per cent. The key findings of the study are:

1. A significant positive relationship exists between underspending of municipal corporations and 'dependency ratio', representing the share of grants received by a corporation in total municipal expenditure.
2. A highly significant negative relationship exists between underspending and 'revenue decentralization', measured as the ratio of a municipal corporation's per capita revenue to state per capita revenue.
3. Efficiency of revenue administration, reflected in own municipal revenues as a proportion of Gross State Domestic Product (GSDP), has a significant negative correlation with the level of underspending.
4. In 10 out of 25 municipal corporations, less than 10 per cent of the cost of services was recovered through user charges and fees; in another six, the cost recovery was between 10 and 20 per cent. Six municipal corporations recovered between 20 and 50 per cent. Only in two corporations was cost recovery more than 75 per cent.
5. Establishment and administration accounted for more than 50 per cent of total municipal expenditure in 11 municipal corporations. Operation and maintenance (O&M) constituted less than 10 per cent in the case of 12. The share of capital expenditure was less than 10 per cent for nine municipal corporations. These included seven with less than 3 per cent share (Mohanty et al. 2007).

The problems of city finances in India are deeply rooted in institutional and administrative factors, including the structure of fiscal federalism and the way in which cities are governed (Ahluwalia, Kanbur and Mohanty 2014; Mohanty et al. 2007; Mohanty 2014, 2016).

URBAN INVESTMENT NEEDS

The McKinsey Global Institute (2010) projects that India needs to spend ₹9.74 million crores on cities by 2030, with ₹5.31 million crores for capital expenditure. The largest demand for capital spending would be for affordable housing, followed by mass transit. If we exclude affordable housing, the capital expenditure requirement till 2030 would be ₹3.54 million crores. The McKinsey study finds that India's annual per capita spending on cities at US$50, including capital and operational expenditures, is 14 per cent of China's US$362, less than 10 per cent of South Africa's US$508, and less than 3 per cent of the United Kingdom's US$1,772. In terms of capital expenditure, India's per capita annual urban spending is US$17 as against US$116 in China, US$127 in South Africa and US$391 in the United Kingdom. The report estimates that India needs to increase the figure eightfold, from US$17 to US$134, raising it from 0.5 per cent of GDP to 2 per cent of GDP a year. Ironically, per capita revenues and per capita 'own' revenues of municipalities in India in 2012–2013 were remarkably small at ₹3,123 and ₹1,681, respectively. Per capita municipal expenditure in 2012–2013 stood at ₹3,116. This comprised of per capita revenue expenditure of ₹1,986 and per capita capital expenditure of ₹1,130 (ASCI 2014).

HPEC (2011) projects that India would need ₹3.92 million crores for core urban infrastructure over the period 2012–2031. If O&M costs are added, the figure would rise to ₹5.92 million crores. The O&M norms adopted by the HPEC suggest that Indian municipalities spend about 20 per cent of what is needed for the efficient delivery of public services. Table 3.19 depicts the expenditure needs of core urban infrastructure sectors.

The problem of urban infrastructure in India is closely linked to the state of municipal finances, resulting in poor creditworthiness of ULBs, absence of capacity to borrow and repay debt. Paradoxically, while spatial planning and infrastructure development benefit many actors in the urban economy in many ways, the principle of benefit taxation is yet to be adopted by Indian cities in a systematic way. Land

Table 3.19 *Expenditure Estimates for Core Urban Sectors (2012–2031; ₹ at 2009–2010 Prices)*

Sector	Total Capital Expenditure (₹ Crore)	Total O&M Expenditure (₹ Crore)	Average per Capita Investment Cost (₹)	Average per Capita O&M Cost Annual (₹)
Water Supply	320,908	546,095	5,099	501
Sewerage	242,688	236,964	4,704	286
Solid Waste Management	48,582	273,906	391	155
Urban Roads	1,728,941	375,267	22,974	397
Storm Water Drains	191,031	34,612	3,526	53
UT	449,426	304,386	5,380	371
Traffic Support Infrastructure	97,985	36,690	945	34
Street Lighting	18,580	4,717	366	8
Total (Core Sectors)	3,098,141	1,812,637	43,385	1,806

Source: HPEC on Urban Infrastructure Report (2011, 69–84).

values in cities are soaring, but the municipalities have not harnessed the power of urban land as a resource. Similarly, in spite of severe traffic congestion in large cities, the principle of congestion charging (CC) is not applied. There is an urgent need for cities to adopt land-based taxes, CC and other innovative instruments to leverage debt from the market to finance lumpy infrastructure projects. Broadening the municipal revenue base, exploiting the sources already assigned to ULBs and adopting innovative methods to design and implement crucially important urban infrastructure projects, especially public transportation, are amongst the key challenges of urban policy.

CHALLENGES OF SPATIAL TRANSFORMATION

India's spatial transformation process poses many challenges. These are linked to increase in the number of urban residents, large sections of whom are poor; concentration of urban population in a limited number of large UAs; premature suburbanization of metropolitan cities; haphazard growth of census towns; mushrooming of slums and squatter settlements; shortage of affordable housing including rental housing; chronic under-investment in infrastructure, especially public transportation; sprawl and uneconomic extension of city boundaries; traffic congestion, pollution and environmental degradation; and precarious state of municipal finances. However, while urbanization presents apparently intractable problems, if managed well, it can usher in unprecedented opportunities for economic development and poverty reduction. The clustering of firms, households and institutions in compact cities, in conjunction with new technologies, will create multiplier effects for economic growth and resource generation for development through externalities. Cities will also create 'home market effects' by creating demand for secondary and tertiary sector production, subject to scale and agglomeration economies. Vibrant cities will drive not only urban rejuvenation and transformation but also rural development and poverty reduction.

While 68 per cent of India's population lives in rural areas, agriculture engages more than 50 per cent of the workforce and contributes only 15 per cent of GDP. Judging from experiences of countries around the world, this contribution is bound to decline steadily as economic growth accelerates. The capacity of agriculture to provide productive employment to rural residents will dwindle. On the contrary, cities with vibrant externalities will catalyze economic growth and employment in the formal and informal sectors for rural–urban migrants and commuters, enabling them to benefit from scale and agglomeration economies. They will also generate resources for financing rural development and poverty alleviation, apart from leading to urban–rural remittances. If rural areas are physically and functionally connected to vibrant cities, urbanization could act as a powerful instrument to improve the lives of millions of the poor and marginalized in villages. It will assist them in escaping poverty and exclusion. But urbanization issues, if not addressed in time, will lead to disastrous social and environmental consequences for rural and urban areas both. The potential role of cities as catalysts of rural development and poverty alleviation needs to be recognized. The paradigm of 'rural versus urban development' must give way to a strategy of 'rural and urban development'.

The trends, patterns and prospects of urbanization in India suggest that the country needs to devote utmost attention to five key challenges of spatial transformation. First, serviced land and floor space must be available for productive economic activities, including affordable housing. Effective spatial planning and land management will be central to promoting economic growth through cities. Second, transport being the most critical factor to service land and floor space, transportation planning and land use planning must be integrated to exploit the synergy between them. The numbers, densities and income structures of Indian cities and the concerns of environment and climate change present a compelling case for a public transportation-led and transit-oriented development strategy. India needs to make significant investments in urban public transport, including mass transit and high-speed rail. Third, as compulsory acquisition of land will be difficult under the new land acquisition regime, innovative ways of urban land assembly must be explored. Fourth, urban planning must take into account the population composition in cities. The needs of the poor for living, working and vending must be incorporated into the planning model itself. Fifth, robust methods of financing urban infrastructure, especially public transit, must be adopted. The challenges of India's spatial transformation are huge. They call for addressing the lacunae in the present approaches to land use planning, transportation planning, land assembly, affordable housing and infrastructure financing. The principles and practices of land, transport and urban economics must be integrated with urban planning, adopting a people-centric approach, to make urbanization a vehicle for India's socio-economic transformation.

4
Economics of Urban Land
A Critique of Master Planning in India

URBANIZATION AND LAND

Urban land lies at the core of the structural and spatial transformation processes of a developing nation. As a country develops, secondary and tertiary activities collocate in cities to benefit from scale and agglomeration. Urbanization leads to more intensive use of land in existing urban centres, annexation of rural areas to municipal jurisdictions and in situ conversion of rural settlements into towns. It calls for land assembly, servicing of land and creation of floor space to meet the demands of housing, workplaces and public infrastructure facilities such as roads, public transit, water supply, sewerage, drainage, parks, playgrounds, etc. However, land assembly and land use decisions by private actors and public agencies affect the externalities of cities which lead to divergences between private and social costs and benefits. Accordingly, city authorities resort to correction mechanisms, with instruments such as spatial planning, zoning, development control, taxation and infrastructure. Density, land use and development patterns in cities thus reflect the operations of land and housing markets as well as policies and regulations followed by governments. Regulations are important for the functioning of urban land markets, but when poorly designed, they act as a drag on the contribution of cities to economic growth and social welfare.

India's journey from 410 million people in cities and towns in 2014 to 820 million in 2051 will be marked by significant changes in the density and mix of land use for residential, commercial, industrial, institutional, recreational and other purposes. Productive economic activities require serviced land and floor space at strategic locations to benefit from agglomeration and network externalities. Infrastructure facilities, especially transportation, are essential to service land and develop floor space. They lead to direct and indirect, short-term and long-term, and local as well as regional impacts. They are instrumental in avoiding suboptimal urban form and dysfunctional cities. However, they are lumpy and need large upfront investments. Serviced land is also vital for housing and employment of the urban poor. These sections, which are squeezed out of the formal land markets, constitute a quarter of India's urban population. For them, location in a central place or an area served by public transport (PT) system is critical to access employment opportunities. Further, compact cities reduce the demand for indiscriminate conversion of fertile agricultural land to urban use and the cost to service such land. They act against unsustainable consumption of non-renewable energy resources and reduce the carbon footprint. The mechanisms adopted by private developers and public authorities to procure, plan, finance, assemble, develop, use and reuse urban land and floor space will be critical for inclusive growth and sustainable development in India.

Urban areas in India suffer from serious problems of land management. They present a picture of over-regulation of land and housing markets and under-planning of local economic growth. Many conspicuous problems of Indian cities such as haphazard development, exorbitantly high land and housing prices in relation to household incomes, sprawl, slums, inadequate housing and workplaces, especially for the poor, insufficient land for public amenities including open spaces, traffic congestion, environmental pollution and lack of resources to finance infrastructure can be traced to their model of urban planning. Known as 'master planning', this model is rooted in the orthodox urban planning theories of the twentieth century. Its legal basis is derived from the Town and Country Planning Act of 1947 in the United Kingdom. The paradigm has not kept pace with the changes in demand for serviced land and floor space in India in tune with the dynamics of cities. Obsession with land use detailing and development control has also diverted the focus of policymakers and administrators from the core considerations of productive efficiency, environmental sustainability and inclusive growth. The neglect of land, transport and urban economics, transportation planning, plan financing and capacity of local authorities to prepare and implement detailed land use plans is conspicuous. Indian cities have not devoted attention to transportation–land use integration, transit-oriented development (TOD), inclusionary zoning (IZ) and using land use zoning and floor space index (FSI) as resource. Master planning, divorced from the economics of cities, has not been able to present a coherent model for financing planned urban development.

This chapter deals with the operation of urban land markets and efficacy of government policies to address market failure. It dwells on interactions between urban externalities, spatial planning, development regulations, infrastructure, local economic development and land management from the perspectives of land and urban economics. Considering the most critical problem of urban land market as one of acute constraints on the supply of serviced land and floor space, it argues for reforms in master planning to suit India's realities. We refer to the peculiar characteristics of urban land and development rights, which in conjunction with government regulations influence the functioning of urban land and housing markets. We critically examine the current model of urban planning focused on the preparation and implementation of master plans, prescribing land use at city, zone and local levels. We highlight the shortcomings of this model. We refer to the difficulties in compulsory public acquisition of land to implement master plans in view of the new land acquisition (LA) law in India. We discuss the constraints in operation of urban land and housing markets due to outdated laws, including rent control and FSI restriction. The chapter also presents a critique of the master planning approach, rooted in orthodox urban planning theories of the twentieth century. It briefly outlines the key elements of urban land policy in India.

MARKET FOR URBAN LAND

The demand for urban land is 'derived'. It primarily arises from the needs of economic activities in secondary and tertiary sectors for floor space. The supply of floor space depends on the availability of serviced land for various urban uses at particular locations, FSI permitted under zoning regulations, access to infrastructure and services, and conditions of real estate. The markets for land and floor space are conditioned by the functions of the city: economic, social and political. City economic activities attract skilled and semi-skilled workers, who need workplaces, housing, public services and recreational facilities. The concentration of firms and households in close proximity leads to external economies and diseconomies of agglomeration. Diseconomies include congestion, pollution, incompatible land uses, decrease in open spaces and health hazards, justifying zoning regulations. Further, urban land markets exclude the poor and low-income groups (LIGs), calling for 'social functions' of the city to address their needs for housing, workplaces and basic services.

Government interventions in urban land markets are called for on considerations such as the characteristics of urban land, externalities associated with density and land use, need for investment in infrastructure to service land and imperative to address the issues of equity and inclusion. These considerations are described as follows:

- *Nature of urban land:* Inherent attributes of urban land such as locational fixity, uniqueness, inelasticity and durability, coupled with indivisibility in infrastructure, create rigidities in the functioning of urban land markets. They encourage monopoly of landownership and speculative hoarding of land assets. Factors such as ill-defined land titles and property rights, informational asymmetries, restrictions on conversion of rural land to urban use, high stamp duties and outdated rent control laws also affect the transactions in property and add to reasons for market failure.
- *Externalities of cities:* Agglomeration and network externalities arise from the collocation and networking of firms, households and institutions in cities. They are closely connected with spatial and functional linkages between economic activities, intensity of land use, density and mix of development, and infrastructure connectivity. Externalities cause divergences between market equilibrium and socially optimal outcome. They call for mechanisms to internalize externalities, including taxation and regulation.
- *Supply of serviced land:* Serviced land is essential for cities to carry out economic activities. But the market lacks incentives to service

land by installing infrastructure facilities such as highways, rail-based transit, water supply, sewerage, storm drainage, etc. These facilities require lumpy investments and are also subject to freerider problems. Further, a part of their benefits spills over the statutory boundaries of municipalities and is captured by non-residents. Moreover, the services generated by major infrastructure projects spread over generations. Thus, the current residents are often reluctant to pay for their full costs.

- *Needs of the urban poor:* Cities attract poor people in search of opportunities. But due to many reasons, urban land and housing prices soar, weeding the poor and LIGs out of formal markets. They force these segments to seek shelter in slums, which are frequently prone to the onslaught of natural and man-made disasters. However, cities need a mix of workers with varying skills to function efficiently. On this reasoning alone, there is a strong economic case for catering to affordable housing, workplace, public transport and basic service needs of the poor and marginalized sections in cities, including rural–urban migrants.

- *Intrinsic merits of regulation:* Unregulated land markets lead to grave socio-economic consequences, including public health hazards, incompatible land uses and socially suboptimal outcomes. Further, the joint development of land parcels often yields better spatial and economic outcomes than when developed in isolation. Urban land markets also do not function without clear ground rules regarding the definition, recording and use of land and development rights.

CHARACTERISTICS OF URBAN LAND

Urban land has peculiar characteristics (Box 4.1). Unlike horizontal land in rural areas, urban land has both horizontal and vertical dimensions. Another key feature is the access of land to public infrastructure facilities and services. Land is geographically fixed, immobile and scarce. Every parcel of urban land has a unique location and development potential; it is not possible to create identical parcels of land in a city. Though the quantity of urban land per se is finite, its supply can be increased for particular purposes by extending city boundaries, changing land use, providing services and going vertical. But each of these alternatives has

Box 4.1 *Characteristics of Urban Land*

Horizontal land: Subdivision of land into parcels for single family homes and extension of city boundary to accommodate new urban uses provide examples of horizontal dimension of urban land. Poor management of horizontal land leads to sprawl, uneconomic extension of costly infrastructure, longer commuting, wastage of energy resources and adverse impacts on agricultural production.

Vertical land/FSI: Subdivision of land for individual apartments in a high-rise building complex is an example of the vertical dimension of land. When cities lack infrastructural facilities and safeguards for environmental protection, high-rise structures can lead to congestion, pollution, noise and other diseconomies.

Immobility: Urban land is physically immobile and can't be moved from one market to another. Due to this, it is subjected to the effects of externalities. The value of urban land is also closely related to it being an immobile factor, impacted by geography and history, attracting durable activities and commanding rent.

Locational fixity: The location of urban land, its geographical features, including distance from employment centres, markets, recreational facilities, highways, public transit and other trunk infrastructure networks are key factors affecting the use and value of land.

Uniqueness: Each parcel of land in a city is unique with unique physical, historical and economic characteristics. No two parcels of land in a city are identical. Urban land is a highly heterogeneous commodity.

Scarcity: Land is physically scarce. User preference for a particular type of land for a purpose or use makes the supply of such land inelastic. Physical features and access to infrastructure and civic services contribute to the scarcity of land at different locations. Rapid urbanization accentuates such scarcity.

Durability: Land and buildings constructed thereon are durable physically, though not economically. A stretch of land remains forever, but deterioration in services with continuous use by owners or occupiers of property can affect its value.

(Continued)

Box 4.1 *(Continued)*

Accessibility: This dimension relates to the connectivity of land to public infrastructure facilities and services such as water supply, sewerage, storm water drainage, solid waste management, fire protection, roads, transit, etc., and to public and private facilities such as offices, shopping malls and recreational centres. Closely associated with accessibility is the concept of serviceability or access to services.

Indivisibility of infrastructure: The utility of urban land crucially depends on the kind, quantity and quality of services it is able to receive due to proximity to public infrastructure facilities. These overheads tend to be indivisible and have implications for the user value and market value of land over a period of time.

Divisibility of ownership: Ownership of land can be segregated from a land asset physically or legally. Landownership can be physically divided by establishing either horizontal or vertical boundaries.

Property rights: The right to use land, to exclude others from its use and to offer its use to others are exclusive, not absolute. Generally, owners have the right to use, sell, trade, lease, subdivide and mortgage their land, while the rights of taxation, regulation and eminent domain are reserved for the state. Tenure insecurity results when property rights are not defined and enforced due to poor land records and inefficient administration. This has implications for the operation of land markets.

Externalities: Adjoining and nearby plots having different owners and uses influence the value of land in an area. The actions of these actors are not priced and so also some public goods such as open space, leading to market failure. Externalities need not always be negative. For example, households benefit from maintaining a close social network, leading to the accumulation of social capital. Moreover, firms locate in close proximity to other firms to reap the benefits of common markets for intermediate goods.

Spatial planning: Physical planning, including zoning, development regulation and provision of public infrastructure facilities and services, plays a crucial role in making serviced land and floor space available for urbanization and economic growth. They affect the development potential, use and value of urban land at different locations.

implications for costs and benefits—private and social. The right to develop urban land is also not entirely a private right. Zoning laws and development control regulations (DCRs) affect the use of such rights. Urban land is an input for housing and infrastructure; land acquisition, land pooling and other mechanisms to assemble land affect the operation of land markets. Locational fixity, land use density and infrastructure connectivity subject urban land to externalities, calling for government interventions. Further, spatial planning, zoning, infrastructure, public services and growth-augmenting policies of government lead to unearned increments in land values, making urban land an ideal instrument to finance the city infrastructure investments, especially transport.

The peculiar characteristics of urban land and the elaborate interventions resorted to by public authorities through spatial planning and regulation make the operation of urban land markets complex. On the supply side, urban land is entangled in a web of complex ownership and tenure rights, obscure titles, poor land records, absence of land information system, high stamp duties, cumbersome procedures for registration of property, multiple laws and authorities for acquisition, transfer, taxation, planning and development of land and an inappropriate model of land use planning that aims at controlling development rather than promoting it. Severe restrictions on land use, FSI and conversion of agricultural land to urban use are, to a great extent, responsible for the exorbitant increase in land values, housing prices and office rents in Indian cities. These factors, along with the concentration of economic activities, speculation in urban land markets and gross under-investment in infrastructure, especially transportation, are leading to an artificial scarcity of serviced land and floor space in central locations in many cities in relation to the demands of local economic growth.

The demand for land in Indian cities presents an uneven picture. There are pockets within cities where demand is high due to historic, geographic and economic reasons, including external economies, zoning regime and access to infrastructure facilities. Excessive pressure on land in such locations is leading to exorbitant land and housing prices, sprawl, uneconomic expansion of municipal boundaries, spotty development, mushrooming of slums and automobile-dependent urbanization. This is creating a heavy pressure on existing infrastructure systems, including transportation, water and wastewater. It is also lead-ing to a large-scale conversion of fertile agricultural land around cities to urban use with adverse consequences for food grain production. These effects have serious repercussions for the carrying capacity of cities, consumption of non-renewable energy resources, greenhouse gas (GHG) emission, carbon footprint and social cost of urbanization. A major adverse social impact of sprawl is the segregation between the rich and the poor. This affects social cohesion in cities and finds expression in crime, drugs, social unrest and the like.

While cities are largely built by market forces, their contributions to growth and welfare are significantly influenced by governmental inter-ventions to enhance the positive impacts of agglomeration economies and mitigate the negative consequences of congestion diseconomies. The numbers, population composition, income distribution structure and density patterns in Indian cities also call for public policies to promote compact, connected, mixed use and public transportation-led urban development. The design of policies and regulatory instruments to address the failure of urban land markets and attain broader social objectives thus assumes crucial significance. This calls for understanding land and urban economics and the factors determining serviced land and floor space in cities, including the role of firms, households, developers and governments.

ECONOMICS OF URBAN LAND

Cities are shaped by markets and governments. They represent a fun-damental trade-off between the external economies of collocation and urban costs. In large cities, such economies reflect in higher wages and amenities. Urban costs manifest in high land prices and housing rents, shortage of civic services, overcrowding, congestion, pollution, crime, slums and the like. Larger cities tend to increase the time and money costs of travel, and the disutility of longer commuting. Urban econom-ics refer to five major factors that shape cities by impacting demand, supply and price of land and housing: agglomeration economies arising due to the clustering of economic activities; spatial equilibrium linked to the choice of location by firms, households and developers; build-ing technology and FSI that permit developers to substitute capital for land; transport technology that connects firms and households to opportunities and influences city form; and government policies that affect land use, construction of buildings, provision of infrastructure, taxation and local economic development (Alonso 1964; Brueckner 2011; Glaeser 2008a; Mills 1967, 1972; Muth 1969).

Apart from agglomeration externalities, a fundamental concept in urban economics is spatial equilibrium. This is based on the insight that if identical individuals are choosing different locations in cities to reside, then these places must be offering an equivalent bundle of net benefits, taking all relevant factors into account—wages, rents, prices, taxes, transport costs, amenities and services. In the simplest model, the city is assumed to be circular, all jobs are located in the central business district (CBD) and residents commute to the CBD for work. The CBD offers high wage due to the economies of agglomeration. A representative resident residing at a distance d from the CBD spends income on (a) consumption of a private good C assumed to be the numeraire, (b) rent for land L that translates to housing and (c) cost of commuting to CBD, assumed to be a linear function of distance d. We assume that the wage offered by CBD is fixed at w and that the representative resident living at distance d from the CBD maximizes utility subject to budget constraint. The constrained maximization problem is captured by the functions (1) and (2) described as follows:

$$U = U(c, L) \tag{1}$$

where U is the utility function, c = consumption of the private good with price normalized to unity and L is the consumption of land.

The budget constraint for the representative resident can be stated as:

$$c + r(d)L + td = w \tag{2}$$

where $r(d)$ = rent incurred by the representative resident living at distance d from CBD, t = transport cost per unit distance, say 1 km, assumed to be constant for simplicity, $r(d)L$ = total land rent, td = total commuting cost and w = wage offered by the CBD.

The constrained optimization problem for the representative resident is equivalent to the unconstrained optimization problem, that is, maximizing U as a function of d and L, namely:

$$\text{Maximize } U = U\,(w - r(d)L - td,\ L) \qquad (3)$$

Differentiating the expression with respect to d gives the following first-order condition for spatial equilibrium:

$$r'(d) = -t/L \qquad (4)$$

If we replace land rent by housing cost, the modified budget constraint can be stated as follows:

$$c + p(d)q + td = w = \text{Constant} \qquad (5)$$

where $p(d)$ = housing cost incurred by a representative resident living at distance d from the CBD, q = consumption of housing or floor space and $p(d)q$ = total cost of housing.

The new reduced form of the spatial equilibrium condition is:

$$p'(d) = -t/q \qquad (6)$$

This equation suggests that a resident living 1 km further away from the CBD, incurring t more in commuting cost, pays t less towards housing, hence t/q less in housing cost per unit area. This expression is called the 'accessibility premium'.

The spatial equilibrium condition (4) or (6) can be made more realistic by relaxing the assumptions and incorporating the behaviour of firms, developers and governments into the model. However, subject to reasonable conditions, the standard theories of urban economics lead to the following general conclusions regarding the operation of urban land and housing markets:

1. Land rent or housing price adjusts to ensure spatial equilibrium. Land goes to that use which bids the most for it—the principle of highest and best land use.
2. Land uses are ordered away from the CBD according to the accessibility premium to land or housing.
3. The household groups with steeper land rent or housing price functions locate closer to the CBD.
4. Land rent and housing price decreases, land and housing consumption increases, structural density and building height decrease

and population density declines as the distance from the CBD increases.

5. More populous cities tend to be spatially larger; higher income or lower commuting cost leads to more populous and geographically extended cities.
6. The poor and LIGs prefer to locate in central city areas in a bid to be close to workplaces and to save commuting costs.
7. Transportation technology shapes cities which extend along highways. Commuters shift from low fixed cost technology like public transport to high fixed cost technology like automobile as they live away from CBD.
8. Limiting city size by fixing rigid growth boundaries leads to higher urban land rents and housing prices, and lower consumption of floor space.
9. Restricting FSI or building height results in a decrease in housing supply, increase in housing price, lower floor space consumption, sprawl and suboptimal urban form.

While the aforementioned conclusions rely on the assumption of competitive land and housing markets in cities, in practice, pervasive regulations by public authorities affect the functioning of these markets. Cities are thus shaped by interactions between market forces and public policies, leading to trade-offs between benefits and costs of agglomeration—to firms, households, developers-builders, etc. The urban planning model needs to consider these trade-offs.

Urban economics does not attempt to literally depict the complex reality of cities. It, however, provides useful concepts and tools to understand why economic growth localizes and to design policies for guiding urban development. Market forces and government policies together determine the benefits and costs of producing, working, living, interacting, learning, shopping, recreating and commuting in cities. The high costs of land and housing, and traffic jams in cities such as Delhi, Mumbai, Bengaluru and Hyderabad are conspicuous. Yet firms and households prefer to locate in these cities to benefit from collocation. They also weigh the costs and benefits of living and working at particular locations within cities. Firms seek to benefit from scale and agglomeration economies and proximity to markets, including those for skilled labour and intermediate inputs. They strive to reduce transaction, trade, transport and tariff costs. Developers choose locations to build new housing to match the demands of buyers, differing in incomes and tastes. Households decide location based on considerations of wages, land, housing and commuting costs and access to infrastructure and services.

While the location choices of actors in the spatial economy are determined by both benefits and costs, physical planners in developing countries are too obsessed with costs. According to them, the primary objectives of land use planning, including zoning are to reduce urban costs in terms of negative externalities such as vehicular congestion and pollution, incompatible land uses and high land prices. However, they overlook the dynamics of agglomeration and network externalities in cities. They also ignore the role of public policies such as highway toll, congestion pricing, motor vehicle taxation, land-based taxes, road capacity expansion, public transit investment and transport–land use integration in mitigating the negative externalities associated with traffic problems. In fact, environmental degradation in Indian cities is largely due to the faulty model of automobile-dependent urbanization, which could be corrected by a public transportation-led and transit-oriented development strategy.

High urban land values and housing prices in a city may not in themselves mean bad or good things. They may simply imply that land and housing markets are severely constrained—by factors such as control of land use and FSI. They may also mean that the city authorities are not making adequate investments in transportation and other infrastructure to service land and floor space. Further, they may imply that land-based financing instruments are not exploited to finance such infrastructure. The Henry George Theorem (HGT) makes a strong case for financing urban infrastructure by taxing the unearned increments in land values due to public policies and investments.

THE HENRY GEORGE THEOREM

Economics highlights the importance of land rent as a source of financing urban development. Adam Smith recognized the nature of land rent as an unearned income and his description of the landowners runs as follows:

They are the only one of the three orders whose revenue costs them neither labour nor care, but comes to them, as it were, of its own accord, and independent of any plan or project of their own. That indolence, which is the natural effect of the ease and security of their situation, renders them too often, not only ignorant, but incapable of that application of mind which is necessary in order to foresee and understand the consequences of any public regulation. (1976 [1776], Book 1, Chapter 11, 277)

John Stuart Mill argued for taxing land rents based on the principle of social justice as follows:

Suppose that there is a kind of income which constantly tends to increase, without any exertion or sacrifice on the part of the owners: ... In such a case it would be no violation of the principles on which private property is grounded, if the state should appropriate this increase of wealth, or part of it, as it arises. This would not properly be taking any-thing from anybody; it would merely be applying an accession of wealth, created by circumstances, to the benefit of society, instead of allowing it to become an unearned appendage to the riches of a particular class.

Now this is actually the case with rent. The ordinary progress of a society which increases in wealth, is at all times tending to augment the incomes of landlords; to give them both a greater amount and a greater proportion of the wealth of the community, independently of any trouble or outlay incurred by themselves. They grow richer, as it were in their sleep, without working, risking, or economizing. What claim have they, on the general principle of social justice, to this acces-sion of riches? (Mill 2001 [1848], 941)

Henry George (1879) in his *Progress and Poverty*, while recognizing land rent as a surplus, made a strong case for its taxation to finance public expenditures. In fact, he advocated a 'single tax' on land value as it was non-distortionary and was also capable of generating adequate revenues to meet the public expenditures needed. His view was that as public investments capitalize into location values, the economic rent to land was the most appropriate form of public finance. The HGT suggests that under certain conditions, the aggregate spending by the government on public goods will generate adequate land rents so as to finance such goods (Arnott 2004; Arnott and Stiglitz 1979; George 1879; Stiglitz 1977).

Though the HGT is criticized for ignoring the growing public spending needs of modern economies, most scholars agree that it provides a good guide to financing local government expenditures in developing countries. When public financial resources are scarce, urban infrastructure facilities are best financed by taxes on owners of land and of other immobile and quasi-immobile factors. These facilities lead to huge unearned increments in land values and rents due to the externalities of cities. The new economic geography (NEG) literature argues that in the presence of strong agglomeration economies, the mobile factors of production tend to be relatively immobile. They gain from 'agglomeration rents', which can be taxed without the tax base vanishing.

Stiglitz (2012) recognizes the merits of the taxation of different types of rents as an instrument to reduce inequalities and distortions in the economy in his book *The Price of Inequality* as follows:

> A basic principle of economics holds that it is highly efficient to tax rents because such taxes don't cause any distortions. A tax on land rents does not make the land go away. Indeed, the great nineteenth-century progressive Henry George argued that government should rely solely on such a tax. Today, of course, we realize that rents can take many forms—they can be collected not just on land, but on the value of natural resources like oil, gas, minerals, and coal. There are other sources of rents, such as those derived from the exercise of monopoly power. A stiff tax on all such rents would not only reduce inequality but also reduce incentives to engage in the kind of rent-seeking activities that distort our economy and our democracy. (2012, 212–213)

The arguments presented by Stiglitz make a strong case for taxing rents as a source to finance the infrastructure gaps in cities. Paradoxically, in spite of strong theoretical merits, the taxation of urban land rent, monopoly rent and externality-induced agglomeration rent have not engaged the attention of policymakers and municipal administrators in developing countries, including India.

BUILDING TECHNOLOGY AND CITIES

Cites are built with brick and mortar. The vertical dimension of urban land or FSI plays an important role in building cities and enabling them to discharge their role as driver of economic growth. Town planning laws and urban development regulations in India, based on the British legal tradition, separate the development right on land from its landownership. This right is regulated through the instrument of FSI, which enables the substitution of capital for land by developers when land is scarce or costly. The FSI regime for designated land use zones or locations in a city depends on the zoning laws, building regulations and master plans in vogue. The importance of FSI derives from the fact that growth-generating and value-creating economic activities require a significant amount of floor space at central locations with high density and access to infrastructure, especially PT.

Indian cities exercise extreme controls on land and development rights through restrictions on land use and FSI. The FSI imposed by a typical city in India is 1.5 as against 5 to 15 in other Asian countries. Stringent restrictions on FSI have resulted in acute scarcity of floor space, especially for the poor and LIGs, in practically all cities in India— Mumbai being an oft-cited case. Interestingly, Shanghai had only 3.65 sq. m of built space per person in 1984. However, by liberalizing FSI, the city increased the figure to 34 sq. m. In contrast, the average space per person in Mumbai was a meagre 4.5 sq. m. While land values and housing prices in Indian cities are exorbitant, FSI restrictions have prevented building more floor space for housing the increasing urban population. Moreover, unlike many cities around the globe, Indian cities have adopted uniform FSI throughout their jurisdictions, without differentiating between locations based on economic potential or accessibility. Thus, they have not been able to harness the external economies of agglomeration linked to density and mix of economic activities. This has also led to non-exploitation of FSI as a resource to finance infrastructure projects to decongest cities. Box 4.2 compares the FSI regimes in India and internationally.

Box 4.2 *Floor Space Index Regime: India and International*

FSI is defined as the ratio of the floor space that can be constructed as per zoning and building regulations to the plot area.

FSI Regime: India

The FSI permitted by Indian cities is extremely low. For example, FSI is 1.2–3.5 in Delhi; 1.2 in central area and 1.8 in suburbs in Ahmedabad; 1.5–2.5 in Kolkata; 1.0–1.5 in Gurgaon and 1.5–2.0 in Chennai. In Mumbai, FSI is 1.33 for the island city; in suburban areas, it is 1.00 subject to additional FSI of 0.33 on payment of fees and fulfilment of certain conditions.

FSI Regime: International

The downtowns of major cities in the world have much higher FSI compared to Indian cities as may be seen from the following figures:

Denver: 17	New York: 15	Los Angeles: 13
Chicago: 12	San Francisco: 9	Vancouver: 9
Tokyo: 20	Singapore: 12 to 25	Hong Kong: 12
Shanghai: 8	Bangkok: 8	

Internationally, FSI is seen to be increasing during the course of urban development. However, FSI in Mumbai has decreased from 4.5 in 1964 to 1.00–1.33 at present, discouraging the redevelopment of dilapidated buildings.

Source: World Bank (2013) and Mohanty (2014).

TRANSPORT TECHNOLOGY AND CITIES

Access to transport infrastructure facilities such as highways, BRT, MRT and HSR is an important dimension of urban land. Transport affects city form and functions by enhancing the 'accessibility' of locations. Accessibility reduces the inconvenience and time to reach valued destinations such as workplaces, residences, schools, shopping malls, recreation centres, bus stops, railway stations and airports. It also facilitates human interaction, information exchange and knowledge transfers, which are key factors in knowledge-led growth. Both urban economics and transport economics highlight the role of 'accessibility premium' in the choice of location by firms and households. This is particularly important for the urban poor and LIGs as residential location determines their access to jobs, education, health care and other basic facilities. Transport economics also refers to the role of major transport projects in generating wider economic benefits (WEBs) by enhancing access to the economic mass. Such benefits arise from the external economies of agglomeration and networking, primarily shaped by market-driven factors, and transportation, largely determined by public policies.

Closely connected with the concept of 'accessibility' is the notion of 'serviceability'. Networked public services in cities such as water supply and sewerage follow the transportation alignment. Transport and other public services enhance the economic potential and social attractiveness of locations. The parameters of accessibility and serviceability influence the supply and demand for 'serviced land', which is critical for the location of workplaces, housing, retail trade and recreation facilities. If the policy concern is to augment serviced land and floor space to enable cities to contribute to economic growth and well-being, then along with the physical dimensions of land and FSI, the attributes of accessibility and serviceability must be given due importance in urban planning and development. When urban land is broadly interpreted and the social benefits of policies such as strategic densification, renewal or expansion of cities exceed the social costs due to factors such as spatial planning and investment in PT, there is no reason why intra-city density and FSI patterns be dictated by the static master plans, disregarding the dynamic market forces and role of public policies.

Accessibility and serviceability dimensions of urban land have other important implications. Investment in infrastructure and public services translate into 'location rents' for properties at vantage locations. They make value capture financing (VCF) of planned urban development possible. Value capture instruments are fair and efficient tools to capture the unearned increments in land. They subscribe to the benefit principle of public finance and are ideal tools to finance lumpy infrastructure projects by requiring the beneficiaries to pay towards costs. They also promote density and prevent sprawl. If an urban development project passes the benefit–cost test, then the rise in land values in the area served by it is expected to exceed the cost. Therefore, project cost can be covered by reclaiming a part of the uplift in land values and rents, leaving the rest to the landowners as net windfall benefits. The scope for VCF offers an important guide for choosing between alternative policies and projects to develop cities.

CITIES AND LAND USE PLANNING

Urban land is not only an input but also an output of urban planning and development. Location decisions of multiple firms, households and developers, and actions by public authorities in the form of planning of land use, installation of core infrastructure, regulation of development and taxation lead to changes in physical form and function of the city. Urban planning, alternatively called 'land use planning' or 'town planning', plays a crucial role in the development, redevelopment, use and reuse of land in urban areas.

Modern urban planning emerged in the latter part of the nineteenth century, following the industrial revolution. It was a response to the problems of overcrowded, polluted and 'killer' cities of Western Europe. Its goal was to secure 'orderly' growth of cities and towns. Urban planning was regarded as a technical activity, linked to physical planning and designing of human settlements. The legal tools for implementation of urban plans consisted of zoning, aimed at controlling the classification of land and its use, and planning permission, aimed at regulating the development of land for different purposes. In essence, zoning regulations aimed at controlling the type and intensity of land use. They prescribed norms for conforming and non-conforming land uses, densities, open spaces, infrastructure, housing, including light and ventilation, fire safety requirements, etc. Zoning laws were supplemented by (a) subdivision regulations, prescribing street layouts, lot sizes, land allocation for public uses, taxes and charges for infrastructure and civic services, etc., and (b) building codes, setting standards of construction, use and maintenance. The Standard State Zoning Enabling Act of 1926 issued by the United States Department of Commerce highlighted the need for zoning as follows:

... lessen congestion in the streets; to secure safety from fire, panic, and other dangers; to promote health and general welfare; to provide adequate light and air; to prevent the overcrowding of land; to avoid undue concentration of population; to facilitate the adequate provision of transportation, water, sewerage, schools, parks, and other public requirements. (United States Department of Commerce 1926, 6–7)

The key objectives of zoning, as articulated by urban planners, are to balance land uses for different purposes, correct for externalities due to factors such as spatial contiguity, pollution, congestion, noise, indiscriminate conversion of agricultural land to urban use and provision of infrastructure facilities. Planners also contend that the joint development of a large number of sites leads to a better pattern of urban land use than if the owners acted independently. Further, activities on adjoining sites affect one another in positive or negative ways, but transaction costs to reach agreements between the private landowners for a socially optimal outcome based on negotiations are exorbitant. Conservation of natural and heritage resources also call for government intervention. Often zoning is advocated to promote affordable housing for low-income groups, public facilities and local economic development. Land taxation is considered as an essential accompaniment to physical intervention in urban land markets to promote desired land uses, including housing and act against speculation.

The master planning model followed in India is borrowed from the 1947 Town and Country Planning Act in the United Kingdom. The master plan, also called 'comprehensive plan', aims at a long-term vision of the built-environment of a designated urban area, usually comprising a city and its urbanizing extensions. It lays down planning guidelines, policies, proposals and space requirement for various socio-economic activities to support the city population during the plan period. The plan provides a blueprint of future development and forms the basis of all future infrastructure requirements. The urban planning system envisages the preparation of a hierarchy of plans: master plan, zonal plan, action area plan and projects. The stated objectives of master planning are to promote public health, safety and general welfare. Recently prepared master plans have included sustainable development as one of the key objectives, in tune with the United Nations

Millennium Development Goals (MDGs) and Sustainable Development Goals (SDGs).

The master planning model as implemented by Indian cities is based on the twin system: zoning for classification of land use, and planning permission for carrying out development in layouts and plots. For example, the Master Plan of Delhi 2021 (MPD 2021) has divided the Delhi development area into land use zones with nine land use categories under the Land Use Plan 2021 (Table 4.1). Developments in each land use zone are to be carried out in accordance with the regulations approved by the Delhi Development Authority (DDA), including those under the Development Code and approved Master Plan—2021. The Development Code aims at promoting quality in built-environment by organizing the most appropriate development of land in accordance with the development policies and land use proposals contained in MPD 2021. The Code is meant to assist the authorities in regulation of land use at two levels: (a) conversion of use zones into use premises or layouts and (b) permission of use activities in use premises.

Table 4.1 *Master Plan for Delhi (2021): Land Use Zoning/Development Code*

Land Use Category	Zoning Code	Description/Activities Permitted
Residential	RD	Residential area
	RF	Foreign mission
Commercial	C1	Retail shopping, general business and commerce, district centre, community centre, non-hierarchical commercial centre
	C2	Wholesale, warehousing, cold storage, oil depot
	C3	Hotels
Industrial	M1	Manufacturing, service and repair industry
Recreational	P1	Regional park

Land Use Category	Zoning Code	Description/Activities Permitted
	P2	City park, district park, community park
	P3	Historical monuments
Transportation	T1	Airport
	T2	Terminal/depot—rail/MRT/bus/truck
	T3	Circulation—rail/MRT/road
Utility	U1	Water (treatment plant, etc.)
	U2	Sewerage (treatment plant, etc.)
	U3	Electricity (powerhouse, substation, etc.)
	U4	Solid waste (sanitary landfill, etc.)
	U5	Drain
Government	G1	President Estate and Parliament House
	G2	Government office/courts
	G3	Government land (use undetermined)
Public and Semi-public Facilities	PS1	Hospital, education, research university/university centre, college, social—cultural, sociocultural complex/centre, police/police headquarters/police lines, fire stations/disaster management centres, religious, burial ground/cremation
	PS2	Transmission site/centre
	PS3	Sport facilities/complex/stadium/sports centre
Green Belt/ Water Body	A1	Plant nursery
	A2	Green belt/agricultural green
	A3	River and water body
Mixed Use		Land use plan consisting of more than one land use zone

Source: DDA (2015).

Typically, a master plan covers a horizon of about 20–25 years and presents a view of the built-up form of the city in its ideal end state. It comprises of a report, land use maps and an implementation framework. The plan prescribes for: (a) allocation of land for designated urban uses, (b) regulation of its development and (c) installation of infrastructure to implement the land use plan. Plan implementation envisages the instruments of legal protection to the plan, zoning, layout, subdivision and building regulations, infrastructure planning, capital budgeting, land and infrastructure development and urban renewal. Other instruments include taxation policy, particularly land and property taxation, land assembly and capacity building for urban planning and plan implementation.

Adopting the comprehensive planning approach that originated in the United Kingdom, master plans in India have been obsessed with land use detailing. They assigned a subsidiary role to public transport. They prescribed 'minimum' lot size and other standards that excluded the poor and LIGs from the planned city. The master planning model also neglected land allocation for housing and workplaces for these sections. It also failed to provide a robust financing strategy to implement the development proposals. The United Kingdom realized the lacunae in the comprehensive, centralized and rigid approach to town planning since the 1960s. However, the master planning approach in India, with infirmities and inadequacies, continues to thrive.

A CRITIQUE OF MASTER PLANNING

The master planning model in India is rooted in the orthodox, modernist urban planning theories. The fallacies of these theories are eloquently highlighted by Jane Jacobs in her seminal book of 1961, *The Death and Life of Great American Cities*. Jacobs criticizes the top-down, prescriptive paradigm that dominated the conventional wisdom on city planning and rebuilding in the twentieth century led by 'Garden City' proponent Ebenezer Howard (1902), 'decentrists': Lewis Mumford (1938), Patrick Geddes (1915), Clarence Stein (1939), Catherine Bauer (1934) and Henry Wright (1935), and 'centrist': Le Corbusier (1933). The history of twentieth-century planning, as Peter Hall (1988) observes, 'represents a reaction to the evils of the nineteenth century city' (p. 7). Urban planners were concerned with the 'chaos' created in cities by rapid industrialization, manifesting in squalor, disease, dirt, congestion, pollution, noise, and overcrowded and unsanitary slums. They emphasized the need for more air and light, spacious housing and cleaner environments for the working classes. To them, urban form was a key factor for maintaining a high quality of life and modern technology made newer urban forms possible. This view has pervaded not only theory but also the practice of urban planning.

Howard's response to the problems of the industrial city was the development of 'garden cities', laid out in a wheel-and-spoke pattern of settlements surrounding central cities. His idea was to combine physical design, economic plan and social harmony. The new satellite towns were to host small communities of single detached residential buildings with ample open space for every man, every woman and every child to live, to play and to develop. The central area of each garden city was to have civic buildings, a park and a shopping arcade. These cities were conceived to be beautiful, healthy, compact, efficient and self-contained—with community services, self-sufficient industries separated from residential areas and agriculture. To be built on cooperation with communal purchase of land at cheap agricultural prices, each garden city was proposed to house a population of 30,000 in the core and 2,000 in the periphery—at a density of 25–30 per acre. It was to contain 3,500 building lots of an average size of 20 ft × 130 ft with minimum space norm being 20 ft × 100 ft. The garden city was to be collectively owned by the occupants. Economic growth would rely on each resident becoming an artisan entrepreneur, producing high-quality goods for the community and generating export sales. The garden city paradigm is utopian and lacked an economic basis; business activities would hardly be present in Howard's utopia. Subsequent garden city development projects eliminated the 'occupant ownership' and 'local industry' components.

Patrick Geddes wanted to place communities in the wider physical, social and economic contexts of the region. He emphasized the need to accept the inevitability of centrifugal forces and plan accordingly. Geddes advocated that planning must start with a survey of natural resources of the region, the human response to these resources and the cultural landscapes created by these relationships. He thought of planning of cities in terms of planning of the whole region in which garden cities were to be rationally distributed. Frank Lloyd Wright, an individualist who wanted the United States to become a nation of individuals, advocated a planned city called 'Broadacres', connected by superhighways. This city carried forward the concept of decentralization from Howard's ideal community to individual family homes in a garden environment. His view was that decentralization would permit each individual to live his or her own lifestyle on his or her own land (Wright 1958).

Le Corbusier, a centrist who believed that cities were not dense enough, conceived of a vertical garden city to decongest city centres by increasing density with high tower blocks surrounded by parks and highways. In his own vision, large strips of land in the historical centre of Paris needed to be levelled and carefully filled with skyscrapers of enormous proportions in a symmetrical grid of streets. The Radiant City of Le Corbusier proposed a density of 1,200 inhabitants per acre to ensure that skyscrapers occupied only 5 per cent of the ground, while 95 per cent was left for gardens and connectivity infrastructure. High-income segments were to be accommodated in lower density luxury housing around courts, with 85 per cent of the site area being open. The famous architect did not offer an economic logic for his proposal.

Modernist urban planning theories in the twentieth century, including Howard's utopia, Wright's Broadacres City and Le Corbusier's Radiant City, adopted a physical view of urban planning. They did not consider the economic fundamentals of cities: people at the centre of development; collocation of households, firms and institutions to reap benefits; external economies of agglomeration and networking; localization of innovation and economic growth; employment in both formal as well as informal sectors, etc. Streets, sidewalks, public spaces, local economic development and informality had no place in these theories. The models ignored the basic premise that cities are the products of processes, shaped by economic interactions and social relations. They grossly neglected the human element in cities. The view that the restructuring of urban form would solve the social crisis in the industrial city proved to be wrong. The quest for a city's form overshadowed its functions, especially the economic and social functions. Jane Jacobs compares Le Corbusier's Radiant City with 'a wonderful mechanical toy' (1992 [1961], 23).

The advocates of modernist urban planning believed that cities require extensive central planning to save them from impending chaos. Jacobs (1992 [1961]) attacked this position on three grounds. First, local and man-on-the-spot knowledge is the most important resource for good planning. Second, local planning is the best way to use local knowledge and resources. Third, decentralized planning helps and maintains the spontaneous order that makes urban life work. Such order results from the voluntary activities of individuals and not one that is created by the government. Jacobs asks the fundamental question: 'who plans?' She convincingly explains how decentralized and market-driven decisions build the foundation of vibrant cities and contribute to their vitality. She argues that large-scale, centralized systems of planning do not deliver. Varied use of urban space, diverse types and use of buildings, small city blocks and a sufficiently dense concentration of people, ensure pedestrian interaction, street life and a dynamic urban environment. Cities evolve and subjecting them to too many technical stipulations and tight controls seriously undermine their capacity to innovate and contribute to economic growth. Ironically, it is political action rather than technocratic planning that has been responsible for the most successful designs of cities around the world.

The orthodox theories of urban planning did not recognize the crucial distinction between the positive effects of density and the negative consequences of overcrowding. They failed to consider the role of density in the efficient functioning of cities due to its links with agglomeration economies. In fact, the modernist urban planners considered density as a problem and advocated the decongestion of cities with self-contained, lower density fringes and suburbs. As Jacobs observes:

> The development of modern city planning and housing reform has been emotionally based on a glum reluctance to accept city concentrations of people as desirable, and this negative emotion about city concentrations of people has helped deaden planning intellectually.

> No good for cities or for their design, planning, economics or people, can come from the emotional assumption that dense city populations are, per se, undesirable. In my view, they are an asset. (Jacobs 1992 [1961], 221)

The master plans of Indian cities are rooted in the anti-density perspective of modernist urban planning theories which has led to very low FSI, resulting in acute scarcity of space for firms and households in cities, including the poor and LIGs.

Modernist urban planning theories articulated not only an anti-density perspective but also an exclusionary approach to city development in the name of modernization and need to provide decent housing to the working class. The garden city approach prompted moving away from slum-infested cities and getting rid of their rat-infested neighbourhoods without addressing their root causes. It resulted in large-scale government-led slum clearance and rehousing subsidy schemes for low-income households in the United Kingdom. The approach was authoritarian. The United States adopted a market-oriented approach, separating commercial and industrial activities from residential uses. The US Supreme Court in the case of *Village of Euclid, Ohio vs. Ambler Realty Company* upheld the constitutional validity of zoning in 1926 on the grounds of protecting public health, welfare and safety. Following this landmark judgement, zoning was extensively adopted by cities in the United States by 1930. Local zoning decisions in that country were not tied to comprehensive city plans. This model of urban planning, combined with factors such as construction of interstate and intrastate highways, low-cost motor fuel, rise in income favouring automobile ownership and individual preference for consumption of larger quantities of land and housing in garden city-type environments with large lot zoning resulted in low-density residential sprawl in the United States. It also resulted in government-led low-income housing projects that, according to Jacobs, became worse centres of delinquency, vandalism and general social hopelessness.

The master planning system in India combines elements of the comprehensive planning approach in the United Kingdom and the exclusionary zoning model in the United States. It suffers from many inadequacies as presented in Box 4.3.

Apart from lacunae in master planning, land use and FSI regulations, urban land management in India is plagued by factors such as restrictions on conversion of agricultural land to urban uses, inappropriate

Box 4.3 *Inadequacies of Master Planning in India*

The master plan is technocratic, mechanical, deterministic and rigid. It starts with the projection of the population of a planning area to the plan horizon year—20–25 years ahead. It mechanically adopts the space norms for an average middle-class household in the city. The increase in population between the base and terminal years is divided by the estimated household size. This gives the projected increase in the number of households, and consequently the residential space needed. The requirements of non-residential space—industry, office, retail, recreational, etc.—are also linked to the number of incremental households. The process produces unrealistic plans, trying to confine the dynamic forces of the city to a static frame based on the extrapolation of past trends. It ignores the economic forces of cities that are inherently dynamic and the role of public policies for economic growth and urban development.

The master planning process treats the space requirement for conservation and transportation as 'residuals'. As a result, the preservation of natural and heritage resources are not given the importance they deserve. While the master plans in the past reserved land for conservation to be secured through compulsory public acquisition of land, such land could not be acquired due to the lack of funds and vested interests. Further, the treatment of transportation as a residual has led to the non-recognition of its critical role as a 'leading' force in planned urban development. This has led to the neglect of regional planning, and spatial and functional integration between the city, suburbs, rural centres, satellite towns and regional growth hubs.

Land use planning and transportation planning have been pursued as separate processes and by separate agencies in India. Neither the master plan nor the transportation plan has thus harnessed the power of transportation–land use integration and land-based financing instruments in internalizing the agglomeration and network externalities of cities for orderly urban development and economic growth.

Being confined to land use planning, master plans hardly address the concerns of integrated development, encompassing location of activities, production, employment, transportation, housing, inclusion and resource mobilization. They do not address the key drivers of growth, such as regional specialization, knowledge externalities and innovation. Master plans, taking a physical view of the city, have neglected the economic forces of urban areas that drive growth through cumulative and circular

(Continued)

Box 4.3 *(Continued)*

causation processes. They have also not relied on economic instruments such as land taxation and congestion pricing to achieve the plan objectives.

Not connecting to economics, master plans have invariably failed to provide a sensible method for their financing. In fact, they keep the financing of development outside the model of spatial planning. Master plans in the past paid no attention to 'agglomeration rents' generated by externalities and windfall gains in land values that the planned urban development process creates. While a tax on vacant land can be a powerful instrument to achieve the master plan objective of promoting land use for housing, hardly any master plan has emphasized the use of such instruments.

Master plans stipulate an elaborate system of regulation to implement their 'grand' vision to the neighbourhood level. Public authorities impose tight controls over the operation of land markets through land use and FSI regulations in the name of plan enforcement. In the past, master plans also relied heavily on compulsory acquisition of land to achieve plan objectives. The failure of such interventions is conspicuous.

The process of master planning leads to a segregated pattern of land use, whereas mixed use is appropriate for an Indian way of urban living, with the majority having no motor vehicles and large sections engaged in informal sector activities. Master plans are formal; they hardly recognize the large informal economies of cities that employ the bulk of the poor. They do not provide adequate space to these segments for living, working and vending.

Master plans tend to be top-down, prepared by professionals. The planning process, being based on a top-driven approach, does not ensure the participation of the majority in cities, comprising the poor and LIGs. In most states in India, urban development authorities are entrusted with the preparation of master plans. These authorities are parastatals, not accountable to the people; unlike the elected ULBs.

Master plans are based on the concept of a completed product, whereas a city's evolution is a process. Planning is not a one-time activity. Plan-making and plan implementation ought to be dynamic processes, linked to the evolving functions of the city. For example, as the service sector enhances its contribution to GDP, a substantial increase in demand for floor space will arise in central locations with access to public transit. However, the master planning process in India is prescriptive and not responsive to the evolving demands for serviced land and floor space.

rent control legislations discouraging rental housing, high stamp duties adversely affecting transactions in property and difficulties in acquisition of land, making land assembly for urban uses as needed by economic growth difficult. As India has to go a long way in the process of urbanization, a robust and realistic approach to urban land policy to guide land use planning and development is called for. However, except for a sporadic attempt through the report of the Urban Land Policy Committee in 1965, the issues of urban land management in India have not engaged the attention of policymakers and planners at the central, state and local levels. The 1965 Policy deliberations also reflected the command and control approach to urban planning and development, typical of the pre-liberalization era.

THE URBAN LAND POLICY COMMITTEE

The GoI recognized the need for a national policy to address the issues of land in the face of fast urbanization in the early 1960s for the first time. The report of the Urban Land Policy Committee (1965) by the Ministry of Health (MoH), GoI, articulated the following objectives of urban land policy in India:

- To achieve the optimum social use of urban land;
- To make land available in adequate quantity, at the right time and at reasonable prices to both public authorities and individuals for planned urbanization;
- To encourage cooperative community effort and bona fide individual builders in the field of land development, housing and construction;
- To prevent concentration of landownership in a few private hands and to safeguard the interests of the poor and the underprivileged sections of the urban society;
- To use land as a resource for financing urban development by recouping the unearned income, which otherwise accrues to the private landowners.

The Task Force on Planning of Urban Development appointed by the Planning Commission in 1983 reiterated some of the aforementioned objectives and articulated the following goals of urban land policy:

- To widen the base of landownership specially to safeguard the interests of the poor and the underprivileged sections of the urban society;
- To encourage socially and economically efficient allocation of urban land such that urban development occurs in a resource–conserving manner and land is used optimally;
- To promote flexibility in land use in response to changes resulting from a growing city.

The major recommendations of the report of the Urban Land Policy Committee 1965 are presented in Table 4.2.

The Urban Land Policy Committee held the view that public intervention in urban land markets through regulation was necessary

Table 4.2 *Urban Land Policy Committee (1965): Major Recommendations*

Subject	Major Recommendations
Measures for developed urban land	• Effective implementation of Master Plan, zoning and subdivision regulations and urban renewal. • Capital improvement plan (CIP), fiscal plan and land use plan to be integrated into city development plan (CDP).
Measures for undeveloped urban land	• Stringent controls on development outside compact areas to avoid uneconomic stretching of infrastructure. • Extension of public utility services to prevent 'spotty development' and encourage compact urban growth. • Future development in undeveloped areas based on 'planned neighbourhoods'. • Conversion tax on change of land use from agriculture to non-agriculture to discourage speculation.
Measures for land in urbanizable limits	• Urbanizable limits to be determined for each city and included in municipal jurisdiction. • Where an extension of municipal limits is not feasible, physical planning be applied to about 8 km beyond such limits.

Subject	Major Recommendations
	• No change to be permitted in the present use of land in an area of 300 ft along all roads and railway lines and in the potential areas in which the town is likely to extend.
	• A high-powered statutory autonomous authority at the state level to gain ownership of land in city urbanizable limits through compulsory land acquisition for orderly urban development.
Measures for land beyond urbanizable limits	• Land use beyond urbanizable limits to be governed by regional land use plan, regulated by an authority, to prevent growth of conurbations, sprawl and spotty development.
	• Power to control ribbon development by prescribing right of way and disallowing developments within a prescribed distance therefrom be legislated by all states and enforced.
Measures for mopping up unearned increases	• Unearned increases in urban land and property values are 'social surpluses' not to be left to speculators and profiteers.
	• A modest levy on planning permission; a conversion tax with differentiated structures for conversion to residential, commercial and industrial uses; a broad-based annual tax on unearned increments in land and property values; shift of property tax base from rental value to capital value; and a lower tax rate on development along with a graduated higher rate on site value to mobilize unearned increments.
	• Five years' time to be given for completing construction on vacant plots following the provision of services, and a heavy tax thereafter increasing with passage of time.

Source: MoH, GoI (1965) and Mohanty (2014).

to maximize the net benefits of planned urban development to the society. It was of the opinion that when left to market forces, the social needs for housing, infrastructure and services would be overlooked. The Committee argued that the compulsory acquisition of land was a must for effectively addressing planned urban development, including supply of adequate housing and provision of infrastructure. It was of the view that large-scale advance acquisition of land would be the way to end speculation in land markets and capture the unearned increases in land values due to spatial planning and infrastructure investment. The surpluses realized by public authorities could then translate into benefits for the community.

In tune with the recommendations of the Urban Land Policy Committee, urban development authorities were set up by states across India. They were entrusted with the tasks of preparing master plans for designated urban development areas along with detailed zonal and local land use plans, acquiring land and undertaking land assembly. Not surprisingly, the performance of such authorities in planning and development has been far from satisfactory. Utopian master plans and elaborate DCRs for plan enforcement have not worked. Plan achievement has drastically fallen short of target. The lack of capacity of local authorities to regulate land markets without creating adverse incentives in the supply of land and floor space for urbanization is obvious. Excessive regulation has also dampened private enterprise. Some desirable recommendations of the Committee such as integration of land use, CIP and financing strategy, and capturing the unearned increments in land values due to spatial planning and infrastructure development have not been put to practice. The argument that the space needs of the poor are better addressed in a public sector-led model of urban development turned out to be incorrect.

The ambitious paradigm of large-scale public acquisition of land to achieve the planners' vision of a grand city has failed. It is not workable as farmers are stiffly resisting the acquisition of their land due to gross underpayment of compensation and deprivation of the huge unearned benefits of development accruing to others. In fact, many land acquisition (LA) proceedings have been stuck in courts for years. Moreover, the compulsory acquisition of land for planned urban development is going to be difficult in view of the requirements prescribed by the new LA law of 2013. Ironically, the Planning Commission Task Force in 1983 had predicted the failure of the model of large-scale public ownership of land as a means of achieving urban land policy objectives. Cities thus need to explore alternative models of land assembly such as land pooling and guided development in the place of compulsory acquisition of land.

DIRECTIONS FOR URBAN LAND POLICY

The master planning model in India has led to an acute scarcity of serviced land and floor space for value-creating and growth-generating economic activities in cities. It has also resulted in exorbitant increases in land values, housing prices and office rents. The adverse impacts of the restrictive land use and FSI regime in India have not been evaluated. However, Cheshire and Hilber (2008) find that planning restrictions typically imposed a 'tax' on office development in England that varied from around 250 per cent of development cost in Birmingham to 400–800 per cent in London. This tax amounted to about 300 per cent in Central Paris, 200 per cent in Amsterdam, but 0–50 per cent in New York. Cheshire et al. (2011) find that the restrictive town planning system in the United Kingdom has severely constrained the supply of land and housing, turning them to something like 'gold' or 'artwork'. It increases housing prices with regressive impacts on low- and middle-income dwelling units, housing market volatility and office rents. It also lowers retail productivity and employment in small independent retailers. Further, it fails to assess the true social cost of brown field versus green field development. Glaeser (2011), Koster, Rietveld and van Emmerren (2011) and Brueckner and Sridhar (2012) find that building height restrictions typically reduce the positive effects of agglomeration economies. The starting point for formulating urban land policy in India is to evaluate the current approaches and practices in land use planning and development control in cities.

The skyrocketing land prices in Indian cities provide ample evidence that the master planning system has led to high social costs by constraining the supply of affordable housing, workplaces and public amenities, especially to the poor and LIGs. These costs are compounded by the long neglect of public transport (PT) investment and transport–land use integration, leading to spotty development, sprawl, uneconomic extension of city boundaries, environmental degradation, wasteful commuting, energy wastage and increased costs of infrastructure and services. Master planning has led to serious adverse consequences for sustainable development. Further, it has perpetrated an exclusionary regime of urbanization—not in sync with the income distribution structure of cities. It has also narrowly focused on the horizontal dimensions of urban land, neglecting the role of 'density', 'FSI' and 'accessibility' parameters in addressing the needs of firms and households as economic growth occurs. Ironically, the concepts of density and FSI are not absolute. Investments in core infrastructure, which create accessibility benefits to locations, provide opportunities for increasing density while reaping the external economies of agglomeration and networking. These investments also support PT-led and transit-oriented development as a strategy to promote environmentally sustainable and socially equitable cities.

Land economics suggests that urban land is a highly heterogeneous commodity. The supply of urban land is influenced by market forces, externalities and government policies, including conversion of agricultural land to urban use, land use zoning, FSI regulation, infrastructure development, land assembly, land and property taxation, rent control, etc. The demand for urban land is 'derived' from the needs of floor space and amenities by firms and households. The recognition of the peculiar characteristics of supply of and demand for urban land is crucial for the design of spatial planning and other interventions in land markets. A model of urban planning that confines land to its horizontal dimensions is ill-suited to address the needs of large and fast-growing cities, challenges of economic growth and imperatives of sustainable development.

The issues of land in all its dimensions, affordable housing, economic growth, employment, infrastructure, basic services, slums, poverty, informal economy, environment, finance and governance in cities are deeply rooted in their economics. The basic tenet of urban economics suggests that cities are the products of trade-offs between centripetal and centrifugal forces. These forces are shaped by five major factors: agglomeration externalities due to the spatial concentration of economic activity; location choice by firms, households and developers-builders based on appraisal of benefits and costs; building technology and FSI; transport technology and connectivity; and government policy, including town planning and real estate development regulations. They influence land use, density and mix of economic activities in locations. They also affect pecuniary variables such as land rents, housing prices and transport costs. Urban economics and spatial planning together shape the form and functions of a city, not urban planning alone. Thus, the obsession of master planners with a predetermined form of an urban area, 20–25 years ahead, and with land use detailing and control of physical development as key instruments to achieve such form is flawed.

Urban economics emphasizes that cities are not merely places. They are centres of value-creating economic activities. They are the creations of people striving to enhance their productivity and welfare. Driven by powerful interactions between market forces, externalities and public policies, cities are inherently dynamic and cannot be confined to static land use plans. Moreover, too much rigidity in spatial planning is detrimental to developing countries like India where much of urbanization is yet to occur and the ever-renewing knowledge economy offers a huge opportunity for leap-frogged development. Knowledge externalities, closely connected with agglomeration and networking forces of cities, are dynamic. These tend to be strong in the large city regions of developing countries when they upgrade from manufacturing to knowledge-based services. Harnessing these externalities calls for a planning model that is responsive to the emerging needs of firms and workers. By ignoring the economic determinants of demand, supply and price of urban land and floor space, the master plans have failed to connect to the dynamics of the spatial economy. They lack strategies for densification, renewal and expansion in tune with the demands of growth. By neglecting land, transport and urban economics, cities have also not been able to harness the power of economic instruments such as land taxation, pricing of FSI, congestion charging (CC), 'polluters pay' and 'growth pays' instruments. They fail to appreciate that the taxation of unearned land rents in cities, arising as a 'residual' is a first-best instrument to finance urban infrastructure.

The oft-cited logic put forth by urban planners that a flexible planning model will lead to discretionary changes in land use and FSI and maladministration, adversely affecting the environment, is not justified. Administrative issues must be addressed by improving governance rather than perpetuating systemic inefficiencies that affect economic growth. The social benefits and costs of urban projects, whether taken up by private entrepreneurs or public agencies, need to be appraised, duly taking into account their direct, indirect and induced effects, including external economies and diseconomies. The urban planning system also leads to benefits and costs, which need to be evaluated. Planning regulations and permissions involve trade-offs and influence the location, scale and mix of economic activities. A static model of urban planning aimed at controlling land use and FSI based on predetermined norms, disregarding the dynamic forces of cities is not suited to address the challenges of economic growth in India. It is also not appropriate for mobilizing resources for plan implementation based on a value capture framework. Economic considerations suggest that India needs to move from a prescriptive and rigid paradigm of urban planning to a responsive and flexibly regulated regime that takes into account the changing functions of the city in the globalizing and increasingly networked world.

Land and urban economics suggest that urban land policy in India must address the factors influencing the choice of location by productive firms and workers; integration of land use and transportation to promote mobility in the labour market; bridging the demand–supply gap for serviced land and floor space by adopting innovative methods of land assembly and liberalizing FSI; investing in leading and decongesting infrastructure, especially MRT and HSR; incorporating the needs of the poor for land and housing; and exploiting urban land and FSI as resource to finance urban development plan. A conspicuous lacuna in India's master planning model is that it is narrowly focused on physical control of land use, density and FSI to attain the development objectives and ignores economic instruments. For example, while a land value tax can be a powerful tool to prevent speculation in urban land market, promote housing and other productive uses and raise resources to finance infrastructure, the tool has been grossly neglected by master planning. Similarly, to address the problems of congestion and sprawl, master plans in the past focused on restricting development rather than adopting fiscal tools such as congestion pricing, motor vehicles taxation, motor fuel levy and parking charges. There is a need to reform urban planning in India by incorporating the principles of economics and adopting economic instruments to supplement the physical planning tools to achieve the objectives of inclusive growth and sustainable development.

5

Economics of Urban Transport
Integrating Transportation and Land Use Planning

TRANSPORT AND THE CITY

Transport makes or mars a city. The pivotal importance of urban transport (UT) derives from its impacts on city form, functions, externalities and economic growth. Transport, along with land use and buildings, shapes the morphology of a city. A key function of the city is to move goods, people, ideas, information and knowledge at low cost. Transport assists cities in discharging this function by making entrepreneurs and workers mobile and enabling them to benefit from face-to-face interaction and collaboration. It balances jobs, housing and public facilities and expands labour markets. Transportation improvements reduce travel time, cost and inconvenience to commuters to reach valued destinations, enhance travel safety and improve the environment. They act against billions of man-hours being 'stuck in traffic'. Transport enhances the productivity of workers and competitiveness of firms. Cities function well when they act as markets for specialized skills needed by growth-generating activities in the secondary and tertiary sectors. These activities locate in cities to gain from scale, agglomeration and networking. One of the key reasons why large cities are important is that they create unified labour markets. The efficiency of these markets, however, depends on the mobility of workers, which is critical for the economic viability of cities. Transport, when integrated with land use, enables cities to function as efficient labour markets (Bertaud 2014).

Transport is an economic activity; it also facilitates, induces and creates economic activity. Transportation investments affect not only transport markets but also goods, labour and land markets. They promote backward and forward linkages, enhance competition, facilitate trade, catalyze growth and generate land value increments to finance infrastructure. Public transport (PT) systems such as mass rapid transit (MRT), bus rapid transit (BRT) and high-speed rail (HSR) act against auto-dependent urbanization, sprawl and greenhouse gas (GHG) emission. Further, they connect the poor to employment opportunities and contribute to inclusive urbanization. UT is the key to economically efficient, environmentally sustainable and socially equitable cities. This is particularly so in developing countries where the structural transformation process favours the location of productive firms and workers in cities to benefit from externalities.

Historically, transport has played a crucial role in the development of cities, regions and nations. Adam Smith recognized the strong positive effects of low shipping costs on the growth of cities located on riverbank or coast. The size of market, division of labour and specialization were directly related to these costs (Smith 1976 [1776]). Baxter wrote in the context of the United Kingdom: 'Railways have been a most powerful agent in the progress of commerce, in improving the conditions of the working classes, and in developing the agricultural and mineral resources of the country' (Baxter 1866). Lord Lugard made the following statement for Africa: 'The material development of Africa may be summed up in one word, transport' (Lugard 1965 [1923]). Rostow observed: 'The introduction of railroads has historically been the most-powerful single indicator to take-offs. It was decisive in the United States, France, Germany, Canada and Russia' (Rostow 1960). India's Economic Survey 2014–15 has articulated the following view:

> Conceptually, there is a strong case for channelizing resources to transport infrastructure in India given the widely known spillover effects of transport networks to link markets, reduce a variety of costs, boost agglomeration economies, and improve the competitiveness of the economy, especially manufacturing, which tends to be logistic-intensive. (Ministry of Finance [MoF], GoI, 2017, Volume I, 91)

The crucial role of transport in urban development stems from its impacts on economic growth through the externalities of cities. A good network of roads coupled with an efficient mass transit system substantially contributes to the 'working efficiency' of the city. For individuals, better access to transport leads to savings in travel time and costs, reduced impacts of negative externalities and changes in household location and commuting patterns. For businesses, the impacts manifest in increased productivity of workers and freight operators, access to new markets and new sources of inputs, and reorganization of production. New growth theory (NGT) suggests that better transportation leads to increased total factor productivity (TFP), a key factor in economic growth. New economic geography (NEG) emphasizes that interactions between scale economies, agglomeration externalities and transportation costs lead to productivity gains and cost savings through circular and cumulative causation processes. Transport economics argues that urban transportation improvements enhance access to the 'economic mass', augment agglomeration economies in nodes, reduce congestion diseconomies in trunks and channelize local economic development in desired directions. They lead to 'accessibility premiums' and 'wider economic benefits (WEBs)' which transcend user time and operator cost savings and reduction in pollution, congestion, noise and accidents. These benefits are not captured by conventional benefit–cost appraisal (Graham 2007; Venables 2007; Vickerman 2008).

Mobility is the key to working efficiency of a city. But unless firms and households are able to choose locations to optimize their objective functions, the efficiency gains from mobility cannot be harnessed for economic growth. Paradoxically, cities in India have not devoted much attention to urban PT, including BRT, MRT and HSR. This is in spite of the fact that considerations of population density and income distribution structure in cities, energy security, environmental sustainability and poverty alleviation call for a PT-based strategy of urban development. The master planning paradigm that Indian cities follow has accorded a secondary role to PT. Obsessed with land use detailing, it has ignored the two-way relationship between land use and transportation. The model is rigid and underestimates the importance of UT for inclusive growth and protection of the environment.

Obviously, when large investments are made in PT leading to benefits of accessibility, the economic potential of the nodes they connect magnifies. Thus, when the master plans artificially restrict land use and density patterns in such nodes, the outcomes of such investments turn out to be suboptimal. The integration of transport and land use is a fundamental requirement of good urban planning.

This chapter dwells on India's urban mobility challenges. It aims at drawing lessons from transport economics, urban economics and NEG to guide integrated transportation–land use planning. Referring to the trends in motorization in India, it refers to transport economics to highlight the economic significance of UT. We focus on the impacts of UT on the spatial economy. We also refer to research in urban and regional planning, including New Urbanism and Smart Growth to highlight the role of urban PT in sustainable development. While calling for a holistic approach to urban planning, financing and development, we present a case for PT-led and transit-oriented development in cities. We argue for significant investments in MRT and HSR projects based on a financing strategy rooted in the principles of benefit taxation, value capture, congestion charging (CC) and intergovernmental partnerships.

INDIA'S URBAN MOBILITY CHALLENGES

Indian urbanization is characterized by a massive increase in urban population and its concentration in large cities. Cities with more than 100,000 population, numbering 468, contained 264.9 million people in 2011. They accounted for 70 per cent of India's urban population. Million-plus cities, numbering 53, had 160.7 million in 2011, accounting for 43 per cent of urban population. These trends have been accompanied by increasing motorization and traffic congestion.

Bourgeoning travel demand, increasing number of personalized vehicles, dwindling share of public transport, severe traffic congestion, fast deterioration in urban environment due to air pollution, increasing risks to pedestrians and cyclists leading to escalation in road accidents and fatalities, lack of integration between transportation and land use, fragmented institutional arrangements and chronic under-investment in transportation infrastructure are amongst the key challenges of urban mobility in India.

Motorization: Trends and Patterns

The number of registered motor vehicles in India increased from 0.3 million in 1951 to 210 million in 2015. While the share of two-wheelers rose from 8.8 per cent in 1951 to 73.5 per cent in 2015, the share of buses declined from 11 per cent to 1 per cent. Table 5.1 presents the trends in the number and composition of registered motor vehicles in India over the period 1951–2015.

Table 5.2 depicts the number and composition of registered motor vehicles in India's metropolitan cities in 2015. The total population

Table 5.1 *Total Number of Registered Motor Vehicles in India (in Million; 1951–2015)*

		Composition (% of Total Vehicle Population)				
Year	Number in Million	Two-wheelers	Cars, Jeeps and Taxis	Buses	Goods Vehicles	Other Vehicles
1951	0.3	8.8	52.0	11.0	26.8	1.3
1961	0.7	13.2	46.6	8.6	25.3	6.3
1971	1.9	30.9	36.6	5.0	18.4	9.1
1981	5.4	48.6	21.5	3.0	10.3	16.6
1991	21.4	66.4	13.8	1.5	6.3	11.9
2001	55.0	70.1	12.8	1.2	5.4	10.5
2006	89.6	72.2	12.9	1.1	4.9	8.8
2011	141.8	71.8	13.6	1.1	5.0	8.5
2012	159.5	72.4	13.5	1.0	4.8	8.3
2013	176.0	72.7	13.6	1.0	4.7	8.0
2014	190.7	73.1	13.6	1.0	4.6	7.7
2015	210.0	73.5	13.6	1.0	4.4	7.5

Source: MoRTH, GoI (2016).

Table 5.2 *Share of Two-wheelers and Cars in Total Number of Registered Motor Vehicles in Million-plus Cities of India as on 31 March 2015*

Million-plus Cities	Total Number of Registered Motor Vehicles	Two-wheelers		Cars	
		Number	% of Total	Number	% of Total
Agra	905,023	741,778	81.96	76,107	8.41
Ahmedabad	3,419,828	2,431,839	71.11	525,891	15.38
Allahabad	897,035	730,758	81.46	72,779	8.11
Aurangabad	426,246	335,725	78.76	19,591	4.60
Bengaluru	5,559,730	3,841,139	69.09	1,088,587	19.58
Bhopal	1,080,477	847,334	78.42	136,627	12.65
Chandigarh	745,520	395,565	53.06	261,752	35.11
Chennai	4,934,412	3,516,062	71.26	860,932	17.45
Coimbatore	1,901,277	1,547,395	81.39	232,751	12.24
Delhi	8,850,720	5,698,242	64.38	2,730,071	30.85
Dhanbad	563,426	427,714	75.91	58,836	10.44
Durg-Bhilai	768,922	644,138	83.77	49,569	6.45
Ghaziabad	751,603	533,808	71.02	152,256	20.26
Greater Mumbai	2,571,204	1,470,175	57.18	797,267	31.01
Gwalior	617,681	487,259	78.89	52,685	8.53
Hyderabad	2,368,818	1,707,714	72.09	402,334	16.98
Indore	1,712,702	1,301,383	75.98	208,005	12.14
Jabalpur	638,219	493,633	77.35	67,445	10.57
Jaipur	2,249,240	1,658,006	73.71	305,445	13.58
Jamshedpur	472,051	351,696	74.50	55,020	11.66
Jodhpur	916,172	650,097	70.96	71,972	7.86
Kannur	188,497	112,851	59.87	43,920	23.30
Kanpur	1,461,530	1,172,577	80.23	147,072	10.06

Million-plus Cities	Total Number of Registered Motor Vehicles	Two-wheelers		Cars	
		Number	% of Total	Number	% of Total
Kochi	605,689	336,316	55.53	171,063	28.24
Kolkata	1,401,638	600,156	42.82	541,432	38.63
Kollam	274,006	175,528	64.06	58,097	21.20
Kota	654,041	512,740	78.40	51,749	7.91
Kozhikode	412,304	289,801	70.29	70,539	17.11
Lucknow	1,709,662	1,361,787	79.65	244,121	14.28
Madurai	954,893	793,510	83.10	68,804	7.21
Malappuram	276,765	151,351	54.69	59,297	21.43
Meerut	525,235	424,975	80.91	63,148	12.02
Nagpur	1,275,575	1,067,160	83.66	108,951	8.54
Nashik	622,206	461,628	74.19	62,473	10.04
Patna	1,018,798	705,298	69.23	135,638	13.31
Pune	2,337,085	1,765,172	75.53	375,267	16.06
Raipur	1,111,745	845,861	76.08	84,377	7.59
Rajkot	979,423	787,608	80.42	93,185	9.51
Ranchi	547,036	356,067	65.09	65,434	11.96
Srinagar	235,614	100,291	42.57	77,043	32.70
Surat	2,459,111	1,912,715	77.78	307,540	12.51
Trichy	763,396	636,961	83.44	58,712	7.69
Thiruvanantha-puram	571,956	349,657	61.13	153,674	26.87
Thrissur	355,491	226,285	63.65	72,994	20.53
Varanasi	768,769	609,656	79.30	55,727	7.25
Vijayawada	610,321	452,403	74.13	53,755	8.81
Vadodara	1,041,818	803,969	77.17	123,509	11.86
Visakhapatnam	730,872	574,135	78.55	79,592	10.89
Total	66,243,782	47,397,918	71.55	11,653,035	17.59

Source: MoRTH, GoI (2016).

of motor vehicles in metropolitan cities in 2015 was 66.24 million. Delhi had the highest number at 88.51 lakhs, followed by Bengaluru (55.60 lakhs), Chennai (49.34 lakhs), Ahmedabad (34.20 lakhs), Greater Mumbai (25.71 lakhs), Surat (24.59 lakhs) and Hyderabad (23.69 lakhs). The largest number of two-wheelers in 2015 was in Delhi at 56.98 lakhs, followed by Bengaluru (38.41 lakhs), Chennai (35.16 lakhs), Ahmedabad (24.32 lakhs), Surat (19.13 lakhs), Pune (17.65 lakhs) and Hyderabad (17.08 lakhs). As regards the number of cars in 2015, Delhi had 27.30 lakhs, followed by Bengaluru (10.89 lakhs), Chennai (8.60 lakhs), Greater Mumbai (7.97 lakhs), Kolkata (5.41 lakhs), Ahmedabad (5.26 lakhs), Hyderabad (4.02 lakhs) and Pune (3.75 lakhs).

Table 5.3 presents the growth in motor vehicles in 22 metropolitan cities of India over the period 2005–2015. As the table shows, 16 out of the 22 metropolitan cities experienced an average annual growth rate of more than 10 per cent; three cities had an annual growth rate exceeding 20 per cent.

Urban Mobility: Key Policy Issues

Data on motorization trends and patterns in India reveal that between 2005 and 2015, the number of motor vehicles registered a compounded annual growth rate (CAGR) of 9.8 per cent vis-à-vis a CAGR of 3.6 per cent in total road length. The number of two-wheelers experienced a CAGR of 10.1 per cent, while cars, jeeps and taxis witnessed a CAGR of 10.7 per cent over the same period. The bulk of these vehicles ply in cities, especially metropolitan cities. However, the length of urban roads experienced a CAGR of 5.0 per cent between 2005 and 2015. While urban areas accounted for only 8.54 per cent of the total road length of India as of 31 March 2015, the number of motor vehicles in 50 million-plus cities was 31.54 per cent of the total number registered in the country in 2015. An obvious conclusion from the trends in motorization is that growth in urban road space has drastically fallen short of the increase in number of personalized motor vehicles plying in cities. The problem is assuming serious proportions in cities such as Delhi and Bengaluru.

Table 5.3 *Growth in the Number of Registered Motor Vehicles in Select Metropolitan Cities (2005–2015)*

Metropolitan City	No. of Motor Vehicles (in Thousands)		Average Annual Growth (%)
	2005	2015	
Ahmedabad	1,632	3,420	10.96
Bengaluru	2,232	5,560	14.91
Bhopal	428	1,080	15.23
Chennai	2,167	4,934	12.77
Coimbatore	682	1,901	17.87
Delhi	4,186	8,851	11.14
Greater Mumbai	1,295	2,571	9.85
Hyderabad	1,433	2,369	6.53
Indore	705	1,713	14.30
Jaipur	923	2,249	14.37
Kanpur	425	1,462	24.40
Kochi	166	606	26.51
Kolkata	911	1,402	5.39
Lucknow	615	1,710	17.80
Madurai	330	955	18.94
Nagpur	770	1,276	6.57
Patna	378	1,019	16.96
Pune	827	2,337	18.26
Surat	692	2,459	25.53
Varanasi	366	769	11.01
Vadodara	586	1,042	7.78
Visakhapatnam	435	731	6.80

Source: MoRTH, GoI (2016).

A second conclusion from the trends in motorization in India is the neglect of PT in cities. This is responsible for severe traffic congestion that is making cities dysfunctional. Cars and two-wheelers account for less than 30 per cent of trips, but they occupy 80 per cent of road space. PT accounted for only 27 per cent of UT in India compared with 49 per cent in the Philippines, Venezuela and Egypt, 40 per cent in South Africa, South Korea and Brazil, and 62 per cent in Bogota. In 2009, only 20 out of 85 Indian cities with a population of half a million had access to bus services. Due to increased congestion, people commute 3–4 hours to work every day in cities like Bengaluru. Efforts by city authorities to augment roads and construct flyovers are nullified by the increase in ownership of personalized vehicles, induced traffic volume and return of congestion.

While India is already facing gigantic challenges of urban mobility, the problems are bound to magnify as the country urbanizes and moves to a higher growth trajectory. The car penetration rate, defined as the number of cars per 1,000 persons, is very small in India compared to that in developed countries and several developing countries. With structural transformation, economic growth, rise in income and increased urbanization, the vehicular penetration rate, including car penetration rate, with attendant problems of congestion, pollution, noise and carbon emission, is bound to go up. This conclusion can be inferred from a comparison of statistics on gross national income (GNI) and vehicular penetration rates for select countries with those for India as presented in Table 5.4.

The trends and prospects of motorization in India suggest that in a business-as-usual scenario, the proliferation of personalized vehicles will increase the demand for road space and traffic congestion in cities manifold. They make a strong case for a strategy of urban transport development and management that includes both supply side and demand side interventions. Indian cities have neglected investments in PT, including MRT and BRT, for long. They have also not used transport demand management (TDM) tools practised elsewhere. In particular, the strategies of transportation–land use integration, transit-oriented development (TOD) and congestion charging have not been given due attention. Cities have not exploited the synergy

Table 5.4 *Vehicular Penetration Rates in Select Developed and Developing Countries (2013)*

Country	GNI per Capita (US$) 2013	Number per 1,000 Persons		
		Passenger Cars	Total No. of Motor Vehicles	Two-wheelers
Developed Countries				
United States	53,470	360	783	27
United Kingdom	41,680	455	517	19
Japan	46,330	466	598	81
Germany	47,270	544	603	50
Australia	65,390	562	711	32
Developing Countries				
Mexico	9,940	203	285	15
Malaysia	10,430	358*	396*	356
South Africa	7,190	110**	162**	6
Brazil	11,690	227	290	108
China	6,560	76	93	70
South Korea	25,920	300	386	42
India	1,570	19	167	123

Source: MoRTH, GoI (2016).
Note: * Data relate to 2012; ** Data relate to 2011.

between agglomeration and network externalities, land use planning, transportation planning, economic development planning and plan financing. The neglect of urban and transport economics in city planning is conspicuous. This has resulted in the lack of a robust strategy to finance UT. The non-recognition of wider economic impacts of UT projects has also accorded them a low ranking in benefit–cost appraisals. Paradoxically, transportation planning and land use planning in India in the past have been pursued as disjointed exercises, the prime example being Delhi. There is a need for urban planners to recognize the economic significance of transport and its impacts on growth by shaping the externalities of cities. They must also appreciate the literature in urban planning dealing with New Urbanism, Smart Growth and TOD. This literature highlights the role of public transit in promoting liveable and sustainable habitats.

ECONOMIC SIGNIFICANCE OF URBAN TRANSPORT

Economics suggests that the demand for transport is derived from the level of economic activity. Firms and households minimize transport costs while choosing that level. This is, however, too naive an assumption as changes in transport costs and benefits lead to differential competitiveness among locations. They influence the returns to firms and lead to changes in location and composition of economic activity. Theories of city formation from von Thunen (1826), Weber (1971 [1909]), Christaller (1933) and Losch (1940) emphasize the role of transport in the location choices of firms. Urban economics and NEG highlight the balancing of centripetal forces of agglomeration economies and transportation accessibility against the centrifugal forces of congestion, land rents, housing prices and immobile factors (Alonso 1964; Fujita 1989; Fujita and Thisse 2002; Henderson 1988; Krugman 1991b; Krugman and Venables 1995; Mills 1972; Muth 1969; Venables 1996). NEG suggests that consumers want to be close to producers to benefit from a variety of goods without incurring transport cost. Producers want to be near consumers or firms with vertical linkages to reap scale economies while satisfying a larger demand. However, a place with a concentration of firms tends to have a larger market. NEG associates demand side and supply side circular and cumulative causation processes with interactions between scale economies, externalities and transport costs.

Transport economics distinguishes between direct and indirect impacts of transport. Direct impacts relate to transport users and suppliers; they operate within the transport market. Indirect impacts, including induced effects, arise outside the transport market—in goods,

Table 5.5 *Direct and Indirect Impacts of Transport Investments*

Market	Key Impact Parameters
Transport Market	• Travel time savings, especially for business travellers and freight operators. • Increased reliability for travellers and freighters. • Efficient logistic operations and supply chain management. • Reduced accidents and increased safety.
Goods Market	• Increased efficiency in combining inputs in production. • Expansion of markets through reduced input and output prices, access to new markets and new sources of raw materials. • Reorganization of production, shifting the production possibility frontier; smoother business interaction and 'just-in-time' management. • Agglomeration economies due to collocation and clustering of firms, workers and institutions in cities. • Stimulation of inward investment, knowledge transfer, innovation and technology diffusion. • Gains from trade: reduction in costs of transport, transaction, tariff and time (4 Ts). • Enhanced competition, alleviation of market failure and promotion of cross-trading between markets.
Labour Market	• Increase in labour market catchment area, reducing labour search, recruitment and training costs. • Expanded pool of specialized labour with industry-specific and cross-industry skills. • Economies of face-to-face interaction and collaboration. • Increased labour market flexibility; better matching of employers and workers, jobs and skills; and job relocation benefits. • Enhanced labour force participation, especially female workers.

(Continued)

Table 5.5 *(Continued)*

Market	Key Impact Parameters
Land Market	• Accessibility premium to land. • Unlocking sites for value-adding developments. • Supporting densification and formation of economic agglomerations. • Benefits of density, proximity and spatial contiguity. • Increase in land values due to enhanced accessibility and serviceability of locations, leading to resource mobilization for infrastructure through value capture instruments.
General	• Triggering growth, which in turn stimulates further growth. • Enhancing welfare. • Promoting social interactions and accumulation of human and social capital. • More consumer choices—access to a variety of goods, services and amenities. • Taking advantage of shifts in geographic and economic opportunities associated with globalization, ICT revolution, innovation, etc.; attracting globally mobile activities. • Impacts on energy use and emission of GHGs. • Developing competitive cities as engines of economic growth. • Enhancing rural–urban linkages; extending money economy to rural areas.

Sources: Mackie, Graham and Laird (2011); Author.

labour and land markets having local, regional and national ramifications. Table 5.5 outlines the impacts of transport investments.

Standard benefit–cost analysis of transportation projects focus on travel time savings. The value placed on such savings is estimated based on the opportunity cost of time lost in reaching valued destinations. However, 'time savings are the base metal of the system, but impact on GDP is the gold' (Mackie, Graham and Laird 2013, 513). In the case of urban PT, such impacts tend to be large due to 'accessibility premiums' to locations and 'WEBs' to firms, households and governments. These benefits include: agglomeration externalities, impacts on outputs in imperfectly competitive markets and effects through labour markets. UT improvements catalyze agglomeration economies by expanding labour markets, enhancing accessibility to the economic mass and increasing returns to density. Lower transport costs also lead to increased output and reduced prices in imperfectly competitive markets. A part of the increase in GDP due to external economies translates into increased taxes on income that can finance urban infrastructure. Further, urban transportation investments induce changes in land use and densities, shape city form, attract value-generating activities, create 'location rents' and facilitate the adoption of value capture instruments to finance urban infrastructure. They also lead to beneficial effects on the environment and contribute to climate change agenda.

URBAN TRANSPORT AND WIDER ECONOMIC BENEFITS

Urban transport affects economic growth through agglomeration externalities in cities. These externalities lead to productivity benefits and cost savings linked to market size, backward and forward linkages, sharing of assets and inputs, specialization, labour market pooling, diversity of economic activity, knowledge transfers and innovation. Empirically, a 10 per cent increase in agglomeration is associated with a 0.7–1 per cent increase in labour productivity in developed countries; bulk of the increase occurs within the first 20 minutes of travel. Productivity gains due to agglomeration externalities seem to be stronger in developing countries compared to developed nations. One-hour commuting time from the location of job in a developing country's city is often regarded as the threshold for agglomeration benefits to taper off. Such benefits are reinforced by transport which connects places that are synergistic, expands markets and reduces congestion. Agglomeration economies constitute a major part of the WEB of UT projects.

Graham (2007) reveals that the initial calculation of agglomeration externalities typically adds 10–20 per cent to conventional user benefits from increasing returns to the economic mass. The inclusion of WEB increased the benefit–cost ratio (BCR) of the East–West rail line in Melbourne by about 40 per cent (Eddington 2008). It raised the BCR for London Crossrail, a 73-mile East–West link involving 26 miles of tunnel in Central London, from 2.55 to between 3.47 and 4.91 (Jenkins, Colella and Salvucci 2011). Recognizing the importance of WEB, the United Kingdom Department for Transport has issued official guidelines for assessing the additional benefits of transportation investments, including those due to agglomeration economies (GoUK 2013).

Venables (2007) adopts the monocentric city model of urban economics to analyse the contribution of transport improvements to economic productivity. Using a spatial computable general equilibrium (SCGE) model, he shows that the external benefits from transport investment can be substantial and these can be measured from the elasticity of productivity with respect to employment density. Transport improvements reduce commuting costs, which in turn facilitates the expansion of employment at the central business district (CBD). This results in increased productivity of workers through agglomeration economies. Workers benefit from higher wages. The landowners gain from higher rents, and government from tax wedge. The incorporation of agglomeration effects on production gives rise to 85–147 per cent additional benefits for commuting journeys compared to standard benefit–cost analysis.

Venables' model assumes that all jobs are located in the CBD. Workers living in different parts of the city commute to the CBD for work. City living imposes costs. There is a trade-off between land rent or housing cost and commuting cost. Spatial equilibrium warrants that workers are indifferent between locations at the margin. The city expands to the point, where commuting cost is high enough to make workers indifferent between living at city edge and working in CBD, and living and working in a non-city location. The spatial equilibrium condition with no tax on wages is:

$$w_u = w_e + \tau d \text{ or } w_u - w_e = \tau d \tag{1}$$

where w_u is the wage at the CBD, w_e is the wage at the edge of the city, τ is the commuting cost per unit distance, assumed to be uniform, and d is the distance to the CBD.

For simplicity, agglomeration economies are assumed to be related to city size; the wage gap $w_u - w_e$ is an increasing function of city population, N_u. Assuming further that the government taxes w_u at the rate t, the condition of post-tax spatial equilibrium is as follows:

$$(1 - t)w_u = w_e + \tau d \text{ or } (1 - t)w_u - w_e = \tau d \tag{2}$$

Figure 5.1 presents Venables' model with pre-tax and post-tax wage gap depicted as increasing function of urban population, N_u due to the presence of agglomeration economies. The equilibrium city size is determined at N_u^* where the post-tax wage gap curve intersects the commuting cost curve C, assumed to be increasing in N_u. When C falls to C^T due to improvements in transportation, the equilibrium moves to N_u^{**}. Let us denote $\eta = N_u^* DB N_u^{**}$, $\alpha = OAD$, $\beta = ABD$, $\varepsilon = AEFB$ and $\delta = GHFE$. The increase in the resource cost of commuting with N_u rising from N_u^* to N_u^{**} is $= OBN_u^{**} - OAN_u^* = \eta - \alpha$; the increase in output is $OHFN_u^{**} - OGEN_u^* = \delta + \varepsilon + \beta + \eta$. Thus, there is a net real income gain of $\alpha + \beta + \delta + \varepsilon$. The area $\alpha + \beta$ captures the commuting cost reduction and ε is the tax wedge effect. The area δ captures the impacts of agglomeration externalities on productivity; it is akin to a measure of the elasticity of productivity with respect to city size.

Venables' model does not consider an important aspect of the role of cities in developing countries, namely providing jobs to rural–urban migrants and commuters. To accommodate this role, one can consider a two-region model with production in the urban region subject to scale economies due to externalities associated with transport investment and production in the rural region subject to diminishing returns. For simplicity, we ignore tax on wages and also effects of reduction in commuting costs. The model is presented as follows:

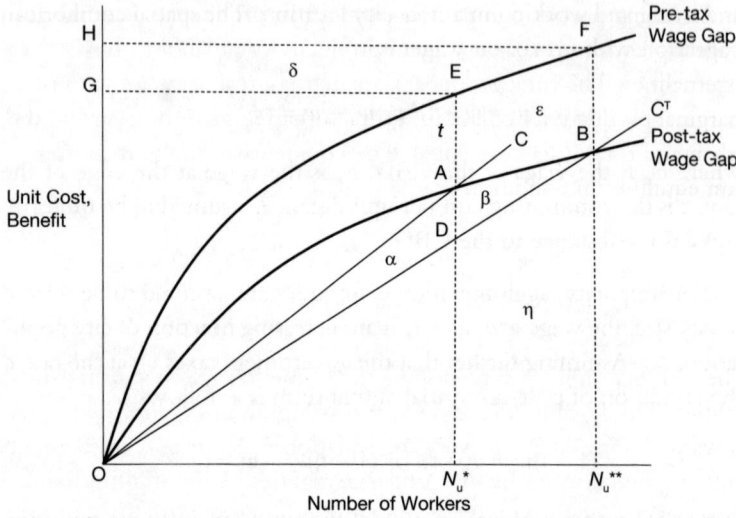

Figure 5.1 *Net Gains from Transport Improvement with Endogenous Productivity*

Source: Venables (2007).

Urban production function: $X_u = g(T)f_u(N_u)$ (3)

where X_u is urban production, N_u is urban population and $g(T)$ represents the agglomeration function that incorporates urban transport T. The production function is assumed to be subject to increasing returns due to external economies of agglomeration.

Rural production function: $X_r = f_r(N_r)$ (4)

where X_r is rural production and N_r is rural population. The X_r function is assumed to be subject to decreasing returns to scale due to overcrowding in agriculture.

Population endowment: $N_u + N_r = N_T$ or $N_r = N_T - N_u$ (5)

where N_T is total population in the economy, assumed to be fixed.

Assuming perfect competition, the urban producers set urban real wage w_u equal to urban marginal productivity of labour oblivious of externalities. The rural producers equate rural real wage w_r with rural marginal productivity of labour. Rural–urban migration occurs till the urban and rural wages are equal. The competitive rural–urban migration equilibrium condition is:

$$w_u = g(T)f_u'(N_u) = w_u(N_u) = w_r = f_r'(N_r)$$
$$= f_r'(N_T - N_u) = w_r(N_u) \tag{6}$$

The w_u function is upward-sloping in N_u due to agglomeration externalities. The w_r function is downward-sloping in N_r and, therefore, upward-sloping in N_u in view of equation 5. Transport investment shifts w_u function up by affecting externalities. Adopting the framework of Venables' model, it can be easily shown that such a shift will lead to real income gains due to: (a) enhanced productivity of existing urban workers, (b) enhanced productivity of rural–urban migrants and commuters and (c) additional benefits to urban workers due to total factor productivity (TFP) growth. Additionally, rural residents benefit due to increase in average product associated with alleviation of diminishing returns. If rural–urban remittances are also taken into account, then the rural residents gain further. When the impacts of UT on the rural economy, urban and suburban land use, protection of the environment and generation of resources through value creation, capture and recycling are added to reduction in commuting costs, tax wedge and agglomeration effects, the economic case for investment in UT becomes compelling. In fact, the precarious state of the urban environment in India, with much of the urbanization yet to take place, suggests that a PT-led and transit-oriented model of urban development may be the most sensible strategy for India to address the urban challenges.

Cities create not only positive externalities but also negative consequences due to congestion diseconomies. Apart from concepts such as accessibility premium, wider economic benefits and value capture financing, transport economics also highlights the importance of congestion charging to correct negative externalities. It suggests that unless drivers are required to pay the full social cost of congesting urban roads during peak hours, those roads will be overused, creating wastage of resources and a dead weight loss to the entire society. The Mohring–Harwitz Theorem (MHT) in transport economics suggests that CC breaks even.

THE MOHRING-HARWITZ THEOREM

Called the 'self-financing' or 'cost recovery' theorem, the MHT states that under certain conditions, the revenues from congestion tolls will be adequate to finance the capacity cost of an optimal-sized public facility such as a highway (Mohring 1972, 1976; Mohring and Harwitz 1962). Lindsay (2009) shows that the result continues to hold in the presence of short-run uncertainty, with additional assumptions. The MHT is of significance to developing countries like India as it addresses the neglected subject of financing PT investments. It shows that the efficient pricing of a congestible public good is consistent with the 'users pay' principle and there will be no need for subsidy. Further, users are not required to pay arbitrarily or excessively; the pricing strategy provides for limiting the charges to marginal social costs. Globally, a number of cities such as Singapore, Stockholm and London have successfully implemented the 'congesters pay' principle by adopting electronic pricing and automated payment methods. When congestion charging is not feasible, motor vehicles tax, fuel tax, parking fees, etc., are considered as surrogates to congestion pricing. 'Congesters pay' is a corollary to the 'beneficiaries pay' principle. Those who cause dis-benefits to the society must pay for the costs of mitigation.

URBAN TRANSPORT AND THE ENVIRONMENT

Urban transport has crucial implications for the environment. The pro-liferation of personalized vehicles in cities is responsible for exorbitant increase in fuel combustion, leading to adverse impacts on the climate. Globally, about 75 per cent of urban air pollution occurs due to this source. Transport accounts for about 22–23 per cent of energy-related

GHG emissions worldwide, and 30 per cent in developed countries. It contributes to the largest share of emissions in automobile-dominated North American cities. What is alarming is that emissions due to transport are increasing at a faster rate than any other sector. Cities are the hubs of fossil fuel activity and unsustainable energy consumption. They consume about 80 per cent of the energy produced globally and account for roughly the same percentage of energy-related GHG emissions (World Bank 2010). The 50 largest cities of the world are responsible for the third highest emission of energy-related GHGs, after China and the United States (Ohshita et al. 2015). Cities are at the forefront of global warming.

Cities are disproportionately affected by climate change impacts, which are manifested in the frequency and intensity of extreme weather events such as cyclonic storms, floods, unseasonal rains, landslides, droughts, heatwaves, intense smog and increased spread of tropical diseases. About 30 million urban dwellers in India, residing in coastal zones are at the risk of rise in sea level due to global warming. While it is the rich in cities who are responsible for the bulk of carbon emissions, the poor are the most vulnerable to disasters induced by climate change. In particular, the residents of slums and squatter settlements, many of which are located in eco-fragile zones, are the worst affected in cities due to disasters. They are also subjected to public health hazards that follow the occurrence of various disasters. Thus, on the considerations of environmental sustainability, public health and social equity, climate change mitigation and adaptation are emerging as important priorities of cities globally.

Cities represent the single largest opportunity to pursue the climate change agenda through environment-friendly transportation and energy-efficient, low carbon development. Investments in PT, including transit, have the potential of creating long-lasting impacts on the environment by shaping city development and urban form. They lead to improved air quality, safer roads, more functional, inclusive and sustainable cities. If India and China resort to per capita carbon emission at the same level as in sprawling United States, the world's carbon emissions will increase by more than 125 per cent. But if they rise only to the level observed in the dense, transit-oriented but prosperous Hong

Kong SAR, China, global carbon emissions will rise by less than 30 per cent (Glaeser and Joshi–Ghani 2015). India, which will contribute the largest share to global urban population between 2014 and 2050, needs to make cities integral partners in the strategy to fight climate change by moving away from automobile-centric sprawl to compact and transit-oriented development. Low carbon emission transport systems need to be combined with sustainable land use planning, including effective management of FSI and densities.

While urban and transport economics underscore the importance of PT investment for city functionality and efficiency, a branch of the planning literature emphasizes its role in the designing and planning of neighbourhoods, communities and cities to make them environmentally sustainable. In particular, the theory and practice of New Urbanism and Smart Growth emphasize the role of PT in creating liveable and inclusive places. These paradigms emerged in the United States, Western Europe and Australia in response to their problems of urban sprawl, traffic congestion and pollution, a consequence of automobile-dependent urbanization. They provide useful lessons to developing countries like India for designing urban and transport development strategies to address the negative effects of increased motorization and overcrowding.

NEW URBANISM AND SMART GROWTH

New Urbanism and Smart Growth emerged in the last four decades as alternatives to low-density, single-use and spread-out urban development that occurred after the Second World War, threatening farmland and open space, raising infrastructure costs, encouraging flight of people and wealth from central cities to suburbs, increasing traffic congestion and air pollution and adversely affecting the environment and quality of life. New Urbanism has architectural roots. It is design-oriented and focused on neighbourhood design. It advocates compact, human-scale urban design with walkable streets, mix of housing and shopping, accessible public places, higher density and less automobile-dependency. Smart Growth is a growth management approach advocated by planners to guide urban development. It has environmental roots and is policy-oriented. It is not so much concerned with urban design as it is with growth promotion.

New Urbanism took roots in the early 1980s in the United States as an urban planning and design paradigm that aimed at creating communities as pleasant places to walk, cycle and use public transit. It advocates a mix of housing, workplaces, retail facilities and public amenities. It suggests densely packed housing, workplaces, commercial sites and recreational spaces to reduce dependence on the car and to promote face-to-face interactions between people from all walks of life. It targets at integrating the natural and man-made environments to promote sustainable urbanization. The key building blocks of New Urbanism are: walkable blocks and streets, houses and shops in close proximity and accessible workplaces and public places. The paradigm calls for the attention of urban planners to Traditional Neighbourhood Design (TND) and TOD. New Urbanism has grown as an international movement to reform the design of the built environment.

Box 5.1 presents the key principles of New Urbanism contained in the Charter of New Urbanism formulated in the United States following the establishment of the Congress for the New Urbanism in 1993.

The Smart Growth movement originated in the United States in the 1990s, in the course of an intense debate on 'growth' versus 'no growth'. This debate was in response to the problems of uncontrolled expansion of urban areas, sprawl and automobile-induced suburbanization. The movement advocated compact, mixed use, walkable, bicycle-friendly and transit-oriented growth with multiple housing and transportation options. The United States Environmental Protection Agency (US EPA) defines Smart Growth as 'development that serves the economy, the community, and the environment. It changes the terms of the development debate away from the traditional growth/no growth question to how and where should new development be accommodated' (US EPA 2004). The paradigm has emerged as a key element in the strategy to make cities and communities economically strong, socially diverse, environmentally sustainable and attractive places to live, work and recreate. The logic and 10 principles of Smart Growth are presented in Box 5.2.

TRANSIT-ORIENTED DEVELOPMENT

Both New Urbanism and Smart Growth advocate TOD, aimed at concentrating growth around one or more transit stations or within a transit

Box 5.1 *Principles of New Urbanism*

The principles of New Urbanism, applied to projects at the full range of scales from a single building to an entire community, are as follows:

Walkability
- Most activities within a 10-minute walk of home and work.
- Pedestrian-friendly street design (buildings close to street, with porches, windows and doors; treelined streets; on-street parking; parking lots and garages behind houses and buildings, often connected to alleys; narrow, slow-speed streets).
- Pedestrian streets free of cars in special cases.

Connectivity
- Interconnected street grid network disperses traffic and encourages walking.
- A hierarchy of narrow streets, boulevards and alleys.
- High-quality pedestrian network and public realm makes walking pleasurable.

Mixed use and Diversity
- A mix of shops, offices, apartments and homes on site. Mixed use within neighbourhoods, within blocks and within buildings.
- Diversity of people—of varying ages, income levels, cultures and races.

Mixed Housing
- Zoning allows a wide range of housing types, sizes and prices in closer proximity.
- Move towards affordability or inclusive housing framework.

Quality Architecture and Urban Design
- Emphasis on beauty, aesthetics, human comfort and creating a sense of place. Human scale architecture and beautiful surroundings nourish the human spirit.

Traditional Neighbourhood Structure
- Discernible centre and edge.
- Public space near the centre.

- Importance of quality public realm; public open spaces function as civic art.
- Contains a range of uses and densities within 10-minute walk.
- Transect planning: highest densities at town centre; progressively less dense towards the edge.

Increased Density
- More buildings, residences, shops and services closer together for ease of walking, to enable a more efficient use of services and resources, and to create a more convenient, enjoyable place to live.
- Design principles applied at the full range of densities from small town to large city.

Smart Transportation
- A network of high-quality trains connecting cities, towns and neighbourhoods together.
- Pedestrian-friendly design that encourages a greater use of bicycles, rollerblades, scooters and walking as daily transportation.

Sustainability
- Minimal environmental impact of development and its operations.
- Eco-friendly technologies, respect for ecology and value of natural systems.
- Energy efficiency to minimize effects on the environment.
- Less use of finite fuels.
- The community connects strongly with surrounding farmland, encouraging land conservation and local food production.
- More walking, less driving.

Quality of Life
- Promote life worth living by creating places that enrich, uplift and inspire the human spirit.

Source: https://www.cnu.org/who-we-are/charter-new-urbanism (accessed 12 July 2018).

Box 5.2 *The Logic and Principles of Smart Growth*

The logic of Smart Growth is based on four propositions:

- Whether its causes are economic forces, consumer preferences or misguided public policies, the dominant form of urban development over the post-war period can be characterized as urban sprawl.
- Urban sprawl can be defined as development that is low density, unplanned, automobile-dependent, homogeneous and aesthetically displeasing.
- Urban sprawl has adverse effects on environmental quality, social cohesion, government finance and human health.
- Urban sprawl, and its associated evils, can be mitigated by policies that promote compact urban growth, mixed land uses, bicycle and pedestrian-friendly environments, public transit, urban revitalization and farmland preservation.

The 10 principles of Smart Growth are:

- Create a range of housing opportunities and choices;
- Create walkable neighbourhoods;
- Encourage community and stakeholder collaboration;
- Foster distinctive, attractive places with a strong sense of place;
- Make development decisions predictable, fair and cost-effective;
- Mix land uses;
- Preserve open space, farmland, natural beauty and critical environmental areas;
- Provide a variety of transportation choices;
- Strengthen and direct development towards existing communities; and
- Take advantage of compact building design.

Source: Knaap and Talen (2005).

corridor. TOD is regional and urban planning, city development and rejuvenation, suburban revitalization and walkable neighbourhoods combined. It calls for connected, compact, walkable, mixed use communities with access to high-quality transit services within a walking distance. The principles of TOD are not entirely new. They were incorporated by many cities in North America and Australia into their planning models after the Second World War to address the problems of sprawl and congestion. However, TOD as a policy paradigm has taken roots only in the last two decades. It is rapidly spreading across nations with the creation of people-friendly communities in city after city. The public has appreciated the model as a tool to create socially attractive places. Real estate developers have rose to the occasion to meet the demand for quality urban places on transit nodes and corridors. The concept of TOD is even more relevant to developing countries like India in view of their urban population densities, income distribution structures and problems of traffic congestion, environmental degradation and social exclusion.

The concentration of development with a TOD approach has several merits. It enables lower stress living without complete dependence on the automobile. It acts against sprawl and uneconomic extension of infrastructure. TOD also promotes city efficiency and contributes to inclusive growth. It facilitates the collocation of productive economic activities and catalyzes external economies of agglomeration while mitigating congestion diseconomies. It is environment-friendly, reduces carbon emission and contributes to the climate change agenda. It promotes inclusion of the poor in urban development. The poor, who do not own a vehicle, benefit by availing efficient transport services to reach workplaces. When designed well, TOD can assist public authorities in raising revenues through land and property taxes, betterment levies and other instruments.

The most effective response to urban sprawl is to increase urban densities and channelize growth around transport nodes and corridors. TOD is a key component of such a strategy. By creating pedestrian-oriented, medium to high-density and mixed use spaces around public transit hubs, this type of development simultaneously constrains unnecessary expansion of city boundaries and encourages PT use. It creates strong links between residential, commercial, institutional and recreational spaces, removing the need to travel long distances for work, shopping or recreation. By ensuring that residents live within a short walk from regular PT services—principally rail lines, but also bus and light rail— TOD makes PT a more convenient option. TOD can also be a major solution to the serious problems of climate change and energy security by creating dense, walkable and public transit-using communities. It can greatly reduce the need for driving and consumption of non-renewable energy. Experience of developed countries suggest that a TOD-type living arrangement can reduce driving by up to 85 per cent.

The success of TOD depends on its design. Box 5.3 presents some key principles to guide TOD designing.

While the principles of Smart Growth and TOD originated in developed countries in response to their problems of automobile-centric urban development, sprawl and traffic congestion, the paradigms make good sense for developing countries like India. Cities in India suffer from problems manifesting in wastage of energy, increased carbon emissions and damage to the environment. These are linked to extreme controls on FSI and land use and lack of investment in PT. However, large cities in India are eminently suitable for TOD in view of their population densities and income distribution structures. Policies that lead to more compact and mixed development and create more multimodal transportation options will lead to cost savings and environmental benefits. Such development makes sense as it is resource-efficient and causes residents to consume less land and energy, own fewer vehicles, require less parking and generate less congestion, traffic risk and pollution. It also enhances productivity due to external economies. Further, TOD tends to be more socially equitable because it expands affordable housing and transport options for the disadvantaged sections. TOD presents a significant opportunity to India to make urbanization efficient, sustainable and equitable. It is a key element of India's National Urban Transport Policy (NUTP).

INDIA'S NATIONAL URBAN TRANSPORT POLICY

India has formulated the NUTP 2014 replacing the earlier policy of 2006 (MoUD 2014). NUTP 2014 recognizes the importance of sustained investment in UT not only as a response to emerging demand but also as a driver of economic growth. It regards UT as a key service that imparts efficiency to the city by providing mobility to workers and enabling them to enhance productivity. The key objective of the policy is to move people rather than vehicles by providing sustainable mobility

Box 5.3 *Transit-oriented Development: Design Principles*

1. Multimodal Transit Station
   Transit is at the heart of TOD and should be designed to connect with, not be isolated from, the surrounding neighbourhood. People should have their choice of transportation modes including cars, bus rapid transit, light rail transit, two-wheelers, auto-rickshaws, cycle rickshaws and bicycles.

2. Interconnected Streets
   An interconnected street pattern is a traditional urban design technique that reduces congestion, encourages travel choice and supports mixed use development. Block lengths should not exceed 400 m.

3. Mixed Use Development
   A mix of diverse and complimentary land uses in a compact pattern allows residents and workers to walk to work or to shop rather than driving for all daily needs.

4. Walkability
   Pedestrian-friendly environments allow walking to be a pleasant, safe and efficient alternative to (or extension of) the automobile. This includes design features such as safe crossing points near transit stations, shaded pedestrian routes and continuous sidewalks.

5. Compact Development
   The scale of TOD approximates the scale of the pedestrian. The extent of neighbourhoods around transit nodes is based on a comfortable walking distance from edge to centre (approximately 400 to 800 m in radius).

6. Street-facing Buildings
   Buildings should be placed near streets, not behind parking areas, to better define the street. Street front retail should be provided to humanize the building wall and activate the sidewalk. Building entrances should be close to transit entrances.

7. Urban Place-making
   TOD is defined as much by its public realm as its private development. Public and semi-public spaces enable the neighbourhood infrastructure to build community bonds, social interaction and community participation.

8. Neighbourhood High Street
   Retail streets provide the goods and services of daily life, activate the street, reduce reliance on the automobile and increase ownership and safety of the pedestrian realm.

(Continued)

Box 5.3 *(Continued)*

9. Streetscape Design
   A highly connected street pattern with design elements coordinated to provide visual interest, pedestrian amenity and a sense of place improves the desirability of walking and shortens the perception of distance.
10. Bicycle-friendly Streets/Parking
    Bicycles are efficient ways to expand a station's service area without relying on automobiles or bus. Bike lanes, bike routes and secure parking make the bicycle an easy option.
11. Urban Parks and Plazas with Minimized Ecological Footprint
    Varieties of public open spaces near transit stations contribute to a sense of place, foster healthy communities and provide places for interaction.
12. Architectural Variety
    Promoting an architectural style that is pedestrian-friendly, contains visual variation and, with improved economics of higher density, higher quality building materials.
13. A Well-designed Transit Station for a High-quality User Experience
    The transit station will be a focal point in mobility hub areas, as the gateway to the regional transit network. Its design will be paramount to ensure a seamless, accessible and attractive customer environment and experience.
14. Reduced Parking Standards
    By reducing parking standards to reflect increased transit use and walking, the amount of site area that can be used for active uses or public amenities increases.
15. Safety and Security
    Developing the pedestrian environment to maximize safety and security will enhance patron experience and transit ridership.
16. Market Acceptance and Successful Implementation
    A TOD is successful when it attracts sufficient jobs and residents to create a vibrant, transit-supportive place. In order to ensure success of a TOD, strategies should be flexible, designed to respond to the diverse nature of the station areas, their surrounding community contexts and area development market.

Source: GEF-World Bank-UNDP (2012).

and accessibility to all citizens—to jobs, education, social services and recreation at affordable cost and within reasonable time. It presents a compelling case for investment in UT as follows:

> There is an urgent need to conserve energy and land, control pollution and 'greenhouse gas emissions', and to alleviate poverty. Urban Transport (UT) is a significant cause and also a solution to these issues. Hence planning and management of UT services and infrastructure require immediate attention. The growth story of India shall be written on the canvas of planned urban development and scripted with the instrument of planned urban mobility solutions. (p. 1)

NUTP 2014 acknowledges the huge deficit in UT services and infrastructure in India—in terms of quantity and quality both. The use of desirable modes: walk, bicycle and PT is decreasing and that of undesirable modes, that is, car and two-wheelers is increasing. As a result, congestion is escalating, urban mobility and road safety are declining and pollution, use of fossil fuel and accidents are rising. All categories of road users in India are facing problems in commuting. The pedestrians do not get a safe and conflict-free path to walk. The cyclists struggle for the right of way with fast-moving motorized modes, many a times risking their lives. The users of PT face long waiting periods, uncertainty in reaching destinations in time and difficult conditions of travel. The proliferation of personal motorized modes is slowing down passenger and goods traffic, leading to significant delays at traffic signals and road junctions. Road users are facing severe stress due to traffic delays, road rage, rash driving and accidents. India's commercial energy demand and emissions will increase by about six to seven times from the levels in 2011 by 2031–2032 if nothing is done to curb the effects.

The key strategies articulated by NUTP 2014 to enhance urban mobility include the following:

- Incorporating UT as an important parameter at the urban planning stage rather than being a consequential requirement.
- Bringing about a more equitable allocation of road space with people, rather than vehicles, as the main focus.

- PT should be citywide, safe, seamless, user-friendly, reliable and should provide good ambience with well-behaved drivers and conductors.
- Walking and cycling should become safe modes of UT.
- Introducing Intelligent Transportation Systems for traffic management.
- Addressing concerns of road safety and trauma response.
- Raising finances through innovative mechanisms.
- Establishing institutional mechanisms for enhanced coordination in the planning and management of transport systems.
- Building capacity (institutional and manpower) to plan for sustainable UT and establishing a knowledge management system to service the needs of all UT professionals, such as planners, researchers, teachers, students, etc.

According to NUTP 2014, a paradigm shift is needed in the approach to UT with three key strategies in transport planning, namely 'avoid, shift and improve'. The policy calls for action to 'avoid' increase in demand for travel both by reducing the number and length of trips, to promote a 'shift' from personal vehicles to MRT and other non-motorized transport (NMT) modes to reduce energy demand and hence pollution in cities and to 'improve' UT by the use of clean fuel and clean vehicle technology. NUTP 2014 suggests a holistic approach to UT that includes transport–land use integration, TOD, TDM, freight traffic management, promotion of PT and traffic planning and engineering interventions such as coordination between traffic signals, traffic calming methods, road signage and stringent enforcement for prioritizing PT modes, non-motorized traffic and pedestrians in congested and environmentally sensitive areas.

NUTP 2014 recognizes the organic link between transportation planning and land use planning. It advocates that both should be developed together to serve the entire population and yet minimize travel needs. It calls for the development of integrated master plans to channel future growth of a city around a pre-planned UT network rather than developing UT after uncontrolled sprawl has occurred. For example, NUTP 2014 recommends the reservation of radial corridors emerging from the city and extending up to 20–30 km for future development. The policy makes a strong case for TOD as follows:

> High density urban growth offers the opportunity for trip lengths to be short. It promotes a high level of accessibility for Non-motorised Transport (NMT). It fosters successful, financially viable PT, and enables cities to have low levels of energy use per person in UT. The Government of India would encourage Transit Oriented Development (TOD) with increased FAR along transit corridors with high density of population....

TOD calls for concentrating housing, jobs, shopping and other activities around transit stations and restructuring urban planning to promote the following objectives:

1. More people to live close to transit services and to use it.
2. A rich mix of uses within walking distance of a transit station.
3. Pedestrian facilities and multimodal connectivity with focus on moving people.
4. Making transit station a gateway to the community.
5. Revising building by-laws and planning norms for cities so as to encourage high FAR and ground coverage along major transit corridors.

Apart from TOD, NUTP 2014 emphasizes TDM to maximize the efficiency of UT by discouraging private vehicles and promoting more effective, healthy and environment-friendly modes of transport. It also emphasizes timely and smooth movement of freight traffic through measures such as staggering of freight and passenger traffic, building bypasses to enable through traffic to go around the city without adding to city traffic and developing parking terminals for freight vehicles outside city limits. The policy has stressed on the importance of PT, including MRT, para-transit and personalized PT. MRT, both rail and road-based and including city bus, is considered the backbone of city transport as they are the only modes that carry a very large number of people using minimum space. Para-transit modes, that is, tempos and mini buses, supplement MRT in large cities and can be the main mode of PT in medium- and small-sized cities. Personalized PT, that is, autos and taxis, and cycle rickshaws, cater to the demand of commuters seeking a substitute for personal transport. NUTP envisages that the GoI would support cities to plan a citywide integrated multimodal PT network comprising all three modes of PT along with first and last mile connectivity for easy access to MRT stations.

MRT is a more sustainable form of UT compared to personal vehicles. It occupies less road space and causes less pollution per passenger-kilometre. Therefore, the GoI has decided to promote investments in MRT as well as undertake measures to make its use more attractive. Towards this end, the GoI would encourage all state capitals as well as other cities with a population of more than one million to start planning for an MRT network. In doing so, they should look at various proven technologies globally and adopt a technology that would best suit the city requirements for the next 30 years and beyond. Cities with population less than a million should plan MRT based on a mix of buses of various sizes. All cities would be mandatorily required to prepare an integrated operation plan which should be reviewed every five years to update and rationalize PT routes. NUTP 2014 recognizes that there is a wide spectrum of MRT technologies. While rail-based systems seem to suit dense cities with limited sprawl and only a few spinal corridors, bus systems seem better where urban densities are low and the city has spread over a large area. NUTP advocates the integration of all modes of MRT to provide seamless journey to the commuter at affordable cost.

Box 5.4 *Transit-oriented Development Policy for Delhi (2013)*

The TOD Policy for Delhi 2013 aims at low carbon emission, high-density, compact, mixed land use and sustainable development by minimizing travel time for citizens, promoting use of PT, reducing pollution and congestion, creating more homogeneous neighbourhoods, having workplaces near residences, creating public amenities within walking distance and providing a safe environment through redevelopment along MRTS corridors in the national capital. The salient features of the Delhi TOD Policy are:

- Development/redevelopment in TOD zone will be incentivized by providing significantly higher FAR of 4.0 on the entire amalgamated plot being developed/ redeveloped. However, these higher norms can be availed only for plots of area of 1 hectare or more for which a comprehensive integrated scheme has to be prepared. In contrast, the minimum scheme area for undertaking redevelopment outside TOD zone is 4 hectares. Within an approved scheme area in TOD zone, development can be taken up in phases for minimum plot size of 3,000 sq. m at a time. Minimum scheme area for development by MRTS agencies such as Delhi Metro Rail Corporation (DMRC), Rapid Rail Transit System (RRTS) and Railways will be 3,000 sq. m.
- Additional FAR may be availed only through Transferable Development Rights (TDRs) for schemes larger than 1 hectare.
- Entire approved layout plan of a scheme will be included in the transit influence zone if more than 50 per cent of the plan area falls inside that zone.
- It will be mandatory to use a minimum of 30 per cent of overall FAR for residential use, a minimum of 10 per cent of FAR for commercial use and a minimum of 10 per cent of FAR for community facilities. Utilization of remaining 50 per cent FAR shall be as per the land use category designated in the zonal plan.
- There shall be a mix of housing types for a wide range of income brackets within communities with shared public spaces/greens/ recreational facilities/amenities, which will minimize gentrification and create community-oriented developments.
- The mandatory residential component covering 30 per cent FAR shall wholly comprise of units of 65 sq. m area or less. Out of these, half of the FAR, that is, 15 per cent of the total FAR, has to be used for units of size ranging between 32 and 40 sq. m. Over and above this, an additional mandatory FAR of 15 per cent, that is, FAR of 0.6 (out of 4.0) has to be utilized for EWS housing. The size of EWS units will range between 32 and 40 sq. m.
- Twenty per cent of land shall be used for roads/circulation areas. Twenty per cent area for green open space shall be kept open for general public use at all times. Further, 10 per cent of green area may be for exclusive use.

Source: MoUD, GoI; DDA (2015).

While NUTP 2014 presents a framework for long-term urban strategy, its real test lies in implementation. The policy envisages that states and cities undertake significant investments in urban PT, integrate transport and land use and implement TOD. Some metropolitan cities in India are implementing MRT and BRT systems. The Mass Rapid Transit System (MRTS) in Delhi, 'Namma Metro' in Bengaluru and Bus Rapid Transit System (BRTS) 'Janmarg' in Ahmedabad are noted examples. Delhi, Ahmedabad, Bengaluru, Hyderabad, Naya Raipur and Haryana have launched TOD schemes. The DDA has formulated a TOD policy in 2013. A notable feature of this policy is that it combines environment-friendly development and social equity. Box 5.4 describes the key features of Delhi's TOD policy.

The success of Delhi's TOD policy will depend on its execution in field. While Delhi has chosen a model based on a top–down and 'one-size-fits-all' approach, Ahmedabad has adopted the Local Area Planning (LAP) route to promote strategic densification along the BRTS corridor. Ahmedabad's model tries to exploit the synergy between transportation, land use and local economic development. It subscribes to a key principle of urban and transport economics that the demand for transport depends on the distribution of economic and social activities and the trade-off between benefits and costs associated with location. These factors have strong localized implications which a pan–city scheme may not be able to address. They point to the importance of strategies such as transport–land use integration, value increment financing (VIF), congestion charging (CC), transportation system management (TSM), etc. Nodes and networks matter due to their links with localized externalities associated with agglomeration of and networking between productive economic activities.

TRANSPORT ECONOMICS AND URBAN PLANNING

The existing and projected population, densities and income distribution structures in India's large city regions and the overriding concerns of the environment and climate change call for a PT-led strategy for urban development in India. However, the master planning model followed by cities accorded a secondary role to urban PT. This is due to the obsession of urban planners with land use detailing based on the premise that land use primarily determines the transportation needs. Master plans have undermined the two-way relationship between transportation and land use. They have also neglected transport economics, which suggests that major transport projects influence the collocation of productive economic activities and the returns to density by catalyzing agglomeration and network externalities. Indian cities have not given due importance to these externalities, including the phenomena of 'accessibility premium' and 'WEB' associated with urban PT. They have also not exploited economic instruments such as benefit taxes, value capture tools and congestion charges to address externalities and raise resources to finance transportation infrastructure. Further, the lack of recognition of the broader economic impacts of major UT investments has led to a low ranking to MRT and HSR projects in the conventional benefit–cost appraisals.

Public transport plays a crucial role in guiding the development of compact, connected, inclusive and sustainable cities. It magnifies the positive impacts of externalities while mitigating their negative consequences. Dispersed development, characterized by fewer transport options, low densities and separation between residences and workplaces, results in adverse consequences for the environment, unnecessary commuting, energy wastage, increased air and water pollution, segregation between the rich and the poor and loss of habitat. It also negatively affects the efficiency of the transport system as the same volume of economic activities and the same number of commuters demand transport that involves increased number and length of trips and journey time. Further, the poor for whom the access to PT is critically important to access remunerative employment opportunities are adversely affected. India needs to make significant investment in urban PT, including MRT and HSR to maximize the net benefits from the externalities of cities. Efforts are also needed to promote 'public transport-led' and 'transit-oriented' development with a focus on inclusion of the poor and enabling rural growth nodes and intermediate towns to benefit from the agglomeration economies in large cities. The paradigm 'connect, connect, connect' is critical for inclusive development in India.

The view held by some physical planners in India that land use planning should guide transportation planning needs to be revisited. While
both the planning streams must be integrated, the fact that Indian cities
have grossly neglected investment in PT for decades suggests that a
PT-led urban development strategy will pay rich dividends for decades
by addressing the concerns of economic growth, inclusion and sustainability. In this context, four strategic reforms are of pivotal importance:
planning and implementing a grid of arterial roads; investing in MRT
and HSR networks in metropolitan city regions to attract economic
growth; integrating transportation and land use planning with a 'leading' role assigned to PT and a TOD strategy focused on inclusion and
adopting economic instruments such as taxation of urban land, purchasable development rights, CC and VIF to supplement growth management instruments while raising resources to finance PT infrastructure.

A Grid of Arterial Road Networks

A recognition of the role to UT in 'leading' development to new area
rather than following it calls for planning and delineation of strategic
transportation networks, including arterial and radial roads, and PT systems in anticipation, and their development in phases. Shlomo Angel,
an eminent planner, presents four simple ways that cities in developing
countries could adopt to expand their areas to meet population growth
in the future. The first step is to project population and the land area
needed. The second step is to secure new municipal boundaries that
include the feasible areas for urban expansion. The third step is to
acquire the right of way for a grid of arterial roads in the expansion
area, connecting the city's existing arterial roads network. Arterial roads
are those which will carry trunk infrastructure lines such as water and
sewer mains, storm water drains, telecommunication networks, etc.,
and also cater to PT services. At last, cities should acquire the land for
public open spaces in the expansion area in advance, before development occurs. Angel suggests that the arterial roads be designed with
about 30 m width to support designated bus lane, bike path and median
apart from regular traffic. Such roads may be located about 1 km apart to
ensure that no individual lives at more than 10–15 minutes of walking

distance from public and private transportation services that will make use of the arterial roads (Angel 2008).

Angel's approach enables cities to add infrastructure inexpensively on a 'just-in-time' basis as their urban footprint expands. It does not rely on top-down master planning schemes that make elaborate prescriptions about land use, density and FSI. The model is non-intrusive and suggests that land development between the arterial roads be market-driven, producing structural and spatial diversities, eloquently emphasized by Jane Jacobs. Such diversities contribute to the vitality of cities. Apart from arterial roads, land needed for radial roads and future MRT and HSR networks must also be reserved. Strong incentives need to be put in place to encourage developments near arterial and radial roads and rail transport corridors. Efforts are also needed to procure land for such projects through town planning schemes (TPSs). The Sardar Patel Ring Road developed by the Ahmedabad Urban Development Authority (AUDA) with land secured free of cost through the TPS presents an excellent initiative for wider replication.

Mass Rapid Transit and High-speed Rail

The goals of efficient, inclusive and sustainable urbanization warrant that India adopts a mix of PT options, planned well in advance. The importance of MRT and HSR can be gauged from the facts the road system in India's large cities will not be able to handle the projected per hour per direction traffic (phpdt). India is only 33 per cent urban, and between 2014 and 2050, the country's urban population would double. Metropolitan cities are already dense and subjected to serious forms of environmental degradation. PT-led development is the only socially desirable strategy for cities. In this regard, transportation planners recommend public transit options for cities depending on projected phpdt: BRT—10,000–15,000; light rail—15,000–35,000, medium rail—30,000–60,000 and heavy rail—55,000 and above. High-speed trains, running at a speed of 250 km/hr or more, are desirable for mega-city regions. The GoI has embarked on an HSR corridor between Mumbai and Ahmedabad at a cost of about ₹98,000 crores with Japanese financial and technical assistance. Considerations of powerful external economies associated with major UT projects make a strong economic case for investment in HSR, connecting cities and emerging growth hubs in mega-city regions. While MRT and HSR involve huge upfront investment, the fact that the country cannot postpone such projects any longer calls for devising innovative financing strategies rooted in a value creation, capture and recycling framework. Land values in large cities of India are exorbitantly high and must be tapped to raise seed money to finance MRT and HSR projects based on intergovernmental partnerships. The R+P (rail plus property) model of Hong Kong offers a good example in this regard.

HSR originated in Japan in 1964, with Japanese national railways launching the Tokaido Shinkansen, connecting Tokyo Central and Shin Osaka—running with a speed of 210 km/hr. By 2017, China has been able to establish and operate an HSR network of about 23,914 km, Japan—3,041, Spain—2,871, France—2,142 and Germany—1,475 km (Hunkar 2017). Some researchers argue that huge investments in HSR and other PT networks have enabled China to drive economic growth through cities and become a superpower. Salzberg at el. (2013), in their studies of HSR projects in China, found the presence of 'WEB' of significant scale—of the same order as, but additional to the direct benefits conventionally measured. Further, these benefits of larger and better connected markets accrue to individuals and businesses even when they do not themselves undertake travel. Transport economics suggest that if the strategies of industrialization, economic growth, urbanization and transportation are combined, HSR will not only be socially worthwhile but also financially viable in India. It will save time and money, reduce pollution, promote energy security, facilitate the emergence of technology clusters, expand tourism, revitalize derelict urban areas and enhance the competitiveness of city regions. It will enable cities to harness the external economies of density, diversity and networking, and benefit from decongestion, integration, inclusion and conservation. It will also spur economic development in tier-2 cities and rural growth centres along the train routes. Further, HSR will lead to unified labour markets, offering opportunities to workers to choose from a wider set of employers and vice versa. India needs to have a strategy to integrate MRT and HSR development programmes with urbanization as part of the strategy of economic growth.

Transportation–Land Use Integration

Transportation–land use integration is perhaps the single-most important tool available to policymakers and planners in developing countries like India to pursue the goals of sustainable and inclusive urban development. The paradigm calls for investment in MRT and HSR in anticipation of economic growth, strategic densification of PT nodes with increased FSI and value-enhancing changes in land use and TSM. Every major transport project needs to be packaged, linking public infrastructure investment, spatial planning, local economic development and plan financing strategies.

Transportation and land use have symbiotic relationships. A well-planned public transportation system, with higher commercial and residential densities at strategic locations and mixed land use development facilitates multimodal travel: walking, bicycle, PT and automobile. Locations with good accessibility tend to have a higher chance of being developed with higher densities than remote locations, unless irrationally restricted by myopic local government policy. The acknowledgement that trip and location decisions codetermine each other has culminated in the concept of 'land use–transport feedback cycle' in the urban planning literature in developed countries. This suggests that the distribution of land uses determines the location of human activities such as living, working, shopping, education and leisure. The geographic spread of such activities calls for trips in the transport system to overcome the impedance of distance. The development of transportation networks leads to opportunities for spatial and functional interactions due to improved accessibility. Differential accessibility codetermines location decisions and results in changes in the land use system.

The two-way relationship between transportation and land use suggests that the land use impacts intended by city master plans cannot be attained without integrating transportation planning and land use planning. Institution and change of land use and density based on zoning regulations lead to changes in demand for transportation. Major transportation investments also call for changes in land use and intensity of development. The benefits of transportation–land use integration can be harnessed only by a flexible planning framework—not rigid master planning. Flexible planning is also necessary to promote TOD as a vehicle of inclusive and sustainable urbanization. The low- and middle-income groups need to be located in public transit nodes with the incorporation of mixed land use, high-density development and affordable housing. Such a strategy will address the problems of traffic congestion. It will also enhance transit ridership and make transit projects financially viable. Further, the strategic densification of transit nodes will facilitate benefit taxation and value capture financing of transit-related infrastructure by exploiting land, FSI and urban planning as resource. In this context, a strong case exists for converting the national and state highways passing through large cities in India to mass transit corridors with TOD by developing bypasses and regional ring roads.

Adoption of Economic Instruments

Both urban planning and transportation planning in India have neglected economic instruments to achieve the objectives of urban development plans. In particular, they have neglected benefit taxation, value capture and congestion charging tools to promote sustainable urban mobility.

Transport creates access, and access creates value. Major PT investments result in the benefits of accessibility which capitalize into land values at vantage locations. Accessibility reduces the time, cost and inconvenience to reach destinations: workplaces, schools, shops, recreation centres, railway stations, airports and the like. It also facilitates human interaction, information flow and knowledge transfer, leading to agglomeration economies. Further, the benefits of accessibility translate into 'residual' land rents. VCF, including benefit taxation, is thus a fair and efficient method to tap such windfalls to finance worthwhile projects. It also promotes density while preventing sprawl. If a transportation project passes the benefit–cost test, the rise in land values in the project–impact area is likely to exceed its cost. Therefore, the project cost can be covered by reclaiming a part of the uplift in land values, leaving the rest to the landowners as net windfall gains. VCF offers a significant opportunity to mobilize seed money to finance UT projects in India.

VCF instruments subscribe to the 'beneficiaries pay' principle and can take many forms. They include land value tax (LVT), land value increment tax (LVIT) and property tax; sale of developer land; sale/lease of project land including project-excess land; sale/lease of development rights; monetization of land assets; joint development mechanisms (JDMs); special assessment districts; betterment taxes and charges and tax increment financing (TIF). TIF is an attractive tool that relies on future increases in tax revenues from a designated project area such as a TOD zone or corridor to finance current infrastructure investments. It aims at promoting development through public authorities earmarking the whole or part of the revenue increments arising from it to service the debt needed to finance. TIF is often supplemented by development financing tools, including developer exactions and impact fees. Exactions require developers to install at their own expense internal infrastructure facilities needed by new development or to pay for publicly provided facilities. Impact fees aim at meeting the external costs of new development that generates demand for system-wide expansion in infrastructure capacity. While value capture instruments target at appropriating and recycling the values generated by spatial planning and infrastructure investment, development financing tools are one-time upfront charges collected from developers to meet the costs of infrastructure.

Indian cities have neglected not only 'beneficiaries pay' but also 'congesters pay' and 'polluters pay' instruments to address their transportation problems. For example, they have not resorted to road user charges to cover the cost of negative social impacts in order to reduce the peak loads of transport infrastructure and congestion, facilitate a switchover to cleaner transport modes and raise resources for decongestion programmes. No city in India has adopted the pricing of UT based on congestion pricing principles. This has led to individual travel behaviour and location decisions increasing motorization and reducing the efficiency of road use. The importance of such charging was recognized by Nobel laureate William S. Vickrey in the following words:

> ... in no other major area are pricing practices so irrational, so out of date, and so conducive to waste as in urban transportation. (Vickrey 1963, 452)

While Singapore, London and Stockholm have adopted electronic road pricing (ERP) to address traffic congestion, cities around the globe have resorted to other instruments. These include: one-time motor vehicle registration tax, annual motor vehicles tax, licensing fee for car ownership, motor fuel levy, pay-at-the-pump charges, highway tolls, parking fees, carbon taxes, emission charges, restriction on entry of vehicles to designated urban zones during peak hours and public transit subsidies. Indian cities need to have access to a toolbox of economic instruments along with spatial planning tools to address congestion externalities and raise resources for public transportation infrastructure.

Urban planning and transportation planning at present are pursued as separate exercises in Indian cities. The paradigms need to be integrated to effectively address the challenges of efficient, equitable and sustainable urbanization. Transport–land use integration, TOD, benefit taxation, VCF and CC need to be pursued as ingredients of a holistic strategy of planned urban development. The issues of lack of capacity to plan and implement projects must also be addressed in tandem. This is critical for managing land and transport, protecting the environment, including the poor in urban development, and raising resources to finance transportation infrastructure. Ironically, most cities in India lack transportation planners and engineers. The limited exercises for transportation planning they undertake are through physical planners. However, physical planning in India also suffers from the utter lack of town planners on one hand, and the obsession of master planning with land use detailing on the other. While reforming master planning, India must create institutional and human resource capacities for integrated land use–transportation planning and value capture financing. The recognition of the 'leading' role of public transport in guiding urban and regional development will be central to the design of such reforms.

6

Urban Land Assembly
Alternatives to Public Acquisition of Land

URBANIZATION AND LAND ASSEMBLY

Demographic and socio-economic factors shape the needs of cities for housing, workplaces and public amenities. They call for changes in the pattern and intensity of land use, utilization of floor space index (FSI) and provision of infrastructure in existing cities, their peripheral areas and rural settlements 'in transition' to urban. The availability of serviced land, floor space and public facilities to support growth is a central issue in India's urbanization. The issue is of crucial significance in view of the difficulties in public acquisition of land for planned urban development under India's new land acquisition (LA) law. It calls for alternative mechanisms of land assembly by private developers and public authorities—procuring, consolidating, developing and subdividing land, servicing it with external and internal infrastructure, renewing derelict areas and creating floor space. Land assembly, along with investment in transportation and other infrastructure, is the primary vehicle for accommodating economic growth and attaining the objectives of economically efficient, environmentally sustainable, socially inclusive and financially viable cities.

Indian cities face a huge constraint of serviced land and floor space. The McKinsey Global Institute (2010) estimates that the country needs 700–900 million sq. m of commercial and residential space each year till 2030. Connecting these spaces requires 2.5 billion sq. m of new roads and 7,400 km of new metros and subways, representing 20 times the infrastructure capacity that has been added in India since 1999. The challenges are daunting due to the malfunctioning of urban land and housing markets and abysmal state of city finances. While the demand for land and floor space in cities is increasing due to urbanization and spatial concentration of economic growth, supply is lagging due to speculation, regulatory restrictions and lack of infrastructure. The widening gap between demand and supply is leading to exorbitant increase in land prices, making housing unaffordable to not only the poor and low-income groups (LIGs) but also the middle class. Further, the patterns of demand for floor space in cities present an uneven picture. Demand is high in some pockets owing to historic, geographic and economic forces including externalities, but supply is severely constrained due to land use and FSI restrictions. These factors are leading to haphazard growth and excessive pressure on infrastructure. Indiscriminate expansion of cities is leading to suboptimal use of land at the urban fringe, culminating in sprawl, wasteful commuting, traffic congestion, pollution and unsustainable consumption of energy. If unchecked, these trends will lead to serious economic, social and environmental consequences for both the city and the countryside.

This chapter deals with the challenges of urban land assembly in India. It takes into account the economics of urban land as well as the context of urbanization. They lead to three overarching propositions to guide land assembly. First, the demand for urban land is 'derived' from the needs of workplace, housing and public facilities such as roads, public transit, water supply, sewerage, drainage, parks and playgrounds, shaped by economic growth. A primary requirement of growth is the availability of floor space for productive economic activities. Second, the numbers, densities and patterns of income distribution in Indian cities, with one-fourth of their residents being poor, high costs of infrastructure, energy security and environmental concerns make it imperative to promote compact, public transportation-led and transit-oriented cities, avoiding sprawl and automobile-dependent urbanization. This strategy has important implications for the management of land and FSI. Third, cities in India have been too obsessed with compulsory acquisition of land for spread-out development while exercising extreme controls over development rights. There is a strong case for cities to optimize the utilization of land available, liberalizing FSI and investing in infrastructure, especially transportation, to guide development.

The most fundamental role of cities is to catalyze growth which requires floor space at strategic locations. Land, with its horizontal dimension, is only one of the factors in this. Other important variables include FSI and infrastructure to service land. They have important implications for the externalities of cities which catalyze growth. With this perspective in view, this chapter discusses the key issues of LA and refers to Indian and international practices of land assembly, including management of land, FSI and infrastructure. It suggests a range of land assembly mechanisms, including strategic densification of growth nodes, renewal of dilapidated areas and infill development in cities; planned expansion of urban areas based on the land pooling model followed by Gujarat and Andhra Pradesh and liberalization of FSI in Hyderabad; development of ring towns and satellite towns connected to metropolitan cities by fast public transport (PT) modes; and promotion of new towns on emerging growth corridors. We advocate a transit-oriented development (TOD) approach based on transport–land use integration with the adoption of spatial as well as economic instruments of urban planning. The chapter also suggests the models of sale and auctioning of development rights in growth nodes with high economic potential based on a transparent regime as practised in Brazil.

LAND ACQUISITION: KEY ISSUES

The Land Acquisition Act, 1894, has been the principal legal instrument to secure land for urban development in India. This law allows for compulsory acquisition of private land for public purpose, including housing, employment and social overheads. As the bulk of the land for urbanization is under private ownership, the development of cities based on LA by public authorities involves many contentious issues as follows:

- The public purpose has to be defined;
- Land can be acquired only through an agency of the government;
- There are restrictions on private rights over land through laws other than the Land Acquisition Act;
- Compensation must be paid to the persons whose land is acquired; and

- The land acquired should be used for the public purpose after the acquisition.

Large-scale acquisition of private land for urban development has been justified by public authorities in India in the past based on the following arguments:

- When land at the outskirts of a city is acquired at a relatively low price (considered to be equivalent to the prevailing agricultural land value), it can preclude speculation that occurs in the event of conversion of agricultural land to urban use;
- All increases in land value are believed to be beneficial to the public at large;
- Land can be made available at affordable prices to low-income households as the private market does not cater to their needs; and
- Supply of land to the public sector is needed to promote orderly planning and development of the city and to minimize the adverse impacts of urbanization on environment.

Over the years, a sizeable quantity of land has been made available for planned urban development across the country through LA. Delhi offers a prime example. The 'Scheme for Large Scale Acquisition, Development and Disposal of Land', initiated by the Delhi Development Authority (DDA) in 1961 has resulted in acquisition of substantial tracts of rural land. However, over time the limitations of the scheme have become conspicuous. The key reasons for difficulties in compulsory public acquisition of private land for planned urban development include the following:

- The procedures prescribed by the Land Acquisition Act are time-consuming. The processes of notification, publication in official gazette, mandatory enquiries, determination of compensation, etc., invariably get delayed;
- Frequent litigations arise due to non-willingness of the landowners to part with valuable land. Prolonged court cases stalled LA proceedings in the past, making land consolidation and infrastructure development difficult; and

- Payment of compensation at below-market rate has been a major hindrance to LA. The deprivation of the landowners of the huge increments in the value of their land reaped by speculators, developers and new buyers of land and housing is a key factor behind their resistance.

All the aforementioned issues have gained considerable significance with the enactment of the Right to Fair Compensation and Transparency in Land Acquisition, Rehabilitation and Resettlement Act, 2013.

In the bank nationalization case, the Supreme Court of India held that the object of the principle of evaluation must be to pay to the owner what he or she has lost, including the benefit of advantages, present as well as future. Vide the 25th Amendment to the Constitution, the term 'compensation' in Article 31 of the Constitution of India was substituted by 'amount'. Consequent to this Amendment, the property of a citizen could be acquired for a public purpose by paying an amount less than 'just equivalent' in money or the market value of the property being acquired. However, subsequent court rulings have gone against the acquisition of property at below-market value. This is an important consideration in LA in India.

The use of the land acquired is another major issue. A Planning Commission Task Force had found as early as 1983 that the land acquired by public authorities was put to uneconomic, wasteful and inefficient use because it was bought cheap. Undoubtedly, the inefficient allocation of publicly acquired land has been a breeding ground for many problems, including corruption and favouritism. The determination of prices of land at different locations did not follow a scientific procedure. The density and development norms prescribed by authorities also tended to be arbitrary.

After land is acquired, it is developed and disposed of by public authorities according to their rules. The method of disposal of land has generally been the leasehold system according to which land was leased for a specified period of time to individuals or organizations. The lease period extended from 10 years (Bengaluru) to 99 years (Delhi). The policy of long-term lease practised in Delhi was expected to achieve a greater degree of control over the use of land, facilitate collection of ground rent on a continuous basis and enable the capture of a portion of land value increment to public account at the time of transfer. This system has, however, been criticized as restricting the spatial mobility of people and encouraging clandestine transactions. Another dimension of land disposal has been the allocation of public land among different categories of people for different purposes. Residential land has often been allocated among low-, middle- and high-income groups at fixed prices. Land for commercial purposes has been sold in public auction with a view to secure the highest price. Evidence, however, suggests that land disposal policies in the past have benefitted the better off segments at the cost of the weaker sections.

Land Acquisition Act, 2013

While there were many outstanding issues of LA such as purpose of acquisition, payment of compensation, disposal of land acquired and its use, the new LA law of 2013 has added procedural complexities that have crucial implications for planned urban development. The new law mandates the LA, rehabilitation and resettlement (R&R) processes to follow a number of key steps as follows:

- *Notification for Social Impact Assessment (SIA) study:* The appropriate government shall issue notification for the commencement of consultation and of SIA study and publish the same as per prescribed procedures.
- *Conduct of SIA:* The appropriate government shall ensure the completion of the SIA study within a period of six months from the date of commencement and make it available to the public.
- *Appraisal by an expert committee:* The appropriate government shall ensure that the SIA report is evaluated by an independent multidisciplinary expert group. The group shall make recommendations within two months from the date of its constitution.
- *Preliminary notification for LA and R&R:* For acquiring land, the appropriate government shall give public notification about the details of the land. The same shall be published as per prescribed procedures.
- *Food security:* No irrigated multicropped land shall be acquired under the Act. Such land may be acquired only in exceptional circumstances, as a demonstrable last resort.

- *Hearing of objections:* Any person interested in any land which is notified for a public purpose may raise objection to the District Collector in writing within 60 days from the notification. The decision of the appropriate government on the objections made is final.
- *Preparation of R&R scheme:* The appropriate government shall conduct a census in the affected area and prepare a draft R&R scheme, including particulars of the R&R entitlements of each landowner and landless persons whose livelihoods are primarily dependent on the lands.
- *Publication of declaration:* After examination and taking decisions, the appropriate government shall make a declaration of the land under the Act along with the summary of the R&R scheme. This should be published as per prescribed procedures.
- *LA award:* After an enquiry into and disposal of objections, if any, raised by persons according to the public notice published, the Collector shall make the LA award in the prescribed form.
- *R&R award:* Under this, the Collector hands over the R&R award to each affected family.
- *Compensation:* The compensation for land acquired to be awarded by the Collector shall be a multiple of the market value—by a factor of at least one to two times. The market value shall be the higher of: (a) the minimum land value, if any, specified under the Indian Stamp Act, 1899, for the purpose of registration of sale deeds in the area where land is situated, (b) the average of sale price for similar types of land being acquired, ascertained from the highest 50 per cent of the sale deeds in the vicinity registered during the preceding three years and (c) the consented amount in the case of acquisition for private companies or public-private-partnership (PPP) projects. Solatium will be paid at 100 per cent of the compensation, including the market value and value of the assets.

The elaborate procedural requirements under the new LA law suggest that compulsory acquisition of land by public authorities for the purpose of planned urban development, including housing, is not going to be an easy task. There is a need to explore alternative models, learning from land assembly practices followed by Indian cities and internationally.

LAND ASSEMBLY PRACTICE: INDIA

Except in Gujarat, where the town planning scheme (TPS) is the primary vehicle for planned urban expansion, the principal mode of land assembly in India has been the compulsory acquisition of land. However, as such acquisition has become increasingly difficult, some states and cities in India have tried to adopt alternative ways to assemble land for urban development. Some key initiatives undertaken by them are presented in the following text.

The Delhi Model

In Delhi, the responsibility of land development is entrusted to the DDA under the Delhi Development Act, 1957. The Land and Building Department of the Government of National Capital Territory of Delhi (GNCTD) acquires land for the DDA, which then undertakes land development for various purposes, including housing, workplaces and public facilities. The DDA also allocates land to private developers for construction of houses. However, over the years, the DDA has failed to fulfil the bourgeoning demand for land and housing. This has led to the growth of unauthorized structures and illegal colonies due to strong market forces. An analysis of land acquisition and development under the land policy of the DDA presents the following picture (Centre for Civil Society 2009, 147):

- Only an average of 777 hectares of land was acquired annually instead of 1,372 hectares intended to meet the targets of development set in the Master Plan of Delhi (MPD) 1962 over the period 1962–1981.
- During 1981–2001, against a planned acquisition of 24,000 hectares, 9,507 hectares were acquired by 2001—only 39.6 per cent of the target.
- Around 14,479 hectares of land was proposed to be developed in the plan period 1961–1981. However, by 1984, the land actually developed for residential purpose was only 7,316 hectares.
- In the various sub-cities envisaged under MPD 2001, of the total 17,493.15 hectares proposed to be developed, only 8,388.15 hectares (47.95%) of serviced land were made available by 2001.

Although the DDA undertook large-scale public acquisition of land for planned development of Delhi, the outcome fell far short of the target. Slums, called jhuggi jhopri (JJ) colonies, mushroomed on a large scale. This was a result of the DDA failing to provide land at affordable prices to low-income communities, including migrants. Suboptimal utilization of land occurred due to spiralling land prices. There was also over-provision of land to well-off groups. The DDA auctioned very few plots at a time. The maximum quoted price was believed to be the actual market price. This provided room for artificially raising the land prices through the creation of deliberate scarcity. Due to these reasons, the model of compulsory acquisition of land is no longer feasible in Delhi. The DDA has accordingly proposed to follow the model of land pooling through the TPS practised in Gujarat. The MoUD, GoI, approved the Land Pooling Policy (LPP) of the DDA in September 2013 (Box 6.1).

The LPP assumes significance as MPD 2021 proposes the construction of 25 lakh additional housing units by 2021, for which 10,000 hectares of land is required. The policy is at initial stages; its implementation crucially depends on the GNCTD declaring 95 villages as development areas and 89 of them as 'urban' villages and providing the needed support.

The Haryana Model

Realizing the role of the private sector in efficient functioning of land and housing markets and the inability of the government to provide sufficient amount of developed land to meet housing needs, there was a consensus on the involvement of the private sector in real estate development in Haryana. In accordance with the Haryana Development and Regulation of Urban Areas Act (HDRUAA), 1985, areas were identified for allocation to private developers to assemble parcels of land which were in excess of the limits prescribed by the Urban Land (Ceiling & Regulation) Act (ULCRA). Private colonizers operated in collaboration with the Haryana Urban Development Authority (HUDA) to develop residential layouts on a large scale. This was to prevent ill-planned and haphazard urbanization in and around growing cities (Box 6.2).

Box 6.1 *Delhi Development Authority: Land Pooling Policy (2013)*

The LPP of the DDA is based on the premise that the government should act as a facilitator of planned urban development. It aims to make the landowners partners in the process. It stipulates that a landowner or a group of landowners who have grouped on their own or a developer—called the 'developer entity'—shall be permitted to pool land for unified planning, servicing and sharing of land for development as per guidelines. The key features of the policy are:

- The LPP will apply to the proposed 'urbanizable' extensions of Delhi for which Zonal Development Plan (ZDP) has been approved. Each landowner will get an equitable return under the LPP irrespective of land uses assigned to his or her land in the ZDP with minimum displacement.
- The land use distribution at the city level for urbanizable areas in the urban extension is: gross residential—53 per cent; commercial—5 per cent; industrial—4 per cent; recreational—16 per cent; public and semi-public facilities—10 per cent; and roads and circulation—12 per cent. For every 1,000 hectares of land pooled, the gross residential distribution provides for about 50,000 housing units for the EWSs—32–40 sq. m in size.
- Two categories of land pooling are envisaged. For category I (land—20 hectare and above), the developer entity will have 60 per cent share (53%—gross residential; 2%—city level public/semi-public use and 5%—city level commercial), while the DDA will retain 40 per cent. For category II (land—below 20 hectares), the developer entity will have 48 per cent share (43%—gross residential; 2%—city level public/semi-public use and 3%—city level commercial), while the DDA will retain 52 per cent.
- Residential FAR of 4.0 for group housing is permitted on net residential land. This is to be exclusive of 15 per cent FAR reserved for EWS housing. Tradeable FAR is also permitted.
- External development charges (EDC) and any other charges incurred for city infrastructure shall be payable by the developer entity on actual cost incurred by the DDA.
- Relief to small farmers, self-penalty on the DDA for delay in approval and flexibility to farmers to trade land or tie up with developers for land pooling are amongst the innovative provisions of the LPP.

Source: MoUD, GoI (2013).

Box 6.2 *The Haryana Joint Development Model*

Haryana experimented with an innovative model of land assembly legally permitting, under a grant of licence from the director of town planning (DTP), private developers to assemble lands from the market through negotiation to develop residential colonies. The salient features of the scheme are:

- Private developers can negotiate on market price with the agricultural and other landowners to purchase land.
- They prepare layout plans for integrated development of residential areas, with all internal infrastructure facilities adopting the space norms specified by the city development plan.
- A developer has to reserve 20 per cent of housing for EWS and LIG; another 25 per cent has to be sold in the market on 'no profit no loss' basis, while the rest 55 per cent can be sold freely in the open market.
- The developer is required to pay 'external development charge' (EDC) to the HUDA in proportion to its development costs for a colony for getting connected to the HUDA's trunk lines of utilities and 'infrastructure development charge' (IDC) towards citywide infrastructure development.
- The DTP is the nodal authority for regulating the functions and activities of the licensed private developers including checking their income and expenditure.

Source: HUDA.

With the adoption of the joint development model, Haryana became the first state in India to formally involve the corporate private sector in acquisition, development and disposal of urban land. Permission for development was subject to evaluation of title, location and extent of the land, capacity of the applicant to develop a colony, its layout and conformity of the development schemes of the colony land with those of the neighbouring areas. The private developers had to furnish a bank guarantee equivalent to 25 per cent of the estimated cost of land development along with an undertaking to carry out and complete the development works in accordance with approved plan. In addition, they had to pay proportionate development charges if the main lines of roads, drainage, sewerage, water supply and electricity were to be laid out and constructed by a public authority. Roads, open spaces, public parks and public health services were to be maintained by the developer for five years after the issue of completion certificate. Thereafter, all such assets were to be transferred to the government or local body free of cost.

Along with the physical infrastructure, the private colonizer was required to provide social amenities such as schools, hospitals, community centres and other community buildings on the lands set apart for the purpose. The developer could bear the cost of providing these amenities or transfer the lands to government. Subsequently, such lands could be allotted to any person or institution in order to develop the required amenities.

The limitations of private sector-led model of land development practised in Haryana are as follows:

1. The demands of the lower income groups and EWSs were largely ignored.
2. The colonizers were mostly profit-oriented and were highly active in the areas adjoining Delhi to exploit the captive demand.

The Haryana model reveals that the private colonizers are not interested in catering to the needs of the entire population both across geographical areas and income groups. This underscores the importance of government in land assembly—facilitating private sector involvement and attending to the special needs of the poor. Moreover, private negotiation is time-consuming and some landowners may not part with their land, making integrated development difficult. Taking these considerations into account, the Government of Haryana has notified a 'land pooling scheme (LPS)' in September 2012 for the development of residential sectors by the HUDA.

The Ghaziabad Model

The Ghaziabad Development Authority (GDA) has implemented a novel scheme for developing land under the Urban Planning and Development Act, 1973, of Uttar Pradesh. This aimed at making funds available for infrastructure in the land development process. The model is applicable in selective residential areas with a minimum size of 50 acres. Its salient features are:

- Planned urban development is envisaged as a joint venture between GDA and private developers.
- The equity sharing between GDA and the private developer is in the ratio of 10:90. This leads to a reduction in the cost burden to GDA and increases comfort to the developer.
- The compensation package streamlines the implementation by reducing litigations and constraints of the traditional LA process.
- The private developer earns revenue from the sale of 60 per cent of plots in the open market.
- The GDA, apart from less investment and free-of-cost public facilities, earns annual revenue of 1 per cent from the private developer (tie-up cost index).

The NOIDA Model

The Noida city was planned adjacent to Delhi by the New Okhla Industrial Development Authority (NOIDA) as an integrated urban area with prime focus on institutional and industrial development. Subsequently, efforts were made to promote integrated urban development, including residential, commercial, institutional, government/semi-government, industrial and recreational activities. These are supported by physical infrastructure such as transportation, electricity, water supply, sewerage, drainage and garbage disposal facilities. The NOIDA Master Plan also provided for recreational amenities and social infrastructure to cater to education, health, social and cultural needs of the people. Other facilities such as telecommunication, marketing, police protection, fire safety, milk supply and petrol stations were also provided as per needs. The Noida Authority has liberalized the payment of compensation for LA to avoid unnecessary litigation by farmers under the Land Acquisition Act. It revises the compensation rates for land every financial year by linking them to the 'consumer price index'. These rates are determined irrespective of location. A separate rehabilitation package in the form of additional 15 per cent on the basic LA rate along with land compensation at a rate of one-fifth of actual plot value is also adopted. Development levies are charged from villagers.

The Government of Uttar Pradesh has permitted Noida, Greater Noida and Yamuna Expressway Industrial Development Authority (YEIDA) to purchase land directly from the farmers. This is meant to help the farmers to get a higher rate of compensation and drastically reduce litigation that has slowed down real estate development. The land use is not defined before acquisition; it could be for any land use.

Negotiated Land Acquisition

The 1984 amendment to the Land Acquisition Act provides that if all the people, who are party to a LA, reach an agreement on the award, the Land Acquisition Collector (LAC), without making any further enquiry and resorting to the determination of compensation for land in the same locality or elsewhere, can make an award. The Greater Noida Authority has successfully used this procedure. It estimated the compensation package for land on the basis of sale price of land registered during the last three years, solatium and interest, and negotiated with the landowners on the basis of these rates. The Authority and the landowners, after several rounds of discussion, agreed upon mutually acceptable rates for the lands acquired. The landowners collected the compensation as worked out by LAC and then filed a reference with the District Judge for enhancement of compensation. Subsequently, the Authority and the landowners filed a compromise deed in the District Court on compensation at the agreed rate based on which the District Judge finalized the same. This method of negotiated LA has been adopted by other states also, including Tamil Nadu and Maharashtra. Some of the benefits of this model are as follows:

- Compensation is paid to the landowners at a rate close to the market value of land pertaining to a short period of 3–4 months preceding the date of LA; the landowners and public agencies both save litigation expenses;
- Speedy acquisition of land is facilitated with lesser risk of land encroachment and consequently a reduction in the cost of land development and housing;
- The landowners cooperate with public agencies and have lesser incentive to collude with private developers for unauthorized development; and

- Public developers are able to estimate the sale price of land on the basis of definite compensation rates and avoid subsequent recovery from land or housing allottees (Town and Country Planning Organisation [TCPO], GoI, 2007).

Town Planning Scheme: Gujarat

The TPS in Gujarat, based on the land readjustment models practised in Germany, Japan, Taiwan and South Korea, is the most promising method of land assembly for planned expansion of cities in India. It ensures the minimal displacement of the landowners, involves their participation in town planning, is farmer-friendly, inclusive, equitable, pro-poor and self-financed. It minimizes strains on the government to undertake planned urban development. The Gujarat Town Planning and Urban Development Act (GTPUDA), 1976, provides the legal framework for town planning in Gujarat. Under this, the government plans and develops designated urban areas by land pooling. An area development authority is made responsible for both macro- and micro-planning. Macro-planning involves delineating a 'development area' around a city coming under the influence of urbanization; micro-planning involves devising TPS for smaller areas.

Urban planning in Gujarat is a two-step process: (a) preparation of a development plan (DP), and (b) formulation and implementation of area development schemes. The DP is a broad-brush vision for the city which clearly marks the new areas to be developed gradually. It gives overall direction to the growth and infrastructure of the city. Every development area is divided into a number of TPS, each catering to about 100 to 200 hectares and including 100 to 250 landowners. The plots within a TPS are developed with public amenities and infrastructure, earmarking land for housing the poor. Developed plots are subsequently returned to the original owners in a reduced proportion of their original plots (OPs) after taking into account the land needed for planned facilities and for sale to meet their costs. A portion of developed land under each TPS is kept with the development authority towards the cost of public infrastructure. The development cost is recovered by selling this portion of land with value enhanced due to planning and development.

Every TPS is legally required to reserve land to the extent of nearly 10 per cent of total area for socially and economically weaker sections (SEWS). The allotment of land is made as per the following standards: 15 per cent for roads; 5 per cent for parks, playgrounds, gardens and open spaces; 5 per cent for social infrastructure such as schools, dispensary, fire brigade and public utilities; and 15 per cent for sale by the appropriate authority to meet the cost of infrastructure in the scheme area. Inclusion, self-financing and equity in land development are the distinguishing features of TPS. Costs and benefits are spread across all the landowners. Betterment charges are levied on them in proportion to the land value increment due to spatial planning. Public participation is mandatory at every step of planning and reorganization of plots. The TPS helps to avoid the complex procedures and costs associated with LA and court litigation. Box 6.3 portrays the TPS process as implemented in Gujarat.

Box 6.3 *Town Planning Scheme Process in Gujarat*

The steps involved in a TPS in Gujarat include the following:

1. Survey of Planning Area
   A detailed survey of the planning area is undertaken covering all topographical and physical details such as buildings, infrastructure, trees, compound walls, water bodies, drains, heritage structures, etc. Every kind of private or public property is marked.
2. Documenting Landownership Details
   All landownership details and cadastral maps are collected and compiled. The details, especially land tenure, are carefully noted as mostly the land tenure is retained when giving back the land to the owners.
3. Preparing the Base Map
   All area records and maps are collected to prepare the 'base map'. These are matched with physical survey of the area. This process is called *melavni* in local language, which means 'matching'. Discrepancies, if any, are resolved. As the base map is prepared, it is sent to the Land Records Department for approval.
4. Marking the Boundary of the TPS
   Taking all the physical and administrative features into consideration, the boundary of the TPS is clearly marked on the

base map. At this stage, a sales map is also prepared using the relevant land prices and sales of land. This also determines the original value of the plots.

5. Marking Original Plots on the Base Map

   The original plots (OPs) are marked on the base map and are given OP numbers. If more than one land parcel belongs to the same person, then these are consolidated and given the same 'OP' number. This simplifies planning and reduces land fragmentation.

6. Tabulating Ownership Details and the Plot Size

   Landownership details, land tenure, OP area, OP number, estimated value of the OP, etc., are tabulated in 'F form'.

7. Layout of the Road

   If any city level road is passing through the TPS, it is first and foremost drawn on the base map. Then, keeping the expected future urban activities and their appropriate locations in mind, a road network is established on the map that maximizes efficiency.

8. Marking the Plots for Public Use and Amenities

   Keeping the proportions of land under public land use and amenities in accordance with the shares prescribed by law, plots for schools, open spaces, health facilities, etc., and for housing the poor and low-income groups are drawn up. The percentage of area allotted to public use is 20 per cent.

9. Tabulating the Final Plot Sizes

   The total land used for public uses is calculated as a proportion of total land in the TPS. This proportion is deducted from each OP and the final plots are given back to the landowners. Efforts are made to ensure that the final plot retains its tenure and is as close to the OP as possible. A semi-final value of the plot is also calculated.

10. Delineating Final Plots

    As the public utilities are drawn up and worked out, the OPs are reconstituted and formulated as per the future plans envisioned. The irregular shapes of the OPs are made regular and the final plots are drawn as close to the respective OPs as possible.

11. Estimating Cost of Infrastructure and Tabulating Betterment Charges

    The costs of the infrastructure, compensation to the landowner, final value of the plot and administrative charges are calculated. The increase in the value of land is also estimated

(Continued)

Box 6.3 *(Continued)*

and betterment charges are levied. Cash flows are tabulated in 'G form'. The 'F form' is completed at this stage.

12. Meeting the Landlords
    A notice inviting all the landlords to meet the Area Development Authority is published in local newspapers. This meeting is called to take suggestions and opinions of the landowners so that a draft TPS can be prepared.

13. Modifying and Approving the Draft TPS
    The suggestions of the landowners are noted and the draft TPS is modified accordingly. The modified TPS is again published in newspapers and after another round of suggestions, it is sent for approval to the state government. When approved, it is called 'Sanctioned Draft TPS'. After approval, the Area Development Authority can take physical charge of the space allotted for roads.

14. Appointment of the Town Planning Officer
    After approval of draft TPS, a Town Planning Officer (TPO) is appointed to look after physical as well as financial prospects of the project. He or she deals with the landowners regarding disputes on physical aspects, or compensation or betterment charges. He or she amends the draft TPS if considered fit, finalizes it and eventually hands over the final plots to the landowners. The TPO divides the 'Sanctioned Draft TPS' in two parts: a preliminary TPS to deal with the physical planning proposal and a final TPS to deal with the financial proposal.

15. Individual Hearing of the Landowners on TPS, Appeal and Finalization
    The TPO gives a hearing to every landowner. If required, the preliminary TPS is modified according to suggestions. After a second round of hearing, the TPS is sent to the state government which must approve it within two months. This is now the Final TPS and is published in local newspapers as the 'Award of the Final TPS'. Any appeals related to betterment charges or compensation are resolved at this stage and the final TPS is modified. After this, it is sent to the state government, which is required to approve the final TPS within three months. Once approved, the drawings and documents are sent to the state's revenue department to update the land records.

Source: Government of Gujarat: Town Planning Department; Ballaney (2008).

Land Pooling Scheme: Andhra Pradesh

The Government of Andhra Pradesh (GoAP) enacted the Andhra Pradesh Capital Region Development Authority (APCRDA) Act, 2014, for developing the 'new capital area' for the state and establishing the APCRDA. The Authority is entrusted with planning, coordination, execution, supervision, financing, funding, promoting and securing the planned development of the capital region and capital city area in Amaravati in Guntur district. The APCRDA Act provides for voluntary LPS for the development of the capital city area. Box 6.4 presents the salient features of the scheme and its progress.

Box 6.4 Andhra Pradesh Land Pooling Scheme

The APCRDA has formulated 'Integrated Smart LPS' for lands in 29 village settlements in Amaravati—the new capital city of Andhra Pradesh, covering 217 sq. km. The LPS, similar to the TPS in Gujarat, is meant to legally consolidate the land parcels owned by individuals or groups of the landowners by transferring ownership rights to the APCRDA.

The LPS provides for land allocation for various purposes as follows: 30 per cent for roads and utility services, 10 per cent for playgrounds and open spaces, 5 per cent for social infrastructure (e.g., schools, health and community facilities) and 5 per cent for housing the poor. A share of the total LPS area is specified for allotment of reconstituted plots to the landowners as per the norms fixed by the state government. Another share is meant for the costs of development of infrastructure and administrative costs.

When the capital is developed, farmers would get back almost 30 per cent of their pooled land in the newly built city. The GoAP has issued orders guaranteeing return of reconstituted land to the owners per every acre of original land surrendered under the LPS—up to 1,000 square yards of residential land and 450 square yards of commercial land depending on the type of land. Apart from these, the landowners or landless families would receive a pension of ₹2,500 every month for 10 years as compensation for the loss of livelihood. Affordable houses would be provided

(Continued)

Box 6.4 *(Continued)*

to the poor and working classes. Under the Mahatma Gandhi National Rural Employment Guarantee Act (MGNREGA), 365 days of employment will be provided. Skill development training with subsidy and interest-free loan up to ₹25 lakhs for self-employment ventures are also arranged.

More than 23,000 landowners have filed consent applications under the LPS covering an extent of approximately 34,690 acres out of 38,581 acres targeted in Amaravati area—as of December 2017. Development agreement have been executed for 33,208 acres, and 59,014 returnable plots have been allotted to 23,903 landowners through 46 lotteries. In Andhra Pradesh Capital Region, about 90 per cent of the land required has been secured through the LPS; the balance missing bits of land are being acquired under the Land Acquisition Act. The acquired lands are also included in the LPS.

It is believed that the LPS strategy would lead to a road of prosperity, not deprivation for the farmers. The present landowners would become landlords of the ultra-modern capital city, and they will also get a means of livelihood under the LPS.

Source: Andhra Pradesh Capital Region Development Authority (APCRDA—Amaravati Project Status Report Edition 3, https://crda.ap.gov.in accessed 15 January 2018.

Land Pooling Scheme, Hyderabad

The Hyderabad Metropolitan Development Authority (HMDA) has embarked upon two types of LPSs—linked to road development comprising areas adjacent to master plan road and metro rail corridors, and township development covering areas exceeding 50 acres. As part of the initiative, the HMDA has completed an innovative LPS at Uppal Bhagath, where about 700 acres were taken over from farmers subject to 1,000 square yards of developed plot being given back for each acre taken. The land was secured in connection with Musi riverfront development and metro rail projects in Hyderabad. It was decided to earmark 10–15 per cent of developed land for commercial space to raise adequate resources to finance the LPS. The HMDA has already 1.10

lakh square yards available under the LPS as its share, which would generate a significant sum of money.

Impressed with the benefits of land pooling in Uppal Bhagath, the landowners in several locations in Hyderabad region, especially those coming under the influence of Outer Ring Road and Metro Rail, have come forward to offer their land to the HMDA for development under LPS. The Government of Telangana has also issued a comprehensive order in 2017 to promote LPSs in Hyderabad metropolitan region. The minimum area for LPS shall not be less than 20 hectares (about 50 acres). The consent of 50 per cent of landowners is necessary to initiate a scheme. The landowners are required to hand over their land to the development entity (DE). Infrastructure development is required to be completed in three years. In case the same does not happen within the time period specified, the DE has to pay 0.5 per cent of the basic value of the land per month to the owners till completion of the scheme. The developable area reconstituted, after deducting the land statutorily required for public open spaces, water bodies, buffer zone, social amenities, road networks, etc., shall be shared between the DE and landowners as per the project cost. However, a minimum of 30 per cent is guaranteed as the owners' share and minimum of 30 per cent as DE's share. The land shared with the DE is towards the cost of development, including internal and external infrastructure and amenities, scheme costs and expenses, lands for capitalization and for partially meeting the expenditure towards the requirements of the statutory development plan. Developed land is to be allotted to the landowners based on lottery.

Magarpatta City Model, Pune

Magarpatta city in Pune, Maharashtra, offers an excellent example of how rural farmers can be partners in urban land assembly to develop a world-class township without displacing them. This township, spread over 430 acres, is located in the outskirts of Pune. The township, with about 9,000 apartments, is home to over 35,000 residents and a working population of 65,000.

A community of 120 farmers took the crucial decision of organizing themselves to set up the Magarpatta Township Development and Construction Company, which prepared the township plan. It is a private limited company, which is efficient as well as democratic in approach. Each family is a shareholder in the company receiving shares according to their landholdings. The company approached the Pune Municipal Corporation and the Government of Maharashtra with an integrated township proposal under the Maharashtra Regional and Town Planning Act, 1966. After receiving approval for the project and change of land use, the township was started in 1994, with farmers as full partners in planned urban development and funds borrowed from the market. Money from the land was used only for asset creation, thereby providing a safety net for the next generation of farmers. All farmers agreed to use a part of the value of their land to buy flats and shops in the township, thereby securing lease rentals. Funding for new business ventures came from banks. Over 250 entrepreneurs in non-agricultural ventures have emerged from the farmer community. These first-generation entrepreneurs account for a gross annual turnover of ₹150–200 crores. The business strategy of the company has ensured that a farmer with 1 acre of land at the time of its formation earns a dividend of about ₹15 to 16 lakhs per year at present (Mohanty 2014).

One issue with the Magarpatta city model is that it did not provide for inclusionary zoning (IZ) or inclusionary housing (IH) to cater to the needs of community service personnel (CSP) and the poor. The farmers-developers could have been granted certain incentives like 'density bonus' or relaxation in urban planning norms to provide for IZ and IH. Such incentives are common in developed countries such as the United States, the United Kingdom and Australia.

Transferable Development Rights: Mumbai

Government authorities rely on recent sale transactions to determine the 'fair price' of land being acquired. However, such transactions may not be reported or recorded correctly due to high transaction cost and black money. The government also lacks funds to acquire the necessary land even at the recorded low rates. This is where the practice of 'TDR', adopted by many countries and some cities in India such as Mumbai and Hyderabad, can be a solution. The Urban Development

Plans Formulation and Implementation (UDPFI) Guidelines prepared by the TCPO, MoUD, GoI (1996), define TDR as follows:

> Development right to transfer the potential of a plot designated for a public purpose in a plan, expressed in terms of total permissible built space calculated on the basis of Floor Space Index or Floor Area Ratio allowable for that plot, for utilization by the owner himself or by way of transfer by him to someone else from the present location to a specified area in the plan, as additional built up space over and above the permissible limit in lieu of compensation for the surrender of the concerned plot free from all encumbrances to the Planning and Development Authority.

Under the TDR concept, the development potential of land partly or fully reserved for public purpose can be separated from the land itself and be made available to the owner in the form of additional FSI. Such award entitles him or her a Development Right Certificate (DRC), which he or she may himself or herself use or transfer to another person. If the FSI granted cannot be used on the land not covered by acquisition, the landowner is free to use the additional FSI on lands located in other parts of the city. Thus, the exorbitant cost of acquisition of urban land for public purposes such as conservation of open space, arterial and radial roads and public transit networks can be met by a system of compensation in kind rather than in cash.

Mumbai is the first city in India to use TDR as an alternative to LA to secure amenities in accordance with development plan. The Municipal Corporation of Greater Mumbai (MCGM) has been adopting the practice under Regulation 34 of the development control regulations (DCRs) for Greater Bombay, 1991. It has used TDR extensively for slum redevelopment and urban renewal. Hyderabad uses TDR to acquire land for the development of master plan roads. Bengaluru has embarked on a scheme of TDR to acquire land for metro rail project.

Road-widening Scheme: Hyderabad

Hyderabad has implemented an innovative 'road-widening scheme' since the 1980s with remarkable success (Box 6.5). By March 2014, the city widened 307 roads with 260 km of length by securing land

Box 6.5 *Road-widening Scheme: Greater Hyderabad Municipal Corporation*

The 'road-widening scheme' implemented by Hyderabad city since the 1990s is a unique initiative to secure land free of cost by using incentive zoning, including TDR as a resource.

The state government empowered the Municipal Corporation with relaxation of zoning and DCRs, and grant of concessional FAR to secure land for widening master plan roads. Vide orders issued in 1998, it delegated powers to the Corporation to relax FAR up to an extent of 1.0, grant concessions in setbacks and ground coverage and accord permission for conversion to commercial use of the land remaining after road widening, if land for road was surrendered free of cost. In particular, the government delegated the authority to grant relaxations in zoning regulations and building rules to the Commissioner of Greater Hyderabad Municipal Corporation (GHMC).

Learning from experience, the state government incorporated the following concessions for road widening by ULBs/development authorities under the Common Building Rules of 2006 and Comprehensive Building Rules of 2012:

* Upon surrendering the area included in Master Plan road network or road required to be widened as per road development plan (RDP) free of cost to the sanctioning authority, the site owner shall be entitled to TDR to be utilized in the remaining land or anywhere within the municipal jurisdiction. Alternatively, the owner shall be allowed to construct an extra floor with an equivalent built area for the area surrendered subject to mandatory public safety requirements or be permitted to avail concessions in setbacks, including front setback.
* The extent of concessions shall be such that the total built-up area after concession shall not exceed the sum of built-up areas allowed (as proposed) on total area without road widening and built-up area equivalent to surrendered area.
* In the case of plots less than 750 sq. m, in addition to concessions in setbacks and height, cellar floor may be allowed keeping in view its feasibility on ground.
* In the case of high-rise buildings, concessions in setbacks, other than front setback, would be considered subject to maintaining minimum clear setback of 7 m on the sides and rear

side, and such minimum setback area shall be clear without any obstructions to facilitate movement of firefighting vehicles and effective firefighting operations.
- The aforementioned concessions shall be considered at the level of sanctioning/competent authority without referring to the state government. The authority may consider any other concessions as deemed fit with the prior approval of the government.

Source: GHMC.

estimated at ₹1,200 crores from the landowners free of cost. The scheme has been popular with the landowners as they perceived that the benefits accruing to them from road widening and development would be much more than the foregone cost of the land surrendered.

Recently, Hyderabad has embarked on a new phase of the road-widening scheme with grant of TDR equivalent to 400 per cent of land surrendered free of cost to property owners to enable them build floor space on the remaining land or avail the benefit of TDR.

FSI Deregulation: Hyderabad

Indian cities resort to stringent controls on FSI. The Master Plans arbitrarily predetermine FSI for different areas in the city. Discretionary relaxations of FSI by planning authorities occur from time to time. These factors are amongst the key reasons behind the mismatch between supply of and demand for floor space. Hyderabad is the first city in India to liberalize FSI by linking the height of building to the abutting road width and open space requirements around the building. Box 6.6 presents the salient features of the innovative scheme.

While conventional FSI regulations in India impose flat areawide restrictions on FSI, the Hyderabad experiment has broken a new ground by allowing for a more dynamic determination of FSI based on the carrying capacity of abutting road and plot size. Though the initiative is criticized by some planners as favouring new areas at the

Box 6.6 *Deregulation of Floor Space Index: Hyderabad*

The government of the erstwhile state of Andhra Pradesh notified the Hyderabad Revised Building Rules, 2006, by Government Order No. 86 dated 3 March 2006. In 2012, the government issued revised consolidated Andhra Pradesh Building Rules, 2012, vide Government Order No. 168 dated 7 April 2012—called GO 168, which contained some modifications and additional features.

GO 86 liberalized floor space restrictions and increased the FSI for all types of properties by changing the basis on which built-up area is controlled, linking it to a formula based on a combination of (a) width of abutting road, (b) building setbacks and (c) special controls in designated areas for fire safety, air traffic clearance or other local reasons. The liberalization of FSI is most significant for large plots on wide streets; properties situated along roads with width of 30 m or more have no applicable building height restriction provided they adhere to the setbacks prescribed. Properties along roads with width from 24 m to 30 m can have height ranging from 30 m to 50 m depending on setbacks which increase with building height. GO 86 also provides for 'skyscraper zones' with minimum height of building permissible at 36 m (12 floors), minimum plot size at 4,000 sq. m and minimum width of approach road at 24 m.

GO 86 stipulates the levy of city level infrastructure impact fee for all buildings with height above 15 m to raise resources for area development and citywide infrastructure. The scales of impact fees for buildings in the GHMC area are as follows:

	Height for Building	
	Above 15 up to 50 m (₹)	Above 50 m (₹)
Occupancy/Use		
Residential	500–1,500	3,000
Commercial/Office	1,000–2,500	5,000
Institutional/Others	300–1,000	2,000

> GO 168, while retaining the key features of GO 86, increased the saleable built-up area across the board, the increase being more than 60 per cent for some categories of property. It also permitted additional building height subject to larger setbacks around the building.

Source: GoAP.

cost of inner city locations, its contribution lies in making the operation of FSI objective, linked it to accessibility and city level impact fees. It is in tune with the principles of urban and transport economics. The formula-based approach to FSI has also freed it from the discretions of planners. The model recognized that keeping FSI rigid in the face of significant investments in infrastructure or economic growth is bound to be inefficient. It has kept land and housing prices in Hyderabad metropolitan area within reasonable limits unlike many other large metropolitan cities in India.

LAND ASSEMBLY PRACTICE: INTERNATIONAL

Internationally, private sector-led land assembly has been the principal vehicle to accommodate urban growth. Governments, however, played a key role through policies and investments in connectivity infrastructure which enabled private developers to exploit the synergy between transportation, density and land use. Some key strategies to promote urban land development that are relevant to India are presented as follows:

Land Readjustment: South Korea

The Government of South Korea started a major urbanization programme in the 1960s when the country witnessed a massive structural shift from agriculture to industry. The share of urban population in South Korea rose from 26.7 per cent in 1950 to 87.8 per cent in 2000. A major contributing factor to this growth was rural–urban migration. As the share of urban population was growing fast, a large number of housing units were required to be provided along with basic services in a short span of time. But the lack of serviced land was a huge bottleneck. It was soon realized that the responsibility to facilitate mass housing had to be shouldered by the public sector. As the government had severe financial constraints for providing civic infrastructure, 'land readjustment' was considered an appropriate method to secure land and housing for the growing urban population. The Korean government later enacted the Housing Construction Promotion Act in 1972 under which the housing units were to be provided by private construction firms. These units required serviced land to cope with urbanization.

A large proportion of the people in Korea who migrated from the 1960s ended up in Seoul. The average number of people migrating to Seoul every month was 22,000. About two-thirds of the annual population growth in Seoul in the 1960s and 1970s was due to the new migrants. As housing and basic amenities were not sufficient to accommodate such a huge increase, the new entrants to the city settled on the banks of streams and mountainsides. These substandard habitats posed serious environmental challenges such as sprawl, deforestation, contamination of rivers and proneness to natural disasters. To address the issues of haphazard development, the Seoul Metropolitan Government prepared the Seoul Metro Area Master Plan in 1966. The plan aimed at developing Seoul as an eco-friendly, transit-oriented and compact city while keeping the future urbanization and economic growth in view.

During the initial stages of urbanization, South Korea used land readjustment to lay foundation for orderly growth of Seoul. It was a tool to obtain land for public utilities and establish an overall spatial framework for sustainable development. The Seoul Metropolitan Government was able to put a grid pattern of planned urban structure with land readjustment. In the beginning, due to the fear of public complaints, the government did not ask for much contribution from the landowners. But this resulted in insufficient infrastructure, including roads. In fact, the percentage of land for roads in 1960 was 8 per cent. Due to this, many plots remained inaccessible to emergency services. From the late 1960s, Seoul adopted a new plan which included more public space for better development. In the first stages of land readjustment project, maximum funding came from national subsidy and municipal bond issuance, but during the later stages, the finances were mobilized by the sale of serviced residential and commercial plots. By using land readjustment, the Government of South Korea accommodated 40 per cent urbanization. This tool paved the way for sustainable urban development in the future, securing space for public services and protecting the environment.

The Finger Plan: Copenhagen

Copenhagen's Finger Plan demonstrates how transportation and land use planning can be integrated to promote sustainable urban development. The Danish Town Planning Institute developed the 'Egnsplan' or Finger Plan in 1947 based on the paradigm of TOD. This Plan aimed at channelizing 'overspill' growth from urban centres based on a cogent regional development strategy that focused on the 'palm of the hand' and 'five city fingers'. The palm rested on the existing core urban region in Copenhagen, and the fingers pointed to directed growth in the peripheral areas. 'Green wedges' were planned between the fingers to minimize the adverse consequences of the built-environment and provide recreational areas to the urban population. The Finger Plan has successfully guided the growth of Greater Copenhagen area for over a generation (Suzuki, Cervero and Iuchi 2013).

The Finger Plan envisaged the channelization of urban growth along city fingers linked to the railway system—suburban trains, regional trains, metros and light rail—and radial roads connected with other road networks that facilitated easy access to central Copenhagen. It aimed at promoting mixed use, high-density commercial and residential development around transit stations, maximizing the use of PT, avoiding urban sprawl and automobile-dependent urbanization and protecting the natural environment. Shopping malls, offices, recreational centres and housing were all planned in pedestrian areas with good bicycle facilities such as cycle lanes and parking, and good connectivity to PT. Box 6.7 presents the salient features of Copenhagen's Finger Plan.

'Transit-First' Policy: Curitiba

Curitiba, Brazil, is known as one of world's well-planned and sustainable cities. The urban form of the city was guided by a long-term

Box 6.7 *Copenhagen's Finger Plan: Transit-oriented Development*

The design of Copenhagen's Finger Plan included five fingers or corridors of development along suburban areas connected through railway lines and directly connecting to the city's CBD. Neighbourhoods around the transit stations were planned to be developed in a TOD fashion with high-density housing and all amenities. The approach aimed at an ordered and integrated 'green' growth at a time when urbanization was extensive and rapid. There were spaces left for farmlands, forests and recreational purposes between the fingers, known as 'green wedges'. A ring road was planned at the end of each finger, linking the Copenhagen Harbour and inner city to industrial locations. Most of the land was developed by the end of the 1960s and the two southernmost fingers were extended.

The Finger Plan was followed by a Regional Plan in 1989. According to this plan, industrial and service activities were to be located within 1 km of station on the rail corridor, which reduced the traffic to CBD. In 1993, the Copenhagen Municipal Plan came, which incorporated the development of Orestad township. In 1995, another plan came, known as the Master Plan which focused on urban development around stations, including light rail mini-metro stations. Metro was believed to be the core of development along with bicycles. Even car parking lots were minimized and made expensive to discourage private car travel.

Orestad offers one of the best examples of successful implementation of the Finger Plan. The township is connected with Copenhagen by an automated, fully grade-separated metro rail line that preceded its development. The construction of metro adopted the sale of publicly owned land with increased development value as a key source. Orestad combines economic activities—jobs, housing, amenities, retail, leisure and education—all based on TOD. It has provided world-class facilities for businesses and helped Copenhagen to remain competitive while reducing pressure on the CBD.

Source: Suzuki et al. (2013).

vision based on its 'Transit-First' policy. The 1965 Master Plan for the city outlined a TOD concept aimed at distributing densities strategically along BRT corridors. It sought to direct urban growth along well-defined radial axes, intensively served by dedicated busways. The plan intended to promote mixed land uses, high-density development at major BRT stations and high-quality urban design that encouraged pedestrian access to BRT. The city government mandated that all medium- and large-scale urban development be located along the BRT corridor. Curitiba's BRT system, with 390 routes served by 2,000 buses, hauls 2.1 million passengers per day (Suzuki et al. 2013).

Curitiba has successfully integrated transportation, land use, urban design and TOD. From the 1970s, the city has implemented a linear growth strategy along structural axes. Each axis comprises a 'trinary road system' with three parallel roadways, located a block apart. The structural axes constitute the first level in a hierarchy of an integrated road system. The central lane of the central road is exclusively dedicated to high-capacity express busway. The two lateral roads cater to through traffic while providing access to adjacent development. In the land parcels situated within one block from a structural axis, the FAR was increased to 6, permitting buildings that could reach a volume of construction six times the plot area, at gross population density up to 600 inhabitants per hectare. The FAR permitted along other routes served by PT was fixed at 4. The city master plan provided for FAR decreasing with distance from the PT network. The owners of properties which could not be developed because of zoning restrictions were allowed to sell a standard FSI as TDR to developers who could use the same for high-density construction along the structural axes.

Sale of Development Rights: Brazil

Brazil has implemented urban planning and financing innovations that are not detrimental to the functioning of land and housing markets. The notion that the private landowners should not be the sole beneficiaries from city planning and public investments was incorporated into the 1988 Constitution of Brazil through Articles 182 and 183. These articles outline the social functions of the city and property by separating the right to own land from the right to build. Emphasizing that private ownership of land cannot override the social functions of the city, they stipulated the levy of charges for any conceded building rights over and above a baseline. The articles were subsequently incorporated into the federal law No. 10.257 of 2001, called the City Statute (*Estatuto da Cidade*). This Act empowered local governments to regulate land development by framing policies to balance individual property rights with collective interest, capture the land value increase due to public action such as infrastructure development or spatial planning, sell air rights above those allowed by zoning scheme and offer tradable development rights. The revenues realized could be used to provide infrastructure and services to targeted areas known as *Operacion Urbanisica* or urban operations (UOs).

Consequent to the City Statute, Brazilian cities have adopted instruments to charge for additional building rights through *Outorga Onerosa do Direito de Construir* (OODC) and auction development rights through *Certificados de Potencial Adicional de Construcao* or Certificate of Additional Construction Potential (CEPACs) bonds, using the following formula:

Private revenue gained
from real estate = LA cost + development cost + real estate margin + additional land value premium
= Revenue (virtual plot − real plot)

Sale of Additional Building Rights: OODC

The instrument of OODC in Brazil is the sale of air rights that enables landholders to make use of their own sites up to the maximum FAR permissible under law (Box 6.8).

Certificate for Potential Additional Construction

The instrument of CEPAC in Brazil aims at restructuring large areas of a city with land-based incentives offered to public–private partnerships, encompassing the local authorities, developers, landowners and other stakeholders as independent investors. CEPAC is a bond issued

Box 6.8 *Charges for Additional Building Rights: Sao Paulo and Curitiba*

In Sao Paulo, the landowner's property development right is limited to a 'basic' FAR which is different from the 'maximum' FAR the area could support. The difference between the maximum FAR and the basic FAR has to be purchased. The basic FAR for most part of the city was fixed at 1.0–2.0 under the 2002 Strategic Master Plan—*Plano Diretor Estrategico* (PDE). This meant a reduction in the FAR permitted earlier in some zones. The maximum FAR, however, can be up to 4 depending on area and land use. The price of undeveloped air rights in Sao Paulo is determined by market forces, though the municipality can reject price offers below its minimum prices. OODC also applies to other types of changes leading to more profitable land use options such as conversion from rural use to urban use or rezoning of areas for renewal or commercial use. The proceeds from OODC paid by property owners to municipal government go to a special urban development fund called FUNDURB (*Fundo de Desenvolvimento Urbano*) meant to finance prioritized urban public investments, including slum upgrading within the city. Sao Paulo earned US$762 million through OODC since 2004 (US$130 million in 2012–2013; Smolka 2015).

Curitiba has been selling building rights since 1991. The city granted higher FAR in some areas as an instrument to promote TOD when the BRT system was installed. Maximum FAR was increased further to attract developers to pay into a special fund earmarked for social housing. The city collected US$17.5 million as ad hoc charges through the sale of building rights in 2011–2012 (Smolka 2013).

The instrument of OODC incorporates two principles for its legitimacy: (a) in order to support additional floor area construction or higher order land use, the local authority needs to undertake investments in public infrastructure and services, and (b) the local authority cannot favour one property over another when granting additional building rights or permitting new land use. Sharing of benefits is a must for sharing of costs. The Brazilian Supreme Court has ruled that OODC is not a tax, rather a charge imposed on the use of additional building rights that are not a part of the owner's assets but a public good that belong to the city as a whole.

Source: Sandroni (2010) and Smolka (2013, 2015).

as an integral part of UOs. UOs are implemented through *Operacoes Urbanas Consorciadas* (Consortia UOs). Urban investments in UOs are expected to be financed through incremental values generated by those investments and changes in land use and zoning as recouped through sale of air rights (Box 6.9).

Box 6.9 *Certificate for Potential Additional Construction: Sao Paulo and Curitiba*

Sao Paulo has adopted the instrument of CEPAC from 1995 to auction building rights. The city issues CEPAC bonds corresponding to additional building rights for purchase by competing developers in public electronic auctions. The idea is that new development potential due to rezoning, permission for additional construction and public investment in infrastructure in designated areas should not be free but auctioned amongst those intending to take advantage of the future economic benefits. A key benefit of CEPAC is that it generates resources upfront to finance urban infrastructure investments. Another is that the price of undeveloped air rights is determined by the market forces, though the municipality can reject offers below its minimum prices.

CEPACs are tradable air rights created by the municipal government and auctioned through the Brazilian Stock Exchange regulated by *Comisao de Valores Mobiliarios* (CVM), the Brazilian Securities and Exchange Commission. CVM regulation 401 requires the municipal government to set minimum price of the CEPAC to keep real estate business competitive. The amount of CEPAC offered for each public auction is also required to be fixed. The amount of CEPACs to be issued corresponds to the additional square meters that the present and future urban infrastructure in the designated UOs can support. The final sale price is determined by auction. In theory, CEPACs can be traded in the securities market, though a secondary market has not developed.

CEPACs present an attractive source of finance for the government as the chances of loss are minimum and profits are large. If CEPACs sell at the minimum price, the local government gets to keep the whole profit. If CEPACs do not sell, the local government does not have to incur much cost and only has to pay for the auction. As the increase in value is expected to be manifold, CEPACs sell at a price greater than the minimum prior. Local governments can access capital markets by these instruments, increasing their capital base. CEPACs are also beneficial to the buyer. They can be used to change the land use or add a floor. They also don't have to be used on a specific land parcel as they can be used anywhere in the designated UO. Lastly, they can be implemented at a chosen time; mostly people like to use CEPAC at a time when real estate demand is strong.

CEPAC revenues are deposited in special escrow accounts earmarked for improvements within the UO. Between 2004 and 2010, Sao Paulo auctioned 638,074 CEPACs valued at around US$722.9 million.

CEPAC revenues part-financed the investment costs of *Linha Verde* (Green Line) UO in Curitiba where a major national highway was converted into an urban avenue along with extension of BRT and promotion of high-density land uses.

Source: Sandroni (2010) and Smolka (2013, 2015).

While CEPACs present many benefits, they also pose challenges. First, they are not a part of comprehensive urban development plan; this might lead to the revenues generated being wrongly spent on non-productive projects. Second, the development potential of UOs could be overestimated or underestimated, leading to an inappropriate amount of CEPACs being auctioned. Third, CEPACs are dependent on real estate cycles. In times of weak real estate, CEPACs do not yield profit. They are also not a recurring source of income, as once the development right is sold, the revenue flow stops. Fourth, CEPACs are prone to speculation due to their direct connection with the real estate market. Fifth, buyers of CEPACs face a number of challenges, being exposed to real estate risks. If CEPACs are bought at a high price, then the weakening of the market harms them. Further, if the CEPAC-funded infrastructure construction is delayed, the buyers run a construction risk. They also run a government risk; new legislation or corruption by government officials might affect CEPACs in a negative manner.

STRATEGY FOR LAND ASSEMBLY

Innovative Indian practice and international experience present useful lessons for designing the strategy for land assembly to meet the land and floor space needs of planned urbanization in India. First, the method of compulsory acquisition of land has not worked. Moreover, its implementation will be difficult under India's new LA law. Thus, there is a need to search for alternative models that do not rely on the acquisition of land by public authorities. The obvious choices are: densification of existing cities and land pooling for expansion of urban areas and development of new townships. Second, the models of land pooling and land readjustment are intrinsically valuable. They are also landowner-friendly, inclusionary and self-financing. They are rooted in a value increment financing framework. However, these methods are yet to be replicated widely across India. Third, the approaches to use density, FSI and zoning as resource through instruments such as density bonus, premium FSI (PFSI), incentive zoning and TDR, charges for additional development rights and sale of additional construction potential are promising. They not only generate resources to finance infrastructure but also contribute to better planning. Fourth, the prime requirement for economic growth is floor space, and not land per se. This warrants a broader approach to manage urban land, including its horizontal and vertical dimensions and accessibility to infrastructure. While cities must be encouraged to innovate, models such as LPS in Gujarat, Amaravati in Andhra Pradesh, Uppal Bhagath in Hyderabad and Magarpatta city in Pune; removal of FSI restrictions, linking height of building to size of plot, abutting road width and impact fee, and using TDR to widen strategic roads in Hyderabad; TOD linked to investment in metro rail in Bengaluru and Hyderabad; transport–land use integration in Copenhagen and Curitiba; and sale of development rights through the instruments of OODC and CEPAC in Brazil offer promising directions to Indian cities to design and adopt robust approaches to land assembly.

Unlike Indian cities which have opted for spread-out development, cities in developed countries and some developing countries have used FSI as a key instrument to promote compact cities and prevent sprawl. This strategy is integrally connected with planned investments in urban and regional infrastructure, especially PT, densification of city centre and a few sub-centres supported by a flexible, incentive-based urban planning regime and management of congestion diseconomies. However, Indian cities in the past have been too obsessed with the acquisition of land, neglecting its vertical dimension and the notion of accessibility to economic mass. Thus, they have not been able to exploit the economies of density and collocation to catalyze economic growth. In fact, they have resorted to stringent controls on density and FSI on the grounds of absence of infrastructure and preventing negative externalities. This is based on a lack of understanding of the 'wider economic impacts' of urban transportation infrastructure through its links with density, land use, agglomeration and networking externalities. While India needs to make significant investments in urban infrastructure, especially public transit, the management of development rights based on a pricing strategy is a neglected area that needs urgent attention.

The considerations of efficient, inclusive, sustainable and financially viable cities suggest that India cannot afford a sprawling and automobile-dependent urbanization. A deliberate PT-led and transit-oriented development strategy, powered by transport–land use integration, strategic densification of key transit nodes with overall liberalization of FSI and land use, infrastructure investments supported by incentive zoning, benefit taxation and value capture financing offers opportunities to reengineer cities and develop new towns. Hyderabad has taken a lead in doing away with restrictions on FSI and linking it to accessibility parameters. Ahmedabad, Hyderabad, Indore, Pimpri-Chinchwad and Bengaluru have adopted policies to significantly increase FSI on planned public transit corridors. For example, Bengaluru allows FSI up to 4.0 for all properties within an influence area of 500 m on either side of the metro rail alignment. A part of the benefit accruing to property owners due to the higher FSI is collected through a cess of 10 per cent on residential buildings and 20 per cent on commercial buildings. The proceeds are to be used to service the debt raised for the project by the Bengaluru Metro Rail Corporation Ltd (BMRCL) and to finance the augmentation of civic infrastructure by other agencies in view of denser urban development due to higher FSI. Bengaluru also uses the instrument of TDR to acquire land for metro rail free of cost.

Traditionally, development rights were considered to be permanently tied to a particular parcel of land. However, in the course of urban planning, the right to own land and the right to develop land were recognized as separate rights. In the first half of the twentieth century, development rights started being sold from the owner of one parcel of land to the owner of another parcel through TDR. The land from which the development rights are sold is called the 'sending area' and the one that receives such rights is called the 'receiving area'. The TDR instrument reduces the intensity of development in the sending area and increases it in the receiving area, affecting agglomeration economies. It also facilitates the mobilization of resources by tapping the unearned increments in land values due to investment in infrastructure and spatial planning. Learning from the experience with TDRs around the globe, Brazil has introduced the sale of development rights in cities through CEPACs. This instrument, linked with investments in public transit, transport–land use integration, strategic densification of key transit nodes and local economic development, has a considerable scope for application in India. However, it requires a robust legal regime, a flexible urban planning framework, an appropriate financing strategy and a government culture that imbibes confidence in the developers. It will work in cities with strong real estate markets.

Whereas the sale or auctioning of development rights based on a TOD framework is appropriate for strategic densification of cities in India, the model of land pooling practised by South Korea, Gujarat, Andhra Pradesh (Amaravati), Telangana (Uppal Bhagath [Hyderabad]) and Maharashtra (Magarpatta city [Pune]) is eminently suitable for planned expansion of urban areas in India. The schemes are based on some fundamental premises: (a) high-quality infrastructure, backed by innovative urban planning, acts as the foundation for the economic success of a city, (b) strong landowners' opposition to public acquisition of land can be addressed by making them partners in planned urban development and (c) voluntary participation by the landowners on a partnership mode to share the fruits of planned urbanization is a financially sound model of city development. They suggest that infrastructure development, when combined with value-adding spatial planning, can generate enormous values to make land assembly in large cities with agglomeration economies self-financing. While the TPS in Gujarat and the LPS in Andhra Pradesh and Telangana are led by public authorities, farmers in Magarpatta, Pune, have voluntarily adopted a LPS to develop a world-class township, facilitated by change in land use by the Pune Municipal Corporation and the Government of Maharashtra. Considering the magnitude of the problem of urban land assembly in India, there is a strong case for facilitating the execution of land pooling/town planning schemes through consortia of the landowners and developers. The current process of approval of such schemes led by public authorities is time-consuming. This needs to be simplified; a time limit of 1 year may perhaps be targeted to complete the process. There is also a need to design incentives to promote urban renewal schemes based on land pooling and value increment financing principles.

With 410 million in cities and towns and another 400 million to be added by 2050, India needs to not only densify but also strategically expand cities and also create new towns. However, the contexts of cities vastly differ from one another and 'one size' will not fit all. International experiences and Indian practices suggest that a combination of strategies may be appropriate for Indian cities. This may include:

- Overall liberalization of FSI accompanied by strategic densification of growth nodes in existing cities, especially those located on planned transit corridors and which can accommodate new growth due to their external economies of agglomeration and resource generation potential. The strategy needs to be accompanied by significant investments in public transit and strategic road networks along with value-adding changes in land use and density to promote TOD.
- Development of underused and unused land and renewal of derelict areas in existing cities with increased densities and appropriate changes in land use while preserving heritage structures, protecting the environment, undertaking decongesting investments and adopting a value creation, capture and recycling strategy to finance development.
- Planned expansion of cities with the development of core infrastructure networks, especially transportation, water supply, sewerage and drainage linking debt repayments to TPS, benefit taxation, congestion pricing and other suitable instruments.
- Development of ring and satellite towns linked to metropolitan cities with strategic connectivity through limited access expressways, public transit or high-speed rail and other infrastructure facilities that make them attractive places for living and doing business.

- Promotion of new towns, especially those on emerging industrial development and freight corridors with the integration of trunk transportation networks and economic activities facilitated by incentives for industrial location.
- Development of census towns and large villages that account for a significant growth in urban population with agro-based and ancillary activities—ensuring connectivity to the nearest cities and regional hubs that can lead to the rejuvenation of rural economies.

The choice of land assembly strategy in particular areas of cities needs to be based on two key tests. First, social benefits exceed social costs, accounting for all internal and external impacts, including wider benefits to the economy. Second, the projects must be financially viable, taking into account feasible changes in land use and density patterns and resource generation potential through user charges, benefit taxes, general taxes and intergovernmental transfers.

7

Urban Land, Transport and the Poor

Case for Inclusionary Zoning and Housing

CHALLENGES OF INCLUSIVE URBANIZATION

A quarter of urban population in India lives in slums. An equivalent percentage lives below poverty line. About 70 per cent of the urban workforce is engaged in informal sector activities and subjected to precarious work conditions. Most of them belong to the 'poor and vulnerable' sections, living at a bare subsistence level without any job or social security. They constitute those whom the economic growth process has, by and large, bypassed. What distinguishes urban poverty from rural poverty is that the former is characterized by multiple non-income vulnerabilities having social, occupational and residential dimensions. These vulnerabilities disproportionately affect the disadvantaged sections in the urban society, especially the aged, the disabled, the destitute, women, children, self-employed, home-based workers, street vendors, waste pickers and casual labourers. Social vulnerability is linked to socially imposed constraints that relate to caste, gender, age, education, health, place of residence and the like. Stratification in the social structure fosters exclusion in land and housing markets, depriving the urban poor of basic entitlements. Occupational vulnerability is manifested in the lack of opportunity for remunerative and secure employment. Residential vulnerability arises from the lack of affordable housing and basic amenities such as water supply, drainage, solid waste management, etc. It finds expression in homelessness, temporary housing without proper roof or walls, lack of tenure security, insanitary living conditions, violent crimes and devastating impacts of disasters. The worst manifestation of residential vulnerability is in slums, presenting precarious living conditions and subjecting the dwellers to serious health hazards and heavy burden of diseases.

According to Census 2011, 2.43 million urban households had no exclusive room, compared to 1.25 million in 2001; 25.34 million were living in one room as against 18.85 million in 2001. The number of households residing in one room or less constituted 35.2 per cent of the total number in urban areas in 2011. More than 4 million urban households in 2011 lived in houses with grass/thatch/bamboo/wood/mud/plastic/polythene as roof material. More than 57 per cent of slum-dwellers did not have access to drinking water within premise; 71 per cent had no drainage or open drainage. According to Census 2011, 27.5 per cent of urban households lived in rental accommodation. As per the NSS 65th Round data, the average monthly rent on hired dwelling in urban areas was ₹1,149 in 2008–2009, nearly double of that in rural areas. A technical group, constituted by the Ministry of Housing and Urban Poverty Alleviation, GoI, estimated that as against the country's urban housing shortage of 18.78 million in 2012, 17.96 million or 95.7 per cent pertains to EWSs and LIGs. The bulk of this shortage (14.99 million) relates to families residing in congested tenements. This phenomenon is explained by the fact that the urban poor seek to be close to workplace, even if it meant subhuman living conditions.

A major bottleneck to affordable homes and workplaces for the poor and low-income households in Indian cities is the lack of well-located, litigation-free serviced land. Cities need these sections to be functional. However, they are deprived of access to serviced land and affordable housing due to extreme market conditions as well as failure of urban planning. The city master plans do not address their land, housing, employment and transportation needs. The slums which provide shelter to the poor and low-income groups (LIGs), and the informal activities which engage the bulk of them hardly find a place in the master plans. The lack of legal recognition to slums and informal sector has also led to frequent evictions of these households from homes and workplaces in the name of master plan enforcement and city modernization drives. This has also made them hostages to 'favours' from politicians and administrators for being incorporated into the legal city and gaining access to public services. Further, the neglect of public transport (PT) by master plans has deprived the urban poor of the mobility needed to access employment opportunities. All these factors have led to an exclusionary regime of urbanization in India. The country needs to undertake urgent reforms in the current system of master planning, including zoning and development control regulations (DCRs). Land use planning and transportation planning need to be integrated. This chapter dwells on the issues of exclusion in urban land and housing markets in India. It makes a case for 'inclusionary zoning (IZ)' and 'inclusionary housing (IH)', which are key paradigms emerging globally to promote inclusive communities and affordable homes. The rest of the chapter deals with the urban informal sector in India, genesis of exclusionary urban planning, perspective on 'right to the city', economic case for inclusionary urban planning, international case studies in IZ and IH, initiatives by Indian states and cities to promote inclusion and strategy for inclusive urbanization in India.

THE URBAN INFORMAL SECTOR IN INDIA

Periodic employment and unemployment surveys (EUSs) conducted by the National Sample Survey Office (NSSO) highlight the importance of the unorganized sector in cities. Between 2004–2005 and 2011–2012, the total employment in the country increased from 457.9 million to 472.4 million. Over the same period, employment in the organized, non-agriculture sector rose from 28.8 million to 47.7 million, whereas employment in the unorganized sector went up from 185.4 million to 209.6 million. Organized sector employment was 6.3 per cent and 10.1 per cent, respectively, of the total employment in 2004–2005 and 2011–2012. Between the two years, more people joined the unorganized sector workforce than the number entering the organized sector. The informal sector workers, comprising those working in the unorganized sector or households, excluding regular workers with social security benefits, and workers in the organized sector without any employment/social security benefits provided by employers, contributed about 46 per cent of the non-agricultural gross value added in India (International Labour Office [ILO] and Women in Informal Employment: Globalizing and Organizing [WIEGO] 2013).

The 68th Round of the NSSO Survey, conducted during July 2011–June 2012, defined the informal sector as consisting of proprietary and partnership enterprises (excluding those run by non-corporate entities such as cooperatives, trusts and non-profit institutions) in the non-agriculture sector and in agriculture-related activities excluding growing crops, plant propagation and combined production of crops and animals without a specialized production of crops or animals (AGEGC). Adopting this definition, the EUS 2011–2012 estimated employment in the informal sector to be about 75 per cent of total usual status employment (principal plus subsidiary) in rural areas and 69 per cent in urban areas. Among the workers engaged in the informal sector in 2011–2012, 98 per cent in urban areas were employed in non-agriculture. Table 7.1 presents a comparative picture of the share of the informal sector in total employment in urban areas between 2004–2005, 2009–2010 and 2011–2012 based on the NSS data. The figures are likely to be larger as the enterprises identified as 'employer's households', which account for employment such as provision of domestic services, are excluded from the definition of the informal sector.

In 2011–2012, the proportion of self-employed, regular wage/salaried employees and casual labourers among urban informal workers was 58 per cent, 27 per cent and 16 per cent, respectively. Ninety-eight per cent of the self-employed, 81 per cent of casual labourers and 40 per cent of regular wage/salaried employees were employed in informal activities. Manufacturing, construction, wholesale and retail trade, transportation and storage industries are the main providers of employment in the informal sector. Seventy-five per cent of informal

Table 7.1 *Proportion of Workers Employed in Informal Sector Enterprises in Urban Areas (%)*

NSS Round	Male	Female	Total
61st (2004–2005)	73.9	65.4	72.2
66th (2009–2010)	68.5	61.6	67.3
68th (2011–2012)	70.4	63.6	69.1

Source: NSSO.

sector workers in urban areas were employed in these industries (77% for male and 66% for females). Seventy per cent of urban informal sector workers were engaged in smaller enterprises (with less than six workers). Most of them were poor. The average daily earning of a regular wage/salaried employee in the informal sector in 2011–2012 was about ₹258 for urban males and ₹194 for urban females. The daily wage rate of a casual labourer in the informal sector was about ₹169 for urban males and ₹113 for urban females. Domestic workers, home-based workers, street vendors and waste pickers constitute the most vulnerable workers in cities. They are informally employed and constituted 33 per cent of total urban employment in 2009–2010—35 per cent of male and 24 per cent of female. These four groups together represented 41 per cent of the total urban informal employment: 44 per cent for male and 29 per cent for female (Mohanty 2014).

A large number of urban informal sector workers did not have a workplace in the conventional sense in 2011–2012. While 9.3 per cent of informal workers did not have a fixed place for work, 3.2 per cent worked from streets with a fixed location. More than 22 per cent of informal urban workers worked from own dwelling unit, structure attached to own dwelling, open area adjacent to own dwelling, detached structure adjacent to own dwelling or employer's own dwelling unit. For female informal sector workers in urban areas, the figure was more than 54 per cent (Table 7.2). The data reveal that a significant volume of economic activities in cities is carried out at home and other non-conventional places of work. These aspects have been completely overlooked by the master planning model in the allocation of land for various economic activities in Indian cities.

GENESIS OF EXCLUSIONARY URBAN PLANNING

The exclusionary urbanization in developing countries, including India, has genesis in their master planning model, rooted in the 'modernist' urban planning theories of the twentieth century. These theories emerged in response to the problems of the industrial city in the nineteenth century, manifesting in unhealthy living conditions of the working class, vanishing green spaces and non-compatible land uses. The 1919 Housing and Town Planning Act in the United Kingdom,

Table 7.2 *Distribution of Informal Sector Workers Residing in Urban Areas by Location of Workplace (2011–2012)*

Location of Workplace	No. of Informal Workers per 1,000		
	Male	Female	Persons
No fixed place	105	35	93
Workplace in rural areas	37	34	37
Workplace in urban areas and located in			
Own dwelling unit	77	400	134
Structure attached to own dwelling unit	35	67	41
Open area adjacent to own dwelling unit	7	16	9
Detached structure adjacent to own dwelling unit	12	20	13
Own enterprise/unit/office/shop but away from own dwelling	245	87	217
Employer's dwelling unit	20	41	24
Employer's enterprise/unit/office/shop but outside employer's dwelling	302	224	288
Street with fixed location	35	20	32
Construction site	94	43	85
Others	29	13	26
Urban areas	857	930	870
Total	1,000	1,000	1,000

Source: NSS 68th Round, (July 2011–June 2012), *Informal Sector and Conditions of Employment in India.* NSS Report No. 557(68/10/2).

which legally recognized the need for town planning, was significantly influenced by the 'garden city' movement led by Ebenezer Howard. This movement was based on the twin ideas of (a) recreating traditional way of life to reverse the chaotic conditions in cities, laden with slums and (b) bringing the aesthetics of the countryside into cities in the interest of physical and spiritual health. In France, the modernist city idea was spearheaded by Le Corbusier in the 1920s and 1930s. The influential architect articulated the view that the society needed to be regulated and controlled, and an ideal city form—neat, ordered and efficient—was necessary. The master panning approach in India is based on a form-centric approach to city development advocated by the orthodox urban planners. This undermines the role of the people in city building and rebuilding.

Cities in developing countries attract the poor, including rural–urban migrants due to their external economies of agglomeration. These economies catalyze employment opportunities in formal and informal sectors. However, the master planning model does not recognize the informal sector. The model also considers slums and unorganized activities antithetical to the notion of a modern city. The 'garden city' of Howard and 'radiant city' of Le Corbusier called for a new order to redesign urban places and cities. Howard proposed scientifically planned garden cities to address the problems of the older industrial cities, infested with smoke-choked, overcrowded and unhealthy slums. Le Corbusier proposed the demolition of narrow streets and slum settlements to give way to efficient transportation corridors, residences in tower blocks planked by 'flowing' open spaces and land uses separated into mono-functional zones. A key problem with these approaches of doing away with slums in the existing cities or creating new cities without slums is that they are 'paternalistic'. They assume that the planners know more about places than the people. Further, they do not address the economics of why slums arise in the first place. As Jane Jacobs observes:

> Conventional planning approaches to slums and slum dwellers are thoroughly paternalistic. The trouble with paternalists is that they want to make impossibly profound changes, and they choose impossibly superficial means for doing so. To overcome slums, we must regard slum dwellers as people capable of understanding and acting upon their own self-interests, which they certainly are. (Jacobs 1992 [1961], 271)

The master planning model is based on the command and control approach to city development advocated by modernist urban planning theories. The master plan reflects a 'technocratic' vision of the city and a 'statist' view of urban policy. It creates a 'virtual city', not connected with the 'real' economy. It advocates a top-down approach with detailed land use to the local level to achieve the plan objectives. It calls for lumpy investment, but ignores the financing strategy altogether. The master plan is 'formal'. The informal sector that engages the bulk of the poor and LIGs in cities of developing countries is excluded from land allocation for various urban uses. Presenting a permanent contradiction between urban order and management, the master planning approach perpetrates an 'exclusionary' model of city development in which many lose and a few gain.

The master plan defines the standards of land allocation for urban activities based on the logic of the middle class. Zoning and development control, the principal instruments for implementing the master plan, prescribe space norms based on the Western standards. These norms are unrealistic and cannot be satisfied by the poor and LIGs, who constitute the majority in cities of developing countries. The planning regulations do not consider the issues of affordability. They practically ignore the existence of the urban poor, driving them to 'self-created' settlements in 'leftover' spaces. Further, the master plan segregates residential use from other land uses following the practice in developed countries, making home-based and other informal sector activities like street vending illegal. UN-HABITAT (2009) rightly observes:

> The most obvious problem with master planning and modern urbanism is that they completely fail to accommodate the way of life of the majority of inhabitants in rapidly growing, largely poor and informal cities. The possibility that people living in such circumstances could comply with zoning ordinances designed for European towns is extremely unlikely. Inappropriate zoning ordinances are instrumental in creating informal settlements and peri-urban sprawl. It could be argued that city governments are producing social and spatial exclusion as well as environmental hazards, as a result of the inappropriate laws and regulations which they adopt. (p. 12)

Zoning rules restrict the use of land for various purposes in different parts of the city. DCRs restrict land development and building construction by imposing norms related to parameters such as subdivision of land, on-site and off-site infrastructure, size of plot, width of access road, ground coverage, setbacks, open space, parking, size of dwelling unit, building height, FAR, population density, space for common facilities, etc. In practice, these regulations have been highly restrictive. They have led to a scarcity of developable land and built-space for housing and other economic activities in cities, and exorbitant increases in land prices and building rents. The urban poor are the worst affected in the process. Minimum plot-size standard raises housing costs by requiring more land. Population density norm limits the number of housing units that can be constructed per hectare of land. FAR restriction reduces the amount of floor space that can be built on a plot of land. In residential areas, this effectively limits the height of buildings as well as the number of dwelling units they can contain. Unrealistically low density and FAR also make urban infrastructure systems, including mass transit, economically unviable. Importantly, the master plan restrictions increase infrastructure and commuting costs, leading to dead weight welfare losses. Bertaud and Brueckner (2005) find that FAR controls in Bengaluru impose significant welfare costs on city residents. They push new developments to the periphery, challenging infrastructure and creating additional commuting cost equal to 3 to 6 per cent of a typical household's consumption—a substantial amount for low-income households.

Master planning in India in the past aimed to control rather than promote development. This approach, based on modernist planning theories, is reflected in town planning regulations and urban planning guidelines. For example, the Urban and Regional Development Plans Formulation and Implementation (URDPFI) Guidelines 2014, issued by the MoUD, GoI, explicitly refer to the following key principles for approval of residential layouts: (a) there would be sufficient light and air in the buildings when constructed; (b) there would be protection against noise, dust and local hazards; (c) there would be sufficient open space for various family needs; (d) the circulation system and access to places are easy and safe from accident point of view; and (e) as far as possible, the plots are of regular shape and size, and are logically arranged in a systematic manner so as to give a regular pattern of development. Undoubtedly, the principles are laudable on the face of them. But in practice, they have led to unrealistic norms and standards which have weeded the urban poor out of formal land and housing markets and the so-called 'modern', 'planned' city.

The URDPFI Guidelines 2014 prescribe elaborate measures to control development in the name of 'development promotion'. They reiterate the requirements of the National Building Code and the norms advocated in the Urban Development Plans Formulation and Implementation (UDPFI) issued by the Town and Country Planning Organisation (TCPO), MoUD, GoI, in 1996. Some controls prescribed by the URDPFI Guidelines, which adversely affect the access of the urban poor to land and housing in the city, are presented in Table 7.3.

Table 7.3 *Urban and Regional Development Plan Formulation and Implementation Guidelines (2014): Salient Development Control Regulations*

Parameter	Controls Prescribed
Means of Access	**Residential Buildings** • Development on plot shall not be permitted without a minimum 6 m width and length of 75 m of access road. • If development is only on one side of the means of access, the prescribed width can be reduced by 1 m. **Non-residential Buildings** • Development on plot shall not be permitted without a minimum 12 m width and length of 200 m of access road. • The width of the means of access shall not be less than the internal access ways in layouts and subdivisions.
Building Control	• In plots of 30 sq. m in residential premises, the maximum ground coverage shall be 75 per cent, FAR—1.5, number of dwelling units—1 and maximum height of building—8 m.
Setbacks	• For a street with less than 7.5 m width, the distance of the building shall at least be 5 m from the centre line of the street. • The minimum front setback shall be 1.5 m in the case of streets fronting the plot up to 7.5 m width—for buildings up to maximum height of 7 m. • The minimum rear setback shall be 1.8 m—for building height up to 10 m.
Open Space	• Fifty per cent of the open area of a plot would be used for proper landscaping and for plantation.

Parameter	Controls Prescribed
Parking	• In residential and mixed land use premises, the parking standard per 100 sq. m of floor area is to be two equivalent car space (ECS).
Low-income Housing	• The minimum size of plot, with ground coverage not to exceed 75 per cent, shall be 40 sq. m in small and medium towns and 30 sq. m in metropolitan cities. • Plot sizes below 30 sq. m but not less than 15 sq. m may be permitted in the case of cluster planning subject to ground coverage of 100 per cent and FAR of 2. • Every dwelling unit should have at least two habitable rooms, first room of minimum 9 sq. m and width of 2.5 m and the other room shall be minimum 6.5 sq. m with minimum width of 2.1 m provided the total area of both the rooms shall not be less than 15.5 sq. m. • In the case of single room tenements, the single multipurpose room shall be of minimum 12.5 sq. m carpet area. • In plotted development, the number of plots per hectare shall be 65–120. • In mixed development, the number of dwelling units (population density) per hectare shall be as follows: Small Towns: 75–100 (335–450) Cities: 100–125 (450–560) Metropolitan Cities: 125–150 (560–675)

Source: MoUD, GoI (2015a).

While the master plans have denied the urban poor a lawful place for living, working and vending in the city, the neglect of investment in PT and the lack of integration between land use and transportation planning have deprived them of access to job opportunities offered by dense, diverse and dynamic agglomerations in cities. The exclusion of lower income groups in the urban planning process is compounded by escalating motorization, declining modal share of PT and increasing sprawl. Master plans, by design, have neglected transport, in general, and PT, in particular. Unaffordable transport results in segregation: spatial, social and economic. If urban transport issues are not tackled as cities grow, islands of plenty in the midst of poverty will dominate the urban spatial structure. Governments will ultimately pay a heavy price to rectify the problems of economically dysfunctional, socially exclusionary and environmentally unsustainable cities.

PUBLIC TRANSPORT AND URBAN POOR

Transport enables cities to function as unified labour markets. It plays a crucial role in reducing poverty by affecting economic growth and addressing the mobility concerns of the poor and LIGs. PT connects these segments to central locations that offer the external economies of density and agglomeration. It enables them to access jobs matching their skill endowments; it also enhances the participation of women in labour force. Further, the access to PT complements the availability of other public services such as water supply, sewerage, drainage, health and education. However, the urban poor in developing countries like India are handicapped due to the long neglect of PT. The lack of infrastructure for non-motorized modes such as walking and bicycling and the absence of fast, reliable and safe PT have disconnected them from opportunities offered by the globalizing and increasingly networked urban economies.

Transport-related expenditures constitute a major share of the monthly expenditure on services by urban residents, especially the poor. NSSO 68th Round (July 2011–June 2012) data find that conveyance expenditures incurred by urban residents amounted to 7.5 per cent of total consumer expenditure. NSSO 72nd Round (July 2014–June 2015) data reveal that the primary modes of transport used by urban residents are buses. About 62 per cent of urban households reported using buses/trams, spending 58 per cent of their monthly expenditure on transport. Nearly 47 per cent reported expenditure on the next most used mode of transport, namely auto-rickshaws which accounted for 18 per cent of their household consumption expenditure on transport. Though walk, public bus and three-wheelers are the principal modes of transport for the majority of residents in cities, especially the poor and LIGs, other modes such as cars and two-wheelers overwhelmingly dominate the transportation scene in Indian cities.

Several countries around the world are investing in public transit to restructure cities and create new satellite towns with focus on moving people, rather than vehicles. Transit-oriented development (TOD) is emerging as a key paradigm to combine environment-friendly and efficient PT with inclusive communities. TOD offers a unique opportunity to cities in India to overcome the constraints imposed by exclusionary planning. Enabling the lower income groups to live and work in places with access to affordable PT will not only enable them to avail remunerative employment opportunities but also save time and cost. It will also generate the density required to make the public transit project economically viable. However, TOD requires significant investments in public transit-related infrastructure and integration of transport, land use and local economic development. The strategy calls for a flexible planning approach that treats every public transit investment as a major project with potential for generating external economies. Such projects need to be meticulously designed, combining the development of mass transit, integration of transportation and land use, location of the poor on transit nodes and corridors, and mobilization of resources on value capture financing (VCF) principle. Interestingly, 1 km wide band of land abutting the 76 km long Sardar Patel Ring Road in Ahmedabad, which was formed by securing land free of cost through the implementation of town planning schemes (TPSs), has been reserved as 'affordable housing zone' in the development plan (DP) for Ahmedabad urban area. Such inclusionary approaches to promote planned urban development have been neglected by the master planning model due to the primacy accorded to land use.

The developed countries have abandoned master planning since long. However, the model thrives in developing countries, perpetrating exclusionary urbanization. The master planning model in India including zoning and DCRs needs to be reformed urgently. This calls for shift from a form-centric theory to a people-centric approach towards urban planning. A fundamental question that arises in cities in developing countries is: whose city is being planned for? The federal government of Brazil tried to address this question by amending the federal constitution and guaranteeing the right of the poor to the city through a federal statute in 2001.

RIGHT TO THE CITY: THE CITY STATUTE

According to the Brazilian Constitution, the Municipality is statutorily responsible for urban planning and implementation of urban policy.

The Master Plan, approved by the Municipal Council, is the basic tool to guide urban expansion, renewal and development. However, the master planning model in Brazil led to exclusionary urbanization as is the case with developing countries like India today. The Master Plan adopted utopian standards that weeded the urban poor out of formal land and housing markets. This resulted in the mushrooming of *favelas* or slums in a bid by the poor to be close to the centres of employment. *Favelas* in Brazil have been a phenomenon of large cities; they came up mostly in eco-fragile zones—flood-prone areas, hill slopes, peripheral areas, environmental preservations, etc., which the Master Plan left out of the formal planning framework. To address the problems, Brazil took the bold steps of amending the Constitution and enacting a federal statute to provide for 'the social function of the city and of property'. These followed a long movement from below, demanding the inclusion of the urban poor and slum-dwellers in the formal city. The National Urban Policy Forum in Brazil, a federation of civil society groups, championed the cause of the universal right to housing and to the city in the 1990s. It singled out the prevailing master planning practice as the main factor responsible for *favelas* and imbalanced cities. Box 7.1 presents the relevant provisions of the Constitution of Brazil and the City Statute regarding the right of urban poor to the city.

Brazil adopted the concept of the 'right to the city' in 2001, when the country was more than 80 per cent urban and many slums in its largest cities had already become dens of drugs, crime and social unrest. A quick lesson for India from the Brazilian experience is that the

Box 7.1 *Brazil: Social Functions of City and Property—The Right to the City*

The Federal Government in Brazil enacted a path-breaking law in 2001, called the City Statute, aimed at addressing the problem of exclusionary urbanization. Based on Articles 182 and 183 of the Brazilian Constitution 1988, the Statute aimed to guarantee 'the right to the city'. Article 182 makes Master Plan compulsory for cities with over 20,000 inhabitants and that the Plan be approved by the City Council. It stipulates that the municipal government may, by means of a specific law for an area included in the Master Plan, demand that the owner of un-built, underused or unused urban land provide for adequate use thereof, subject successively to compulsory parcelling and land tax rates that are progressive in time. Thus, the Brazilian Constitution authorizes the state to require developers to provide for particular uses of vacant land including housing the low-income communities. It also provides for the levy of a progressive vacant land tax (VLT) over time, if urban land is left unused. Article 183 stipulates that an individual who possesses an urban area of up to 250 sq. m, for five years, without interruption or opposition, using it as his or as his family's home, shall acquire domain of it, provided he or she does not own any other urban or rural property. The right shall not be recognized for the same holder more than once and public real estate shall not be acquired by prescription.

The City Statute has four main elements: (a) interpretation of the Brazilian Constitution on the contours of the 'social function of the city and of property' in the process of city development; (b) creation of new instruments of planning and urban order by the municipality; (c) promotion of a process to ensure the democratic management of cities; and (d) identification of legal instruments for regularizing favelas in public and private urban areas. Article 2 of the City Statute stipulates that the purpose of urban policy is to give order to the full development of the social functions of the city and of urban property through guidelines for urban planning. These include: (a) guarantee to the right to sustainable cities—right to urban land, housing, environmental sanitation, infrastructure, transportation and public services, to work and leisure for current and future generations; (b) democratic administration through participation of the community in the formulation, execution and monitoring of urban DPs, projects and programmes; (c) integration of urban and rural activities based on a regional approach to socio-economic development; (d) regularization of landownership and urbanization of areas occupied by low-income populations through special urban planning and environmental norms; and (e) equality of conditions for public and private agents in the promotion of activities related to the urbanization process, serving the social interest.

Source: Federal Law No. 10.257 of Brazil, 10 July 2001; Mohanty (2014).

country must mainstream the slums and integrate slum-dwellers with the formal urban economy. This must start from the current stage of development itself, when the urbanization level is less than the one-third mark. It may be appreciated that slums arise due to the failure of not only land and housing markets but also the urban planning system. Social capital building is a key requirement for economic growth to be sustainable, and this calls for urban policy to accord the slum-dwellers and urban poor access to land tenure and affordable housing. The 'right to the city' paradigm of Brazil, supplemented by the inclusionary zoning (IZ)/inclusionary housing (IH) approach adopted by several countries around the world provide useful guidance to make India's urbanization process inclusive.

INCLUSIONARY ZONING AND HOUSING

The extreme land and housing markets in cities exclude the lower income households. Realizing this, many developed countries have incorporated 'IZ', 'IH' and 'mixed income housing' into their land use planning frameworks. While the models to promote inclusionary planning differ between countries, the basic approach in IZ, alternatively called IH, is to create affordable housing for the urban poor through the market. IZ policies have been adopted by the United States, Canada, the United Kingdom, Ireland, France, Belgium, Spain, the Netherlands, Italy, Australia, New Zealand, Colombia, South Africa, Israel, Malaysia and India (Gujarat state). The United States and Canada adopt decentralized land use regulation at state or provincial level for IH; Ireland and Spain centrally mandate it; England and France centrally enable its use and Italy promotes IH as a local initiative (Calavita and Mallach 2010). These countries supplement government-led social housing by IH in market-led programmes. In the sections that follow, we use the term 'IZ' to cover IZ, IH and mixed income housing.

IZ refers to a range of land use policies aimed at capturing the gains from rising real estate values due to factors such as urban planning, public investment and economic growth. The gains captured are used to mitigate the impacts of market-led development on the affordability of housing. IZ programmes link the approval for market-rate housing and commercial real estate to the supply of affordable housing units for lower income households at below-market rates. Although the definition of IZ differs between countries and cities, it generally requires the developers to reserve a percentage of land being developed or floor space being constructed for lower income households. In the United States, IZ programmes typically require the developers to sell or rent 10 to 30 per cent of new residential units to low- and moderate-income households. They are based on a mandatory requirement under the city zoning regulations or a scheme of 'incentive zoning' outside the purview of the zoning code. They enable the LIG households to live in MIG and HIG neighbourhoods.

The arguments for IZ cut across the principles of 'beneficiaries pay', 'congesters pay', 'exacerbaters pay' and 'growth pays'. They stress the need for sharing the benefits of rising real estate values due to public policies and programmes with the disadvantaged sections of society. Researchers argue that the extreme real estate markets in cities make housing to these segments unaffordable. IZ programmes enable them to access greater employment prospects, higher quality schools and hospitals, and better community facilities. A strong case for IZ is also presented in terms of the social value of integration and the long-term affordability in housing market. Social integration is a public good that has implications for the foundations of economic growth. IZ acts as an instrument to promote socially cohesive and inclusive development. Empirical studies reveal that while IZ serves relatively more advantaged sections in the group of low-income households, the access to opportunities it provides at the bottom of the pyramid is remarkable.

ECONOMICS OF INCLUSIONARY ZONING

There are conflicting views on the economic impacts of IZ as an instrument to provide affordable housing to very low, low or moderate-income households. Economists contend that any form of control on housing or house rent is distortionary as it reduces the quantity and quality of housing. They argue that price control leads to shortage in supply. Some compare IZ with a rent control regime that imposes price restriction on a portion of new development, requiring the developers to sell or rent the so-called 'affordable' units at below-market rates. Others argue that the imposition of price control on a part of new development will not discourage housing production as much as price control on the whole development, but it will discourage housing nonetheless. By acting as a tax on housing production, it will raise the price of non-price-controlled housing and thus decrease the amount of new housing.

The arguments against IZ run as follows. IZ leads to two markets for new homes: price-controlled or below-market rate and non-price-controlled or market-rate housing. The price-controlled segment will have many features of markets with rent control such as shortages and discouragement of production. IZ mandates that if developers want to build non-price-controlled units, they must also provide a certain number of price-controlled units. This implies that unless the 'affordable' units are subsidized by government or some charity, the price-controlled units will cause an economic burden on development. When subsidies do not cover the costs of below-market rate units, IZ will act like a tax on production of market-rate housing. When a sizable number of housing units in a development are sold at below-market rate, the cost of the development will rise. Thus, the developer must increase the price of the market-rate housing units much above what is warranted by the market to compensate for the discounts. As a result, the price of such housing will go up and finally housing production will fall. The arguments are based on the premise that the developer bears the cost of subsidy on the below-market rate units.

· Although the developers may appear to bear the burden of below-market rate housing units under IZ, standard microeconomics suggests that they would end up passing on a part or all of this effective tax onto buyers of housing or sellers of undeveloped land. If housing costs are very high, they could push land prices so low that some landowners would choose not to sell at all. If this occurred, less housing would be produced and prices increase. However, the distribution of the incidence of the tax between the buyers and sellers will be determined by actual market conditions, specifically the relative elasticities of housing demand and housing supply. The effect of IZ on housing supply will be similar to that of a tax on housing. The housing supply curve will shift up by the tax equivalent of IZ. The reduction in supply of market-rate housing due to IZ will be smaller with inelastic demand compared to when demand is elastic. The market price after IZ will be higher than that before IZ. But the burden of IZ will be split between buyers and sellers. If demand for housing is inelastic, a relatively larger burden will fall on the buyer than on the seller.

Not only the slope of housing demand but also of housing supply and land supply functions will affect the impact of IZ on the production and price of housing, and sharing of IZ burden between buyers and sellers. It is important to note that the slopes of demand and supply curves vary between cities and sub-markets within a city. Further, factors such as income, tastes and preferences, interest rate, population size, etc., affect land and housing market outcomes under IZ. However, as the position of supply and demand curves isolates the relationship between the price and quantity, given the exogenous variables, it provides useful information for analysing the economic impacts of IZ. A careful examination of the pre-IZ and post-IZ supply and demand curves for land and housing, and their elasticities—the economics of IZ—is necessary before arriving at any conclusion on the impacts or efficacy of an IZ programme. This will inform how the burden of IZ is likely to be split between the housing developers, landowners and market-rate homebuyers.

A study conducted by the Lincoln Institute of Land Policy has examined the economic impacts of IH with focus on the following four questions (Jacobus 2015):

1. Is it fair to ask one group (developers) to solve a broader social problem?
2. Will housing developers pass on the cost to homebuyers and tenants?
3. Will inclusionary policies prevent new development and make the housing problem worse?
4. Can IH work in every type of housing market?

The economic arguments and evidence considered by the study are summarized as follows:

Fairness of Inclusionary Zoning

New developments create positive and negative impacts on the community, including windfall gains to a lucky group of the landowners and developers, and escalated demand for affordable housing. Thus, it is fair to ask the gainers from spatial planning, infrastructure investment and growth-augmenting policies by public authorities to compensate for the impacts generated by developments and to share a portion of their unearned increments with the disadvantaged groups. The operation of market forces suggests that the housing units added in a given market will put some downward pressure on the price of the existing units. But the new units built primarily for higher income residents will command higher rents, and the new residents who can afford such units will create demands for more lower wage workers in the area, leading to a greater demand for housing. The larger effect could thus be an upward pressure on housing costs. The whole picture must be taken into account while gauging the fairness of IZ.

Costs of Inclusionary Zoning

Basically, there are three elements in the price of a new house: (a) land cost; (b) cost of building (including fees, permits, design, construction, etc.); and (c) developer's profit. As the local real estate market determines the prices of market-rate units, the developer of one project cannot influence the overall market price or rent. When a city imposes an IZ requirement, it may increase a developer's cost of production. But the developer cannot really pass those costs on to homebuyers or tenants, because the new units must still be competitively priced in the overall market. In the long run, land prices may adjust to absorb the costs of the IZ as developers avoid projects that do not earn profits. Further, competition between developers may force them to earn 'normal profits' absorbing the IZ requirements as a 'cost of doing business'. Thus, the costs of IZ may be absorbed by a modest decline in land prices or a reduction in 'super-normal profits' of developers, or a combination of both.

Impact on New Development

There is no conclusive evidence that IZ diminishes the supply of housing by prompting the landowners to withhold the sale of land due to reduction in its price and therefore increase housing prices. While the production rate of market-rate housing units may fall with the imposition of IZ, city jurisdictions are most likely to adopt IZ policies at the peak of the business cycle. When the market forces demanding new development are strong, IH will not cause a fall in the production of market-rate housing. Thus, it is possible to design IZ programmes that do not affect the market price of housing.

Offsetting Opportunity Costs

When incentives are offered, it does not make sense to talk about the cost of IZ in isolation. The whole economic picture must be considered. At the centre of IZ is the concept of 'residual land value' linked to the theory that the landowners capture whatever is left over after the costs of development, including payments to other factors are met. When a city imposes IZ, the developers are likely to incur more costs and forego some revenues, representing the 'opportunity cost' of complying with IZ. However, in the long run, higher costs would prompt them to bid less for developable sites, leading to a reduction in land value and their profit margin returning to 'normal' levels. Moreover, most IZ programmes do not impose additional costs; they rather offset costs (at least, in part), with various incentives provided to developers. The most common incentive is density bonus or extra FSI under which the developers are granted the right to build more units than permitted normally. Other incentives include favourable changes in zoning. Such dispensations can lead to increased income to developers to offset the cost of providing affordable units at below-market rate.

Taking various economic considerations into account, Jacobus (2015) concludes that IZ policies are fair. They are instruments to mitigate the adverse impacts of new development and to share the benefits of rising real estate values with low- and moderate-income households. Regarding the possibilities of developers shifting the cost of IZ to homebuyers and tenants and IZ programmes adversely affecting housing production, the study suggests that, if properly designed, they will not lead to adverse effects. On the question of whether IZ can work in all types of markets, the study clarifies that it works well when the real estate markets are booming and creating unearned increments. When real estate prices are very low, housing rents and sale prices would be too low to support the requirements of IZ even if cheap land is available and zoning incentives are provided. Jacobus (2015) observes:

> It is entirely reasonable to ask real estate developers to help address the pressing need for more affordable housing, because developers and landowners benefit financially from the conditions that give rise to the shortage of decent, well-located homes for lower-income residents. But inclusionary programs need to be designed with care to ensure that their requirements are economically feasible. While developers are not able to pass on the cost of compliance to tenants and homebuyers, there is some risk that poorly designed inclusionary requirements could slow the rate of building and ultimately lead to higher housing costs. Policymakers can avoid this unintended consequence by offering developers flexibility in how they comply and by calibrating requirements and incentives so that the net economic impact on projects is not too great. At some level, inclusionary housing can be implemented in most housing markets, but the stronger the local real estate market, the greater the potential for inclusionary housing to make a meaningful difference. (Jacobus 2015, 17)

Empirically, IZ programmes are observed in communities where land and housing prices are booming. Economic feasibility requires that these programmes must be designed to suit local conditions. The principal factors determining feasibility of housing development include: public policy (zoning, density, land use mix and design requirements); market feasibility (demand for space, achievable price relative to the production cost); capital (cost and availability of funds, including equity and bank loans); and land (availability and acquisition cost). IZ requirements intersect with market feasibility and land. Market feasibility depends on the intensity of demand and adequacy of returns, taking into account efforts, risks, cost of funds and cash flows. It varies between sub-markets with differing demands for housing, prices, rents, construction costs, and availability and cost of land. In some areas, housing prices and rents may be high to cover construction costs, but land may be too costly. However, if zoning permits the developers to build with greater density, they will be willing to incur higher cost of land per unit of housing. The 'residual land value' serves as a measure to assess the feasibility of housing development with IZ. With a set of capital and operating costs and projected cash flows, a higher residual land value means that the developers would be able to pay more for land. When agglomeration externalities in cities are strong, they capitalize into 'agglomeration rents' and residual land values are likely to be high. These considerations suggest that IZ programmes need to be tuned to local market conditions (Williams et al. 2016).

INCLUSIONARY ZONING: INTERNATIONAL PRACTICE

The key approaches to IZ and IH adopted internationally are presented as follows:

United States

State laws in the United States provide for 'impact fees' as one-time charges, levied by local government to make the developer pay a 'fair share' of the cost of on-site and off-site public facilities necessitated by new development. Impact fee legislations cover a vast range of new infrastructure facilities, including roadways, streets, water supply, sewerage, storm water drainage, solid waste management, underground utilities, electricity supply, fire protection and low- and moderate-income housing. State laws also enable municipalities to implement IZ by requiring the developers to construct below-market rate housing units for sale or rent in market-rate developments. Over time, the concept of IZ in the United States has evolved to include a broad spectrum of possibilities, including (a) mandatory requirement for affordable housing, coupled with offsets against the cost of providing such housing, (b) incentive-linked zoning that is voluntary, but results in the production of affordable housing when incentives are availed and (c) negotiated development approval that either sets land aside for non-market development or produces affordable housing based on a policy framework articulated in local plans.

Inclusionary zoning/housing originated in the United States in the early 1970s as a reaction to the close nexus between racial segregation in the society and land use regulation system that fostered it through exclusionary zoning. The concept took roots in 1971 in Fairfax County, Virginia, which passed a mandatory zoning ordinance. This required the developers of more than 50 units of multi-family housing to include at least 15 per cent of the dwellings within an affordable range that was defined to address the housing needs of households between the 60th and 80th percentile of median household income. This ordinance was subsequently struck down by the Virginia Supreme Court. However, in the nearby Montgomery County, Maryland, a similar ordinance, passed in 1973, has survived till date, with refinements, improvements and remarkable results. More than 500 cities and counties in 27 states and the District of Columbia in the United States have adopted an IZ policy. The common approach is to use the zoning power with local authority to require or encourage the development of below-market rate houses for low- and moderate-income groups when according approval of real estate projects.

New Jersey and California states are the pioneers in IZ programmes. The New Jersey's Supreme Court in Mount Laurel Case, 1975, granted powers to municipalities, developers and lower income people to approach the court directly to seek a judicial declaration of compliance with their affordable housing duties and rights. The decision mandated communities to use their zoning powers to provide realistic opportunities for the production of affordable housing to low- and moderate-income households. The Court included a constitutional obligation on all parties to create a 'fair share' of regional low- and moderate-income housing through IZ/IH or similar policies and zoning practices. It also provided immunity to towns from civil law suits attempting to demonstrate compliance through participation in the administrative process. Further, the Court's ruling permitted citizens with low income and developers the right to challenge legally under certain circumstances. Each municipality was mandated to develop an 'adequate housing plan' to bring the town in compliance with its 'fair share' of regional and prospective needs by setting aside 15–20 per cent of its total housing units for affordable housing.

The scope and design of IZ programmes in the United States vary between states, counties and cities. Box 7.2 summarizes the salient features and impacts of such programmes.

Montgomery County in Maryland has established an exemplary track record of IZ through its 'Moderately Priced Dwelling Unit

Box 7.2 *United States: Inclusionary Zoning and Housing Policies*

Mandatory Versus Voluntary Status: Most policies are mandatory; some are voluntary. Some mandatory programmes apply only in the context of zoning changes. Some impose inclusionary requirements only on large single-family home projects; others prescribe IZ on all types of projects.

Set-aside Requirement: Set-aside requirements are mostly between 10 and 20 per cent of total number of units. Some programmes require only 5 per cent of the new units to be sold at a discount; others warrant a percentage as high as 30 per cent. IZ-mandated units can be for sale or rent.

Eligibility and Term: Most IZ programmes fix income eligibility requirements aimed at households earning between 60 and 120 per cent of the area median income. Many define the time period for which affordability must be maintained—varying from 10 to 99 years.

Development Types and Location: Some IZ policies exempt projects from IZ requirement depending on project size (number of units) and type (condominium, redevelopment or adaptive use). Some impose neighbourhood-specific requirements.

Opt-outs: Some jurisdictions require developers to construct below-market rate housing units in the proposed development itself; others permit such units in another location. Some IZ policies allow developers to make payments in lieu of inclusionary units. Such payments usually go to a local housing fund.

Incentives: Generally, IZ programmes offer incentives to developers for providing affordable housing units: non-monetary, monetary or both. Non-monetary compensations include upgraded zoning, density bonus, waiver of subdivision requirements, design relaxation, reduction in street width or setbacks, reduced parking requirements and fast-track permission. Monetary compensations include lowered permit fees, impact fee waiver or deferral, tax abatements and direct subsidies from local, state and federal sources.

(Continued)

Box 7.2 (Continued)

Impact: IZ policies have achieved significant new below-market rate housing production in some markets which include Fairfax County, Virginia; Montgomery Country, Maryland; Palm Beach County, Florida and the whole of Southern California. Three issues are common in jurisdictions that have not been able to achieve the IZ objectives: (a) weak development market conditions; (b) poor design of IZ programme, inconsistent administration and weak enforcement; and (c) lack of adequate development incentives.

Source: Knaap, Bento and Lowe (2008), Hickey, Sturtevant and Thaden (2014) and Williams et al. (2016).

Program' launched in 1973. This has led to the production of more than 10,000 affordable housing units in the County in 25 years. Portland, Oregon, has followed the 'Metropolitan Housing Rule' from the 1970s. State law there provides for mingling of apartments for HIGs and LIGs in residential developments. Boulder, Colorado, mandates 20 per cent of housing units to be affordable. In the Bay Area in California, 72 per cent of cities followed IH policies as of 2014. Most policies require the developers to designate between 10 and 15 per cent of their units as affordable. Davis, California, requires 15 per cent IH. Boston, Massachusetts, has adopted a new Inclusive Development Plan (IDP) in 2015. This applies to projects financed by the city, being developed on city or government property and those that require zoning concessions. Projects that provide 13 per cent of the total number of housing units on-site affordable fulfil the city's obligation. New York City has rezoned previously classified 'industrial' land on the Brooklyn Waterfront and other land parcels to 'residential' and allocated a strong density bonus to developers who agreed to meet the city's affordable housing targets. The city's IH programme created about 2,700 permanently affordable rental housing units between 2005 and 2013 (Crispell, Gorska and Abdelgany 2016; Mohanty 2014).

New York City has launched 'Mandatory Inclusionary Zoning (MIZ)', linking new affordable housing to land use regulation. Called Zoning for Quality and Affordability (ZQA), the programme is expected to be the strongest IZ effort in the United States. The city has recognized the need 'to modernize obscure and outdated zoning rules'. The new rules allow developers to build taller buildings (usually 10 to 20 ft higher, but in some cases more) if they construct affordable apartments for seniors, long-term care facilities or provide affordable housing through the IZ. They remove barriers to affordable housing development on narrow sites by eliminating specific height restrictions for these lots. Nobel Laureate Paul Krugman has reportedly endorsed the New York City's MIZ initiative to permit taller and denser buildings on the logic of making the city more affordable for more people.

United Kingdom

The Town and Country Planning Act, 1990, in the United Kingdom permits negotiation between a developer and the local authority to achieve socio-economic objectives. Section 106 (1) of the Act stipulates that any person with an interest in land may, by agreement or otherwise, enter into a planning obligation, enforceable by the local planning authority:

(a) restricting the development or use of the land in any specified way; (b) requiring specified operations or activities to be carried out in, on, under or over the land; (c) requiring the land to be used in any specified way; or (d) requiring a sum or sums to be paid to the authority on a specified date or dates or periodically.

Section 106 agreements are known as 'planning obligations'. These are legalized and regularized under various planning acts and government circulars. Planning obligations typically require new housing developments to provide a proportion of total units for affordable housing to low- and moderate-income households. They aim at creating mixed and inclusive communities.

Town planning law in the United Kingdom does not mandate IZ based on a fixed percentage or pre-established requirement for affordable housing as the technique is based on negotiation between the local authority and the developer. Local authorities are authorized to regulate the development of land, requiring new housing projects to provide affordable housing to lower income segments. They specify the type, location, number and timing of such housing, and the financial contributions that the developer has to pay towards the provision of infrastructure and services. The Unitary Development Plan 2002 of London stipulated that 25 per cent of the new residential developments should be affordable, if provided on-site. If the affordable units are provided off-site, then the figure would be 33 per cent. Payments in lieu will be the cost of providing the 33 per cent affordable units off-site.

Section 106 agreements have been instrumental in creating around 40 per cent of affordable housing units in the United Kingdom by 2005; availability of additional subsidies in the form of social housing grant has played a key role in this outcome. However, many research studies have detected problems in negotiations with developers due to the poor negotiating capacity and the lack of market awareness on the part of local authorities. Furthermore, the number of affordable housing units built is found to be substantially below the forecast figures (Mohanty 2014).

Other Countries

Australia follows a system of 'Development Contributions' levied on new developments based on law. They take three forms: (a) contribution in kind—land gifted to public authority by the developer for roads, drains and public facilities like open spaces, schools, health centres, etc.; (b) work-in-kind—public infrastructure facilities constructed by developer and handed over to the public authority on completion; and (c) monetary charges—financial contributions towards acquisition of land for public use or provision of infrastructure and affordable housing. Since the 1980s, municipalities in Australia, while granting development permission, are requiring the developers to incorporate a certain proportion of affordable housing in proposed developments or make an in-lieu monetary contribution for equivalent number of units of specified standard to be provided elsewhere in their jurisdiction. Law also permits negotiations with developers to make contributions. For example, under Section 94 of the Environmental Planning and Assessment Act of 1979 in New South Wales, a developer seeking a development or rezoning permit can be required to provide or bear the capital and recurrent cost of public infrastructure facilities and services, recreation, environmental conservation and affordable housing. There is no limit to contributions that can be negotiated and these can be in lieu of or in addition to development contributions. South Australia uses density bonus and other incentives to promote IH; it has a 15 per cent mandatory affordable housing target for all new developments (Renewal SA 2013).

Several provinces and cities in Canada have adopted IZ policies. Since 1988, Vancouver has been requiring 20 per cent of the houses in all major developments to be affordable. Ontario uses tools such as exemptions in development charges and property taxes on new residential developments to provide affordable housing units. Planning law in Ontario links affordable housing to planning permissions for building at densities or heights greater than that are currently permitted on sites designated for new residential developments. It also allows second suites in single detached houses as a right to expand affordable rental housing. The 2004 Master Plan of Montreal formally committed the city to making 30 per cent of all new housing units affordable. It established the following guidelines: (a) 15 per cent of new housing units be reserved for social housing, targeting households with low or very low incomes and (b) another 15 per cent to be affordable and built by the private sector, targeting households with moderate incomes. Some modest financial assistance was made available along with density bonus to developers. The provision of affordable housing was negotiated specifically in large developments that required major changes to the approved master plan or zoning, such as a change of use to residential, or an increase in permitted density or height or public investment in basic infrastructure or environmental improvements. Reportedly, Montreal's IH policy, which was based on a voluntary approach, revealed after two years of implementation that the goal was surpassed—39 per cent of new housing in Montreal met the affordability targets, both in very low- and moderate-income categories.

In Belgium, national law requires all cities to make 20 per cent of housing affordable. The 2007 Land Act of Spain prescribes that a minimum of 30 per cent of the newly built housing units must be affordable. Ireland's Planning and Development Act, 2000, amended in 2002, requires the local authorities to guarantee that a maximum of 20 per cent of new development projects are intended for affordable housing. Article 55 of the French *loi SRU* (Solidaritéetrenouvellementurbains), enacted in 2000, explicitly embodied a national policy of social inclusion mandating that every met-ropolitan community above a certain population size should designate at least 20 per cent of its total housing stock as social housing. While the Act did not require IH, it became a spur for individual communes to impose inclusionary requirements on private developers. That, in turn, led the national government to pass legislation in 2006 explicitly authorizing local IH programmes. Malaysia imposes an IH quota of 30 per cent and a defined ceiling price for inclusionary houses, for all private developers in developments beyond a certain threshold size (Mohanty 2014).

Globally, IZ and IH policies are being increasingly adopted to pro-mote affordable housing and social inclusion. Local authorities generally require 10–30 per cent of the housing units constructed under market-led programmes to be affordable. They apply IZ to greenfield as well as brownfield developments; both ownership and rental housing units are encouraged with a focus on long-term affordability. Three key les-sons emerge from international experiences with IZ and IH. First, the efficacy of IZ depends on the state of the real estate market. IZ does not work when the demand for market-rate development is sluggish. When the development environment is strong, IZ programmes can yield a sizable number of new affordable housing units even with-out any incentives to developers. However, when market forces are weak, developers require a combination of incentives and subsidies. Second, the success of IZ policies is significantly dependent on their design. When designed properly, IZ requirements do not lead to much adverse impacts on the production of new housing. The structuring of requirements and incentives is crucial. Third, housing developers generally target moderate-income households under IZ programmes; they require higher incentives and subsidies from the municipalities to build affordable houses for LIGs. The poorest of the poor segments need special dispensations from the government, including public housing.

INCLUSIONARY ZONING: INDIAN INITIATIVES

The central government and some state governments in India have tried to promote affordable housing for the EWSs and LIGs through IZ and IH. Key national initiative include the National Urban Housing and Habitat Policy (NUHHP) announced in 2007 and the Jawaharlal

Nehru National Urban Renewal Mission (JNNURM) launched in 2005. Important state level initiatives include the TPS in Gujarat; Slum Rehabilitation Scheme (SRS) in Maharashtra; Affordable Housing Policy in Rajasthan; MPD 2021, Land pooling and TOD policies in Delhi; the Patta Act in Madhya Pradesh; and Land Sharing Model in Vijayawada, Andhra Pradesh. The brief features of these initiatives and key lessons from their implementation are presented in the following text.

NUHHP 2007 and JNNURM

NUHHP 2007 stipulated that 10–15 per cent of the land in every new public/private housing project or 20–25 per cent of FSI/FAR, whichever is greater, be reserved for EWS/LIG housing. The reform agenda of the JNNURM included the reservation of at least 20–25 per cent of developed land in all housing projects (both public and private) for EWS/LIG categories with a system of cross-subsidization, that is, charging higher prices to other groups to subsidize the low-income households. The implementation of the national stipulations regarding IZ and IH under the NUHHP and JNNURM called for the structuring of appropriate incentives to developers at the state and city levels. However, hardly any such incentives were offered to make the IZ requirements economically feasible for developers. Ironically, long before the NUHHP 2007 and JNNURM, the TPS in Gujarat promoted an impressive regime of IZ and has been implementing the same.

Town Planning Scheme: Gujarat

The Gujarat Town Planning and Urban Development Act (GTPUDA), 1976, prescribes urban planning in two steps: DP for designated urban development area and TPS for constituent smaller areas of approximately 100–200 hectares to implement the DP. The TPS promotes planned, self-financed and inclusive urban development. An innovative feature of the TPS is the reservation of land for housing the socially and economically weaker sections (SEWS). Section 40(j) of the GTPUDA provides for:

> ... the reservation of land to the extent of ten percent; or such percentage as near there to as possible of the total area covered under the

scheme, for the purpose of providing housing accommodation to the members of S.E.W.S.

The allocation of land for other urban uses under a TPS are: 15 per cent for roads, 5 per cent for parks, playgrounds, open spaces and gardens, 5 per cent for social infrastructure such as schools, fire stations, dispensaries and public utilities and 15 per cent for sale by the planning authority to meet the cost of infrastructure development in the scheme area. The remaining lands are returned to the landowners, as near as possible to their original lands—with substantially increased land values. The TPS facilitates the procurement of land for infrastructure and affordable housing free of cost. It has enabled the Ahmedabad Urban Development Authority (AUDA) to form the 76 km long Sardar Patel Ring Road without incurring the cost of LA.

The TPS relies on the value of planning in making urban development self-paying while catering to the needs of lower income groups for affordable housing. The land sale component yields adequate revenues to meet the costs of infrastructure to service the TPS in accordance with the urban planning norms. Betterment charges are levied on the landowners in proportion to the land value increment likely to accrue to them due to the TPS. The scheme has enabled large cities in Gujarat to procure significant extents of land for catering to the land needs of the disadvantaged sections of society for affordable housing. To cite an example, Surat city was able to secure 394 hectares of land for housing the urban poor and LIGs. This facilitated the construction of a large number of houses for such sections by the Surat Municipal Corporation (SMC) under the Basic Services to the Urban Poor (BSUP) sub-mission of the JNNURM (Shorey 2009). The TPS in Gujarat demonstrates the potential of IZ as an instrument to secure land for affordable housing through the urban planning process itself.

Slum Rehabilitation Scheme: Maharashtra

In December 1995, the Government of Maharashtra launched the SRS with the formation of the Slum Rehabilitation Authority (SRA). The scheme is based on using land locked in slums as a resource to promote slum redevelopment with affordable housing and infrastructure without burdening the exchequer. The slum-dwellers are provided rehabilitation tenements free of cost, with cross-subsidization through a sale component based on the grant of additional FAR as incentive. The developer is allowed to construct houses for sale in the open market under that component to meet the expenditure on rehabilitation buildings and earn a profit. With a screening process, eligible slum-dwellers are given in-situ rehabilitation while non-eligible slum-dwellers are removed from the land occupied. Projects submitted by developers with 70 per cent consent of eligible slum-dwellers are entertained. Initially the cut-off date for eligibility of slum-dwellers under the SRS was 1 January 1995; this was subsequently extended to 1 January 2000.

The key features of the SRS initiative are as follows: (a) there is no financial investment by the government, (b) a slum-dweller gets a self-contained one bedroom flat with alcove/kitchen, water closet toilet and bathroom with a carpet area of 269 sq. ft, (c) an amount of ₹20,000/- per tenement is recovered as a maintenance deposit from the developer to meet the maintenance cost of the rehabilitated building, (d) rehabilitated tenement allotted to a slum-dweller cannot be sold for a period of 10 years, (e) saleable built-up area allowed for every 1.0 sq. m of rehabilitated construction is as under: rehabilitation—1.00 sq. m; city area—0.75 sq. m; suburban area—1.00 sq. m and Dharavi slum area—1.33 sq. m. In practice, progress under the SRS has been tardy due to issues such as landownership disputes, preparation of correct list of eligible slum-dwellers, securing consent of slum-dwellers, poor quality of construction and administrative bottlenecks.

Affordable Housing Policy: Rajasthan

In 2009, the Government of Rajasthan announced 'Affordable Housing Policy' to address the problems of affordable housing for the EWS and LIG segments based on a multi-pronged approach. The policy envisaged incentive-linked IH through five models: mandatory requirements for public and private developers, projects of private developers on private land, on land acquired by public authorities, on government land for rental housing and outright sale and slum housing on PPPs. The 2009 Housing Policy of the state government has been revised with the launching of Chief Minister's Jan Awas Yojana (JAY) in 2015.

The new housing policy of Rajasthan requires private developers to make the following reservations for housing the poor and low-income segments: construction of flats—7.5 per cent of residential FAR and plotted development—10 per cent of residential saleable area for the EWS and LIG segments with plot area of 30–45 sq. m for EWS and 45–75 sq. m for LIG, respectively. The developers are granted incentive FAR equal to 50 per cent of the standard FAR with exemption from betterment levy. Hundred per cent waiver of land conversion/land use change charges and building plan approval charges for the EWS/LIG component are also provided for. The FAR proposed for EWS/LIG shall not be counted in the calculation of FAR for the main project even if the EWS/LIG units are constructed in another location in the same urban area. In the case of projects of private developers undertaking affordable housing on their own land with 50 per cent of land area reserved for EWS/LIG housing and the remaining 50 per cent for market-rate residential development, incentive FAR up to 2.25 will be available without betterment levy for the complete project, including the FAR consumed for EWS/LIG housing. Development norms and requirements, sale prices of affordable housing units and procedure for allotment of houses to eligible beneficiaries are subject to regulations issued under the housing policy.

Master Plan of Delhi 2021

MPD 2021 embarks on a multi-pronged strategy for affordable housing to the urban poor through: (a) rehabilitation of slums and JJ clusters, (b) redevelopment and reconstruction in resettlement colonies, (c) new housing for the urban poor and (d) night shelters in colonies. To create affordable housing units, private developers are provided with incentives in the form of higher FAR, part commercialization of land, provision of TDR and adoption of cooperative resettlement model under which tenure rights are provided through cooperative societies. Low-income households are also provided with relaxed planning norms covering land use, plot size, density, FAR, ground coverage, setbacks, space for commercial use, and physical and social infrastructure. Land is also reserved for new housing for EWS and LIG segments. It is mandatory for developers of group housing to provide a minimum 15 per cent of FAR or 35 per cent of dwelling units, whichever is higher, for community service personnel and EWS/LIGs. Redevelopment schemes and industrial housing are the two ways to achieve this in old built-up areas. In urban extensions, the acquisition and development costs of land for the urban poor are to be borne by the rest of the project through cross-subsidization, and EWS and LIG housing is promoted by handing over reserved lands to the designated agency.

Table 7.4 *Delhi Master Plan 2021: Planning Norms for Informal Shops/Units*

S. No.	Use Zones/Use Premise	No. of Informal Shops/ Units
1	Retail Trade: Metropolitan City Centre, District Centre, Community Centre, Convenience Shopping Centre	3 to 4 units per 10 formal shops (to be provided in informal bazaar/service market components)
2	Government and Commercial Offices	5 to 6 units per 1,000 employees
3	Wholesale Trade and Freight Complexes	3 to 4 units per 10 formal shops
4	Hospital	3 to 4 units per 100 beds
5	Bus Terminal	1 unit for two bus bays
6	Schools: Primary/Secondary Senior Secondary/Integrated	3 to 4 units 5 to 6 units
7	Parks: District Parks Neighbourhood Parks	8 to 10 units at each major entry 2 to 3 units
8	Residential	1 unit/1,000 population
9	Industrial	5 to 6 units per 1,000 employees
10	Railways Terminus/MRTS Stations	To be based on a survey at the time of project preparation

Source: DDA (2015).

MPD 2021 provides for space norms to facilitate informal sector activities, including service markets, informal bazaars and street vending in unobjectionable areas as presented in Table 7.4.

Land Pooling Policy: Delhi

The LPP of Delhi 2013 aims at promoting inclusive urban development with the landowners as partners. A landowner, or a group of landowners, who have grouped on their own or a developer, called the 'developer entity', shall be permitted to pool land for unified planning, servicing and subdivision or sharing of land for development as per prescribed norms and guidelines. Each landowner is expected to get an equitable return under the LPP notwithstanding the uses assigned to their land in the zonal development plan (ZDP) with minimum displacement. The LPP is applicable to urbanizable areas in the urban extension of Delhi for which ZDP is approved. The land use distribution at the city level for the proposed 'urbanizable extensions' adopted by the LPP is: gross residential—53 per cent; commercial—5 per cent; industrial—4 per cent; recreational—16 per cent; public and semi-public facilities—10 per cent; and roads and circulation—12 per cent. The policy envisages that for every 1,000 hectares of land pooled, the gross residential distribution will provide for about 50,000 dwelling units for EWS housing (32–40 sq. m size). Residential FAR of 4.0 for group housing will be applicable on net residential land which is exclusive of the 15 per cent FAR reserved for EWS housing. Tradeable FAR will be permitted subject to conditions.

Transit-oriented Development Policy: Delhi

The TOD Policy of Delhi aims at low carbon emission, high-density, compact, mixed land use, and inclusive and sustainable development of Delhi by promoting the use of public transport. Under the policy, development/redevelopment in TOD zones will be incentivized by providing significantly higher FAR of 4.0 on the entire amalgamated plot being developed/redeveloped. Additional FAR could be availed through TDR, for schemes larger than 1 hectare. Entire approved layout plan of a scheme will be included in the influence zone if more than 50 per cent of the plan area falls in the zone. It will be mandatory to use a minimum of 30 per cent of overall FAR for residential use, a minimum of 10 per cent of FAR for commercial use and a minimum of 10 per cent of FAR for community facilities. Utilization of the remaining 50 per cent FAR shall be as per the land use category designated in the zonal plan. There shall be a mix of housing types for a wide range of income brackets within communities with shared public spaces/greens/recreational facilities/amenities, which will minimize gentrification and create more community-oriented developments. The mandatory residential component covering 30 per cent FAR shall wholly comprise of units of 65 sq. m area or less. Out of these, half of the FAR, that is, 15 per cent of the total FAR, has to be used for EWS units of size ranging between 32 and 40 sq. m. Over and above this, an additional mandatory FAR of 15 per cent has to be utilized for EWS units.

The Delhi TOD Policy stipulates that 50 per cent of the EWS housing stock shall be retained by the developer entity and disposed only to the apartment owners, at market prices, to house CSP working for the residents/owners of the group housing. These will be developed by the developer entity at the respective group housing site/premises or contiguous sites. The remaining 50 per cent of the dwelling units are to be sold to the DDA for EWS housing purposes. The sale to the DDA/local bodies would be at the base cost of ₹2,000 per sq. ft as per the Central Public Works Department (CPWD) Index of 2013 (plus cost of EWS parking) which shall be enhanced as per CPWD escalation index at the time of actual handing over and can be developed by the developer entity at an alternative nearby site. Necessary commercial and public service facilities shall be provided by the entity for this separate housing project. The entity shall be allowed to undertake the actual transfer/transaction of saleable component under its share/ownership to prospective buyers only after the prescribed land and EWS housing component are handed over to the DDA.

The Patta Act: Madhya Pradesh

The Madhya Pradesh government passed the Madhya Pradesh Nagariya Kshetron Ke Bhoomihin Vyakti (Pattadhruti Adhikaron Ka Pradan Kiya Jana) Adhiniyam, 1984, called the Patta Act. The objective was to provide leasehold rights to landless persons residing in government-owned land in urban areas; the lease could be given for land up to an extent of 50 sq mt. The Act was amended in 1998, 2003 and 2008, and covers all urban areas in the state. Section 3(1) of the Act provides for a cut-off date limiting the application of the Patta Act to occupation of land by landless persons before 10 April 1984. Section 3(3) provides that the leasehold rights are not transferable other than by way of inheritance. Two types of pattas were given under the Patta Act. Permanent patta for 30 years was assigned to those living in settlements that were to be improved and rehabilitated in-situ. Temporary patta was given to those living in settlements that were to be relocated. Such patta automatically expired after a family relocated to another site with permanent patta. Out of total 40,600 plots identified in slums, 20,790 were provided with tenure rights in the initial phase of the programme.

Amendment to the Patta Act in 1998 declared 31 May 1998 as the new date of eligibility. Along with this, plot areas for different categories of cities were also revised, ranging from 100 to 600 sq. ft. Lease rent per square feet per year for 10 years was introduced at the rate of ₹1 for Nagar Panchayats, ₹1.50 for other towns and ₹2.00 for the cities of Bhopal, Indore, Jabalpur, Gwalior and Raipur. Three categories of patta were introduced: (a) for registration of disputed cases, (b) permanent lease of 30 years and (c) temporary lease of 1 year. Introduction of Mohalla Samitis was done with the intent of empowering the local community for management and development of allotted land, social welfare activities and redressal of grievances. An amendment to the Patta Act in 2003 allows pattas to be mortgaged for housing loans from banks, registered housing societies or government organizations. Subsequently, the cut-off dates have been advanced to 31 May 2003 and 31 December 2007.

Land Sharing Model: Vijayawada

The Government of Andhra Pradesh (GoAP) assembled 226.54 acres of land under the jurisdiction of Vijayawada Municipal Corporation for inclusive expansion of the city through an innovative instrument of land sharing at Gollapudi and Jakkampudi villages. Under the BSUP component of the JNNURM, 40 per cent of the assembled land was allocated for housing the poor and low-income segments. This was done based on a partnership between landowning farmers and the state government. After conversion of agricultural land for urban use, layout approval and plotted development, 60 per cent of the land was returned to the landowners. Internal and external infrastructure facilities in the designated area were provided by municipal authorities free of cost.

The Land Sharing Model in Vijayawada proved to be a win-win situation for both the landowners and the public authorities. Under the conventional LA, the farmers would have received an estimated compensation of ₹58.4 lakhs per acre. In the Land Sharing Model, farmers got a fully developed 1,800 square yards plot per acre of land. The value of the developed land, worked out by the Vijayawada Municipal Corporation, ranged between ₹5,000 to ₹10,000 per square yard. Thus, the farmers got ₹90 lakhs to ₹180 lakhs per acre in the model of 60:40 land sharing as against ₹58.4 lakhs per acre in traditional LA. In addition, they saved on land use conversion, registration, development and betterment charges and layout development as well as infrastructure connectivity costs. By resorting to conventional LA, the government would have spent ₹5,292 lakhs to compensate the farmers. However, the amount spent for infrastructure development on the farmers' share of land (60%) was only about ₹4,600 lakhs. This indicated a saving of ₹692 lakhs for the government through the Land Sharing Model (Mohanty 2014).

STRATEGY FOR INCLUSIVE URBANIZATION

Nearly 50 per cent of gross value added in non-agricultural activities originates from the informal sector. About 70 per cent of the urban workers are informally employed. More than 25 per cent of the urban population in India lives in informal settlements. However, the urban planning system in India has failed to provide space for dwelling, working and vending by the urban poor and LIGs. There are four key reasons as to why urban planning in India can be called exclusionary. First, the city master plans impose multiple controls on development based on the standards of developed countries. This has led to acute scarcity of land and built-space for the city as whole, adversely affecting all sections—not only the lower income groups. Second, the DCRs set unrealistic land development and housing norms, which the urban poor just cannot satisfy. For example, the draft Mumbai Metropolitan Regional Plan stipulates the minimum size of plot at 500 sq. m. Plots larger than 1,000 sq. m can be subdivided but subject to plot sizes not exceeding 200 sq. m each. These sizes are too large for sites and services, and affordable housing to lower income groups. Third, the master plans do not recognize slums and informal economic activities, largely carried out in non-conventional workplaces. This has led to frequent evictions of the urban poor from homes and workplaces in the name of plan enforcement and promoting 'world-class' city. Fourth, master planning has grossly neglected public transport by its very design; it accords primacy to land use and a subsidiary role to transport. This has severely restricted the mobility of the urban poor and their access to remunerative employment opportunities offered by globalizing urban economies.

While some inclusionary initiatives have been adopted by state governments in India, the shortage of affordable housing is so huge that only a multi-pronged approach can make a dent on the problem. This approach must include rental housing and ownership housing undertaken by beneficiaries, sites and services, and social housing implemented by public authorities, and IZ/IH led by private developers. While IZ programmes cannot be a panacea to the gigantic problem of housing the EWS and LIG in India, the experiences of developed countries suggest that they have a significant potential to secure land and housing for the lower income groups in market-led programmes. A key merit in such programmes is that they provide the poor access to employment opportunities as new developments occur. However, IZ programmes do not work in all housing markets; they need to be carefully designed, taking into account the market conditions. In this context, the model of IZ followed by Gujarat through the TPS is promising. The scheme is intrinsically valuable as it regards the landowners-farmers as partners with government in the process of inclusive, planned and self-financed urban development. This model needs to be propagated widely. Additionally, IH practices, backed by incentives to developers depending on the economic viability of projects, as followed internationally need to be explored.

Evidently, IZ is one of the few successful strategies available to local authorities around the world to accommodate the otherwise-excluded low-income communities in asset-rich and employment-generating localities. The poor need homes where developments occur and create a demand for their services. IZ facilitates their access to job opportunities and to quality services such as schools and hospitals. The construction of affordable housing through IZ, however, is not based on a concept of charity as many think. The developers must be required to mitigate the adverse 'impacts' of new development, including those pertaining to affordable housing without burdening the existing residents or the local authority. Moreover, they benefit from unearned increments due to spatial planning and infrastructure invest-ment made by public authorities, leading to buoyancy in the urban land and housing markets. Apart from these considerations, the developers are provided with zoning incentives to make IZ financially viable such as relaxation of planning norms and provision of density bonus. Such incentives are possible only when the urban planning model is flexible, not rigid as in India.

IZ can be promoted in India in three ways. The first is to provide for land reservation for socially and EWSs in TPSs as in Gujarat state, rooted in a value creation process. The second is to impose a modest IZ requirement within the existing zoning framework, where the devel-oper bears the cost of subsidizing to the extent of being compensated in the form of incentives and cost offsets. The third way is to link IZ with a strategy of 'up-zoning' of particular areas in order to gain from land value creation and capture. Imposing IZ within an existing state of zoning is a static view of urban planning. The main problem with such an approach is that the developer loses the motivation to bargain with the landowners to get land at a lesser rate as he or she is assured that his or her profit margin will not be cut and he or she will be compensated by government authorities. A more appropriate solution is to link IZ to favourable zoning changes in large parcels of land, accompanied by investment in public transport infrastructure and a strategy of TOD so as to recapture the gain in land value. In such cases, the IZ requirements could even be more than a customary range of 10–20 per cent. By linking IZ to value-enhancing rezoning and TOD, a better integra-tion of land use, transportation and affordable housing can be effected.

A dynamic urban planning approach would combine up-zoning and infrastructure development with IZ rather than imposing it with the existing state of zoning and then giving incentives to developers.

Inclusionary urbanization in India requires a larger policy shift in which developers are called upon to shoulder a part of the wider social repercussions of development. 'Beneficiaries pay', 'congesters pay', 'polluters pay', 'exacerbaters pay' and 'growth pays' are widely accepted principles internationally to address the adverse impacts of new development; India may not be an exception. However, planning and local authorities must address the hurdles that prevent developers from contributing a 'fair share' of affordable housing. This calls for removing the constraints in operation of land and housing markets with liberalization of density norms and FSI—a good example provided by Hyderabad. The problem of affordable housing in large cities has to be solved by the developers themselves rather than the government as developments in these cities have the ability to mitigate the adverse impacts they create. Agglomeration externalities in such cities lead to exorbitant increases in 'residual land values'. In smaller cities, the government needs to bear a part of the cost of providing houses to the urban poor at lower than the market rate. In reality, the private developers would bear a part of the burden of subsidizing EWS and LIG units, but not at the cost of 'normal' profits. They will meet the burden when compensated in the form of cost offsets and incentives, including connectivity infrastructure. This aspect needs to be kept in mind while considering the role of developers in inclusive urbanization. The approach to IZ needs to be rooted in a value creation, capture and recycling strategy that combines spatial planning, infrastructure development, land use zoning and customized incentives to developers to suit the local contexts. The 'design' of inclusionary programmes is important; blanket prescriptions will not work.

8

Financing Urban Development Plan
Benefit Taxation and Congestion Charging

FINANCING CHALLENGES OF CITIES

A conspicuous failure of urban planning in India is that while the master plans present a grand vision of city development, they narrowly focus on land use and development control regulations (DCRs) to realize the vision. They do not provide for robust instruments to finance core urban infrastructure facilities needed for economic growth, especially transportation. The result is an enormous backlog in the capital expenditure required by cities. According to the McKinsey Global Institute (2010), India needs to spend ₹9.74 million crores on cities by 2030, including ₹5.31 million crores for capital works. The largest demand for capital spending would come from affordable housing, followed by mass transit. If we exclude affordable housing, the capital expenditure needed by cities till 2030 would be ₹3.54 million crores. HPEC (2011) projects the requirement of cities over the period 2012–2031 at ₹5.92 million crores, excluding affordable housing. This includes ₹3.92 million crores towards capital expenditure. More than 70 per cent of the capital spending would be for the transportation sector, including roads, public transit and traffic management. Whether one adopts the McKinsey or the HPEC projections, there is no doubt that the investment needed to sustain the contribution of cities to India's economic growth is colossal. The only practical way to meet such needs is to resort to debt financing. However, robust mechanisms must be in place to repay the debt. Ironically, the total revenue of all ULBs in India in 2012–2013 stood at only ₹0.1 million crores. In most municipalities, the revenues mobilized are not even adequate to meet their staff expenses and pension liabilities. Indian cities lack a sound strategy to finance their development plans and projects.

Countries around the world have adopted a range of instruments to finance urban infrastructure during their development transition phases. These include:

- 'Own' revenue surplus of municipalities and local infrastructure entities;
- Dedicated user charges, benefit charges, fees, taxes, including benefit taxes and general taxes;
- Borrowings from financial institutions and capital market through various instruments, including revenue and general obligation bonds;
- Budget appropriations or capital grants from central and state governments;
- Partnerships between central, state and local governments through national schemes;
- Private sector participation and PPPs;
- Special purpose vehicles or off-budget agencies to finance, develop and operate infrastructure, adopting a mix of revenue instruments, including equity and debt; and
- Land-based financing tools, including taxes and charges, development financing instruments and value capture mechanisms.

While some Indian cities are exploring a combination of the aforementioned methods to finance infrastructure, mechanisms for sustained funding of planned urban development are yet to be firmly grounded. This calls for studying the principles of urban public finance and international practices in financing congestible local public goods to draw lessons to design a robust strategy.

The urban public finance literature highlights the following 'golden rules' to guide the choice of revenue instruments to finance particular types of public expenditures in cities, including infrastructure (Bahl and Linn 1992):

- Where the benefits of public services are measurable and accrue to readily identified individuals in a jurisdiction, user charges are the most appropriate financing instruments;
- Local public services such as administration, traffic control, street lighting and security, which are services to the general public in the sense that identification of beneficiaries and measurement of benefits and costs to individuals are difficult, are most appropriately financed by taxes on local residents;
- The cost of services, for which significant spillovers to neighbouring jurisdictions occur (e.g., health, education and welfare), should be financed substantially by state or national intergovernmental transfers; and
- Borrowing is an appropriate source to finance capital outlays on infrastructure projects, particularly public utilities, roads and transit, where investment requirements are large and benefits accrue to generations.

User charges are the first-best instruments to finance local public services; they act as market prices. Where charging is not feasible, benefit charges and earmarked benefit taxes levied on local residents are appropriate. They act as surrogate user charges. General taxes and intergovernmental transfers are necessary when user charges, benefit charges and benefit taxes are not adequate. Borrowing is the most desirable instrument for long gestation projects whose benefits spread over generations. This principle makes the earmarking of project-specific and general revenues of ULBs or infrastructure entities based on benefit taxation to service the debt obligations a key issue in urban public policy.

Cities constitute the tax bases of governments. Agglomeration and network externalities, spatial planning and local public goods are key factors that create unearned benefits in cities. Large cities in India are particularly subjected to exorbitant increases in land values. The owners of land at vantage locations reap windfalls, reflecting differential zoning, access to infrastructure and policies to spur local economic growth. Thus, benefits taxes, especially those linked to land rents, score high as tools of local public finance based on the 'equity' principle. Further, land being immobile, these taxes are 'first-best' instruments of public finance in terms of the 'efficiency' criterion. Similarly, congestion charging (CC) is a socially optimal way of mobilizing resources to augment the capacity of congested public facilities. It subscribes to the principle that those who create negative externalities for the society must pay towards the mitigation costs. However, benefit taxation and CC instruments are yet to be adopted by cities in India in a systematic way to finance congestible local public goods. This is perhaps due to a lack of appreciation of the key principles of economics in urban planning. In this background, the present chapter refers to theories of benefit taxation, including land-based financing and CC as well as their empirical applications. Theory is important as it contributes to conceptual clarity, consistency and coherence in policymaking. Practice matters as it conveys which policies work, and which do not.

This chapter is focused on the resource mobilization strategy to promote planned urban development in India. It recognizes that the context of fiscal federalism matters. But while recognizing the institutional constraints, the principles of public finance and lessons from land, transport and urban economics can guide the choice of appropriate instruments to implement urban development plans. We particularly refer to the paradigms of benefit taxation propagated by Wicksell (1964 [1896]) and Lindahl (1919), land value taxation advocated by Henry George (1879) and congestion charging articulated by Mohring and Harwitz (1962). These theories make a good sense for cities in developing countries like India which are faced with serious problems of free ridership in civic services, congestion and resistance from taxpayers to pay local taxes. Moreover, due to the pervasive externalities of cities, 'beneficiaries pay' and 'congesters pay' are the most legitimate instruments to finance congestible local public goods. The fundamental problem in local government is how to provide services matching the preferences of residents. This makes linking the benefits from civic services to local taxes a desirable strategy to promote accountability. We argue for earmarked benefit taxes, including land-based taxes, congestion charges and other hypothecated revenue sources to repay the debt incurred for implementing urban infrastructure projects such as arterial and radial roads, mass rapid transit (MRT) and high-speed rail (HSR).

THE GENERALIZED BENEFIT PRINCIPLE

Urban economics and new economic geography (NEG) suggest that when external economies are vibrant in cities, value capture instruments present an opportunity for self-financed or even a surplus-generating process of urban development. Resulting from the collocation of firms, households and institutions, agglomeration and network externalities lead to enhanced productivity. They reduce the costs of transporting goods, people, ideas, information and knowledge (Duranton and Puga 2004; Glaeser 2008a, 2011; Jacobs 1969, 1984; Lucas 1988; Marshall 1890; Puga 2010; Rosenthal and Strange 2004). Further, they create unearned 'land rents' and 'agglomeration rents' that can be captured and recycled to finance urban infrastructure. A recent body of research in NEG suggests that agglomeration rents accrue not only to immobile factors such as land but also mobile factors such as skilled labour and capital. These can be taxed without the tax base disappearing (Anderson and Forslid 2003; Baldwin and Krugman 2004; Borck and Pfluger 2006; Ludema and Wooton 2000). Stiglitz (2012) also refers to other forms of rents, including monopoly rents. Thus, municipalities can make the beneficiaries of rents pay for investments that benefit them disproportionately. As a corollary, those causing 'disbenefits' or negative externalities in the urban economy must pay for their mitigation.

The externalities of cities are linked to market forces and public policies such as land use zoning and infrastructure development. Spatial planning and investment in core urban infrastructure facilities lead to direct, indirect and induced effects. The definition of benefits in the urban context thus goes far beyond those accruing to the direct users of services. Transport economists also argue that major UT projects lead to significant benefits because of agglomeration externalities. However, the externalities of cities also result in negative consequences when exceeding a certain threshold. Agglomeration diseconomies manifest in overcrowding, congestion in infrastructure networks, pollution, environmental degradation and increased vulnerability to disasters. They call for externality-correcting mechanisms, including capacity augmentation in infrastructure and CC. But actions by governments through decongestion programmes also result in benefits to locations. Thus, a city's development process is marked by differential benefits to actors in the spatial economy, carving out a case for benefit taxation. This paradigm logically embraces the 'users pay', 'beneficiaries pay', 'polluters play', 'exacerbaters pay', 'congesters pay' and 'growth pay' principles. We pool these together under the broad caption of the 'generalized benefit principle' and regard it as the cornerstone of urban public finance in developing countries like India.

The generalized benefit principle is central to the design of a sound municipal finance system in a developing country for a number of reasons. First, by establishing a close link between expenditures and revenues, it facilitates the accountability of municipalities in service delivery. Second, the principle acts against taxpayers' resistance, increasingly becoming common as people care about how their 'own' money translates into benefits for them and their city. Third, it emphasizes that while, as a first resort, the services provided by local governments should be paid for by users, beneficiaries gaining indirectly due to externalities must also contribute to urban development. Fourth, worthwhile projects that pass the benefit–cost test should be in a position to generate adequate values to finance them. Thus, in a way, the generalized benefit principle guarantees the availability of adequate resources to facilitate debt financing of local public goods.

THE WICKSELLIAN CONNECTION

Knut Wicksell, in his theory of 'just taxation', articulated the view that taxes for public programmes should be mobilized from those who benefit from them. His idea contradicts the mainstream public finance view that there is no quid pro quo in taxation as it falls under the sovereign powers of the state. Wicksell's concept was extended by Erik Lindahl to what has come to be known as 'Lindahl pricing'. This mechanism suggests that individuals benefitting from a public service should pay according to the marginal benefits received. While the theoretical formulations of Wicksell and Lindahl are criticized by mainstream public finance theorists, the merits of linking expenditures to revenues are increasingly being recognized in the literature of local public finance and governance. If the aim of public policy is to ensure that the local government functions efficiently, it is important to establish as clear a linkage between expenditure and revenue decisions as possible—what Breton (1996) calls the 'Wicksellian Connection'. The benefit principle, in the sense of tax–service linkage, is the hallmark of good local governance. It makes a strong case for matching local expenditure responsibilities with revenue resources, revenue capacities with political accountability and benefit areas with financing areas (Bird and Slack 2015).

The 'Wicksellian Connection' provides guidance for reforming the system of financing cities in developing countries like India. Researchers in urban public finance have advocated the following methods to apply the concept:

- Municipalities should charge for services as far as possible. When services are measurable and beneficiaries identified, they should be paid for by direct user charges.
- Where municipal services are characterized by problems of measurement and/or identification of beneficiaries, specific and generic benefit taxes are appropriate sources of financing.
- Municipal property tax may be treated as a surrogate user charge aimed at recovering the costs of collective civic services;
- Property tax burden should be lower for non-residents; relatively high tax rates may be applied to properties that benefit from vibrancy in the urban economy;
- Local payroll and goods and services taxes can be used to tax non-residents who benefit from civic services.
- As land is immobile and the value of urban land increases due to investment in planned infrastructure development, land value tax (LVT) and land value increment tax (LVIT) are ideal instruments to recoup the cost of such development.
- Dedicated benefit taxes such as motor vehicle tax, motor fuel tax, transport tax and special assessments in transit-impact zones are appropriate for financing public transportation infrastructure.
- Property, sales, goods and services, excise and income taxes can be regarded as benefit taxes for working, living and transacting in the city.

The 'Wicksellian Connection' makes a strong case for 'earmarking' user charges, benefit charges and benefit taxes to raise seed money for debt financing of urban infrastructure. The concept, powered by the merits of land taxation and CC, has the potential for not only mobilizing adequate resources but also enforcing accountability and transparency in local government.

Nobel laureate Buchanan (1963) considers 'earmarking' as a first-best operational way to address the fundamental normative problem of public economics: providing services to match peoples' preferences while recovering the costs. Earmarking introduces market prices into the budgeting process and facilitates rational choice by taxpayers. The efficacy of earmarking, however, depends on the following conditions:

- Expenditure specificity: Expenditures to be financed by earmarked revenues are well defined and specific in that taxpayers can identify their obvious benefits;
- Tight earmarking: The linkage between earmarked revenues and expenditures is tight at the margin; and
- Strong benefit linkage: Revenues are in the form of direct user charges such as payments for services and indirect user charges such as specific benefit taxes for infrastructure.

The case for earmarking to finance core urban infrastructure in India is justified for at least two reasons. First, such infrastructure, especially public transportation, has been neglected for decades and this has serious adverse implications for economic growth. In the absence of dedicated funding, there is little chance that MRT and HSR would receive the attention they deserve from policymakers. Second, cities generate enormous values to immobile and quasi-immobile factors, especially urban land, disproportionately benefiting some lucky agents in the economy. This makes 'value creation, capture and recycling' an elegant strategy to finance city development plans (CDPs) by earmarking value increments to leverage debt financing.

The value creation process in cities is a result of the operation of not only market forces but also public policies. Such policies relate to spatial planning, developing core infrastructure, channelizing local economic development to particular locations, densifying growth centres, decongesting over-crowded areas, renewing derelict localities, improving services and inducing economic growth. In fact, the experience of developing countries suggests that the market value of rural land adjacent to a metropolitan city can rise by more than 10–20 times if such land is simply included in the master plan. Factors such as conversion of agricultural land to urban use, institution of zoning, change of land use, assignment of development rights through instruments such as floor space index (FSI)/floor area ratio (FAR), transferable development rights (TDRs), density bonus, and investments in highways and public transit lead to agglomeration and network externalities. Such externalities translate into windfall gains to owners of properties at particular locations. Increased capacity in the infrastructure systems leads to enhanced serviceability and accessibility of locations, leading to 'location rents', 'accessibility premiums' and wider economic benefits (WEBs).

Apart from plans and projects, regulatory policy and taxation regimes also cause differential benefits to locations in cities. CC strategies contribute to rejuvenation of decaying central areas by revitalizing agglomeration economies and augmenting business prospects. The beneficiaries of decongestion programmes should, therefore, pay for their costs based on the generalized benefit principle. If a part of the windfall gains due to planned urban development and redevelopment projects is escrowed to repay the debt incurred to finance them, a self-sustained process of planned urban development could be set in motion. Benefit taxation instruments, including land-based taxes, fuel tax, transport tax and CC tools, are ideal sources to finance CDPs. The master plans of cities in India in the past have hardly discussed the relevance of these instruments in internalizing the externalities of cities while raising revenues for financing their development proposals. This is due to the neglect of economic theory and lack of appreciation of international practices, especially those relating to land taxation and CC.

URBAN LAND TAXATION: THEORY

Adam Smith attributed land rent to the good government of the state and regarded it as a 'proper' subject of taxation.

> Both ground-rents and the ordinary rent of land are a species of revenue which the owner, in many cases, enjoys without any care or attention of his own.... Ground-rents and the ordinary rent of land, are therefore, perhaps, the species of revenue which can best bear to have a peculiar tax imposed upon them.
>
> Nothing can be more reasonable than that a fund which owes its existence to the good government of the state should be taxed peculiarly, or should contribute something more than the greater part of other

funds, towards the support of that government. (1976 [1776], Book V, Chapter II, Part II, Article 1, 843–844)

Smith presented the case for taxation of land rents based on three key principles as follows:

1. *Efficiency:* Taxes on land rents are non-distortionary and neutral in terms of effects on resource allocation and productive behaviour. As land is immobile, the incidence of land tax falls on the landowner, and not on development.
2. *Equity:* It is just to tax away surpluses that arise more due to extraneous factors such as progress of society, community effort or social enterprise than due to individual endeavour. Land tax aims at recouping a part of the unearned benefits accruing to the landowners from public investments. The tax is progressive in that only households who own land pay any tax at all. Those owning more valuable lands pay more.
3. *Benefit:* People should pay for government actions which benefit them. Spatial planning and infrastructure development in cities lead to a significant transfer of wealth from a large number of taxpayers to a small number of property owners who gain disproportionately from increased land values.

The logic for taxing land rents advanced by Adam Smith was extended by Henry George in his *Progress and Poverty* (1879). George declared that the value of undeveloped land was unearned. It did not owe to any initiative or sacrifice by the landowner; it rather arose from the demand for a fixed supply of land whose value went up due to public expenditures. Thus, if land were taxed more heavily, it would not affect productive behaviour. The extent of land available would also not decrease; nor would the demand for land decline because of land's productive use. George further argued that landlords had no moral right to claim land values, land rents or land value increments which resulted from the progress of society. His view was that as public investments capitalized into location values, the economic rent to land was the most appropriate form of public finance. Apart from presenting a case for land tax based on equity, efficiency and benefit considerations, George also argued that such a tax would generate adequate revenues to meet the public expenditures needed. He propagated 'the single tax movement', stating that a 100 per cent tax on the annual rental value (ARV) of land was warranted. This has led to the Henry George Theorem (HGT), which states that under certain assumptions, the beneficial effects of expenditures on a public good translate into adequate land rents to finance such expenditures. A version of HGT is presented in a simple mathematical model as follows (Arnott and Stiglitz 1979; Atkinson and Stiglitz 1980; Stiglitz 1977; Wellisch 2004).

Consider a competitive economy producing and consuming a private good X and a public good G. Each individual consumes the same amount of private good equal to x. Land rents are equally distributed between all individuals. We describe the economy as follows:

$$\text{Private Good Production Function: } Y=f(N) \tag{1}$$

where $Y=$Output of private good and $N=$Population or labour force

$$\frac{\partial Y}{\partial N} = f'(N) = \text{Marginal product of labour} \tag{2}$$

$$\text{Endowment Constraint: } Y=f(N)=xN+G \tag{3}$$

where $x=$Consumption of private good and $G=$Consumption of public good.

$$\text{Utility Function of the Representative Individual: } U=U(x, G) \tag{4}$$

The welfare maximization problem of the society is: Maximize $U=U(x, G)$ subject to $f(N)=xN+G$. Combining (1), (3) and (4), this exercise can be reduced to the following unconstrained maximization problem:

$$\text{Maximize } U = U\left(\frac{f(N)-G}{N}, G\right) \tag{5}$$

The first-order conditions for utility maximization are:

$$\frac{\partial U}{\partial x}\left[Nf'(N) - f(N)+G\right]\frac{1}{N^2} = 0 \text{ or } G = f(N) - Nf'(N) \tag{6}$$

$$\frac{\partial U}{\partial x}\left(-\frac{1}{N}\right)+\frac{\partial U}{\partial G}=0 \text{ or } \frac{\partial U}{\partial x}=N\frac{\partial U}{\partial G} \tag{7}$$

Figure 8.1 depicts the determination of the socially optimal level of the public good at G^*.

Condition (7) depicts the Samuelsonian rule for efficient provision of public good. The marginal product of labour under competitive conditions will be equal to real wage so that wage payment $=Nf'(N)$. Thus, condition (6) implies that the optimal level of public good equals the aggregate land rents (total production – wage payment), the HGT. This result is, of course, dependent on the oversimplistic assumptions of the model presented. However, it highlights the spirit of the argument that 'residual' land rents in cities could generate a substantial amount of revenues to finance local public goods.

CONGESTION CHARGING: THEORY

Mohring–Harwitz Theorem (MHT) in transport economics suggests that under certain conditions, an optimally designed and priced public infrastructure facility such as a highway should, in principle, be self-financing (Mohring 1972, 1976; Mohring and Harwitz 1962). Thus,

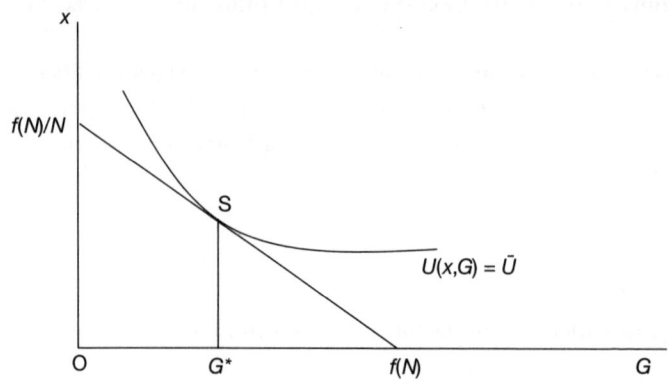

Figure 8.1 *Henry George Theorem: Utility Maximization*

there will be no need for subsidy. A simple version of the theorem is presented in the following mathematical model.

Consider a congestible public good, say a highway, with the number of users $= x$ and capacity $= c$ so that a measure of capacity utilization $= \dfrac{x}{c}$. Let the cost of congestion in the public facility to an individual user or the private trip cost (PTC) be represented by:

$$g = g\left(\frac{x}{c}\right) \tag{8}$$

where $g'\left(\dfrac{x}{c}\right) > 0$ due to congestion externalities.

Aggregate congestion cost $= xg\left(\dfrac{x}{c}\right)$ and therefore the marginal social cost of highway travel or the social trip cost (STC) with no change in capacity $= g\left(\dfrac{x}{c}\right) + \dfrac{x}{c}\, g'\left(\dfrac{x}{c}\right)$. This expression suggests that the STC curve will lie above the PTC curve as $g'\left(\dfrac{x}{c}\right) > 0$.

Figure 8.2 shows the PTC and STC as upward-sloping functions of trips. Private travel demand, as a function of PTC, is downward-sloping, showing that the number of trips falls as PTC increases. T_p is the equilibrium number of trips which will occur under free market conditions, determined by the intersection of the PTC curve and the travel demand curve. T_S is the socially optimal number of trips, determined where the STC curve intersects the travel demand curve. As $T_S < T_p$, a Pigovian congestion toll equal to SR will be needed to reach the socially optimal outcome T_S and eliminate the dead weight loss equal to the Harberger's triangle ASB.

Let K be the construction cost per unit of capacity. We assume for simplicity that the total construction cost $= cK$. The total cost to the society $=$ aggregate highway construction cost $+$ aggregate congestion cost:

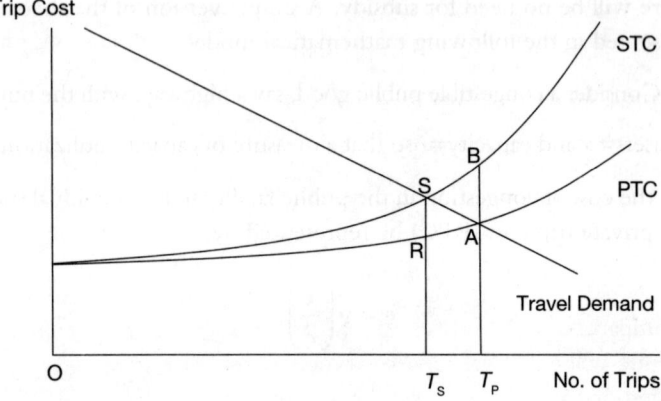

Figure 8.2. *Congestion Pricing Model*

$$C = cK + xg\left(\frac{x}{c}\right) \tag{9}$$

where C = Total social cost

The society's optimization problem can be stated as finding the capacity c that minimizes the total cost C. The first-order condition for optimization is:

$$\frac{\partial C}{\partial c} = K - \left(\frac{x^2}{c^2}\right)g'\left(\frac{x}{c}\right) = 0 \text{ or}$$

$$cK = \text{Construction cost} = \left(\frac{x^2}{c}\right)g'\left(\frac{x}{c}\right) \tag{10}$$

Consider now the congestion pricing of the highway once the optimal capacity has been installed. Each additional road user increases every other user's congestion cost by $\dfrac{\partial g}{\partial x} = \left(\dfrac{1}{c}\right)g'\left(\dfrac{x}{c}\right)$. As there are x number of users who suffer this externality damage, each user will be required to pay a Pigovian toll equal to $x\left(\dfrac{1}{c}\right)g'\left(\dfrac{x}{c}\right)$ when a congestion pricing scheme is adopted. As the total number of persons paying this congestion toll is x, the total revenue from congestion charge will be equal to:

$$R = x\left(\dfrac{x}{c}\right)g'\left(\dfrac{x}{c}\right) = \left(\dfrac{x^2}{c}\right)g'\left(\dfrac{x}{c}\right) \qquad (11)$$

A comparison of (10) and (11) reveals that the aggregate congestion toll revenue will equal the total construction cost of highway. Thus, the congestion pricing breaks even. This result—the MHT—is one of the arguments put forward by transport economists in favour of the CC scheme adopted by cities such as Singapore, London and Stockholm.

The results from the MHT are subject to the simplified assumptions of the model presented. However, it amply highlights the economic case for CC and that such charges can generate sufficient resources to finance congestible public goods. What is needed is the political will to levy such charges—directly or through surrogate instruments such as motor vehicles tax and fuel tax.

A MODIFIED HENRY GEORGE THEOREM

We now combine the HGT and the MHT into a single model following Wellisch (2004, 93). Let us consider N identical households evenly spread over a city having a fixed land area equal to T. Each household is assumed to derive utility from consumption of a private good X, housing H and a congestible local public good Z. The consumption good is assumed to be the numeraire, that is, with price equal to unity. Housing is produced by land only, and each unit of land translates into one unit of housing. We also assume that the rent to land is distributed equally among all the households, meeting their cost of housing. The utility function of the representative individual, subject to standard neoclassical assumptions, is expressed as:

$$U = U(x, h, z) \qquad (12)$$

where x, h and z represent the consumption of good X, H and Z, respectively.

We further assume that each household has an income w, spent on the private good X and public good Z.

Let the cost of the congestible local public good Z be represented by the function:

$$C = C(Z, N) \qquad C_Z > 0, \ C_N > 0 \qquad (13)$$

where Z=production of public good, N=population and C is increasing in Z and N.

The endowment conditions for the society are simply stated as:

$$Nw = Nx + C(Z, N) \qquad (14)$$

$$T = Nh \qquad (15)$$

In (14), we assume that the city is self-sufficient. Condition (15) reflects our simplified assumption regarding housing; the demand for housing is equal to the city's land area.

The society's optimization problem can simply be stated as follows:

$$\text{Maximize } U = U(x, h, z) \text{ subject to}$$
$$Nw = Nx + C(Z, N) \text{ and } T = Nh \qquad (16)$$

Forming the Lagrangean $L = U(x, h, z) + \lambda[Nw - Nx - C(Z, N)] + \mu(T - Nh)$, the first-order conditions for optimization yield the following results:

$$\frac{\partial U}{\partial x} = \lambda N \text{ or } U_x = \lambda N \qquad (17)$$

$$\frac{\partial U}{\partial h} = \mu N \text{ or } U_h = \mu N \qquad (18)$$

$$\frac{\partial U}{\partial Z} = \lambda \frac{\partial C}{\partial Z} \text{ or } U_Z = \lambda C_Z \qquad (19)$$

$$\frac{\partial L}{\partial N} = 0 \text{ implying } \lambda(w - x - C_N) = \mu h \tag{20}$$

Dividing (19) by (17), we have the Samuelsonian condition for efficient supply of the local public good:

$$N\frac{U_z}{U_x} = C_Z \tag{21}$$

From (17) and (18), we get $\dfrac{\mu}{\lambda} = \dfrac{U_h}{U_x}$. Applying this result in (20), we have

$$w - x - C_N = \frac{U_h}{U_x} h \tag{22}$$

Combining (14), (15) and (22),

$$C(Z,N) = Nw - Nx = \frac{U_h}{U_x} Nh + NC_N$$

$$= \frac{U_h}{U_x} T + NC_N = R + NC_N \tag{23}$$

In (23), we have R equal to the aggregate land rent as $\dfrac{U_h}{U_x}$ is the marginal rate of substitution between housing/land and private good, which equals the relative price ratio in equilibrium, that is, rent to land as the private good has unity price. NC_N is equal to total revenue from a Pigovian congestion toll.

Equation (23) shows that the cost of the congestible public good at the social optimum equals land rents plus Pigovian congestion toll. This result can be called the modified HGT which also takes into account the MHT. It may be noted when there is no congestion, that is, $C_N = 0$, the original Henry George result holds. Equation (23) can be rewritten as:

$$\frac{C(Z,N)}{N} = \frac{R}{N} + C_N \qquad (24)$$

The left-hand side in (24) shows the reduction in the cost of public good when a new individual is added to the city. We assume that the new entrant bears an equal share of the cost of public good. The right-hand side reflects the increase in cost that the new entrant to the city imposes on the existing residents. This is divided into two parts. First, as the entire land rent in the city is assumed to be divided equally among all the residents, the share of all the existing residents in the city falls by the average aggregate land rent. Second, the cost of providing a given amount of public good increases the marginal congestion cost due to the additional demand placed on the public facility by the new individual.

The modified HGT as presented does not consider the agglomeration externalities in cities. However, the result (24) is generic; it states that an optimal city size or population results when the marginal benefits and the marginal costs associated with an increase in population are balanced. It also reveals that land rent taxation and CC are highly desirable instruments to finance congestible local public goods. Rents in cities arise due to externalities, spatial planning, public investment in infrastructure and other factors. They include not only land rent but also other kinds of rents such as 'agglomeration rent' and 'monopoly rent'. As the externalities in cities of developing countries tend to be large when they upgrade from primary to secondary and knowledge-based services, these cities should, in principle, be generating a large quantum of rents. Thus, when the taxation of various types of rents is combined with congestion charges, these cities should be in a position to generate substantial revenues to support debt financing of infrastructure. Depending on the nature of benefits and costs, a system of local taxation and charging can thus be put in place based on the benefit principle to ensure that there is no shortfall in spending. Unfortunately, the paradigms of benefit taxation and CC have not engaged the attention of urban policymakers in India. Such tools need to be adopted and suitably designed by Indian cities, taking into account international experience and their existing contexts.

URBAN LAND TAXATION: PRACTICE

The practice of urban land taxation in all countries is embroiled in long debates, vehement discussions and vested interests. Sir Winston Churchill made the following arguments in support of land value increment taxes during the debate in British Parliament over the 1909 People's Budget:

> ... the landlord who happens to own a plot of land on the outskirts or at the centre of one of our great cities ... watches the busy population around him making the city larger, richer, more convenient, more famous every day, and all the while sits still and does nothing. Roads are made, streets are made, railway services are improved, electric light turns night into day,... water is brought from reservoirs a hundred miles off in the mountains—and all the while the landlord sits still. Every one of those improvements is effected by the labour and at the cost of other people. Many of the most important are effected at the cost of the municipality and of the ratepayers. To not one of those improvements does the land monopolist as a land monopolist contribute, and yet by every one of them the value of his land is sensibly enhanced. He renders no service to the community, he contributes nothing to the general welfare; he contributes nothing even to the process from which his own enrichment is derived....

> At last the land becomes ripe for sale—that means that the price is too tempting to be resisted any longer—and then, not till then, it is sold by the yard or by the inch at ten times, or twenty times, or even fifty times, its agricultural value....

> In fact, you may say that ... the unearned increment on the land is reaped by the land monopolist in exact proportion, not to the service, but to the disservice done. (Speech made to the British House of Commons on 4 May 1909, www.andywightman.com/docs/churchill. pdf, accessed 24 August 2018)

The key points in Churchill's arguments are reiterated in country after country over the course of history.

The Report of the National Commission on Urban Problems 1969 in the United States made the following observations:

> The owners of the land can go to Hawaii and rest languidly on the beaches or make prolonged safaris into the inmost regions of Africa.

They may study Shakespearean literature at Stratford–upon–Avon or Zen Buddhism in Japan or ponder urban problems in Washington. They can go up in space capsules or down a hole in the ground. They will become richer and richer without trial or sweat. For as Dr Johnson once remarked in another connection here are 'riches beyond the dreams of avarice'. (National Commission on Urban Problem 1969, 396)

The Committee on Urban Land Policy in India, appointed by the then MoH, GoI, observed in their report of 1965 as follows:

While discussing the various measures for tackling the problems in the developed and undeveloped urban land we had stated that unearned increases in urban land and property values being in the nature of 'social surpluses' must be mopped up for the benefit of the society as a whole. After all development in and around a town takes place as a result of Government and municipal development activities and there is no reason why the huge profits should be allowed to be digested by speculators and profiteers.... The Third Five Year Plan also recommends the mopping up of unearned increases in urban land and property values as a measure to combat speculation and also as a measure to achieve social and economic equity. We also unreservedly endorse this idea. (MoH, GoI, 1965)

The Vancouver Action Plan of the United Nations Conference on Human Settlements 1976 contained the following statement.

The unearned increment resulting from the rise in land values resulting from change in use of land, from public investment decision, or due to the general growth of the community must be subject to appropriate recapture by public bodies (the community). (United Nations 1976, Recommendation D.3)

The observations in policy documents around the world suggest that Henry George was a visionary who distinguished between the returns to labour and capital, which are earned and the returns to land, which are unearned. George, of course, did not visualize the kind of effects that planned urban development could usher in for the landowners due to the externalities of cities capitalizing into land rents, site values, agglomeration rents and monopoly rents. However, he implicitly recognized the paradigms of 'beneficiaries pay' and 'value capture financing'. Thus, George laid the foundation for a system of benefit taxation in cities linked to public policies such as spatial planning and infrastructure development. In fact, the modern argument for taxation of urban land to finance planned urban development makes George even more relevant to countries like India today. A strong case for the taxation of urban land value arises when land is considered as not only an input but also an output in the process of planned urban development. A tax on urban land promotes density and agglomeration economies. It acts against sprawl and uneconomic extension of costly infrastructure to city boundaries. A compact city also minimizes the use of non-renewable resources, including energy. It positively contributes to energy security and climate change agenda. Urban land taxation also promotes housing and productive use of land for commercial, industrial, institutional and other purposes. It discourages the investment of scarce capital in idle land assets for speculative gains. Further, by bringing brownfield sites to appropriate uses, it eases pressure on green belts, forests and conservation areas. Thus, an urban land tax is considered a 'green tax', contributing to the objectives of sustainable development.

Why is that the Henry George tax, in spite of its strong theoretical merits, so neglected in developing countries like India? Apart from political economic factors, a key reason for this is the obsession of master planners with the physical dimensions of urban land, ignoring its role as a resource. The master plans in the past have hardly discussed the financial implications of spatial planning, infrastructure development and urban externalities for factors such as land use, FSI and density. The urban planning process in India has neglected the concept of benefit taxation, including land-based revenue instruments. The master plans searched for plan financing outside the framework of urban planning.

Internationally, land-based instruments of financing CDPs and projects fall into three groups as follows:

1. *Land-based taxes:* These are levied under the sovereign powers of the state, generally exercised through ULBs. They include property tax, stamp duty/property registration tax, LVT, site value rating (SVR), LVIT, vacant land tax (VLT), land use conversion tax, tax on planning gain, tax on development gain, etc.

2. *Development financing tools:* These are upfront payments in connection with development of land undertaken by private developers with permission from the local authority. They include developer exactions, development charges, external development charges (EDCs), development impact fees (DIFs), planning obligations, development contributions, town planning schemes (TPSs), etc. They subscribe to 'growth pays', 'polluters pay' and 'exacerbaters pay' principles.

3. *Land Value Capture (LVC) instruments:* These are post-development levies meant to capture the increments in land values due to spatial planning, infrastructure development and other factors. These include LVT, LVIT, sale of developer land, lease/sale of extra project land/excess condemnation, lease/sale of development rights, monetization of land assets, joint development mechanism (JDM), special assessment district, business improvement district, betterment charges, tax increment financing (TIF), etc.

Table 8.1 presents the key instruments of land-based taxes and charges followed by countries internationally, indicating where they are practised, to guide cities in India in the design of their DP financing strategies.

CONGESTION CHARGING: PRACTICE

CC is based on 'congesters pay' principle. It usually takes the form of a surcharge on motorized private travel along designated congested roads, aimed at curbing travel demand, combating air pollution and mobilizing revenues to finance public transport (PT). Congestion charges have been effective in reducing traffic volume, travel time, travel time variability, vehicle kilometres travelled and emission of air pollutants such as carbon dioxide. The cases of Singapore, London and Stockholm, which present prime examples of the innovative application of congestion pricing are presented in the following text (International Council on Clean Transportation 2010; Mohanty 2016; Wang et al. 2017).

Singapore

The population of Singapore was 5.47 million in 2015, with about 45 per cent of households owning cars. From 1975 onwards, the city state has

Table 8.1 *A Toolbox of Land-based Instruments*

S. No.	Revenue Instrument	Description	Where Practised
A. Land-based Taxes			
1.	Property Tax	Imposed on both land and buildings based on capital value, rental value or unit area method (UAM). The trend is to shift to a capital value base to exploit the ongoing increases in property values.	All over the world. Most cities in India follow the unit area-based property tax linked to location, plinth area and use of building
2.	Stamp Duty/ Property Registration Tax	Paid by buyer/seller (buyer in India) on any transfer of registered property title or other property rights to another party.	All over the world. In India, the buyer pays the tax. In some cities like New York, the tax is shared between the buyer and seller
3.	LVT	Based on the capital value of land or specific characteristics/parameters of land.	Taiwan, Australia, Denmark
4.	LVIT	Based on increases in land values between two dates.	Taiwan, Germany, Denmark, South Korea, Latin America
5.	Land Gains Tax (LGT)	Gains in land value when land is held beyond a certain period—paid by seller of land, in addition to capital gains income tax. The tax applies only to gains attributed to land, not buildings.	United States (Vermont State), Canada (Toronto)
6.	VLT	Based on capital value of land held idle beyond a pre-specified period—generally at a rate higher than that applied to built-up property.	Latin American Countries, Taiwan, South Korea, Andhra Pradesh, Telangana

(Continued)

Table 8.1 (*Continued*)

S. No.	Revenue Instrument	Description	Where Practised
7.	Real Property Gains Tax	Chargeable on gains arising from disposal of real property or of interest, options or other rights in or over land as well as the disposal of shares in real property companies.	Malaysia
B. Development Financing Tools			
1.	Developer Extractions	Based on land use regulations to make land developer or builder contribute towards on- and off-site infrastructure works warranted by new development—through negotiation.	United States, Canada, Shanghai, Thailand (Bangkok)
2.	Development Charges	Charges collected by local planning authorities under law while granting permission for development. These include internal (on-site) and external (off-site) development charges.	India (EDC—HUDA)
3.	DIFs	Charges under law on new development to pay for impact—towards the cost of a broad range new infrastructure or expansion of old infrastructure facilities, especially those located outside the boundaries of such development (off-site), but are required to serve the new development.	United States. The city of Hyderabad in India levies impact fee, but the instrument is yet to be adopted by other cities

4.	Planning Obligations	Covers the installation of infrastructure, financial or in-kind contributions, or provision of affordable housing based on negotiation between developer and local authority as condition of planning permission under the town planning law.	United Kingdom
5.	Development Contributions	Local authorities collect development contributions from developers towards shared local and regional infrastructure facilities as conditions of permission for development or rezoning.	Australia
6.	Land Readjustment/ Land Pooling	Based on pooling or sharing of land—in-kind instrument; farmers/landowners are partners in planned urban expansion, sharing costs and benefits.	South Korea, Taiwan, Japan, Latin America, Gujarat, Andhra Pradesh (new capital at Amaravati)
C. LVC Methods			
1.	Sale of Developer's Land	Real estate developers install internal and external infrastructure in layouts and recover costs of through sale of land or housing.	Developed countries, India
2.	Lease or Sale of Extra Project Land/Excess Condemnation	Lease or sale of land in vicinity of major public infrastructure facilities such as highways and mass transit after development; often accompanied by rezoning, value-adding land use and enhanced development rights.	Hong Kong, France, Australia.
3.	Lease/Sale of Development Rights	Lease or sale of FSI/additional zoning/land use/ development rights than normally permitted.	Brazil, India (Karnataka State—Bengaluru Metro)

(Continued)

Table 8.1 (*Continued*)

S. No.	Revenue Instrument	Description	Where Practised
4.	TDRs	Transfer of development right from one zone of a city to another zone subject to fulfilling the master plan requirements.	United States, Brazil, India (Mumbai, Hyderabad)
5.	Monetization of Land Assets	Selling or leasing some of the publicly owned unused or underused lands with rezoning and enhanced property values.	India (Mumbai), Egypt (Cairo), Turkey (Istanbul), South Africa (Cape Town)
6.	JDM	A form of partnership between a public authority and a private developer to build a real estate project on land owned or controlled by a public authority.	Japan
7.	Special Assessment District	Local governments set geographical boundaries within which differential taxes are imposed on land and property whose values are expected to increase due to new infrastructure and spatial planning.	United States, Canada, Europe
8.	Betterment Taxes and Charges	Charges based on land value increments due to infrastructure development and spatial planning in a designated benefit area or citywide.	Latin America (Colombia: Bogota), Argentina, India (Hyderabad)
9.	Value/TIF	Public authorities earmarking the whole or a part of the revenue increments arising from a value-creating venture executed over a designated geographical area to service the debt incurred.	United States, Australia

Source: Mohanty (2016) and University of Hyderabad–HSMI (2017).

been implementing a series of innovative initiatives to curb traffic congestion by raising the cost of vehicle ownership and use. These include area licensing scheme (ALS), vehicle quota system, certificate of entitlement, park and ride, weekend car and off-peak hour road pricing, electronic road pricing (ERP), free pre-peak travel on mass rapid transport and complementary measures such as transport–land use integration, higher vehicle and parking taxes and public transit improvement. The proliferation of private vehicles is discouraged through a vehicle quota system that employs an open bidding process for certificates of entitlement to own a vehicle. This is combined with high initial registration cost (around 150% of the vehicle's market value). There is also an annual road tax that increases with engine capacity, and a surcharge on older vehicles. The city imposes higher parking fees in areas with a high concentration of vehicles.

Singapore introduced the ALS for vehicles entering the central zone in 1975. The scheme provided for cordon pricing by time of day and vehicle class via a manual paper permit system. This was replaced by a fully automated ERP from 1998. The funds secured through congestion charges are dedicated for public transportation improvements. The traffic volume in Singapore reduced by 44 per cent after the adoption of ALS, and 10–15 per cent compared to ALS after the introduction of ERP.

Greater London

The population of Greater London was 8.54 million in 2014, with population density of 5,432 persons per sq. km. The share of various modes of transport in London was: 45 per cent public transport, 32 per cent private transport, 2 per cent cycling and 21 per cent walking. Car ownership ratio was 329 cars per 1,000 persons in 2015. London initiated CC scheme in 2003. The charging zone included 21 sq. km inside the Inner Ring Road of Central London in 2015. The charging period is between 7.00 AM and 6.00 PM from Monday to Friday, excluding other time intervals in the day, holidays and certain periods. All motor vehicles entering the CC zone are subject to the congestion charge, with some exceptions. The daily charge, which was £5/day in 2003 increased to £8/day in 2005 and £11.50/day in 2014. Net revenue from congestion charge is required to be reinvested in PT by law. Eighty per cent of the same is used for transit and

20 per cent for other transportation improvements in Greater London area. Automated number plate recognition (ANPR) system is used to track payment compliance and identify violators.

The share of journeys by PT across London increased from 37 per cent in 2003 to 45 per cent in 2015 due to CC; that of private transport dropped from 41 per cent to 32 per cent. Carbon dioxide emissions decreased by 15–20 per cent by 2008. Congestion charge revenue has emerged as an important source of financing public transit investment, non-motorized transport (NMT) and transport demand management (TDM) in London.

Stockholm

Stockholm started CC from 2006 based on cordon pricing by time of the day. The charge ranged from 10 SEK to 20 SEK (about US$1.50 to US$3.0) per crossing of delineated cordon line into and out of city centre with a daily maximum of 60 SEK. It applied to 34 sq. km of area. Implementation was initially based on detecting vehicles with a combination of automatic licence plate recognition and transponders. The system has since shifted to cameras, which automatically detect the licence plates. The scheme has led to an annual travel time saving of 600 million SEK (US$85 million) apart from other benefits.

CC as practised in Singapore, London and Stockholm is not only theoretically elegant but also environmentally beneficial. The principle could be applied in metropolitan cities of developing countries like India, with a mix of taxes, charges and spatial planning instruments. Congestion charges in central zones, where feasible, may be levied and supplemented by instruments such as motor vehicle tax, motor fuel tax, business licensing fee and parking charges. Expert committees in India in the past have recommended a sharing of motor vehicles tax levied by state governments with municipalities. Such sharing is justified based on CC principles and the imperative to expand capacity in the UT system. A dedicated city surcharge on motor fuel tax may be desirable to finance highways and public transit as in the case of developed countries. Further, there is need for levying appropriate parking charges to curb travel demand. The municipal corporation of Hyderabad, apart from levying parking charges, collects special parking fees from new developments in layouts which have not provided adequate parking facilities in accordance with norms. The amounts are required to be spent for the construction of public parking facilities in the city.

FINANCING INNOVATIONS BY CITIES IN INDIA

While there has been no systematic attempt by Indian cities to levy 'beneficiaries pay' and 'congesters pay' charges, some states and cities have resorted to innovative land-based instruments and other mechanisms to finance urban infrastructure and services as discussed in the following text (Mohanty 2014, 2016).

Property Tax Reform: Hyderabad and Bengaluru

Property tax–GDP ratio in India, less than 0.2 per cent at present, is one of the lowest in the world. This is even lower than that in many comparable developing countries. While the ratio is around 2 per cent for developed countries, it is about 0.6 per cent for developing countries. Studies suggest that property tax–GDP ratio in India has the potential of increasing to 0.8 per cent with a reasonable effort. Experiments by municipal corporations such as Patna, Hyderabad, Ahmedabad and Bengaluru also reveal that with modest reforms, the collection under property tax could be increased significantly. The Self-assessment Scheme (SAS) introduced by Hyderabad city in 1998, adopting a simple UAM led to a 70 per cent growth in property tax in 1999–2000 even when the effective tax rate was reduced by two-thirds. This was by correcting the historic inequities in the property tax system. An enforcement-led drive resulted in a growth of 59 per cent in property tax collection in Hyderabad in 2013–2014.

The Greater Bengaluru Municipal Corporation launched an optional self-assessment of property tax scheme in 2000 due to which tax collection increased by 33 per cent during 2000–2001. Learning from the optional regime, Bengaluru shifted to a mandatory scheme in 2008 by amending the Karnataka Municipal Corporations (KMC) Act, 1976, to provide for self-assessment based on unit area value (UAV). The city is divided into six zones based on the ready reckoner property values notified by the Registration Department of Government of Karnataka. For each zone, UAVs per square foot are determined linking buildings to location, type of construction, built-up area, use and age. Due to the new scheme, which involved geographic information system (GIS) mapping of 1.9 million properties with each property assigned a unique identification number, property tax collection in Bengaluru increased by 39 per cent between 2009–2010 and 2010–2011. The tempo of property tax growth is continuing; with tax collection increasing from about ₹1,020 crore in 2010–2011 to more than ₹2,100 crore in 2016–2017.

While Bengaluru presents a laudable case of property tax reforms in India in recent times, the Economic Survey 2016–2017 has estimated that the city collects less than 20 per cent of its property tax potential. This reveals that other cities in India may be collecting relatively far less. Reforms in land and property taxes present the most promising agenda for Indian cities to leverage external resources for sustained funding of city infrastructure and services. International experience suggests that shift to a fully capital value-based property taxation offers a desirable direction for reforms.

Town Planning Scheme: Gujarat

TPS has been the principal instrument to promote self-financed process of urban development in Gujarat for decades. It offers a robust alternative to compulsory acquisition of land, being more beneficial to the landowners and also more equitable. Based on the concept of land pooling, the TPS promotes planned urban expansion without straining the public exchequer. New areas to be opened up for development in accordance with the statutory DP of a city are clearly marked and divided into smaller areas of about 100 to 200 hectares, typically involving 100 to 250 landowners. Each such area is called a TPS. The plots within a TPS are developed in terms of public amenities, infrastructure, housing for the poor, etc. Developed plots are subsequently returned to the original owners in a reduced proportion of their OPs after taking into account the land needed for public facilities. A portion of developed land in the TPS is kept with the land pooling authority to meet the cost of infrastructure. The development cost is recovered by selling this land with appreciated value. Land allotment in a TPS follows the following norms: 15 per cent for roads, 5 per cent for parks, playgrounds, gardens and open spaces, 5 per cent for social infrastructure such as schools, dispensary, fire brigade and public utilities, nearly 10 per cent for the SEWS and 15 per cent for sale to meet infrastructure cost. The TPS has recently been applied by Andhra Pradesh government with the name of 'land pooling scheme (LPS)' to pool about 35,000 acres in 29 villages to build the state's new capital at Amaravati in Guntur district.

External Development Charges: Haryana

The HUDA has been levying EDC on land colonizers to finance off-site infrastructure. Under the HDRUAA, 1975, external development works are defined to include water supply, sewers, drains, necessary provisions for disposal of sewage, sullage and storm water, roads, electrical works, solid waste management and disposal, slaughter houses, colleges, hospitals, stadium/sports complex, fire stations, grid sub-stations, etc., and any other work which the Director of Town and Country Planning (DT&CP) may specify for being executed outside a colony/area for its benefit. The Act mandates the developer to pay 'proportionate development charges' in the external development works to be carried out by the government or the local authority. The proportion in which and the time within which such payment is to be made are determined by the DT&CP. EDC revenues have enabled the HUDA to undertake external infrastructure projects of regional importance such as highways, water supply canals, transmission and distribution mains and regional parks.

Land Monetization: Mumbai

With the objective of creating a secondary suburban commercial and office node in Bandra Kurla Complex to relieve congestion in Central Mumbai, the Mumbai Metropolitan Region Development Authority (MMRDA) has undertaken since the 1980s the development of a 553-acre site from marshland and industrial slums. It has combined long-term lease of land (for 80 years) to private developers with permission to take up high-density construction to generate resources for city and regional development. The developers are responsible for all on-site and approach infrastructure at their own expense. The price per square metre of land sold, which was ₹30,000 in 1993, went up to ₹42,500 in 1995

(Diamond Bourse), ₹86,000 in 2000 (Citibank), ₹153,000 in January 2006 (Convention Center) and ₹504,000 in November 2007 (Commercial Complex and Car Park). In just two land auctions of 2006 and 2007 involving 13 hectares, the MMRDA mobilized about ₹51 billion. The MMRDA is using the land lease proceeds for major regional infrastructure projects, including Mumbai urban transit. Bandra Kurla Complex provides an excellent example of how unused or underused land assets with government can promote planned urban development while generating sizable resources for on-site and off-site infrastructure facilities.

Dedicated Cess: Bengaluru

From the 1990s, Karnataka has been earmarking taxes and charges for MRTS, water supply and ring road projects. The following sources were hypothecated for Bengaluru MRTS to start with: (a) 'MRTS' cess on development permission fee; (b) cess on sales tax on petrol, diesel and other goods; (c) 5 per cent cess on luxury tax on lodging charges above ₹750 per day, profession tax, betting tax and motor vehicles tax; (d) 5 per cent additional stamp duty; and (e) 15 per cent additional licensing fee on liquor manufacturing and selling. For mobilizing resources to bring Cauvery water to Bengaluru city, Karnataka levied 'Cauvery Water Cess' on land in UAs for which development permission or change of land use was sought, with different rates for conversion to residential, commercial, industrial, public and other uses and for land development. To develop ring road around Bengaluru, a 'Ring Road Surcharge' was also levied on conversion of land in Bengaluru metropolitan area to various uses.

The Government of Karnataka has recently introduced certain innovative measures to create a dedicated resource pool to finance the Bengaluru Metropolitan Rail (BMR) project as discussed in the following text.

Cess on New Layouts/Developments

A cess is levied in Bengaluru at the rate of 5 per cent of market value of land and/or building in future property developments and new layouts. This is credited to Metro Infrastructure Fund and shared between the

BMRCL, Bangalore Water Supply and Sewerage Board (BWSSB) and Bengaluru Development Authority (BDA) in the ratio of 65 per cent, 20 per cent and 15 per cent, respectively, to finance the metro directly by the BMRCL and to augment other civic infrastructure by other agencies to complement the metro system.

Cess on Additional Floor Area Ratio

FAR up to 4.0 is allowed for properties lying within an impact area of 500 m on either side of the metro rail alignment in Bengaluru. A part of the benefit accruing to property owners due to the higher FAR is harnessed through a cess of 10 per cent for residential buildings and 20 per cent for commercial buildings. The cess proceeds are shared between the BMRCL, Bruhat Bengaluru Mahanagara Palike (BBMP), BWSSB and BDA in the ratio of 60 per cent, 20 per cent, 10 per cent and 10 per cent, respectively, for servicing the senior term debt raised by the BMRCL and for financing the augmentation of civic infra-structure by other agencies.

Transferable Development Rights

TDR is permitted in lieu of compensation for land acquired for transit project in Bengaluru. The BMRCL will issue TDR in lieu of com-pensation for acquisition of land. Systemic improvements are proposed to make the TDR scheme more market-friendly and beneficial to all stakeholders.

Town Planning Charges: Hyderabad

Hyderabad has introduced several innovative land-based charges col-lected in the town planning process. It collects external betterment charges in addition to development charges and betterment charges to recoup the costs of infrastructure facilities such as trunk water and sewer lines, major roads, regional parks, etc. When layouts and build-ings are approved, these charges are collected at the prescribed scales. Hyderabad is also the first city to levy 'impact fee'. Further, the city collects value addition charges per square metre of built-up area in the high-tech city area where an information technology hub has been set up. For widening major roads, additional FSI, zoning concessions and TDRs are granted to the landowners surrendering land free of cost. An open space contribution at 10 per cent of land value is collected from proposed developments in layouts that did not provide adequate open space as statutorily required. Some of the important land-related charges levied by the GHMC are presented in the following text.

Betterment Charges

The GHMC collects 'betterment' and 'external betterment' charges at the time of according approval to layouts and construction of buildings as follows:

1. *Betterment charges:* Charges linked to increase in land values due to the provision of on-site or internal amenities like water supply, sewerage, drainage, roads, etc.
2. *External betterment charges:* Charges linked to increase in land values due to laying of off-site or external facilities, including arterial roads, radial roads, flyovers, regional parks, etc.

Area and City Level Impact Fees

The GHMC collects impact fees from builders of homes/apartment complexes and the landowners/developers for converting land on designated commercial roads from 'other' uses to 'commercial'. The fees are required to be spent on implementing city capital improvement and decongestion plan, including road-widening works, link roads, slip roads, parallel roads, junction improvements, traffic signals, flyovers, overbridges, underbridges and modern lighting on major roads, development of major drains, major parks, etc. The GHMC also collects city level infrastructure impact fee on built-up area above 15 m height in multi-storied buildings, excluding the stilt parking floor. The scale of fees depends on the nature of building, height and location. The amount collected is required to be escrowed—50 per cent for infrastructure development in the same area and the balance 50 per cent for city level capital infrastructure improvements.

Road-widening Scheme

Hyderabad has been implementing an innovative 'road-widening scheme' since the 1980s with remarkable success. By March 2014, the city has widened 307 roads with 260 km of length by securing land estimated at ₹1,200 crores from the landowners free of cost. This has been possible by granting them zoning relaxation incentives such as additional FSI, reduce setbacks and TDR in lieu of the land surrendered. The scheme has been very popular with the landowners as they perceive that the benefits due to the increase in land values and business opportunities would be far more than the foregone cost of land surrendered for the road-widening scheme.

URBAN PLAN FINANCING STRATEGY

Cities in India lack a coherent strategy to finance their DPs. These plans are expected to be implemented through area-based and city-wide projects. In conjunction with land use zoning and DCRs, urban plans and projects lead to local, citywide and regional impacts: physical and financial. They generate benefits, values and rents which can be captured and recycled to achieve the planning objectives. Major urban infrastructure projects, especially public transit, create 'accessibility premium' to locations and 'WEB' to the economy. They catalyze agglomeration and network externalities which capitalize into 'location rents'. The externalities also make the so-called mobile factors in cities quasi-immobile, gaining from 'agglomeration rents'. Further, the need for correcting negative externalities in cities accords a unique place to 'CC' as an instrument of urban management as well as a tool to raise resources. However, Indian cities have not harnessed the potential of impact fees, benefit taxation, value capture and CC instruments. They have not exploited 'location rents' and 'agglomeration rents' to raise resources for projects which lead to such rents. Principles of land, transport and urban economics suggest that taxes on various forms of rents in cities, arising as 'residuals' in the spatial economy, are ideal sources to 'leverage' debt from the market to finance planned urban development.

A key problem with urban planning in developing countries like India is that the master plans searched for financing instruments outside the planning model. Ironically, the TPS in Gujarat, which includes financing as an integral part of the strategy of planned expansion of cities, is yet to be adopted by most states. Cities have thus not tapped the power of land, impacted by spatial planning, infrastructure and externalities, as a resource. This is a paradox as taxes on land values and rents are regarded as 'first-best' instruments to finance urban infrastructure. Developed countries have also exploited these resources to finance cities during their urban transition. Land-based taxes and charges subscribe to efficiency, equity, benefit and ability to pay principles. Similarly, congestion taxes and charges satisfy many criteria of a good local resource. Theory and practice both suggest that the paradigm of value creation, capture and recycling, combined with instruments of benefit taxation, CC and dedicated funds, offers a significant opportunity to cities in developing countries like India to come out of their vicious circle of 'poor quality public services—lack of willingness to pay by taxpayers—inadequate resources—lack of investment in urban infrastructure'. When cities do not have a current revenue surplus, the use of planned urban development as a resource can be a smart strategy to mobilize future revenue surpluses to sustain debt financing of development programmes. Major urban infrastructure projects call for lumpy investments, lead to benefits that spread over generations and jurisdictions, and capitalize into tax bases of different levels of government. While such investments need to be financed by long tenor debt in terms of the golden rules of urban public finance, they can create adequate debt-servicing capacity when intergovernmental partnerships and revenue instruments are designed based on the benefit principle. In this context, the TIF approach, extensively used in the United States, offers a promising strategy to finance CDPs in India.

Tax Increment Financing Approach

TIF hypothecates future revenues to finance current infrastructure programmes. It aims at planned development and renewal of designated areas with the local authorities earmarking a part or whole of the incremental revenues, including taxes, charges and special levies arising from such projects to service the debt incurred to finance them. Originally started by California in 1952 to raise local matching funds to secure federal grants, the importance of TIF can be gauged from the fact that it is called the 'only game in the town'. As many as 49 out of 50 states in the United States have TIF-enabling legislations. In Australia, the instrument is known as value increment financing (VIF).

TIF is based on the general rule: 'growth pays it way'. The instrument is flexible. TIF projects can be executed by public authorities or private partners or both. Tax increments can be used to secure a bond, leverage an upfront investment or undertake development on a 'pay-as-you-go' principle. Sometimes, the tax increments are supplemented by other instruments such as special assessment, impact fee and betterment levy. The TIF principle can be applied to projects for geographically delineated areas or the city as a whole (Mohanty 2014, 2016).

While the modalities of a TIF vary between cities, it essentially allows a local authority to 'ring-fence' tax increments within the 'TIF district' to finance a project that contributes to such increments. A TIF represents a reallocation of a part of revenues accruing to the local authority to the TIF entity. The TIF authority, usually a special purpose vehicle of public authorities, including the local government or a PPP, first assesses the suitability of a development area for TIF. It then carves out the TIF district and prepares a TIF development plan with line estimates. The plan follows the state and local planning norms. It is prepared involving the local government, state authorities, community groups, private developers and other stakeholders. The TIF authority issues tax-free or taxable bonds or resorts to other forms of debt to meet the upfront costs. Often TIF infrastructure bonds are 'revenue bonds', tied to future revenue streams including user charges and taxes in the TIF district. Credit rating of these bonds to meet capital market norms ensures that the bonds are subjected to rigorous scrutiny. Over a period of time, the TIF results in development, leading to increments in land, property and other tax bases in the district. The tax increments over and above the pre-TIF tax revenues are used for debt servicing. The total tax revenues for the TIF district returns back to the original taxing authority at the close of the TIF term, which may range from 5 to 25 years, depending on the type and scale of development (Figure 8.3).

The TIF approach is generic. It may include LVT, property tax, other benefit taxes, congestion charges, development impact fees and

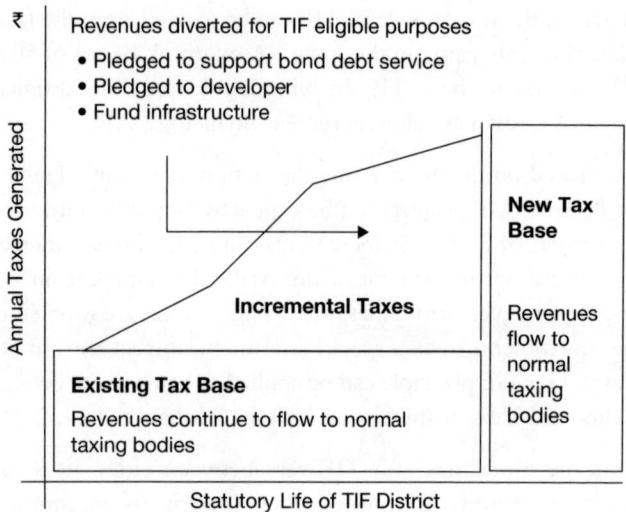

Figure 8.3 *The Basic Tax Increment Financing Model*
Source: Peterson (2014).

value capture instruments such as betterment levies to arrive at 'revenue increments' for being escrowed to service the debt incurred for value-creating infrastructure development projects. A general formulation of TIF symbolically relying on the property tax base only is presented as follows:

Let V = property value in the TIF district, μ = tax rate applied to all properties in the city, λ = value capture rate applied to the TIF district, θ = incremental rate of change in property value in the TIF district due to development. Then, the property tax in pre-TIF period $t-1$ and post-TIF period t can be calculated by the following formulae:

$$\text{Base Tax Revenue} = \mu V_{t-1} \tag{25}$$

$$\text{Value Capture Revenue} = \lambda(V_t - V_{t-1}) \tag{26}$$

But as property value in the current year equals property value in the previous year, augmented by the rate of change in such value, the expression (26) can be rewritten as:

$$\text{Value Capture Revenue} = \lambda((1+\theta)V_{t-1} - V_{t-1}) \qquad (27)$$

The aforementioned expression can be simplified as follows:

$$\text{Value Capture Revenue} = \lambda\theta V_{t-1} \qquad (28)$$

Adding the two revenue calculations, that is, (25) and (28) and dividing the total by the tax base in order to obtain an overall property tax rate, we have

$$\text{Overall Property Tax Rate} = \frac{\mu V_{t-1} + \lambda\theta V_{t-1}}{V_{t-1}(1+\theta)} = \frac{\mu + \lambda\theta}{1+\theta} \qquad (29)$$

Equation (29) provides guidance to municipal administrators in applying the value capture principle and determining the tax revenues that can be escrowed to finance worthwhile TIF projects. The formulae presented earlier can be modified depending on assumptions regarding the taxes and charges are to be included under TIF, their rates and the value capture rates.

TIF offers several advantages to ULBs: (a) development pays for itself, (b) value-creating and resource-generating investments are induced, (c) lacunae in the current methods of collecting upfront contributions through development charges, which discourage development, are addressed, (d) a market test for infrastructure funding through debt contributes to a rigorous selection of projects, (e) long-term spatial planning and funding are facilitated, (f) authorities attempt to avoid time- and cost-overruns in project implementation as debt payment is linked to revenue generation, (g) an equitable approach to funding infrastructure is promoted by spreading cost over generations and making beneficiaries pay and (h) the current fiscal problems of ULBs do not act as a stumbling block for the financing of value-creating projects.

Critics of TIF raise issues as follows. First, TIF expenditures, incurred by a special purpose vehicle, may be subject to less rigorous public scrutiny than other types of municipal expenditures. Second, the TIF district may not be able to raise the predicted tax revenues and the resulting lack of funds could threaten the efforts to rejuvenate the TIF district. Third, TIFs may simply accelerate developments that would have occurred anyway. Fourth, by freezing property taxes at a time when local authorities are experiencing growth in demand for services as a result of area revitalization, TIFs cut into the authority of the local governments to raise revenues. Finally, TIFs target developments and future resources to designated areas at the expense of overall growth of the municipal jurisdiction or of areas outside the TIF district.

Most criticisms of TIF are targeted at design issues, not the core concept. TIF brings home an important message that there is no free lunch. Project costs, whether incurred by public authorities or private developers under a PPP, will need to be recovered. With revolts by taxpayers from time to time, TIF is seen to be the only versatile instrument available to cities in the United States to undertake new development ventures. In India too, with current revenue sources of municipalities precarious, and free ridership problems, the model offers a promising way to address the real concerns of financing CDP. In principle, a robust development plan that passes the cost–benefit test should be in a position to finance itself. When pervasive externalities of cities are recognized as the fundamental forces driving urban economic growth, the instruments of benefit taxation, including land-based taxes and congestion charges, are expected to raise adequate resources to finance development plans. A TIF approach will also promote efficiency, accountability and fiscal discipline in local government. Cities in India need to prepare for the implementation of TIF in a big way to come out of the present low level equilibrium trap that perpetuates poor services, weak finances and under-investment in infrastructure. The strategy is inherently suitable for being linked to municipal bonds or other forms of debt to finance city development projects.

Municipalities in the United States have extensively issued municipal bonds to raise resources for implementing urban infrastructure projects, including those under TIF: revenue, general obligation and hybrid. Revenue bonds are based on anticipated revenue streams from projects; general obligation bonds are predicated on the strength of general revenues of the bond-issuing authority. Hybrid bonds are based on the strength of both. It is apparent that in view of the precarious position regarding cost recovery for services, most cities in India are not in a position to issue pure revenue bonds to finance major development projects. Inelastic project-based revenues suggest that the marketing of pure revenue bonds on a project-specific basis alone may not be feasible. Thus, efforts may be necessary to structure revenue bonds with general obligation covenants. The revenue-generation potential of projects and general revenues of municipal authority may supplement each other to improve the marketability of bonds. These considerations suggest that at the present stage of India's evolution, cities may need to combine project-financing and citywide resource mobilization strategies. They may also need to combine both current revenue surpluses and future tax increments to leverage external resources. The present guidelines of the Securities and Exchange Board of India (SEBI) for regulating municipal bonds, issued in 2015, need to be revisited to incorporate the aforementioned observations.

Debt financing of planned urban development based on a TIF model can be sustained only when the local authority is creditworthy and is in a position to raise adequate resources to contribute seed money and service debt. In this context, the logic of benefit taxation, land-based taxes, CC and TIF points to the importance of structuring planned development programmes, bankable projects, revenue instruments and escrow mechanisms. Based on theoretical principles and best practices, we suggest that the tools of urban planning and economics must be combined in the strategy of financing urban infrastructure to harness the synergy between spatial planning, infrastructure development and local economic growth for creating, capturing and recycling values in cities during India's urban transition. Apart from the TPS in Gujarat, some promising instruments in this regard include: densification of select growth nodes, purchasable development rights, DIFs, betterment levy, land value taxation, capital value-based property tax, sharing of real estate transfer tax and dedicated fund for transport with a 'transport tax' or a share in motor vehicle and motor fuel-related taxes. We also emphasize the need for VIF partnerships between local, state and central governments in the spirit of cooperative federalism and advocate a statutory share in the GST for ULBs.

Strategic Densification of Nodes

Density in India's large cities is very high, but FSI precariously low. FSI is hardly more than 2 in India's metropolitan cities; it is 1.2–3.5 in

Delhi, and 1.5 in Chennai. In Mumbai, FSI is 1.33 for the island city; in suburban areas, it is 1.00, subject to additional FSI of 0.33 as incentive on payment of fees and fulfilling certain conditions. Internationally, FSI is seen to increase during the course of development. However, in Mumbai, FSI has decreased from 4.5 in 1964, discouraging the redevelopment of dilapidated buildings. Downtowns in international cities have much higher FSI: Denver—17, New York—15, Los Angeles—13, Chicago—12, San Francisco—9, Vancouver—9, Tokyo—20, Singapore—12–25, Hong Kong—12, Shanghai—8 and Bangkok—8. Sao Paulo follows FSI of 1 as a right to the landowner, but additional FSI up to 5 is permitted through a system of incentive zoning and TDR.

Internationally, high FSI and public transit accessibility go together to benefit from economies of collocation, density and networking. However, FSI in Indian cities is uniform over large areas. While a strong case exists for increasing FSI in India's large cities with a liberalized FSI regime as in Hyderabad, a paradigm of strategic densification based on TOD, accompanied by investment in fast PT systems such as BRT, MRT and HSR, is desirable. To make TOD succeed, a proactive, flexible and transparent land use policy that promotes transportation–land use integration and harnesses the benefits of density and accessibility to facilitate VCF, including TIF, is necessary. Robust methods of financing PT development and improvement programmes based on mechanisms such as dedicated funds and PPPs need to be explored.

Purchasable Development Rights

Brazil is implementing the scheme of building rights called OODC. This is based on a basic FSI cap on the landowner's building rights beyond which a fee is charged. Sao Paulo has also adopted CEPAC from 1995, involving the auctioning of building rights. The idea is that new development potential due to rezoning, permission for additional construction and investment in infrastructure in designated urban areas should not be free but auctioned amongst those intending to take advantage of future economic benefits. The city issues CEPAC bonds corresponding to additional building rights for purchase by competing developers in public electronic auctions regulated by CVM, the Brazilian Securities and Exchange Commission.

The models of OODC and CEPAC as practised in Brazil are transparent and market-friendly. They are based on sound economic principles and may be adopted by cities in India while taking up TOD-linked strategic densification programmes through TIF-based projects. Hyderabad and Bengaluru have introduced FSI charges in areas benefitting from major transport improvements such as strategic road redevelopment and rapid transit. Such initiatives need to be replicated widely.

Development Impact Fees

DIFs are charges paid by new development towards the cost of infrastructure facilities needed, especially those located outside the boundaries of such development (off-site), affecting citywide infrastructure systems. Impact fees are common in the United States, levied under state laws. These are 'one-time' charges imposed by local government to make developers pay a 'fair share' of the cost of public facilities and services warranted by new development. Impact fees shift a part of the burden of such facilities from municipal general revenues to developers. The principal characteristic of impact fees, which differentiate them from the conventional developer exaction instruments, is the financing of 'off-site' infrastructure facilities needed to support new development.

Impact fee legislations in the United States cover a wide range of public facilities intrinsic and extrinsic to development. These include: roadways, waterworks, wastewater collection and treatment, solid waste collection equipment and disposal, hazardous and toxic waste disposal, underground utilities, electricity generation and distribution, street lighting, protection of environmental resources, harbour, port and airport improvements, mass transit facilities and equipment, tree planation, etc. State laws concerning impact fees mandate the preparation of CIP for newly developing areas in accordance with planning norms and earmarking of impact fees to finance the same. The US Supreme Court has outlined three tests to determine the legal validity of impact fees:

1. *'Reasonably related' test:* Impact fee must demonstrate a reasonable relationship between the fee or exaction and the demand for infrastructure generated by new development.

2. *'Rational nexus' test:* Essential nexus between the conditions of development permission and 'legitimate state interests' must be established.

3. *'Proportionality test':* There must be a 'rough proportionality' between a development's projected impacts and the fee.

Impact fees are regarded as the most 'rational' step in the evolution of local government financing of infrastructure in the United States. There is a strong case for Indian cities to adopt such fees. Hyderabad has already made a beginning, defining 'impacts' to include local, area-specific and citywide effects. Impact fees can supplement other revenue instruments in TIF projects.

Betterment Levies

Land value gains in cities due to spatial planning and infrastructure projects tend to be huge. However, cities may not be able to capture such betterment through general benefit taxes like property tax. Special benefits call for specialized instruments to exploit them. Difficulties, however, arise in segregating the factors that lead to betterment. These are related to (a) demarcation of benefit area, (b) disaggregation of sources of increase in land values such as spatial planning, change in land use, permission for development, owner's initiative, initiatives of other developers, economic growth, external economies, etc., and (c) determination of base and rate of the levy, given that land prices increase much before public investments actually occur. However, these issues can be resolved by opting for a moderate rate of levy. International experiences suggest that when countries tried to extract 80–100 per cent of the betterment, they faced stiff resistance and the scheme failed. To address the problem of segregating the sources of betterment, it may be appropriate to adopt a moderate levy of 25–30 per cent applied citywide or to well-demarcated zones. The models of *Participacion en Plusvalias* in Colombia and *Contrubuciones de Mejoras* in Argentina are worth adopting. The 'betterment levy' and 'external betterment levy' models practised in Hyderabad city also offer guidance for other cities in India.

Urban Land Value Taxation

While municipal laws of some states in India explicitly provide for the levy of VLT based on the capital value of land, the definition of property in all the states includes land. However, the tax is grossly neglected by cities throughout India. What makes VLT desirable in the urban context is that it promotes urban development in accordance with the objectives of CDP, apart from subscribing to the benefit principle. Spatial planning calls for the allocation of land for desired urban uses such as residential, commercial and infrastructure. VLT can act as an instrument to not only prevent speculation in land but also promote housing and other productive activities. Keeping the experience of Andhra Pradesh and Telangana in view, a VLT at 0.5 per cent of the capital value of land in municipal corporations and 0.2 per cent in municipalities may be appropriate to start with. These rates are low compared to international benchmarks, but can yield substantial revenues as most Indian cities are spread out and occupy large areas. The tax rate on vacant land may be set higher than that on built-up property to discourage speculation in land and promote housing activities.

Capital Value-based Property Tax

In most cities in India, property tax is levied on ARV or UAM. As rents or unit area rates do not keep pace with economic growth, cities have not been able to benefit from the ongoing increases in capital value of property due to spatial planning, infrastructure development, agglomeration economies and growth-augmenting policies of governments. Property tax has thus not been a buoyant source of municipal revenue. In tune with international practice, there is a need for Indian cities to shift their base of property tax from rental or unit area basis to capital value of property. At least the metropolitan cities may move to capital value-based property taxation. The UAV method followed by the Greater Bengaluru Municipal Corporation presents a good model for adoption to start with. The MCGM has also adopted a variant of the capital value system of property tax with laudable features. However, the Bengaluru and Mumbai models combine the capital value and UAMs. None of them is able to capture the increase in land

and property values due to urbanization, economic growth, spatial planning and infrastructure development as they occur. However, they can be regarded as innovative experiments in the process of shifting to a full-fledged capital value-based property tax system.

Real Estate Transfer Tax

As land and property values in cities soar due to urban planning interventions and investments made by various levels of government, public finance theory suggests that the ULBs be provided with access to real estate transfer tax or stamp duty. A city surcharge on stamp duty paid by the property buyer as prevailing in Andhra Pradesh, Telangana and Tamil Nadu may thus be considered by other states in India. Further, a tax on the seller of property who benefits significantly from spatial planning and investments made by the local government may perhaps be considered. This may be subject to appropriate deduction under the capital gains tax levied under the provisions of income tax. All land and property transfer taxes may be earmarked for city and regional infrastructure facilities, including freeways and public transit.

Dedicated Fund for Urban Transport

'Beneficiaries pay' and 'congesters pay' principles make a case for dedicated funding of UT. Since 1971, all establishments in France located in a UT area and employing more than nine persons are mandated to pay a percentage of their wage bill as *versement transport* or 'transport tax' to fund PT projects. This is a hypothecated payroll tax credited to *autorite organisatrice de transport urbain*, the urban regional transport authority responsible for regional and urban PT. In 2000, this tax accounted for about 40 per cent of the total transportation spending in France. The transport tax has provided a stable source of funding for the development or extension of 10 light rail transit systems in France since 1985. While payroll tax and piggybacked income tax have been adopted by some developed countries to finance PT, the access of cities to such sources in India requires a constitutional amendment. However, as recommended by the Central Finance Commissions, the existing ceiling on profession tax may be enhanced and the tax may be dedicated towards funding major UT projects, benefitting the commuters to work.

In the United States, gasoline and diesel taxes are largely dedicated to financing highways under the National Highways Act, 1956, and Highway Revenue Act, 1956, through the Highway Trust Fund (HTF). A mass transit account (MTA) was created under this fund by the Highway Revenue Act of 1982. About 85 per cent of the HTF revenues goes to highway account and the remaining to MTA. California has been dedicating gasoline tax for transportation projects since 1923. Fuel excise tax on gasoline and diesel, truck weight fee—a fee on commercial vehicles based on weight, representing compensation for wear and tear in roadways—and fuel tax swap (additional excise tax on gasoline in lieu of sales tax) accounted for the bulk of the state spending on public transportation in 2011.

The GoI has established a dedicated fund called Central Road Fund from the collection of cess on petrol and high-speed diesel. The accrued amounts are distributed for development and maintenance of national highways, state roads, rural roads, rail overbridges and underbridges, and road safety measures as per the provisions of the Central Road Fund Act, 2000. The principle of benefit taxation makes a strong case for sharing of central and state taxes on motor fuel to raise seed money for urban PT, including BRT, MRT and HSR, and leverage external resources or participating in PPP, availing viability gap funding.

Case for Cooperative Federalism

Principles of benefit taxation, covering instruments such as land-based taxation, CC, value creation, capture and recycling, TIF and dedicated funds provide useful guidance for the design of urban development plan financing strategy in India. However, the benefits and values created by spatial planning and infrastructure projects in large cities do not confine to the boundaries of municipal jurisdictions. The municipalities also do not have the necessary revenue instruments with them to tap the values created due to their efforts. Thus, a city development model based on the TIF framework can work effectively only when appropriate VIF partnerships between local, state and central governments are instituted.

The Smart Cities Mission in India rightly envisages the implementation of innovative area-based and citywide projects based on intergovernmental partnerships. Obviously, the success of such projects depends on how they are structured, financed and implemented. Area-based projects are similar to 'special assessment district' or 'business improvement district' projects implemented in developed countries. They lead to 'localized' benefits in the project area and 'spillover' benefits in the broader development district or project-impact zone. They are suitable for debt financing with loan servicing linked to revenue increments in the form of user fees, internal and EDC, impact fees, 'up-zoning' charges, VLT, property tax, betterment levy and other land-based instruments. The financing of citywide projects needs a broader approach as they usually lead to benefits spilling over city boundaries due to externalities. Such benefits translate into tax increments for all levels of government. Major urban infrastructure projects such as MRT and HSR thus warrant intergovernmental partnerships. They call for hypothecation of increments in benefit taxes and charges, including those levied by higher levels of government. In this context, income tax, payroll tax, GST and transport tax can be regarded as benefit taxes for living, working and transacting in the city (Bahl and Linn 2014). While the municipalities in India do not have access to these taxes, even land as a tax base is not fully available with them.

Under the current framework of fiscal federalism in India, whereas the municipalities can levy property tax, including VLT, they do not have access to many land-based revenue sources. Even the fixation of property tax and VLT rates requires permission from the state government. The central government has the exclusive power to levy tax on capital gains in land and property. State governments are authorized to impose land use conversion tax, non-agricultural land assessment, property transfer tax and stamp duty. Urban development authorities, which are parastatals, levy charges for institution and change of land use with reference to the master plan. They are empowered to impose internal and EDC and impact fees. Water and sewerage boards do not have the authority to impose water and sewerage betterment levies. Though the municipalities have power to levy betterment charges, they are often reluctant to share these charges with the water and sewerage boards. Thus, the tax increments occurring to various public authorities due to the implementation of a TIF project may not be available to the local government or the project-sponsoring authority such as a metro rail corporation, which has to incur a huge debt to finance projects. These issues are critically important and must be addressed by appropriate revenue-sharing mechanisms and intergovernmental partnerships in the spirit of cooperative federalism.

The TIF approach to promote planned urban development is rooted in a value creation, capture and recycling framework. The efficacy of this framework demands that the authority creating benefits in the form of value increments must be in a position to capture and recycle them to sustain further infrastructure investments. While there is a strong case for adoption of the TIF principle by Indian cities with 'in-kind' initiatives such as TPS in Gujarat, LPS in Andhra Pradesh and Telangana, and Magarpatta city development model in Pune, Maharashtra, the issue of repayment of project debt must be addressed in right earnest. This calls for combining uplifts in land-based taxes and charges, including town planning charges with predictable contributions from the central and state governments who benefit from increments in their tax bases. In this context, a statutory sharing of GST, which has subsumed a number of municipal taxes, to repay the debt mobilized by municipalities from the market for major urban projects, is worth considering. A strong case also exists for dedicated taxes to finance MRT and HSRs such as fuel tax in the United States and transport tax in France. They lead to wider economic impacts. It must be realized that when there is no TIF, there is no increase in the tax base of any level of government: local, state or central. But when a TIF project is implemented successfully, all the governments stand to gain. VIF partnerships thus need to be structured based on the benefit principle of public finance to facilitate debt financing of urban DPs and projects. The principle can be extended to PPPs also.

9

Reforming Urban Planning in India

Integrating Land, Transport and Urban Economics

THE URBAN REVOLUTION AND INDIA

India must harness the opportunity ushered in by the Urban Revolution. Nothing else will bring so much benefit to the people of India as urbanization. Vibrant cities will enable millions in rural and urban areas to escape poverty and exclusion. They will catalyze external drivers of economic growth by facilitating the collocation of productive economic activities. Agglomeration and network externalities of cities will increase the productivity of workers and reduce the transaction costs to firms. These externalities are closely connected with scale economies, density, and backward and forward linkages in the spatial economy. Scale economies, arising from an increase in the volume of economic opportunities, spread fixed costs and risks over a large number of actors. Density, occurring from the clustering of diverse activities and actors in close quarters, reduces the cost of interacting, organizing, producing, transacting, transporting, consuming and providing services. Density and networking lead to collaborative efficiency, learning and innovation. However, they call for spatial planning and infrastructure, especially transportation, to maximize the positive effects of externalities while minimizing their negative consequences. Urban planning and development of public transport (PT) systems in anticipation as well as in response to growth are key instruments that India must utilize to benefit from the Urban Revolution. The country must act fast as the window of opportunities from urbanization will remain open only for a limited period of time. Dense, diverse, networked and dynamic cities will shape India's form and future.

While the opportunities presented by urbanization to India are huge, the challenges faced by cities are daunting. Haphazard growth, sprawl, crumbling infrastructure, rudimentary PT, traffic congestion, air pollution, piling garbage, lack of sewerage and sanitation facilities, huge shortage in affordable housing, mushrooming of slums, exclusionary land use, crime, social unrest and vulnerability to disasters are some of their conspicuous features. These problems are deeply rooted in the planning, financing and governance systems of cities. In particular, the master planning paradigm in India, based on the 1947 Town and Country Planning Act in the United Kingdom, has failed to deliver the desired outcomes. This is a serious concern as urban planning, infrastructure development, transport–land use integration and taxation are amongst the limited instruments available with policymakers and planners to achieve the goals of economically efficient, socially equitable, environmentally sustainable and financially viable cities. These instruments are of paramount importance to achieve the United Nations' Sustainable Development Goals (SDGs), aimed at making cities inclusive, safe, resilient and sustainable.

The crucial importance of urban planning in a developing country stems from the fact that it enables cities to perform their fundamental role as drivers of structural and spatial transformation. Cities facilitate economic growth and catalyze employment opportunities for millions, including rural–urban migrants and commuters. They fail when they cannot discharge these functions effectively, especially when they are unable to create remunerative jobs in thriving businesses which the workers can access without being subjected to long commute, congestion and pollution. A key role of urban planning is to assist cities in realizing their economic potential while protecting the environment and promoting inclusion. The importance of urban infrastructure, especially transportation, lies in the fact that it connects people to opportunity and business to prosperity. India must make the best use of the instruments of urban planning and just-in-time infrastructure development for economic growth and poverty reduction.

Urban planning and transportation infrastructure, when integrated, link density, land use, housing, employment, local economic development and resource mobilization. They contribute to the following objectives:

1. *Economic:* Catalyzing agglomeration economies; maximizing the beneficial effects of externalities while minimizing their negative consequences; promoting mobility in labour market; supporting economic growth and creation of job opportunities; generating resources for socio-economic development through the creation, capture and recycling of values.

2. *Social:* Facilitating social interaction, inclusion and integration; promoting learning, networking and building social capital; addressing affordable housing and workplace needs of the poor and marginalized groups; protecting heritage precincts and sites of outstanding natural beauty for posterity.

3. *Environmental:* Ensuring clean water, clean air, public health and safety; avoiding urban sprawl; contributing to energy security and climate change agenda; reducing vulnerability to the impacts of disasters; conserving ecology and preventing degradation of the environment.

However, India is far from attaining the aforementioned objectives due to the outdated master planning system that fails to integrate land use, infrastructure and local economic development. This is demonstrated by the JNNURM, the first major national urban initiative in India with substantial funding from the central government.

LESSONS FROM THE JNNURM

The JNNURM was launched in 2005 as a demand-driven and reform-linked national initiative to address the challenges of urbanization. It aimed at providing central grants to ULBs for infrastructure development and provision of basic services to the urban poor. It comprised of four sub-missions. The Urban Infrastructure and Governance (UIG) and Basic Services to the Urban Poor (BSUP) components applied to 65 select cities of national importance. The Urban Infrastructure Development Scheme for Small and Medium

Towns (UIDSSMT) and Integrated Housing and Slum Development Programme (IHSDP) catered to other cities and towns. The JNNURM mandated the preparation of city development plan (CDP) as a key requirement for seeking central grants, which ranged from 35 per cent to 90 per cent of project cost depending on the category of the city. The CDP was expected to provide an overarching framework within which projects could be identified and executed. The JNNURM also prescribed the implementation of 23 reforms, aimed at improving urban planning, financing and governance. The release of central grants was linked to achievement by ULBs and state governments with regard to reform milestones agreed to between the GoI and the state government.

The JNNURM provided step-by-step guidelines for the preparation of CDP. These include: (a) in-depth analysis of existing situation in the city, covering demographic, economic, financial, physical, infrastructural, environmental, institutional and other aspects along with SWOT (strengths, weaknesses, opportunities and threats) analysis; (b) development of a perspective of the city; (c) formulation of strategy to bridge the gap between 'where the city is' and 'where it wants to go'; and (d) preparation of City Investment Plan (CIP) and financing strategy. The process was envisaged to be consultative. However, a critical study of the JNNURM reveals that even though the CDP was to prioritize city needs based on available finances in a participative manner, this did not happen. In most instances, the CDP was prepared by consultants, and not deliberated in the Municipal Council. Stakeholder consultation was more of a formality. Further, the CDP did not link the financing strategy of the city with its master plan. Ironically, the master plan is statutory, whereas the CDP is not. Lastly, it was expected that Detailed Project Reports (DPRs) would flow from the CDP. However, this did not happen in several cases. Many cities already had projects which needed funds. The same were posed for central grants under the JNNURM irrespective of their linkage to the CDP (Sivaramakrishnan 2011).

All the projects under the JNNURM were targeted for completion by 2012. However, an evaluation by the Public Accounts Committee of the Parliament of India in April 2015 found that while the Mission envisaged a central grant support of ₹100,000 crore, the Planning

Commission allocated ₹66,085 crore during the 7-year mission period. The actual budgetary provision made based on the progress of the JNNURM was ₹45,066 crore. Against this amount, ₹40,584 crore was released by 2011–2012 (Public Accounts Committee 2015). A review of the JNNURM in 2016 shows that the overall completion rate of projects approved under UIG was 38 per cent; for UIDSSMT it was 43 per cent. For BSUP and IHSDP, the completion rate was 13 per cent and 10 per cent, respectively. Table 9.1 provides a summary picture on the progress of the four sub-missions of the JNNURM as of 2016. Table 9.2 presents a picture on the completion of various categories of projects sanctioned under the UIG component of the JNNURM.

While the JNNURM contributed significantly to bring urban issues to the forefront of public policy, the tardy progress in its implementation was a result of several factors. First, the CDPs were prepared by consultants, not 'owned' by cities. Many projects that sought central grant had no organic links with the Master Plan or CDP. The thorny issues of land availability for projects were not addressed while preparing DPRs. Second, many states and cities were not able to provide matching share mandated by the scheme. Third, project formulation, implementation and monitoring capacities at the city level were abysmal; institutional and human resource constraints in governance were pervasive. Fourth, the implementation of reforms to improve urban planning, mobilize resources, promote inclusion and enhance efficiency in service delivery was not seriously pursued. Reform conditions under the JNNURM were relaxed from time to time to enable the release of

Table 9.1 *Progress of Projects Under the JNNURM at a Glance (2016)*

Programme	No. of Projects Approved	No. of Projects Completed	Completion Rate (%)
UIG	599	233	38
UIDSSMT	1,148	494	43
BSUP	478	66	13
IHSDP	1,034	86	10

Source: www.jnnurm.nic.in (accessed 1 July 2016).

Table 9.2 *Sector-wise Details of Progress of Projects Under UIG as of 2014*

Sector	No. of Projects Approved	No. of Projects Completed	Completion Rate (%)
Drainage/Storm Water	76	29	38
Roads/Flyovers	104	60	58
Water Supply	186	71	38
Urban Renewal	10	4	40
Sewerage	122	35	29
Other UT	17	12	71
MRTS	22	7	32
Solid Waste Management	46	13	28
Parking Lots and Spaces on PPP Basis	5	0	0
Development of Heritage Areas	7	2	29
Preservation of Water Bodies	4	0	0
Total	599	233	38

Source: www.jnnurm.nic.in (accessed 1 July 2016).

central funds. There were also problems in the design of reforms. For example, the reform relating to property tax called for raising collection efficiency to 85 per cent during the Mission period. While the ratio of collection to demand was reckoned as a measure to monitor the reform, there was no attempt by any city to estimate the property tax base and arrive at the correct demand. Moreover, due to central and state grants being readily available through the JNNURM, there was very little 'own' effort by ULBs to raise funds from the market. Ironically, only three municipal bonds were issued in India during the 7-year mission period, mobilizing a meagre ₹1,500 crore. The JNNURM did not make an appreciable impact on the systems of urban planning, infrastructure financing and governance.

THE SMART CITIES MISSION

The GoI has launched three major missions replacing the JNNURM in 2015: Smart Cities Mission, Atal Mission for Rejuvenation and Urban Transformation (AMRUT) and Housing for All by 2022. The programmes aim to make India's urbanization process efficient, sustainable and equitable. In particular, the Smart Cities Mission targets at promoting economic growth, strengthening governance and improving service delivery to urban residents through support to 'smart' cities, selected based on a national competitive process. Smart cities will strive to provide infrastructure facilities that use 'smart' solutions to improve civic services. The Mission is slated for implementation from 2015–2016 to 2019–2020. The GoI has committed central support of ₹48,000 crores to 100 smart cities, with each city getting ₹100 crores per annum for five years. States and ULBs are expected to mobilize an equivalent amount based on a 50:50 sharing pattern between the centre and the state. The central and state shares will act as seed money to attract local body and external resources. The funds from various sources will be used to develop core urban infrastructure facilities by promoting convergence and synergy with other schemes. Some of the key features of smart cities are presented in Box 9.1.

Unlike the JNNURM, which emphasized the preparation of CDP to formulate projects, the Smart Cities Mission is focused on promoting innovative projects that can be scaled up. It refers to four models to guide the formulation and implementation of area-based and citywide projects for replication across cities. These are:

1. *City improvement (retrofitting):* Develop an existing built-up area greater than 500 acres to achieve the objective of the Mission to make it more efficient and liveable.
2. *City renewal (redevelopment):* Replace the existing built-environment in an area of more than 50 acres and enable co-creation of a new layout, especially enhanced infrastructure, mixed land use and increased density.
3. *City extension (greenfield development):* Develop a previously vacant area of more than 250 acres, using innovative planning, plan financing and plan implementation tools with provision for affordable housing, especially for the poor.

Box 9.1 *Smart Cities: Key Features*

1. Promoting mixed land use in area-based developments—planning for 'unplanned areas' containing a range of compatible activities and land uses close to one another in order to make land use more efficient. The states will enable some flexibility in land use and building by-laws to adapt to change;
2. Housing and inclusiveness—expand housing opportunities for all;
3. Creating walkable localities—reduce congestion, air pollution and resource depletion, boost local economy, promote interactions and ensure security. The road network is created or refurbished not only for vehicles and PT but also for pedestrians and cyclists, and necessary administrative services are offered within walking or cycling distance;
4. Preserving and developing open spaces—parks, playgrounds and recreational spaces in order to enhance the quality of life of citizens, reduce the urban heat effects in areas and generally promote eco-balance;
5. Promoting a variety of transport options—TOD, PT and last mile para-transport connectivity;
6. Making governance citizen-friendly and cost-effective—increasingly relying on online services to bring about accountability and transparency, especially using mobiles to reduce cost of services and providing services without having to go to municipal offices. Forming e-groups to listen to people and obtain feedback and use online monitoring of programmes and activities with the aid of cyber tour of worksites;
7. Giving an identity to the city—based on its main economic activity, such as local cuisine, health, education, arts and craft, culture, sports goods, furniture, hosiery, textile, dairy, etc.;
8. Applying smart solutions to infrastructure and services in area-based development in order to make them better, for example, making areas less vulnerable to disasters, using fewer resources and providing cheaper services.

Source: Ministry of Housing and Urban Affairs, GoI. See www.smartcities.gov.in (accessed 25 July 2017).

4. *Pan-city initiative:* A pan-city initiative in which at least one smart solution is applied covering larger parts of the city.

While smart cities call for smart ways of structuring, financing and implementing projects, the experience of the JNNURM suggests that these must be built on the basic foundations of good urban planning, financing and governance. The objectives of economically efficient, environmentally sustainable, socially inclusive and financially viable cities cannot be attained without reforming the current system of urban planning.

STATE OF URBAN PLANNING IN INDIA

The master planning model in India is rooted in the modernist urban planning theories of the twentieth century. It aims at a grand vision of an urban area with a perspective of 20–25 years and realizing the same through the enforcement of land use plans at multiple levels: regional, city, zonal and local. The approach is top-down, technocratic and rigid. It neglects the role of public transport in sustainable and inclusive development. It is also exclusionary—not in sync with the income distribution structure of cities. Plan implementation relies on centralized control to attain development goals. Ironically, master planning is based on the concept of a finished product, whereas a city's evolution is a process. It pays scant attention to the economics of cities. Due to this, master plans have also failed to present a coherent strategy to finance their development proposals. Urban planning in India needs to be reformed urgently to enable cities to discharge their economic and social functions. This calls for studying the evolution of town planning in the United Kingdom from where India borrowed master planning, understanding the shortcomings in the current approaches to urban plan formulation and implementation, incorporating the principles of land, transport and urban economics into regional and urban planning and replicating the practices that have worked in India and elsewhere.

The United Kingdom recognized the need for town planning in the Housing and Town Planning Act of 1909. This law was a response to the 'garden city' movement led by Ebenezer Howard, who propagated principles of layouts and architectural design to create spacious, treelined avenues for housing the working population. It empowered public authorities to restrict private development not in conformity with stated town planning principles. It empowered—but not compelled—local authorities to develop town planning schemes (TPSs). The Town and Country Planning Act, 1947, legislated that 'all' land use in the future should conform to the plans approved by the local authority. This marked the beginning of 'master plans'. The law separated land development right from ownership. It prescribed that no 'material development' could occur without permission from the appropriate planning authority; ownership alone could not confer the right to develop land. The act assigned overarching powers to local authorities to undertake compulsory acquisition of land to implement their land use plans. Further, it stipulated that all development value—difference between the value of land with permission to develop and existing use value—vested in the state.

The urban planning system in the United Kingdom consists of national planning policy guidelines, regional strategies till recently and local development frameworks. National restrictions include Town Centre First, Green Belt, Sites of Special Scientific Interest (SSSIs) and Areas of Outstanding Natural Beauty (AONBs). While some national guidelines prevail, urban planning in the United Kingdom has undergone drastic changes since 1947. The Town and Country Planning Act of 1968 propagated the concept of development plan (DP) comprising structure and local plans to replace the detailed master plan. The structure plan was envisaged to be a strategic DP, presenting a broad framework of policies and strategies looking forward up to 20 years. Local plans were to be prepared in accordance with structure plans. The Planning and Compulsory Purchase Act, 2004, prescribed the replacement of structural plans by Regional Spatial Strategies (RSS) and Local Development Documents (LDDs). The Localism Act, 2011, has done away with regional strategies and mandated local and neighbourhood plans to reflect the aspirations of people. It aims to make urban planning more democratic and participatory by recognizing neighbourhood planning as a right of the community to shape 'places'. The Cities and Local Government Devolution Act, 2016, empowers combined local authorities with directly elected mayors to use area planning and other instruments to promote economic growth in partnership with the central government.

While urban planning in the United Kingdom has moved away from an interventionist approach to a decentralized regime, the master planning model, with dictatorial connotations, thrives in India. Aiming to be comprehensive, it accords primacy to land use. It neglects strategic aspects of development such as core infrastructure, economic growth, social equity and environmental sustainability. Master plans are obsessed with blueprints delineating detailed land uses for various activities; they hardly focus on implementation. They are not tuned to exploit the limited instruments available for executing plans, including timely development of infrastructure, transport–land use integration, regulation and taxation. Rooted in anti-density perspective of modernist urban planning, master plans undermine the role of clustering of economic activities in catalyzing the external economies of agglomeration in cities. The state of urban planning in India owes to the professional training and ideology of planners at the top of the town planning profession, obsession with standards of the Western countries, vested interests of policymakers, administrators and consultants, inappropriate legislative basis of spatial planning, technocentric approach, lack of peoples' participation in planning and inadequate attention to the economics of cities. The key problems of urban planning in India relate to definition of development, strategy of planning, approach to plan formulation, financing and implementation, and capacity.

Restrictive Definition of Development

Section 10 (2) of the Town and Country Planning Act, 1947, in the United Kingdom defines development as 'the carrying out of building, engineering, mining or other operations in, on, over or under land, or making any material change in the use of any building or other land'. This narrow definition has literally been adopted by the town planning laws of states across India. To cite an example, the Maharashtra Regional and Town Planning Act, 1966, has defined development as:

> … carrying out of building, engineering, mining, or other operations in or over or under land, or the making of any material change, in any building or land or the making of any material structural change in heritage building or its precinct, and includes demolition of any

existing building, structure or erection or part thereof and reclamation, redevelopment and layout and sub-division of any land.

The aforementioned definition is inappropriate for a developing country like India. It does not capture the broader concepts of development, including 'inclusive growth' and 'sustainable development'. A key role of urban planning is to assist cities in becoming economically efficient, socially equitable, environmentally sustainable and financially viable. However, the master plans of Indian cities in the past largely confined to planning and development of land, that too with a narrow focus on its horizontal dimension. They did not devote much attention to the vertical dimension of land, represented by floor space index (FSI). Other aspects of land such as 'access' to infrastructure, especially PT and impacts of density-related externalities on land use were not accorded due importance. The dimensions of density, FSI and accessibility of urban land are important due to their links with agglomeration and network externalities and the imperative need for compact cities to address the concerns of the environment and climate change.

Focus on Form, Neglect of Functions

A master plan regards the physical form of an urban area 20–25 years ahead as the ultimate goal of urban planning. It prescribes land use, density, FSI and infrastructure networks at different levels to attain this goal. It implicitly assumes that the form of a city shapes its functions, ignoring the rational and social processes of designing space that place the citizen at the centre of the city. This goes against a basic concept in land, transport and urban economics that the demand for land, floor space and infrastructure is 'derived' primarily from the needs of economic activities. Such needs depend on the momentum of economic growth, largely determined by market forces. They are closely connected with the location decisions of firms, households and developers-builders, leading to externalities of agglomeration and networking in cities. These externalities call for actions by governments to support density at the emerging nodes of value creation and mitigate congestion in the infrastructure networks. In this context, just-in-time investment in infrastructure, especially PT, is of critical importance. Urban economic theory suggests that the functions and structure of a city are determined simultaneously by the dynamic interactions between market forces and public policies, not by urban planning alone. A city is not an artwork; city planning is not a physical science.

The preoccupation of urban planners in India with land use detailing and controlling development has diverted their attention from the core issues of urbanization such as employment generation and social inclusion. A key economic function of the city is to create remunerative jobs, including those for rural–urban migrants and commuters. However, master plans in India have not devoted much attention to the drivers of inclusive economic growth. They are static, while cities are dynamic. The master plans have also neglected the social functions of the city—to protect the collective rights of inhabitants to a decent life. They have ignored the land and affordable housing needs of the urban poor and low-income groups (LIGs) who constitute the majority in cities. Master plans are formal and do not incorporate the workplace needs of informal economic activities which engage the urban poor. This poses a fundamental question: for whom is the master plan prepared? It also raises the issue: do the planning teams in cities have the skill sets needed to undertake complex economic projections for the plan horizon year 20–25 years ahead?

Conservation and Transport as Residuals

The master planning process is mechanical. It considers the projection of population of the urban area as the first step in plan formulation. The increase in population between the base and plan horizon year is projected and divided by an estimate of household size. This gives the increase in number of households. That number is multiplied by the space norm for an average middle-class household in the city fixed by the planners, yielding the land required for residential use. The projections of land needed for non-residential uses—office, retail, industry, community, recreation, etc.—are tagged to the economic projections and space norms for the relevant activities. This methodology treats land uses for conservation and transportation as residual elements in the planning process. This has led to the neglect of environment and PT. The master plans have failed to address the mobility needs of the urban poor and LIGs, who constitute the majority in Indian cities. These groups need residences near PT nodes and corridors so that they can access the emerging job opportunities in cities. Further, the master plans have promoted segregated land uses as in the West, whereas mixed uses are appropriate for Indian cities, with the majority owning no motor vehicle and large numbers engaged in informal sector activities.

The treatment of transport as a residual in the urban planning chain undermines its crucial role in 'guiding' local economic development and affordable housing. This has led to cities not being able to exploit the wider economic benefits (WEBs) of transportation investments through agglomeration economies at nodes of economic growth. It has also led to a lack of spatial and functional integration between the city, suburbs, rural areas, satellite towns and emerging growth corridors. Paradoxically, land use planning and transportation planning are pursued as disjointed exercises in India. Neither the master plan nor the transportation plan is able to exploit the power of integrated planning to promote economic growth and sustainable development.

Neglect of Transport-Land Use Integration

A major shortcoming in master planning is that it takes land use as the basis for transportation planning. The opposite view is perhaps more appropriate for a developing country like India that has to undergo structural transformation for decades. When resources are scarce, investments in PT can play a key role in guiding the location of productive economic activities. Transport economics also suggests that the relationship between land use and transportation is two-way. Transport–land use integration is perhaps the single-most important instrument available with planners in developing countries to incorporate the goals of sustainability and inclusion in urban development strategy. However, master plans in India have neglected this tool due to their one-sided view that land use determines the needs for transportation.

Some metropolitan cities in India are executing rapid transit projects to address the concerns of mobility. The full benefits of metro rail, with a capacity to handle 50,000–80,000 phpdt, can be achieved only by densifying transit nodes and corridors, increasing transit ridership to make the metro operationally viable and generating adequate resources to finance transit infrastructure. This requires planned increases in FSI and beneficial changes in land use. It also calls for coordinated planning and development of feeder infrastructure. However, metro rail projects in India are being executed in isolation—without value creating and sharing partnerships between the transit authority, the urban planning authority, other infrastructure entities and the municipality. This has crucial implications for financing planned urban and regional development. Transit projects lead to a massive transfer of resources to land and property owners from the future buyers and renters apart from benefiting them through transit construction subsidy. However, the transit agencies do not possess the legal instruments needed to mobilize the windfall increments in land and property values due to their investments.

Long Process of Plan Formulation

A conspicuous drawback in master plan formulation in India is the inordinately long process. For example, the first Master Plan of Hyderabad started in 1965, but came into force in 1975. Its revision was initiated in 1995, but the notification of the revised plan took place in 2008. The second Master Plan of Mumbai began in 1977, but was completed in 1994. Preparatory activities for the second Master Plan of Delhi were launched before 1980, but the plan came into operation in 1990. Experience shows that not only master plans but also zonal development plans do not get ready for years. Further, local area plans take a very long time to prepare. In the meantime, haphazard growth occurs in anticipation of future trends; large-scale violations of master plan become too conspicuous. Unauthorized constructions mushroom, especially in urban fringes and areas earmarked for public facilities, including conservation. Ironically, the planning practices followed by Indian cities reveal that though the master plans claimed to be rigid, discretionary changes in land use and FSI have occurred on a fairly large scale. Such changes reduced the space earmarked for public uses. Master plans of cities, while eyeing for too many unimportant details, neglected their core infrastructure needs, including PT networks and their financing.

Gross Neglect of Plan Financing

India, while borrowing the urban planning model from the United Kingdom, has not followed the plan financing system in that country. There has been little attempt by Indian cities to mobilize the 'development value' created through the urban planning system. Most cities have not resorted to innovative land-based plan financing instruments adopted by other countries such as impact fee, developer exaction, infrastructure cess, special assessment district, betterment levy, purchasable development right and tax increments financing. Master plans in India lack a coherent strategy to finance their development proposals due to failure to incorporate the economics of cities into the urban planning process.

The sources of financing city plans in the United Kingdom include, apart from substantial grants from the central government, 'planning obligations' and 'community infrastructure levy'. Central grants often exceed 70 per cent of the municipal revenues. Section 106 of the UK Town and Country Planning Act, 1990, stipulates that any person interested in land in the area of a local planning authority may, by agreement or otherwise, enter into and enforce a 'planning obligation' (a) restricting the development or use of the land in any specified way; (b) requiring specified operations or activities to be carried out in, on, under or over the land; (c) requiring the land to be used in any specified way or (d) requiring a sum or sums to be paid to the authority. The community infrastructure levy was introduced under the Planning Act, 2008, and came into force through the Community Infrastructure Levy Regulations 2010. This is a hypothecated levy collected from developers at the time of according planning permission towards the cost of infrastructure in the local area.

Interestingly, the history of town planning in the United Kingdom presents a century of efforts by policymakers to design innovative instruments to capture the windfall benefits accruing to the landowners and developers due to spatial planning and infrastructure investment (Table 9.3). Such efforts are missing in India.

Table 9.3 *United Kingdom: Evolution of Taxation of Planning/ Development Gain (1909–2008)*

Measure to Extract Planning/Development Gains	Description of Levy	Years
Betterment Charges (Housing and Town Planning Act of 1909)	50% levy on increases in land values due to TPS.	1909–1932
Betterment Charges (Housing and Town Planning Act of 1932)	Not exceeding 75% levy on increases in land values due to TPS.	1932–1947
Development Charge (Housing and Town Planning Act of 1947)	100% of tax on increase in land value arising due to planning permission or a levy equal to development value of land.	1947–1953
Capital Gains Tax (Finance Act, 1965, and Capital Gains Tax Regulations 1967)	Capital gains tax at 30% on gains arising on the disposal of capital assets, including land.	1967
Betterment Levy (Land Commission Act, 1967)	40% of net development value realized through land transaction or development.	1967–1971
Development Gains Tax (Finance Act, 1974)	Tax on disposal or notional disposal of land or building with development value.	1974
Development Land Tax (Development Land Tax Act, 1976)	Tax of 80% on development value of land with intention to increase it to 100%; rate reduced to 60% in 1979.	1976–1985
Planning Obligation (Town and Country Planning Act, 1990: Section 106)	Contributions from developers negotiated by local authority towards cost of specific public facilities as condition of planning permission.	1990–
Community Infrastructure Levy (Planning Act, 2008, and Community Infrastructure Levy Regulations 2010)	Hypothecated local levy to fund new infrastructure in addition to developer contribution under Planning Obligations.	2010–

Source: Town and Country Planning and other Acts in the United Kingdom; Mohanty (2014, 2016).

Multiplicity of Plans and Authorities

Indian cities are subjected to multiple plans prepared by multiple authorities. These plans lack an integrated approach. Recognizing this, the JNNURM introduced the concept of 'CDP'. However, the mission failed to recognize that while a master plan was statutory, a CDP was not. The JNNURM also introduced city mobility plan and slum-free city plan. Over the years, there has been a move by government programmes to proliferate urban plans without organic links between them. These include perspective plan, district development plan, metropolitan development plan, city utility and infrastructure plan, city investment plan, heritage conservation plan, disaster management plan, environmental conservation plan, city sanitation plan, etc. While each of these plans has a purpose, the lack of integration between them undermines their usefulness. Moreover, while the capacity of cities to prepare plans and projects is limited, they are severely constrained by the lack of resources to finance them. Thus, most urban plans remain unimplemented. Some of them die with discontinuation of the schemes which prescribed them. The multiplicity of authorities also leads to plans working at cross-purposes, resulting in over-regulation of land development.

The institutional structure for urban plan preparation, financing and implementation in India is fragmented. For example, the authorities involved in planning and development of Delhi include: DDA, DMRC, Delhi Urban Art Commission, New Delhi Municipal Council, three municipal corporations, Delhi Jal Board, Delhi Urban Shelter Improvement Board, Government of National Capital Territory of Delhi, National Capital Region Planning Board and Ministries of Urban Development, Home and Railways, GoI. The issues of coordination between these authorities are most obvious in the context of transport–land use integration needed to implement the new TOD policy of Delhi. This policy was approved by the GoI in July 2015. It aims at promoting walk to work and checking congestion and pollution. It targets to reserve 45 per cent of developed land for affordable housing—for the poor and LIGs, and the middle class. Further, the policy aims to bring 20 per cent of Delhi's development area under TOD zone, with FSI of 4 to densify Delhi. However, except one project approved for East Delhi, not much progress has been achieved to promote TOD in the national capital region. This is due to the lack of win–win partnerships between authorities to cooperate, design and finance TOD, which warrants a huge upfront investment. The new Metro Rail Policy issued by the GoI in August 2017 calls for adopting value capture financing (VCF) instruments and TOD to raise resources to finance PPP in metro, including betterment levy. Ironically, the power to levy betterment and other value capture taxes does not vest in the authority investing in metro rail. The state government concerned has to facilitate such levies and make the proceeds available to the transit authority.

Pervasive Constraints of Capacity

Effective urban planning calls for a six-step process: (a) defining priority objectives, (b) developing a strategy consistent with objectives, (c) identifying and quantifying inputs, (d) identifying and quantifying outputs, (e) projecting and monitoring outcomes and (f) projecting and monitoring citywide impacts (Bertaud 2003). These tasks call for instituting capacity, including human resource and management information systems (MISs), which is lacking in India. While urban planning is focused on plan formulation and development control, critical aspects such as plan financing, project implementation and monitoring of outputs, outcomes and impacts are grossly neglected.

The capacity for regional and urban planning in India is severely constrained by the lack of planners: physical, transportation, environment, social, economic and the like. Only about 2,100 master plans have been notified in the country. For many of these plans, the zonal and local area plans are not complete. With more than 7,900 cities and towns in India, including 53 metropolitan cities requiring Metropolitan Development Plans and more than 650 districts requiring District Development Plans as mandated by the Constitution of India, the country needs a huge increase in the number of town and country planners from the current level of about 4,500. An expert group set up by the Ministry of Human Resource Development (MHRD), GoI, has projected the requirement of urban planners in the country by 2031 at 300,000 (MHRD, GoI, 2011). However, there are only 21 recognized institutions in the country, producing nearly 600 qualified planners annually. While the existing planning resources in the country need to be optimally used, planning education in India must be given a significant impetus to create a pool of qualified town and country planners to address the challenges of urbanization.

Marginalized Role of Municipalities

A key question in urban planning in India is: Who plans for the city? The Constitution (74th Amendment) Act, 1992, mandates that urban planning, including town planning, is a legitimate function of elected municipalities. However, under the provisions of urban development and town planning laws of most states, the task of urban planning is assigned to urban development authorities and other parastatals. These laws envisage that such authorities devolve the tasks of urban planning to municipalities. However, the preparation of urban DPs in practice continues to remain with parastatals. While plan implementation is entrusted to municipalities in some states, their involvement in the plan formulation process is marginal. In some cities, the municipalities are not even authorized to approve building plans. In most states, the urban planning process remains centralized. The JNNURM tried to alleviate the problem by including a reform that required states 'to ensure meaningful association/engagement of ULBs in planning functions of parastatals as well as delivery of services to citizens'. This reform has not made a dent on the urban planning system in the country. Municipalities in India continue to play a marginal role in the planning of their cities.

While the URDPFI guidelines 2014 issued by the GoI (MoUD 2015a) have tried to address some of the lacunae in master planning, there remains a conspicuous need to incorporate the economics of cities, including land and transport economics into the model of urban planning.

NEW GUIDELINES FOR URBAN PLANNING

The URDPFI guidelines replace the guidelines issued by the Town and Country Planning Organisation (TCPO) in 1996. These are stated to be 'comprehensive for promoting balanced and orderly regional and urban planning and development'. They acknowledge the criticism that the urban planning in India is 'rigid' and 'static', with 'little regard to investment planning' and the plan formulation and approval processes 'taking a very long time'. They highlight the emerging needs of urban settlements due to rapid growth in urban population, globalization of the economy, advances in information and communication technologies and cities becoming 'more dynamic'. They also refer to 'a new dimension to the planning process' due to 'new emerging aspects' such as regional development, inclusive planning, sustainable habitat, land use and transport integration at the planning stage, service level benchmarks, disaster management imperatives and governance reforms.

The URDPFI guidelines recommend an urban and regional planning system comprising of: (a) core area planning and (b) specific and investment planning. Core area planning includes a set of four interdependent plans: (a) a long-term 'perspective plan' with vision and policy orientation, (b) a sustainability-based long-term 'regional plan' (and 'district plan') aimed at optimization of regional resources for development, (c) a comprehensive long-term settlement plan as 'DP' for urban and peri–urban areas and (d) a short-term rolling 'local area plan' within the framework of DP. Specific and investment planning comprises of a set of three plans: (a) a rolling special purpose plan for special purposes within the framework of 'DP', (b) annual plans to translate the physical and fiscal resource requirements of DP/local area plan and (c) project/research focused on execution. The new guidelines cover planning system framework, planning process, contents of plans, resource mobilization for plan implementation, regional planning approach, urban planning approach, sustainability guidelines, simplified planning techniques, infrastructure planning, simplified development promotion regulations and general recommendations. They recognize the need for modifying the guidelines depending on the context of the city to make the planning process 'efficient and dynamic'.

The planning system recommended by the URDPFI guidelines 2014 includes statutory plans as well as non-statutory plans prescribed under various national policies and programmes from time to time (Table 9.4).

The URDPFI guidelines indicate the contents of various plans. For example, the contents prescribed for a DP include five broad heads: existing conditions and development issues, assessment of deficiencies

Table 9.4 *Planning System Framework in India: The URDPFI Guidelines (2014)*

Planning System	Scope and Purpose of the Plan	Time Frame	Indicative List of Plans
Perspective Plan	To develop vision and provide a policy framework for urban and regional development.	20–30 years	Long-term perspective vision document, concept plan, mission statement
Regional Plan	To identify the region and regional resources for development within which settlement (urban and rural) plan to be prepared and regulated by District Planning Committee (DPC).	20 years	Regional plan (mobility plan), sub-regional plan
DP	To prepare a comprehensive DP for urban areas, peri-urban areas under control of development authority/ metropolitan planning committee.	20–30 years (review every 5 years)	District DP (mobility plan), city/metropolitan DP (mobility plan), master plan, city utility plan (30 years), revised DP
Local Area Plan	To detail the sub-city land use plan and integration with urban infrastructure, mobility and services.	5–20 years (review every 5 years)	TPSs, zonal plan/sub-city plan, ward committee plan, coastal zone management plan, urban redevelopment plan

(Continued)

Table 9.4 (Continued)

Planning System	Scope and Purpose of the Plan	Time Frame	Indicative List of Plans
Specific and Investment Planning			
Special Purpose Plan	To identify the needs of special areas which require special plan within the framework of the DP.	5–20 years (within city utilities 30 year plan)	CDP (as per the JNNURM), comprehensive mobility plan (as per the JNNURM), city sanitation plan (as per the JNNURM), disaster management plan (as per the National Disaster Management Authority [NDMA]), slum redevelopment plan (as per Rajiv Awas Yojana (RAY)), tourism master plan, environmental conservation plan, heritage conservation plan
Annual Plan	To translate DP in the context of annual physical and fiscal resource requirement. To monitor plan implementation with performance milestones.	1 year	Investment plan, audit and monitoring plan
Project/ Research	To focus on project-related investments, costing and returns, and studies required prior to or post-plan formulation. This should be a continuous process to support planning and implementation at all stages and promote innovation in practice.	5–20 years	Pre-feasibility and feasibility study, DPR, schemes and sub-projects, surveys and studies, projects such as Riverfront Development.

Source: MoUD (2015a).

and projected requirements, vision and mission, development proposals and implementation plan. Table 9.5 presents the indicative contents of various plans.

Some welcome features of the URDPFI guidelines are: (a) 'DP' to replace 'master plan', (b) 'development promotion regulations' to substitute 'DCRs', (c) overarching DP for a metropolitan region to be in the form of a 'structure plan', providing a broad framework and flexibility for urban planning, (d) 'DP' and 'mobility plan' to be integrated to ensure 'transport-oriented spatial planning', (e) planning at the local level to be mainly guided by urban design approach focusing on mobility, accessibility and connectivity, (f) planning process to be simplified and (g) land to generate fund for infrastructure development. However, the guidelines have three major shortcomings. First, they do not address the multiplicity of plans prescribed by multiple authorities, leading to overlapping contents, regulations and conflicting signals to actors in the spatial economy. In fact, they exacerbate the problem by prescribing the plans advocated under special purpose schemes, some of which have already been discontinued. Second, the guidelines focus on horizontal land and call for the projection of land requirements for various uses. They underplay the crucial role of vertical land, 'density' and 'accessibility' in the spatial organization of economic activities and distribution of demand for floor space. Third, they do not provide for adequate flexibility to address the needs of economic growth as it occurs. Location and land use decisions by firms, households and developers are shaped by interactions of market forces and public policies, not urban planning alone. Such interactions are influenced by economic variables, including land values, housing prices, transport costs and externalities. They make cities inherently dynamic and call for a flexible planning strategy that is responsive to the needs of economic growth and structural transformation.

The new urban planning guidelines advocate four steps in plan preparation: survey, analysis, synthesis and projection. They prescribe demographic and economic projections which, along with space norms fixed by the planners, determine the land allocation for various uses. The guidelines underscore the need to consider the following aspects in making economic projections: existing and proposed hierarchy of

Table 9.5 *Contents of Various Urban Plans: The URDPFI Guidelines (2014)*

Broad Head	Contents
Analysis of Existing Scenario and Development Issues	• Background • Demographic profile • Land profile • Economic profile • Infrastructure profile • Environmental profile • Shelter • Administrative profile • Maps and plans • Gap analysis
Projected Requirements	• Population • Economic base and employment • Shelter • Transportation • Social infrastructure • Physical infrastructure • Land requirement for various uses: residential, commercial, industrial, public and semi-public, parks, playgrounds and open spaces, transport and communication, special areas, agriculture and water bodies • Assessment of disaster management infrastructure
Development of Vision	• Vision based on existing conditions, development issues and stakeholders' consultations • Goals and objectives • Guiding principles for plan formulation
Development Proposals	• Land use plan • Comprehensive mobility plan • Infrastructure plan/utility plan • Special area planning • Development promotion rules/regulations • Annexures: detailed scaled maps
Implementation Plan	• Priorities: classification of projects/development proposals • Phasing • Proposal for land resource mobilization • Investment strategy • Institutional set-up

Source: MoUD (2015a).

commercial areas, dispersal of commercial and industrial activities, environmental restrictions on industrial development, urban poverty alleviation, workforce and employment in different sectors, etc. However, they do not explain the mechanics of how market-led variables, interacting with policy-related factors, produce the projected spatial and economic outcomes. They rightly observe that the likely demands of land development in cities rest on the composition of economic activities, their 'scale', 'possible location' within a city or a region and 'broad relationships between such activities' (MoUD 2015a, 258). However, they do not dwell on 'scale economies' arising in secondary and tertiary production, 'agglomeration economies' associated with collocation of firms, workers and institutions, and 'network economies' resulting from linkages between economic activities in cities. These factors lead to significant 'non-linearity' in the movement of economic variables that makes projections covering a period of 20–25 years a difficult task. They also require economic planning skills in cities, which are grossly wanting at present. Further, they call for a flexible approach to urban planning capable of accommodating the needs of economic growth as it occurs and as it is affected by major investment projects.

The URDPFI guidelines provide for changes in land use with approval from a high-powered regulatory authority at the state level chaired by the chief minister. They suggest that the authority be entrusted with the following functions:

- Assess and monitor the overall regional/urban planning in the state;
- Observe and evaluate the impact of planning on other elements of the development system;
- Guide the preparation of perspective plan for the state which should provide the frame for all regional and urban DPs in the state;
- Be responsible for guiding land utilization based on suitability and proposed structure of transportation networks;
- Guide the state for development, focusing on protection of environmentally sensitive areas, natural forms, natural vegetation, water bodies, etc.
- Function as an appellate authority to address the related grievances;
- Review the functioning of agencies to overcome multiplicity, duplication and gaps.

Further, the regulatory authority is required to examine plan modifica-
tion requests and permit (mid-term) land use changes, guided by 'large
developments', 'social interest' and 'need for all'. This stipulation is not
simply practical, given the large number of cities and towns in a state
and the range of critical functions exercised by a chief minister. It will
not accord the flexibility needed by urban planning to respond to the
economic dynamics of cities.

INCORPORATING THE ECONOMICS OF CITIES

Cities make little sense without a reference to their economic
functions—catalyzing growth and employment while generating
public finance for socio-economic development. However, the master
planning model neglects the economics of cities, including land and
transport economics. This is perhaps due to differences in the approach
adopted by planners and economists to address the urban problems. As
Richard Arnott observes:

> Economists and planners are often at loggerheads. Economists see the
> strengths of markets; planners see their weaknesses. When a market
> fails in some respect, economists favour pricing solutions, while plan-
> ners favour regulatory solutions. Economists tend to be pragmatists;
> planners tend to be idealists. Economists generally respect consumers'
> tastes, while planners often challenge them. Though the philosophical
> differences between economists and planners are difficult to reconcile,
> a more productive dialogue between the two groups is possible if each
> better understands the language and the logic of other. (2012, 51)

Arnott's view may be exaggerated. However, there can be no dispute
that urban planning will perform better if it incorporates the key principles of land, transport and urban economics.

Cities are the creations of numerous actors striving to benefit from
density, scale and networking. They form to exploit the external
economies of collocation. These economies are returns to density and
networking, manifesting in productivity gains and cost savings. The
externalities of cities, however, lead to divergences between market
and social outcomes, calling for public policies to address negative
consequences such as overcrowding, congestion and pollution. Cities

grow when the benefits to people from living, working and transacting in cities outweigh the costs. Location decisions of producers, workers, developers and other actors in the economy involve important trade-offs between benefits and costs. An evaluation of these trade-offs is essential for the effective design of urban planning and projects. Thus, an 'a priori' conclusion regarding the appropriateness of a city's structure may not be warranted.

The Economic Approach to Cities

The economic approach to cities calls for a people-centric rather than a place-centric design of urban policy (Glaeser 2008b). It is based on three pillars of economics. The first is: people respond to incentives—financial and non-financial. The second pillar is 'no arbitrage equilibrium'. This is exemplified by Nobel Laureate Milton Friedman's oft-cited statement that there is no such thing called a 'free lunch'. This implies that households balance the benefits of wages and amenities against the costs of housing and commuting in choosing locations. Firms compare the benefits of productivity with wage costs while deciding where to locate and how many workers to hire. Developers-builders balance the cost of housing production, including land cost with the price of housing while deciding where to build and whether to build more or taller buildings. The third pillar is that good policies expand the range of choices for individual actors in an economy. Interacting with market forces, they influence the decision-making by firms, households and developers-builders. The economic approach emphasizes the need for urban policy to focus on people and anticipate the mobility of workers and firms.

While the master planning model is not people-centric, it relies on regulation as the primary instrument to achieve the plan objectives. It is based on the premise that the control of land use, density, FSI and other spatial planning parameters will lead to the desired city form. The economic approach to cities, however, emphasizes the role of pricing, taxation and incentive-based development instruments in shaping spatial and economic outcomes. It also suggests that regulation can be more effective, when implemented in conjunction with economic instruments such as land taxation and congestion pricing. For example, the development of a public transit system connecting growth nodes, when combined with favourable changes in land use, increased FSI and taxation of unused and underused land in such nodes can incentivize the location of value-creating and high-density developments there, leading to agglomeration economies. The economic approach further suggests that the urban planners need to study the signals provided by prices regarding the operation of real estate markets to design timely interventions. They must monitor the spatial trends and patterns in land values and land rents, housing prices, office rents, transport costs, etc., and their impacts on resource mobilization to finance urban infrastructure.

Urban Economics and Planning

Urban economics highlights the interactions between land and housing markets, externalities and public policies in shaping the spatial economy. It refers to five major factors influencing city structure:

- location choice by firms, households and developers-builders based on appraisal of benefits and costs;
- agglomeration economies arising from the collocation of economic activities in the secondary and tertiary sectors, leading to benefits of density;
- building technology and FSI that permit developers to substitute capital for land by going vertical;
- transport technology that extends labour market catchment area and expands the choice sets of employers and workers; and
- government policy affecting land development and use, including spatial planning, regulation, land taxation, development of infrastructure, provision of civic services and promotion of economic growth.

The aforementioned factors interact in complex ways, influencing city function and form. Accordingly, a static view of the optimal structure of a city, density of a development area or a strategy to disperse economic activities from a central location without evaluating their socio-economic impacts is bound to have serious limitations.

Research refers to the interplay between opposing forces in determining outcomes in the spatial economy. Urban economics highlights the role of external economies and urban costs in the location decisions of firms, households and developers. New economic geography emphasizes the tension between centripetal and centrifugal forces in determining regional specialization and agglomeration of economic activities. Key centripetal forces are: (a) market size: producers prefer larger markets due to consumers' preference for a variety of goods (demand linkage); a concentration of suppliers of intermediate inputs locally reduces the costs of other producers (cost linkage); (b) thick labour markets: the agglomeration of many economic activities leads to the emergence of markets for specialized skills to match the requirements of firms; and (c) pure external economies such as knowledge spillovers that promote learning. Main centrifugal forces include: (a) transport costs; (b) immobile factors such as land and natural resources; (c) barriers to trade; (d) rise in land and housing costs; and (e) pure external diseconomies such as congestion. The interactions between various centripetal and centrifugal forces shape spatial and economic outcomes, not urban planning or government action alone.

Land Economics and Planning

Land economics explores the relationships between land and housing markets, urban economics and spatial planning. It recognizes the multiple dimensions of urban land—as an input, an output and a resource. It clarifies that the demand for urban land is derived primarily from the demands of economic activities for floor space, and not land per se. While the supply of land can be increased by adding rural areas to urban jurisdictions, that is, by 'building out', the availability of floor space to support greater intensity of economic activities in particular locations can be increased by enhancing FSI, that is, by 'building up'. Both the horizontal and vertical dimensions of urban land are affected by public investments in infrastructure and urban externalities which lead to unearned increments in land values at vantage locations. Urban land is a highly heterogeneous commodity and the obsession of urban planners with long-term projection of horizontal land for various economic activities, ignoring other dimensions is thus misplaced. While cities must strive to discharge their fundamental functions to drive growth and generate employment, the urban planning system should be able to cater to the land use, floor space and accessibility needs of value-generating economic activities in cities in an integrated fashion as economic growth unveils.

The basic model of location and land use in cities assumes that workers commute to the CBD to reap the benefits of higher wages due to agglomeration economies. In the process, they balance the cost of land and housing against the cost of commuting to work while choosing residential location. The model predicts that land rent, housing price, building height and population density fall with increase in distance from the CBD. Further, rising population and greater demand for housing with increase in income make outward urban expansion of growing cities inevitable. More complicated models of land and urban economics suggest that the combined effects of market forces and public policies determine the prices and costs faced by producers, workers, consumers and developers. In particular, they influence land rents, housing prices and transport costs. Land economics regards the rent to land as a 'residual' or an 'unearned increment' and an ideal object of taxation. Trends in land values, housing prices and commuting costs present useful information on the demand and supply for land, floor space and transport in cities. They provide useful directions to planners for alleviating the constraints in real estate markets and mobilizing resources to finance urban infrastructure. When urban planners fix rigid land use, density and FSI norms up to the plot level, they fail to make use of the valuable information supplied by the market. Land economics also suggests that the constraints imposed by urban planning on the operation of markets lead to significant inefficiencies in the allocation of land for economic activities and dead weight welfare losses. Planners need to take into account the cost of land use planning, not benefits alone.

Transport Economics and Planning

Transport makes or mars a city. It affects city functions and structure. Transport economics highlights the importance of 'accessibility premium' to locations and 'WEB' to the economy due to public transportation investments. These benefits significantly raise the benefit–cost ratio of major transport projects that would have otherwise received a low ranking under the conventional appraisal methods. The impacts of UT on the environment and mobility of the poor, and on increase in land values that could finance planned urban infrastructure constitute other important reasons why UT needs significant attention from the planners. However, the master planning model in India has accorded a secondary role to transport. It regards land use as the basis for transportation planning. Emphasizing the two-way relationship between transportation and land use, transport economics counters the argument by urban planners that transportation should follow land use. In fact, in cities of developing countries like India, with much of urbanization yet to occur, UT has a crucial role in promoting sustainable and inclusive development apart from meeting the mobility needs of the people. The capacity of the transport system to connect workers to jobs in less than 1 hour commuting time is critical for enabling cities in developing countries to function as efficient labour markets.

Obviously, when a major transportation project like MRTS in Delhi, BRTS in Ahmedabad, Bandra-Worli Sea Link in Mumbai, Super Corridor in Indore and Mumbai-Ahmedabad HSR is planned, it will be inefficient to leave the land use and density patterns in the project-impact zones unchanged on the ground that the master plan did not envisage any change. Transport economics highlights the significance of UT in guiding planned urban development in view of its impacts on agglomeration and networking economies, labour market mobility, economic growth and social inclusion. The urban poor, who have been excluded from land and housing markets by the design of master planning, deserve a new deal through the allocation of land and workplaces at locations with easy access to PT. Transport economics also emphasizes the role of major UT projects in leading to unearned increments in land values that can be captured to raise resources. The structuring of such projects and the design of plan implementation and financing instruments must be pursued together to explore the power of PT in reengineering cities.

REFORMING URBAN PLANNING IN INDIA

The master planning model in India aims at a predetermined built form for an urban area and prescribes detailed land use zoning and development control as the principal instruments to achieve the same. It ignores the dynamic interactions between spatial and economic forces in shaping the structure and functions of a city as it evolves. In the process, it neglects two powerful factors in urban economic growth, namely 'density' and 'accessibility'. It also neglects economic instruments, including pricing, taxation and fiscal incentives to achieve the planning and development objectives. Master plans overlook the fact that outcomes in cities are shaped by the actions and interactions of numerous firms, households and developers–builders. These actors choose locations and make operational decisions based on appraisal of benefits and costs, shaped by market forces and public policies both, not spatial planning alone. Rigid land use plans, drilled down to the neighbourhood level, reduce the degrees of freedom available to such actors. They stifle enterprise, initiative and innovation, much needed for cities to discharge their fundamental role as drivers of economic growth, providers of employment opportunities and generators of public finance for development. Further, the dynamic interactions between market forces, externalities and public policies make the tasks of long-term economic projections and spatially distributing them difficult. Confining the destiny of a city in a developing country to a static spatial frame based on mechanical considerations is inherently flawed.

While the drawbacks of a form-based and land use-centric urban planning model to address the needs of socio-economic transformation in India are obvious, there is yet another compelling reason why the country cannot afford the 'utopian' master plans and their instrumentalities. The pervasive lack of capacity in urban planning is too conspicuous to be ignored. It is simply not possible for 4,500 odd town planners in the country to develop and implement the large number of detailed plans prescribed by the URDPFI guidelines. Moreover, too many plans, based on disjointed exercises carried out by multiple authorities lead to serious issues of contradiction, coordination and implementation. Ironically, weak plan implementation has been the most pervasive problem of urban planning in India. A key reason for this is the failure of master plans to present a coherent strategy to finance their development proposals. By neglecting land and transport economics, these plans have not been able to exploit density, accessibility and development as tools for financing urban infrastructure. The master planning model, rooted in the modernist urban planning theories of the twentieth century and the Town and Country Planning Act of 1947 in the United Kingdom, is not suitable for cities in developing countries like India.

The inherent lacunae in the master planning approach are obvious when one asks the fundamental questions: for whom is the master plan prepared? Who prepares the plan? Who implements the plan? These questions were eloquently addressed by Jane Jacobs in her critique of the modernist urban planning theories (Jacobs 1992 [1961]). Referring to the significance of dense, diverse and dynamic cities, Jacobs emphasized the need for a people-centric and decentralized planning strategy to harness the energy of the people for collaboration and innovation. However, the technocratic master plans in India have not focused on the needs of the majority in cities. While Indian cities are predominantly inhabited by the poor and low-income households, with about 66 per cent having no exclusive room, one room or two rooms, the master plans have allocated land based on the space norms for the middle-class households. A key direction for reforming master planning is to incorporate the economic approach to cities. This approach is intrinsically valuable as it places people, not space, at the centre of development. Key elements in this approach include: people-centric planning; optimization of planned objectives subject to constraints; recognition of initial conditions and history; density as a source of agglomeration economies; accessibility to the economic mass as a source of WEB; transport–land use integration as an instrument to tap the synergy between density, accessibility and development; economic tools such as pricing of development rights, land taxation, congestion charging and fiscal incentives for development to supplement physical planning instruments and value creation, capture and recycling as the foundation for the strategy to finance urban DP.

People-centric Urban Planning

As Jane Jacobs argues, the most important agents in an urban system are the people themselves whose actions and interactions over time produce the urban phenomena. It is the people who organize and modify bits and pieces in cities, creating the urban structure. Jacobs observes: 'cities are fantastically dynamic places, and this is strikingly true of their successful parts, which offers a fertile ground for the plans of thousands of people' (1992 [1961], 14).

Jacobs refers to the web way of thinking about cities which generate important externalities due to their networking properties. She regards cities as living organisms with internal ability to regenerate continuously despite unpredictable shocks. They are integrated systems in which many variables interact in complex ways and lead to multifaceted social, economic and cultural life. The 'organized complexity' of cities arises from the interrelationships of 'systems', of 'processes' and of 'self-organization'. The various elements in a city function together synergistically. Decentralized actors organize into something greater than the sum of their individual parts. Jacobs also highlights the importance of diversity in city vitality. She identifies four generators of diversity: mixed uses, short blocks, buildings of different ages, state of repair and uses, and density. According to her, density facilitates diversity, and diversity creates richness of urban life. They reinforce each other. Although the modernist planning theories blame density for crime, pollution, congestion and many other urban problems, Jacobs convincingly argues that a high concentration of people is important for civic life, economic growth and well-being. Urban planning in India needs to be people-centric and exploit the collocation of population in cities as a resource while addressing the negative externalities. This calls for decentralized planning with a key role for elected municipalities and ward committees in urban planning as envisaged in the Constitution (74th Amendment) Act. This may be subjected to structural plans in the form of metropolitan and district DPs focused on infrastructure and conservation.

Optimization with Constraints

Economic principles refer to optimization subject to constraints, including those related to resource mobilization, management capacity and plan implementation. While master plans aim at the 'first-best' outcome, economic considerations call for exploring the 'second-best' or a lower order solution when the first-best is not feasible. The economic approach calls for optimal utilization of resources, taking the binding constraints into account. In this context, environmental considerations call for carrying capacity-based planning, protecting natural and heritage resources and addressing climate change and energy security. These concerns are so overwhelming that cities in India cannot simply afford a planning model founded on the automobile. The country needs to move people, not vehicles. Further, equitable urbanization calls for the allocation of adequate space to the poor and LIGs for living, working and vending at locations with easy access to PT. The overriding considerations of sustainability and equity suggest that urban planning in India must be rooted in a public transportation-led and TOD framework. It must also fully utilize the spatial and economic instruments available, including transport–land use integration, CC and taxation of unused and underused land to promote TOD.

Significance of Initial Conditions

The economic approach to the city refers to the importance of history and initial conditions in the design of urban development strategy. Urban economics suggests that history and geography matter significantly for cities. NEG refers to the role of 'circular and cumulative causation processes', 'lock-in effects' and 'path dependence' in regional specialization and polarization of economic activity. These factors emphasize the role of the 'context' in designing city development policies and programmes. Blanket prescriptions cannot lead to the desired outcomes. The prevailing conditions must be taken into account, and this calls for avoiding the wholesale restructuring of habitations and addressing the incentive structures of various actors in the spatial economy. The fact that Indian cities have followed a highly restrictive model of urban planning for long suggests that the liberalization of this regime, accompanied by investments in public transportation infrastructure, would offer significant opportunities for urban economic development along with resource mobilization based on instruments such as impact fee, land-based taxes, betterment levy and congestion charges.

Master planning in India in the past has been exclusionary. On one hand, the norms set by DCRs such as minimum size of development, maximum FSI, minimum size of plot and dwelling unit, maximum plot coverage, minimum setback, minimum number of parking spaces per unit of housing, minimum permissible width of approach road and other standards have led to an inequitable planning regime in which some gained while many lost. On the other, the assignment of higher FSI and land use such as commercial, office or high-density residential has resulted in huge windfall benefits to a lucky group of owners of land at vantage locations. In the past, even a fraction of such unearned increments has not been mobilized to meet the cost of planned urban development that led to such benefits and to compensate the losers. When cities move to a liberalized, PT-led and transit-oriented regime, considerable unearned increments will arise to some actors in the spatial economy again. A strong case exists for linking the liberalization of FSI and land use with mobilization of resources to finance public transportation infrastructure and allocation of adequate space for the urban poor for living, working and vending to correct for historical inequities.

Benefit and Costs of Density

Density, powered by accessibility, is a critical resource to promote planned urban development and support tertiary sector activities subject to scale economies during a country's development transition. It is the key to reaping benefits of agglomeration and network externalities. Further, it leads to 'location rents' that can be exploited to finance infrastructure. The economic approach to cities calls for strategic densification of cities, with focus on a few centres and sub-centres rather than spreading development too thinly. However, poorly managed density can lead to negative environmental consequences. Thus, a strategy to increase density needs to be combined with decongestion programmes, including investment in transportation infrastructure and CC. These programmes must be 'designed' and not 'predetermined', considering both benefits and costs to firms, households, developers-builders and the society as a whole. What the society ought to be concerned with is 'benefits minus costs', not costs per se. If the social benefits of density exceed the social costs, taking into account direct, indirect and wider economic impacts of spatial planning and public transportation investments, the same must be promoted. The arguments of the twentieth-century planners to justify town planning solely on considerations to eliminate the negative effects of clustering are one-sided. They undermine the positive role of density in facilitating interactions, face-to-face contact, human capital accumulation, labour market efficiency and returns to sharing of local public goods. They also fail to recognize that the concept of density is not absolute; its impacts are shaped by the mix of economic activities and their access to PT networks.

Angel (2012) calls urbanization a project. The urbanization project is complete in the developed world. It is ongoing in developing countries. Every project has its own economics and calls for appropriate designing so as to maximize net benefits, that is, benefits minus costs. This requires the structuring of spatial planning and investment in infrastructure, especially transportation together through schemes such as urban expansion, renewal and new township development. The designing of such schemes must aim at maximizing the social benefits from density and accessibility while minimizing the costs of overcrowding. Only an urban planning model that provides flexibility in regard to density, FSI and land use as infrastructure investments and economic growth occur can exploit the economies of agglomeration, mitigate the diseconomies of congestion, maximize the potential of growth-generating activities and mobilize resources for plan implementation. Economic principles suggest that zero pollution or zero congestion is not socially optimal.

Approach to Urban Plan Formulation

Economic considerations suggest that the formulation of urban plans must take three key considerations into account. First, it must recognize the global, national and regional imperatives and constraints in achieving the goals of efficient, inclusive, sustainable and financially viable cities. Second, the actors in the urban economy, including firms, households and developers-builders must have sufficient freedom to respond to market forces, externalities and public policies. Third, the limited resources available for plan implementation with public authorities—density, accessibility, value creation and benefit taxation—must be harnessed with a system of incentives and disincentives to various actors in tune with the planning and development objectives.

A reversal in the present sequence in urban planning is warranted. Planning needs to first assess the carrying capacity of the urban region, determined by environmental constraints. The conservation of natural and heritage resources must be non-negotiable and the starting point in the plan formulation chain. Conservation plan needs to be followed by transportation plan, including a grid of planned arterial and radial roads as well as BRT, MRT and HSR networks, covering a horizon of at least 20–25 years. Traffic-generating commercial, institutional and public activities and high-density housing for the lower and MIGs may be located around transit nodes and corridors. This strategy will promote PT ridership and make the public transit system financially viable. Allocation of land for high-income housing may be the last step in the planning process. A structural planning approach without prescribing detailed land use to the neighbourhood level will enable appropriate response by decentralized actors to the generators of economic momentum and government policies and investment programmes.

Pivotal Role of Public Transport

The pivotal role of PT infrastructure in planned urban development derives from the fact that it leads to agglomeration economies by enhancing accessibility to the economic mass while also reducing traffic congestion and enhancing mobility. Transportation has been the most important resource for cities in developed countries to channelize local economic development. The importance of innovative transportation planning is singularly demonstrated by the 1811 'Grid Plan' of Manhattan, New York. During the nineteenth century, the built-up area of Manhattan increased sevenfold along the grid plan. 'No invisible hand guided Manhattan towards rectangular blocks of private property embedded in a public grid of avenues and streets. A real hand did that of John Tandel Jr., the engineer hired by a state commission to survey the island' (Fuller and Romer 2014, 3). The government acquired land for roads as per the vision plan and protected the same from encroachment for decades. It took up the development of the grid and connectivity infrastructure in a phased manner. It required the landowners to finance the cost of construction of road adjacent to their properties based on the benefit principle. This led to increase in their property values far more than what they paid through betterment levies.

A strategy of transport-led urban development calls for delineating the land needed for arterial and radial roads and rail-based PT networks well in advance so as to add infrastructure inexpensively on a just-in-time basis as urbanization occurs. This approach does not rely on a top-down master planning regime prescribing controls to the plot level. It relies on land development between the arterial roads and around transit corridors by households, firms and developers, facilitated by incentives through schemes such as TPS in Gujarat. Efforts may also be made to procure land for major transportation networks through the planning process. In this regard, the development of Sardar Patel Ring Road in Ahmedabad with land secured through the TPS presents an excellent example. The revised DP for Ahmedabad metropolitan area has demarcated 1 km area around the 76 km ring road as Residential Affordable Housing (R-AH) zone, permitting FSI of 4 for the construction of residential units of 36–80 sq. m of built-up area.

Transportation-Land Use Integration

Transport creates access, and access creates value. Major transport projects lead to network externalities, accessibility premiums and WEB. Maximizing such benefits and making the projects financially viable often call for beneficial changes in land use, density and other planning parameters in transport nodes and corridors. When transport–land use integration is facilitated, it promotes PT ridership and enhances the returns to public investment. It also makes value increment financing (VIF) of such investment possible. These considerations warrant a flexibly regulated and incentive-linked urban planning regime. For example, incentives such as 'access' of large developments to major roads, enhanced FSI in designated transport zones, say, 500 m of transit alignment, and suitable relaxation of other development control norms can promote the objectives of transport-led planning and TOD. Key guiding principles to incentivize TOD are: providing access to PT within 15 minutes of walk and a commuting time to work of 1 hour.

Efforts to promote TOD call for other complementary policies aimed at discouraging automobile ridership, encouraging PT, developing town centres and sub-centres, enhancing regional connectivity and imposing a graduated vacant land tax (VLT) that discourages idle landholding. In order for a transportation project to generate the largest beneficial impacts, the transit authority and the local government must work closely. The local government must be in a position to exploit zoning and land management tools to promote developments that support transit ridership. It must also be equipped with fiscal instruments to capture the unearned increments in land values to repay the debt incurred for financing transit. The need for flexible land use planning in coordination with other complementary policies is demonstrated by many successful public transit projects around the world such as Hong Kong, Singapore, Seoul, Toronto, Copenhagen, Curitiba and Bogota.

Focus on Plan Implementation

A strategic planning approach will accord flexibility for the operation to economic forces. However, it will not be adequate to achieve the objectives of efficient, inclusive and sustainable urban development. Cities must have the financial and managerial resources to implement infrastructure projects and deliver services. Policymakers and planners must appreciate that the instruments available for plan implementation, especially land assembly, are limited, constraining their degrees of freedom. While innovation is the hallmark of great cities, there are many good practices in India and elsewhere which can be customized and replicated. These practices highlight the importance of structuring plan implementation instruments. They include, but are not limited to, TPS in Gujarat; LPS in Amaravati in Andhra Pradesh, Uppal Bhagat, Hyderabad in Telangana and Magarpatta city, Pune in Maharashtra with the landowners–farmers as partners; drastic liberalization of FSI linked to abutting road width and size of plot along with the levy of impact fee in Hyderabad; integrated transportation–land use planning in Copenhagen and Curitiba; auctioning of development rights through CEPAC in Brazil, use of land use zoning and FSI as resource to raise resources for metropolitan transit in Bengaluru; PPP for construction of metro in Hyderabad with focus on using land as a resource; inclusionary zoning (IZ) with reservation of land for socially and economically weaker sections (SEWSs) through the TPS in Gujarat and location of R-AH zone along the Sardar Patel Ring Road in Ahmedabad and land-sharing partnership with farmers for affordable housing in Vijayawada, Andhra Pradesh.

Value Increment Partnerships

Public finance principles suggest that borrowing is the most appropriate instrument to finance lumpy urban infrastructure projects such as MRT and HSR whose benefits spread over generations and jurisdictions. However, the debt incurred for such projects, whether executed by a public authority or a PPP, will have to be repaid. This calls for escrowing revenues: project-based and general. In this connection, a tax increment financing (TIF) approach, often considered 'the only game in the town' in the United States, is worth adoption by Indian cities. This approach aims at earmarking future revenue increments due to infrastructure investments and supporting policies to repay the debt incurred for their financing. TIF focuses on planned development and renewal of designated urban areas with the public authorities 'ring-fencing' a part or whole of the incremental taxes, charges and special levies associated with such ventures. The success of a TIF strategy depends on its design.

Land, transport and urban economics highlight the importance of benefit taxation and CC in the design of financing strategy to implement urban plans. They emphasize that spatial planning and infrastructure development, in conjunction with agglomeration and network externalities, provide significant opportunities for resource mobilization in cities through 'users pay', 'beneficiaries pay', 'congesters pay', 'exacerbaters pay' and 'growth pays' instruments. In particular, land value taxation is an ideal source to raise seed money for financing urban transportation infrastructure, which capitalizes into land values due to enhanced accessibility and increased intensity of development, often facilitated by favourable changes in zoning and increased FSI. While the structuring of financing instruments is crucial for the success of urban plans and projects, economic considerations suggest that a combination of land-based taxes, development financing, VCF, CC and dedicated funding instruments will be appropriate for Indian cities. As major urban projects lead to tax increments for all levels of government, a strong case for value-creating intergovernmental partnerships with earmarking of benefit taxes exists to finance them in the spirit of cooperative federalism. The options for dedicated funding of major urban transportation projects such as arterial and radial roads, BRT, MRT and HSR include transport tax as in France and fuel tax as in the United States, linked to municipal bonds. A city share in GST, which has subsumed a number of local taxes such as octroi and entry tax, presents an appropriate option in the present context of fiscal federalism in India.

Urban Planning as a Resource

Indian cities have not harnessed urban planning as a resource. They are under-planned and over-regulated. They are also under-funded and under-managed. While urban finance and governance are important subjects in their own rights, this book has primarily focused on urban planning and incorporating the key principles of economics to improve the same. Cities in India are under-planned due to the neglect of infrastructure planning and development, especially transportation—in anticipation as well as in response to economic growth. They have thus not exploited the power of transport–land use integration to promote local economic development. Indian cities are also over-regulated due to their restrictive land use, density and FSI regimes, perpetrated by master planning. This model has neglected the economics of cities, land and transport economics, in particular. It has also mastered over the people, especially the poor. The master plan approach needs to be reformed to make urban planning, in conjunction with 'just-in-time' investment in transportation infrastructure an instrument to accelerate India's structural, spatial and socio-economic transformation process. The country must shift from a prescriptive, technocratic, rigid, land use-based and detailed master planning regime to a responsive, people-driven, flexible, transport-led and strategic planning paradigm, aimed at promoting development rather than controlling it. Urban planning must place people at the centre of development and enable cities to effectively discharge their economic and social functions. Urban growth needs to be managed and accommodated, not controlled.

This book takes the view that cities in developing countries like India are economic powerhouses and must not be artificially confined to rigid spatial frames based on inadequate data and inappropriate projections, disregarding their economic dynamics. It does not, however, suggest that the economic approach to cities should replace the physical planning strategy. It emphasizes that urban planning must incorporate the key principles of land, transport and urban economics to be an instrument of economic and social development. The planning system must harness the power of density, accessibility, externalities, transportation–land use integration, benefit taxation, CC, VIF and win-win intergovernmental partnerships based on a benefit-sharing principle. Promoting sustained investment in PT systems to catalyze economic growth and making urban planning responsive to such investment are some key directions for reforming urban planning in India. This book suggests a two-tier approach: structural plans, focused on conservation and infrastructure, and local area plans, focused on TOD, transport–land use integration, IZ and resource mobilization based on value creation, capture and recycling. The focus of urban planning needs to shift from detailed land use plans to a modular development approach led by PT. Dense, diverse and networked cities, distinguished by their transportation and communication grids, land use intensities, spatial planning innovations and dynamic drivers of economic growth will shape India's form and future.

Bibliography

Administrative Staff College of India (ASCI). 2014. *Municipal Finances and Service Delivery in India: A Study Sponsored by the Fourteenth Finance Commission, Government of India.* Hyderabad: ASCI.

Ahluwalia, Isher, R. Kanbur and P. K. Mohanty. 2014. *Challenges of Urbanisation in India.* New Delhi: SAGE Publications.

Alonso, William. 1964. *Location and Land Use.* Cambridge, MA: Harvard University Press.

Andelson, Robert V., ed. 2000. *Land-value Taxation around the World.* Malden, MA: Blackwell.

Anderson, C. 2006. *The Long Tail: Why the Future of Business is Selling Less of More.* New York, NY: Hyperion.

Anderson, John E. 2009. 'A Review of the Evidence on Land Value Taxation'. In *Land Value Taxation: Theory, Evidence, and Practice*, edited by Richard F. Dye and Richard W. England, 99–128. Cambridge, MA: Lincoln Institute of Land Policy.

Anderson, Fredrik and Rikard Forslid. 2003. 'Tax Competition and Economic Geography'. *Journal of Public Economic Theory* 5 (2): 279–303.

Andhra Pradesh Capital Region Development Authority. 2015, 20 June. *Notification for Preparation of Land Pooling Schemes for Amaravati (Capital City) Area.* Amaravati: Andhra Pradesh Capital Region Development Authority.

Angel, Shlomo. 2008. 'An Arterial Grid of Dirt Roads'. *Cities* 25 (3): 146–162.

———. 2012. *Planet of Cities.* Cambridge, MA: Lincoln Institute of Land Policy.

Arnott, R. 2004. 'Does the Henry George Theorem Provide a Practical Guide to Optimal City Size?' *The American Journal of Economics and Sociology* 63 (5): 1057–1090.

———. 2012. 'What Planners Need to Know about the "New Urban Economics"'. In *Oxford Handbook of Urban Economics and Planning*, edited by Nancy Brooks, Kieran Donaghy and Gerrit Jan-Knapp, 51–78. Oxford: Oxford University Press.

Arnott, R. and Joseph E. Stiglitz. 1979. 'Aggregate Land Rents, Expenditure on Public Goods, and Optimal City Size'. *Quarterly Journal of Economics* 93 (4): 471–500.

Atkinson, A. B. and Joseph E. Stiglitz. 1980. *Lectures on Public Economics.* London; New York, NY: McGraw-Hill.

Augustyn, Robert T. and Paul E. Cohen. 1997. *Manhattan in Maps.* New York, NY: Rizzoli International Publications.

Bahl, Roy and Johannes Linn. 1992. *Urban Public Finance in Developing Countries.* New York, NY: Oxford University Press.

Bahl, Roy and Johannes Linn. 2014. *Governing and Financing Cities in the Developing World*. Cambridge, MA: Lincoln Institute of Land Policy.

Bahl, Roy W., Johannes F. Linn and Deborah L. Wetzel, eds. 2013. *Financing Metropolitan Governments in Developing Countries*. Cambridge, MA: Lincoln Institute of Land Policy.

Bahl, Roy, Jorge Martinez-Vazquez and Joan Youngman, eds. 2008. *Making the Property Tax Work: Experiences in Developing and Transitional Countries*. Cambridge, MA: Lincoln Institute of Land Policy.

Baldwin, Richard and Paul Krugman. 2004. 'Agglomeration, Integration and Tax Harmonization'. *European Economic Review*, 48 (1): 1–23.

Baldwin, Richard E., Rikard Forslid, Philippe Martin, Gianmarco Ottaviano and Frederic Robert-Nicoud. 2003. *Economic Geography and Public Policy*. Princeton, NJ: Princeton University Press.

Ballaney, Shirley. 2008. *The Town Planning Mechanism in Gujarat, India*. Washington, DC: World Bank Institute.

Barker, Kate. 2004. *Review of Housing Supply*. London: Her Majesty's Treasury.

———. 2006. *Review of Land Use Planning*. London: Her Majesty's Treasury.

Bauer, Catherine. 1934. *Modern Housing*. Boston, MA: Houghton Mifflin.

Baxter, R. Dudley. 1866. 'Railway Extension and Its Results'. *Journal of Statistical Society of London* 29 (4): 549–595.

Bertaud, Alain. 2003. *The Use and Value of Urban Planning*. Accessed 1 November 2017, http://alain-bertaud.com

———. 2014, 19 February. 'Cities as Labour Markets'. *Working Paper No. 2*, Marron Institute of Urban Management, New York University, New York.

Bertaud, Alain and Jan K. Brueckner. 2005. 'Analysing Building Height Restrictions—Predicted Impacts, Welfare Costs'. *Regional Science and Urban Economics* 35 (2): 109–125.

Bhagat, Ram B. 2014. 'Urban Migration Trends, Challenges and Opportunities in India'. *Background Paper for World Migration Report 2015*, International Organisation for Migration. Accessed 31 August 2016, https://www.iom.int

Bird, R. M. and E. Slack. 2004. *International Handbook on Land and Property Taxation*. Cheltenham: Edward Elgar.

———. 2015. 'Local Taxes and Local Expenditures: Strengthening the Wicksellian Connection'. In *Interaction Between Local Expenditure Responsibilities and Local Tax Policy: The Copenhagen Workshop*, edited by Junghun Kim, Jorgen Lotz and Niels Jogen, 43–66. The Korea Institute of Public Finance and the Danish Ministry for Economic Affairs and the Interior.

Borck, Rainald and Michael Pfluger. 2006. 'Agglomeration and Tax Competition'. *European Economic Review* 50 (3): 647–668.

Breton, A. 1996. *Competitive Governments*. Cambridge: Cambridge University Press.

Briscoe, B., B. Odlyzko and B. Tilly. 2006. 'Metcalfe's Law Is Wrong'. *IEEE Spectrum* 43(7): 34–39.

Brookings Institution. 2015. *Global Metro Monitor 2014: An Uncertain Recovery*. Metropolitan Policy Program, Brookings. Washington, DC: Brookings Institution. Accessed 30 June 2016, https://www.brookings.edu/wp-content/uploads/2015/01/bmpp_gmm_final.pdf

Brueckner, Jan. 2011. *Lectures in Urban Economics*. Cambridge, MA: The MIT Press.

Brueckner, Jan K. and Kala Seetharam Sridhar. 2012. 'Measuring Welfare Gains from Relaxation of Land Use Restrictions: The Case of India's Building-height Limits'. *Regional Science and Urban Economics* 42 (6): 1061–1067.

Brugman, Jeb. 2010. *Welcome to the Urban Revolution: How Cities Are Changing the World*. New York: Basic Books.

Brulhart, Marius and Federca Sbergami. 2009. 'Agglomeration and Growth: Cross-country Evidence'. *Journal of Urban Economics* 65 (1): 48–63.

Buchanan, J. M. 1963. 'The Economics of Earmarked Taxation'. *Journal of Political Economy* 71 (5): 457–469.

Buckley, Robert. 2005. *Macro Linkages with Municipal Finance: An Overview*. Accessed 3 July 2018, http://www.world Bank.org/uicconference

Burrows, E. G. and M. Wallace. 1999. *Gotham: A History of New York City to 1898*. New York, NY: Oxford University Press.

Button, Kenneth. 2010. *Transport Economics*, 3rd ed. Cheltenham, UK and Northampton, MA: Edward Elgar Publishing.

Cairncross, Frances. 1997. *The Death of Distance: How the Communications Revolution Will Change Our Lives*. Boston, MA: Harvard Business School Press.

Census of India. 1971, 1981, 1991, 2001, 2011. Registrar General and Census Commissioner, Government of India, New Delhi.

Centre for Civil Society. 2009. *State of Governance: Delhi Citizen Handbook*. New Delhi: Centre for Civil Society.

Chauvin, Juan Pablo, Edward Glaeser, Yeran Ma and Kristina Tobio. 2016, 3 May. *What Is Different about Urbanisation in Rich and Poor Countries? Cities in Brazil, China, India and the United States*. Harvard University and NBER. Accessed 30 July 2017, https://scholar.harvard.edu/files/yueranma/files/urbaniza-tion_in_rich_and_poor_countries_jue.pdf

Cheshire, P. C. and C. A. L. Hilber. 2008. 'Office Space Supply Restrictions in Britain: The Political Economy of Market Revenge'. *The Economic Journal* 118 (529): F185–F221.

Cheshire, Paul C., C. A. L. Hilber and I. Kaplanis. 2011. 'Land Use Planning: the Impact on Retail Productivity'. *Centerpiece* 16 (1): 25–28.

Cheshire, Paul C., Max Nathan and Harry G. Overman. 2014. *Urban Economics and Urban Policy: Challenging Conventional Policy Wisdom*. Cheltenham, UK and Northampton, MA: Edward Elgar Publications.

Christaller, Walter. 1933. *Central Places in Southern Germany*. Englewood Cliffs, NJ: Prentice Hall.

Crispell, Mitchell, Karolina Gorska and Somaya Abdelgany. 2016. *Inclusionary Zoning Policy Brief*. Berkeley, CA: Urban Displacement Project, University of California.

Clayton, Frank A. and Geoff Schwartz. 2015. *Is Inclusionary Zoning a Needed Tool for Providing Affordable Housing in the Greater Golden Horseshoe?* Toronto, ON: Ryerson University.

Combes, Pierre-Philippe, Gilles Duranton, Laurent Gobillon, Diego Puga and Sebastien Roux. 2012. 'The Productivity Advantages of Large Cities: Distinguishing Agglomeration from Firm Selection'. *Econometrica* 80 (6): 2543–2594.

Corbusier, Le. 1929. *The City of Tomorrow and Its Planning*. London: John Rodker.

———. 1933. *The Radiant City*. London: Faber and Faber Limited.

Danish Ministry of the Environment. 2015. *The Finger Plan: A Strategy for the Development of the Greater Copenhagen Area.* Copenhagen: The Nature Agency.

Delhi Development Authority. 2015. *Master Plan for Delhi—2021.*

de Soto, H. 2000. *The Mystery of Capital: Why Capitalism Triumphs in the West and Fails Everywhere Else.* New York, NY: Basic Books.

Dye, Richard F. and Richard W. England. 2010. *Assessing the Theory and Practice of Land Value Taxation.* Cambridge, MA: Lincoln Institute of Land Policy.

Duranton, Gilles and Diego Puga. 2004. 'Micro-foundations of Urban Agglomeration Economies'. In *Handbook of Urban and Regional Economies,* Vol. 4, edited by J. Vernon Henderson and Jacque Thisse. Amsterdam: North-Holland.

Duranton, Giles, J. Vernoon Henderson and William Strange. 2015. *Handbook of Regional and Urban Economics,* Volumes 5A and 5B. Amsterdam: North-Holland.

Eddington, R. 2006. *The Edington Transport Study—The Case for Action: Sir Rod Eddington's Advice to Government.* London: Her Majesty's Stationary Office.

———. 2008. *Investing in Transport: East West Link Needs Assessment.* Melbourne: Government of Victoria.

Finance Commission of India. 2009. *Report of the Thirteenth Finance Commission.* New Delhi: Government of India.

———. 2015. *Report of the Fourteenth Finance Commission.* New Delhi: Government of India.

Florida, Richard. 2002. *The Rise of the Creative Class.* New York, NY: Basic Books.

———. 2005. 'The World Is Spiky'. *The Atlantic Monthly* 296 (3): 48–51.

———. 2008. *Who's Your City? How the Creative Economy Is Making Where to Live the Most Important Decision of Your Life.* New York, NY: Basic Books.

———. 2011. 'Globalisation: Part I'. In *Wiley-Blackwell Companion to Human Geography,* edited by John A. Agnew and James S. Duncan. New York, NY: Wiley.

Florida, R., T. Gulden and C. Mellander. 2008. 'The Rise of the Mega Region'. *Cambridge Journal of Regions, Economy and Society* 1 (3): 459–476.

———. 2012. 'Global Metropolis: Assessing Economic Activity in Urban Centres based on Night-time Satellite Images'. *The Professional Geographer* 64 (2): 178–187.

Freire, Maria Emilia and Hernando Garzon. 2014. 'Managing Local Revenues'. In *Municipal Finances: A Handbook for Local Governments,* edited by Farvacque-Vitkovic and Mihaly Kopanyi, 147–214. Washington, DC: World Bank.

Friedman, Thomas K. 2006. *The World Is Flat: A Brief History of the Twentieth Century.* New York, NY: Farrar, Strauss and Giroux.

Fox, Justin. 2014, 3 November. 'The World is Still Not Flat'. *Harvard Business Review.* Accessed 3 July 2018, https://hbr.org/2014/11/the-world-is-still-not-flat

Fujita, Masahisa. 1988. 'A Monopolistic Competition Model of Spatial Agglomeration: A Differentiated Product Approach'. *Regional Science and Urban Economics* 18 (1): 87–124.

———. 1989. *Urban Economic Theory: Land Use and City Size.* Cambridge: Cambridge University Press.

Fujita, Masahisa and Jacques-Francois Thisse. 2002. *Economics of Agglomeration: Cities, Industrial Location, and Regional Growth.* Cambridge: Cambridge University Press.

Fujita, Masahisa, Paul Krugman and Anthony J. Venables. 1999. *The Spatial Economy: Cities, Regions, and International Economy*. Cambridge, MA: MIT Press.

Fuller, Brandon. 2017. Expanding *Opportunity for the Urban Poor*. Centre for Development and Enterprise (CDE) Commissioned Research Series Paper. Accessed 20 November 2017, www.cde.org.za

Fuller, Brandon and Paul Romer. 2014. 'Urbanisation as Opportunity'. *Working Paper No*. 1, Marron Institute of Urban Management, New York University, New York. Accessed 15 September 2017, https://marroninstitute.nyu.edu

Geddes, Patrick Sir. 1915. *Cities in Evolution: An Introduction to the Town Planning Movement and to the Study of Civics*. London: Williams & Norgate.

GEF-World Bank-UNDP. 2012, November. Sustainable Urban Transport (SUTP) Project India: GEF-SUTP *Newsletter* 2 (8).

George, Henry. 1879. *Progress and Poverty*. New York, NY: Robert Schalkenbach Foundation (centenary edition, 1979).

Ghemawat, Pankaj. 2007, March–April. 'Why the World Isn't Flat'. *Foreign Policy*: 54–60. Accessed 30 August 2016, www.ForeignPolicy.com

Ghemawat, Pankaj and Steven A. Altman. 2014. *DFL Global Connectedness Index 2014*. Accessed 30 August 2016, http://www.forschungsnetzwerk.at/downloadpub/2014_dhl_gci_2014_study_dhl.pdf

Glaeser, Edward L. 2008a. *Cities, Agglomeration and Spatial Equilibrium*. Oxford: Oxford University Press.

———. 2008b, January. 'The Economic Approach to Cities'. *Discussion Paper No*. 2149, Harvard Institute of Economic Research, Harvard University, Cambridge.

———. 2011. *Triumph of the City: How Our Greatest Invention Makes Us Richer, Smarter, Greener, Healthier, and Happier*. New York, NY: Penguin Books.

Glaeser, Edward L. and Abha Joshi-Ghani. 2015. *The Urban Imperative: Towards Competitive Cities*. New Delhi: Oxford University Press and World Bank.

Graham, D. J. 2007. 'Agglomeration, Productivity and Transport Investment'. *Journal of Transport Economics and Policy* 41 (3): 317–343.

Government of Andhra Pradesh. 2014. *Andhra Pradesh Capital Region Development Authority (APCRDA) Act 2014 (Act 11 of 2014)*. Hyderabad: Government of Andhra Pradesh.

Government of the United Kingdom (GoUK). 2013. *Transport Analysis Guidance*. Department for Transport. Accessed 15 October 2016, https://www.gov.uk/guidance/transport-analysis-guidance-webtag

———. 2014. *Innovation Report 2014: Innovation, Research and Growth*. Department of Business Innovation & Skills. Accessed 5 December 2016, https://www.gov.uk/government/publications/innovation-report-2014-innovation-research-and-growth

Hagman, Donald G. and Dean J. Misczynski, eds. 1978. *Windfalls for Wipeouts: Land Value Capture and Compensation*. Chicago, IL: American Society of Planning Officials.

Hall, Bronwyn H., Jacques Mairesse and Pierre Mohnen. 2009. 'Measuring the Returns to R&D'. *Working Paper No*. 15622, National Bureau of Economic Research, Cambridge, MA.

Hall, Peter. 1988. *Cities of Tomorrow: An Intellectual History of Urban Planning and Design in the 20th Century*. Oxford: Blackwell Publishing.

Hall, Peter. 2009. 'Looking Backward, Looking Forward: The City Region in the Mid-21st Century'. *Regional Studies* 43 (6): 803–817.

Henderson, J. Vernon. 1974. 'The Sizes and Types of Cities'. *American Economic Review* 64 (4): 640–656.

———. 1987. 'General Equilibrium Modelling of Systems of Cities'. In *The Handbook of Regional and Urban Economics*, Vol. 2, edited by Edwin S. Mills, 927–956. Amsterdam: Elsevier.

———.1988. *Urban Development: Theory, Fact, and Illusion*. New York, NY: Oxford University Press.

———. 2000. 'How Urban Concentration Affects Economic Growth'. *Working Paper No.* 2326, World Bank Policy Research, Washington, DC.

———. 2003. 'The Urbanization Process and Economic Growth: The So-what Question'. *Journal of Economic Growth* 8 (1): 47–71.

———. 2005. 'Urbanization and Growth'. In *Handbook of Economic Growth*, edited by Philippe Aghion and Steven N. Durlauf. Amsterdam: North-Holland.

Hensher, David A. and Kenneth J. Button. 2008. *Handbook of Transport Modelling*. Amsterdam: Elsevier.

Hickey, Robert, Lisa Sturtevant and Emily Thaden. 2014. *Achieving Lasting Affordability Through Inclusionary Housing*. Cambridge, MA: Lincoln Institute of Land Policy.

High Powered Expert Committee (HPEC). 2011. *Report on Indian Urban Infrastructure and Services*. The High Powered Expert Committee (HPEC) for Estimating the Investment Requirements for Urban Infrastructure Services, New Delhi.

Hong, Yu-Hung. 2007. 'Assembling Land for Urban Development: Issues and Opportunities'. In *Analyzing Land Readjustment: Economics, Law, and Collective Action*, edited by Yu Hung Hong and Barry Needham, 3–34. Cambridge, MA: Lincoln Institute for Land Policy.

Howard, Ebenezer. 1902. *Garden Cities of Tomorrow*. London: S. Sonnenschein & Co. Ltd.

Hunkar, David. 2017, 21 June. *High Speed Rail Lines in the World by Country 2017*. Accessed 21 March 2018, www.topforeignstocks.com

International Council on Clean Transportation. 2010. *Congestion Charging: Challenges and Opportunities*. Accessed 30 September 2017, www.theiccct.org

International Labour Office (ILO) and Women in Informal Employment: Globalizing and Organizing (WIEGO). 2013. *Women and Men in the Informal Economy: A Statistical Picture*. Accessed 3 July 2018, www.ilo.org

International Union of Railways. 2017. *High Speed Rail: Fast Track to Sustainable Mobility*. Accessed 3 July 2018, www.uuic.org

Jacobs, Jane. 1992 [1961], December. *The Death and Life of Great American Cities*. Edition, New York, NY: Vintage Books Edition. Originally published in 1961: New York: Random House.

———.1969. *The Economy of Cities*. New York, NY: Random House.

———. 1984. *Cities and the Wealth of Nations*. New York, NY: Random House.

Jacobus, Rick. 2015. *Inclusionary Housing (A Policy Focus Report): Creating and Maintaining Equitable Communities*. Cambridge, MA: Lincoln Institute of Land Policy.

Jaramillo, Samuel. 2001. *The Betterment Levy and Participation in Land Value Increments: The Colombian Experience*. Cambridge, MA: Lincoln Institute for Land Policy.

Jenkins, J., M. Colella and F. Salvucci. 2011. 'Agglomeration Benefits and Transportation Projects'. *Transportation Research Board* 2221 (1): 104–111.

Joshi, Rutul and Prashant Sanga. 2009. *Land Reservations for the Urban Poor: The Case of Town Planning Schemes in Ahmedabad*. Ahmedabad: Centre for Urban Equity, CEPT University.

Kanemoto, Y. 1980. *Theories of Urban Externalities*. Amsterdam: North Holland.

Kennedy, C. A. 2011. *The Evolution of Great World Cities: Urban Wealth and Economic Growth*. Toronto: University of Toronto Press.

Knaap, Gerritt-Jan, Antonia Bento and Scott Lowe. 2008. *Housing Market Impacts of Inclusionary Zoning*. College Park, MD: National Center for Smart Growth Research and Education.

Knaap, Gerrit and Emily Talen. 2005. 'New Urbanism and Smart Growth: A Few Words from the Academy'. *International Regional Science Review* 28 (2): 107–118.

Koster, H. R. A., P. Rietveld and J. N. van Emmerren. 2011. 'Is the Sky the Limit? An Analysis of High-rise Office Buildings'. *SERC Discussion Paper No. 86*, SERC, London.

KPMG. 2014. *Decoding Housing for All by 2022: India's Commitment to Inclusive, Sustainable, and Affordable Development*. Accessed 16 August 2016, https://assets.kpmg.com

Kraatz, Judy A., Johanna Mitchell, Annie Matan and Peter Newman. 2015. *Rethinking Social Housing: Efficient, Effective & Equitable*. Brisbane: Sustainable Built Environment National Research Centre (SBENRC).

Krugman, Paul R. 1979. 'Increasing Returns, Monopolistic Competition, and International Trade'. *Journal of International Economics* 9 (4): 469–480.

———. 1980. 'Scale Economies, Product Differentiation, and the Pattern of Trade'. *American Economic Review* 70 (5): 950–959.

———. 1981. 'Intra-industry Specialization and the Gains from Trade'. *Journal of Political Economy* 89 (5): 959–973.

———. 1991a. *Geography and Trade*. Cambridge, MA: MIT Press.

———. 1991b. 'Increasing Returns and Economic Geography'. *Journal of Political Economy* 99 (3): 483–499.

———. 1993. 'First Nature, Second Nature, and Metropolitan Location'. *Journal of Regional Science* 33 (2): 129–144.

———. 1995. 'Innovation and Agglomeration: Two Parables Suggested by City–Size Distributions'. *Japan and the World Economy* 7 (4): 371–390.

———. 2007. 'The "New" Economic Geography: Where Are We?' In *Regional Integration in East Asia*, edited by Masahisa Fujita. New York, NY: Palgrave Macmillan.

Krugman, Paul R. and A. J. Venables. 1995. 'Globalization and the Inequality of Income'. *Quarterly Journal of Economics* 110 (4): 857–880.

Kundu, Amitabh and L. Saraswati. 2012, 30 June. 'Migration and Exclusionary Urbanisation in India'. *Economic & Political Weekly*, 47 (26–27): 219–227.

Kuznets, Simon. 1955. 'Economic Growth and Income Inequality'. *American Economic Review* 45 (1): 1–28.

———. 1966. *Modern Economic Growth*. New Haven, Connecticut: Yale University Press.

Lall, Somik V. and U. Deichmann. 2006, 22 July. 'Fiscal and Distributional Implications of Property Tax Reforms in Indian Cities'. *Economic & Political Weekly* 41 (29): 3209–3220.

Lefmann, O. and K. K. Larsen. 2000. 'Denmark'. In *Land-value Taxation Around the World*, edited by R. V. Andelson, *The American Journal of Economics and Sociology* 59 (5): 185–205.

Lincoln Institute of Land Policy. 2011. 'Land-based Financing for Brazil's Municipalities'. *Land Lines*. Accessed 3 July 2018, https://www.lincolninst.edu/sites/default/files/pubfiles/1953_1274_LLA111004.pdf

Lindahl, Erik R. 1919. *The Justness of Taxation*. Lund: Lund University.

Lindsay, R. 2009. 'Cost Recovery from Congestion Toll with Random Capacity and Demand'. *Journal of Urban Economics* 66 (1): 16–24.

Lösch, Auguste. 1940. *The Economics of Location*. New Haven, CT: Yale University Press.

Lucas, Robert E., Jr. 1988. 'On the Mechanics of Economic Development'. *Journal of Monetary Economics* 22 (1): 3–42.

Ludema, Rodney and Ian Wooton. 2000. 'Economic Geography and the Fiscal Effects of Integration'. *Journal of International Economics* 52 (2): 331–357.

Lugard, Fredrick D. 1965 [1923]. *The Dual Mandate in British Tropical Africa*, 5th ed. London: Frank Cass & Co.

Mackie, Peter, Daniel Graham and James Laird. 2011. 'The Direct and Wider Impacts of Transport Projects: A Review'. In *A Handbook of Transport Economics*, edited by Andre de Palma, Robin Lindsay, Emile Quinet and Roger Vickerman, 501–526. Cheltenham, UK and Northamton, MA: Edward Elgar.

Mahadevia, Darshini. 2001, May. 'Sustainable Urban Development in India: An Inclusive Perspective'. *Development in Practice* 11 (2/3): 242–259.

Mahadevia, Darshini and Rutul Joshi. 2009. *Subversive Urban Development in India: Implications on Planning Education*. Centre for Urban Equity, an NRC for Ministry of Housing and Urban Poverty Alleviation, Government of India, CEPT University.

Mahadevia Darshini, Rutul Joshi and Rutul Sharma. 2009. *Approaches to the Lands for the Urban Poor, India*. Centre for Urban Equity, CEPT University, Ahmedabad.

Mallach, Alan. 1984. *Inclusionary Housing Programs: Policies and Practices*. New Brunswick, NJ: Centre for Urban Policy Research, Rutgers University.

Marshall, Alfred. 1890. *Principles of Economics*. London: Macmillan.

———. 1920. *Principles of Economics*, 8th ed. Macmillan: London.

Mathur, Om Prakash. 2013, 1 June. 'Finances of Municipalities: Issues Before the Fourteenth Finance Commission'. *Economic & Political Weekly* 48 (22): 23–27.

Mathur, Om Prakash, D. Thakur and N. Rajadhyaksha. 2009. *Urban Property Tax Potential in India*. New Delhi: National Institute of Public Finance and Policy.

McCluskey, J. William and Riel C. D. Franzsen. 2013. 'Property Taxes in Metropolitan Cities'. In *Financing Metropolitan Governments in Developing Countries*, edited by Roy W. Bahl, Johannes Linn and Deborah L. Wetzel, 159–181. Cambridge, MA: Lincoln Institute of Land Policy.

McKinsey Global Institute. 2010. *India's Urban Awakening: Building Inclusive Cities, Sustaining Economic Growth*. McKinsey and Company, www.mckinsey.com/mgi.

———. 2012. *Urban World: Cities and the Rise of the Consuming Class*. McKinsey and Company, www.mckinsey.com/mgi.

Melo, P. C., D. J. Graham and R. Noland. 2009. 'A Meta-analysis of Estimates of Urban Agglomeration Economies'. *Regional Science and Urban Economics* 39 (3): 332–342.

Mill, John Stuart. 2001 [1848]. *The Principles of Political Economy*, Book 5. Kitchener, Ontario: Batoche Book.

Mills, E. S. 1967. 'An Aggregate Model of Resource Allocation in a Metropolitan Area'. *American Economic Review* 57 (2): 197–210.

———. 1972. *Studies in the Structure of the Urban Economy*. Baltimore: Johns Hopkins Press.

Ministry of Finance (MoF), Government of India. 2016. 'Putting Public Investment on Track—The Rail Route to Higher Growth', Chapter 6. In *Economics Survey 2014–15*, 89–101. Ministry of Finance, Government of India, New Delhi.

———. 2017. 'From Competitive Federalism to Competitive Sub-federalism: Cities and Dynamos', Chapter 17. In *Economic Survey 2014–15*, 300–314. Ministry of Finance, Government of India, New Delhi.

Ministry of Health (MoH), Government of India. 1965. *Report of the Committee on Urban Land Policy*. Ministry of Health, Government of India, New Delhi.

Ministry of Housing & Urban Poverty Alleviation (MoHUPA), Government of India. 2010. *Report of the Committee on Slum Statistics/Census*. National Buildings Organisation (NBO), New Delhi.

———. 2012. *Report of the Technical Group on Estimation of Urban Housing Shortage*. National Buildings Organisation (NBO), New Delhi.

———. 2013. *Annual Report 2012–13*. Ministry of Housing & Urban Poverty Alleviation, Government of India, New Delhi.

———. 2015. *Compendium of Best Practices in States*. Ministry of Housing & Urban Poverty Alleviation, Government of India, New Delhi.

Ministry of Human Resource Development (MHRD), Government of India. 2011, July. *Report of the Committee of Experts in Town Planning and Architecture for Policy Guidelines to Energise Architecture and Town Planning Education in the Country*, Government of India, New Delhi.

Ministry of Road Transport & Highways (MoRTH), Government of India. 2016. *Road Transport Year Book (2013–14 and 2014–15)*. Ministry of Road Transport & Highways, Government of India, New Delhi.

Ministry of Statistics and Programme Implementation (MoSPI). 2006. *Provisional Results of Economic Census 2005: All India Report*. Central Statistical Organisation, New Delhi.

Ministry of Urban Development (MoUD), Government of India. 1985. *The Report of the Committee on Octroi*. Ministry of Urban Development, Government of India, New Delhi.

———.1996. *Urban Development Plans Formulation and Implementation (UDPFI) Guidelines*, Town and Country Planning Organization, Ministry of Urban Affairs and Employment, Government of India, New Delhi.

———. 2013, 5 September. *Delhi Land Pooling Policy*. Ministry of Urban Development, Government of India, New Delhi.

———. 2014. *National Urban Transport Policy*. Ministry of Urban Development, Government of India, New Delhi.

Ministry of Urban Development (MoUD), Government of India. 2015a. *Urban and Regional Development Plan Formulation and Implementation (URDPFI) Guidelines*. Town and Country Planning Organization, Ministry of Urban Development, Government of India, New Delhi.

———. 2015b, 13 July. *Transit-oriented Development Policy for Delhi*. Ministry of Urban Development, Government of India, New Delhi.

Ministry of Urban Development, Government of India and World Bank. 2013. *Land-based Fiscal Tools and Practices for Generating Additional Financial Resources*. Capacity Building for Urban Development Project (CBUD). Ministry of Urban Development, Government of India, New Delhi and World Bank.

Mishra, Alok Kumar. 2017. 'Is Urban Planning in India Exclusionary? The Case for Inclusionary Zoning and Housing in India'. *Shelter* 18 (2): 8–19.

Mitchell, Stephen R. and A. J. M. Vickers. 2003. 'The Impact of Jubilee Line Extension of the London Underground Rail Network on Land Values'. *Working Paper No.* 035M1, Lincoln Institute of Land Policy, Cambridge, MA.

Mohan, Rakesh. 2006, 5 June. 'Asia's Urban Century: Emerging Trends'. Key note address delivered at the Conference of Land and Policies and Urban Development, Lincoln Institute of Land Policy, Cambridge, MA.

Mohanty, P. K. 2003. *Reforming Property Tax: The Approach of Municipal Corporation of Hyderabad*. Hyderabad: Center for Good Governance.

———. 2014. *Cities and Public Policy: An Urban Agenda for India*. New Delhi: SAGE Publications.

———. 2016. *Financing Cities in India: Municipal Reforms, Fiscal Accountability and Urban Infrastructure*. New Delhi: SAGE Publications.

Mohanty, P. K., B. M. Mishra, R. Goyal and P. D. Jeromi. 2007. 'Municipal Finance in India—An Assessment'. *Study No.* 26, Department of Economic Analysis and Policy, Reserve Bank of India, Mumbai.

Mohring, H. 1972. 'Optimisation and Scale Economies in Urban Bus Transportation'. *American Economic Review* 62 (4): 591–604.

———. 1976. *Transport Economics*. Cambridge, MA: Ballinger.

Mohring, H. and M. Harwitz. 1962. *Highway Benefits: An Analytical Framework*. Evanston, IL: Northwestern University Press.

Mumford, Lewis. 1938. *The Culture of Cities*. New York, NY: Harcourt Brace and Company.

———. 1961. *The City in History*. San Diego, CA: Harcourt.

Musgrave, Richard A. 1959. *The Theory of Public Finance*. New York, NY: McGraw-Hill.

Musgrave, R. A. and P. B. Musgrave. 1989. *Public Finance in Theory and Practice*, 4th ed. New York, NY. McGraw-Hill.

Muth, Richard. 1969. *Cities and Housing*. Chicago, IL: University of Chicago Press.

Myrdal, G. 1957. *Economic Theory and Under-developed Regions*. London: Duckworth.

———. 1974. 'What Is Development?' *Journal of Economic Issues* 8 (4): 729–736.

Nathan, Max and Harry G. Overman. 2011. 'What We Know (and Don't Know) about the Links Between Planning and Economic Performance'. *Policy Paper No.* 11, Spatial and Economic Research Centre (SERC), London School of Economics. Accessed 30 September 2017, www.spatialeconomics.ac.uk

National Commission on Urban Problem. 1969. *Building the American City—Report to the National Commission on Urban Problem to the Congress and to the President of the United States*. Washington, DC: US Government Printing Office.

National Family Health Survey. 2007. *NFHS-3, 2005–06: India*. International Institute for Population Sciences (IIPS) and Macro International. Accessed 5 March 2016, rchiips.org/nfhs/NFHS

National Institute of Urban Affairs. 2010, March. *Best Practices on Property Tax Reforms in India*, submitted to the Ministry of Urban Development (GOI), New Delhi.

National Sample Survey Office, Ministry of Statistics and Programme Implementation, Government of India. 2006. NSS 59th Round (January–December 2003). *Report on Household Ownership Holdings in India*. National Sample Survey Office, Ministry of Statistics and Programme Implementation, Government of India, New Delhi.

———. 2010a. 'NSS 65th Round (July 2008–June 2009)', *Report No. 534, Some Characteristics of Urban Slums*. National Sample Survey Office, Ministry of Statistics and Programme Implementation, Government of India.

———. 2010b. 'NSS 65th Round (July 2008–June 2009)', *Report No. 535, Housing Conditions and Amenities in India 2008–09*. National Sample Survey Office, Ministry of Statistics and Programme Implementation, Government of India.

———. 2011, December. 'Level and Pattern of Consumer Expenditure 2009–10', *NSS Report No. 538*. National Sample Survey Office, Ministry of Statistics and Programme Implementation, Government of India.

———. 2012, January. 'NSS 66th Round', *NSS Report No. 539, Informal Sector and Conditions of Employment in India*. National Sample Survey Office, Ministry of Statistics and Programme Implementation, Government of India.

———. 2013, June. 'NSS 68th Round, (July 2011–June 2012)', *Report No. NSS KI (68/1.0), Key Indicators of Household Consumer Expenditure in India*. National Sample Survey Office, Ministry of Statistics and Programme Implementation, Government of India.

———. 2014, January. 'NSS 68th Round (July 2011–June 2012)'. *Employment and Unemployment Situation in India*. National Sample Survey Office, Ministry of Statistics and Programme Implementation, Government of India.

———. 2016, June. 'NSS 72nd Round (July 2014–June 2015)', *Key Indicators of Household Expenditure on Services and Durable Goods*. National Sample Survey Office, Ministry of Statistics and Programme Implementation, Government of India.

Nick, Brunick, Lauren Goldberg and Susannah Levine. 2003. *Large Cities and Inclusionary Zoning*. Wellesley Institute. Accessed 4 July 2018, www.wellesleyinstitute.com/wp-content/upload

Nico, Calavita and Alan Mallach, eds. 2010. *Inclusionary Housing in International Perspective: Affordable Housing, Social Inclusion and Land Value Recapture*. Cambridge, MA: Lincoln Institute of Land Policy.

Norregaard, John. 2013. 'Taxing Immovable Property: Revenue Potential and Implementation Challenges', *IMF Working Paper WP/13/129*. Washington, DC: International Monetary Fund.

NYU Furman Centre. 2015. 'Creating Affordable Housing Out of Thin Air: The Economics of Mandatory Inclusionary Zoning in New York City'. In *Housing for an Inclusive New York: Affordable Housing Strategies for a High-Cost City.* Accessed 4 July 2018, http://furmancenter.org/files/NYUFurmanCenter_CreatingAffHousing_March2015.pdf

O' Brien, R. 1992. *Global Financial Integration: The End of Geography.* London: Chatham House.

Ohmae, K. 1990. *The Borderless World: Power and Strategy in the Interlinked Economy.* London: Harper Collins.

———. 1995. *The End of the Nation State: The Rise of Regional Economies.* London: Harper Collins.

Ohshita, Stephanie, Lynn Price, Nan Zhou, Nina Khanna, David Fridley and Xu Liu. 2015. *The Role of Chinese Cities in Greenhouse Gas Emission Reduction.* Stockholm Environment Institute. Accessed 2 September 2017, https://www.sei-international.org

Organisation for Economic Co-operation and Development (OECD). 2011. *Revenue Statistics 2011.* Accessed 4 July 2018, http://www.oecd-ilibrary.org/taxation/revenuestatistics-2011_rev_stats-2011-en-fr

———. 2012. 'General Government Accounts: Public Finance and Employment: Revenues'. *OECD National Accounts Statistics*, OECD, Paris.

Ortuzar, Juan de Dios and Luis G. Willumsen. 2001. *Modelling Transport*, 4th ed. Chichester: John Wiley & Sons.

Oxford Economics. 2017. *Global Cities 2030—Future Trends and Market Opportunities in the World's Largest 750 Cities.* Accessed 31 August 2017, www.oxfordeconomics.com

Parker, Geoffrey G, Marshall W. Van Alstyne and Sangeet Paul Choudary. 2016. *Platform Revolution—How Networked Markets Are Transforming the Economy and How to Make Them Work for You.* New York, NY: W.W. Norton & Company.

Patel, Shirish B. 2005, 13 August. 'Housing Policies for Mumbai'. *Economic & Political Weekly* 40 (33): 3669–3676.

———. 2016, 5 March. 'Housing for All by 2022'. *Economic & Political Weekly* 51 (10): 38–42.

Patricia M. Austin, Nicole Gurran and Christine M. E. Whitehead. 2013, September. 'Planning and Affordable Housing in Australia, New Zealand, and England: Common Culture; Different Mechanisms'. *Journal of Housing and the Built Environment* 29 (3): 455–472.

Prahalad, C. K. 2005. *The Fortune at the Bottom of the Pyramid: Eradicating Poverty Through Profits.* New Delhi: Pearson Education/Wharton School Publishing.

Prahalad, C. K. and Stuart L. Hart. 2002. 'The Fortune at the Bottom of the Pyramid'. *Strategy + Business* 26: 1–14.

Peterson, George E. 2009. *Unlocking Land Values to Finance Urban Infrastructure.* Washington, DC: World Bank.

Peterson, Sarah Joe. 2014. 'Tax Increment Financing: Tweaking TIF for the 21st Century'. *Urban Land.* Washington, DC: Urban Land Institute.

Planning Commission, Government of India. 2006. *Towards Faster and More Inclusive Growth: An Approach to the Eleventh Five Year Plan 2007–2012.* New Delhi: Government of India.

———. 2008. *Eleventh Five Year Plan 2007–2012.* New Delhi: Government of India.

Planning Commission, Government of India. 2013. *Twelfth Five Year Plan 2012–2017*. New Delhi: Government of India.

———. 2014. *Report of Expert Group to Review the Methodology for Measurement of Poverty*. New Delhi: Government of India.

Porter, Michael E. 1990. *The Competitive Advantage of Nations*. New York, NY: Free Press.

Prakash P. 2013. 'Property Tax Across G20 Countries: Can India Get it Right?' *Oxfam India Working Paper Series XV*, Oxfam India, New Delhi.

Public Accounts Committee. 2015. *Eighteenth Report—Jawaharlal Nehru National Urban Renewal Mission*. New Delhi: Lok Sabha Secretariat.

Puga, Diego. 2010. 'The Magnitude and Causes of Agglomeration Economies'. *Journal of Regional Science* 50 (1): 203–219.

Rao, Govinda M. 2013. 'Property Tax System in India: Problems and Prospects for Reform'. *Working Paper No. 2013-114*, National Institute of Public Finance and Policy, New Delhi.

Renewal SA. 2013. *Delivering an Inspiring Urban Future*. Annual Report. Adelaide: Government of South Australia.

Rodríguez, D. A. and C. H. Mojica. 2008. 'Land Value Impacts of Bus Rapid Transit: The Case of Bogotá's Bus Rapid Transit'. *Land Lines*. Cambridge, MA: Lincoln Institute of Land Policy.

Romer, Paul M. 1986. 'Increasing Returns in Long-run Growth'. *Journal of Political Economy* 94 (5): 1002–1037.

———. 1990. 'Endogenous Technological Change'. *Journal of Political Economy* 98 (5): 71–102.

———. 1994. 'The Origins of Endogenous Growth'. *Journal of Economic Perspectives* 8 (1): 3–22.

Rosenthal, Stuart S. and William C. Strange. 2004. 'Evidence on the Nature and Sources of Agglomeration Economies'. In *Handbook of Regional and Urban Economics*, Vol. 4, edited by J. Vernon Henderson and Jacque Thisse, 2119–2171. Amsterdam: North-Holland.

Rostow, W. W. 1960. *The Stages of Economic Growth*. Cambridge: Cambridge University Press.

Rothwell, Jonathon. 2012. 'Housing Costs, Zoning, and Access to High Scoring Schools'. *Metro Policy Program at Brookings*, Washington, DC.

Salon, Deborah and Sharon Shewmake. 2011. *Opportunities for Value Capture to Fund Public Transport: A Comprehensive Review of the Literature with a Focus on East Asia*. ADB and ITDP. Accessed 5 March 2016, https://www.itdp.org

Salzberg, Andrew, Richard Bullock, Ying Jin and Wanli Fang. 2013. 'High-speed Rail, Regional Economics and Urban Development'. *China Transport Topics No. 08*, World Bank Office, Beijing.

Sandroni, P. 2010. 'A New Financial Instrument of Value Capture in Sao Paulo: Certificates of Additional Construction Potential'. In *Municipal Revenues and Land Policies*, edited by Gregory Ingram and Yu-Hung Hong, 218–236. Cambridge, MA: Lincoln Institute of Land Policy.

Scholte, Jan Aart. 2000. *Globalization: A Critical Introduction*. Basingstoke: Macmillan.

Schwartz, Heather L., Liisa Ecola, Kristin J. Leuschner and Aaron Kofner. 2012. *Is Inclusionary Zoning Inclusionary? A Guide for Practitioners.* RAND Corporation Technical Report. Accessed 4 July 2018, https://www.rand.org/content/dam/rand/pubs/technical_reports/2012/RAND_TR1231.pdf

Shorey, S. P. 2009. *Model Inclusive Zoning & Development Control Regulations for Indian Cities.* National Resource Centre, School of Planning and Architecture, New Delhi.

Sivaramakrishnan, K. C. 2011. *Re-visioning Indian Cities—The Urban Renewal Mission.* New Delhi: SAGE Publications.

Slack, Enid. 2011. The Property Tax—In Theory and Practice. *IMFG Papers on Municipal Finance and Governance,* Munk School of Global Affairs, University of Toronto, Toronto, Ontario.

Smith, Adam. 1976. *An Inquiry into the Nature and Causes of the Wealth of Nations.* Chicago, IL: University of Chicago Press (Cannan's edition of the *Wealth of Nations* was originally published in 1904 by Methuen & Co. Ltd. First Edition in 1776).

Smolka, Martim O. 2007. La regulacion de los mercados de suelo en America Latina: Cuestiones claves. Reported in Peterson (2009).

———. 2013. *Implementing Land Value Capture in Latin America (Policy Focus Report): Policies and Tools for Urban Development.* Cambridge, MA: Lincoln Institute of Land Policy.

———. 2015. 'Value Capture: A Land Based Tool to Finance Urban Development'. Presentation at International Property Tax Institute and Centre for Urban Research and Land Development at Ryerson University, Toronto, 2 February 2015.

Spiller, Marcus and Mitra Anderson-Oliver. 2015. 'Revisiting the Economics of Inclusionary Zoning'. *SGS Economics and Planning Occasional Paper.* Accessed 4 July 2018, https://www.sgsep.com.au/assets/Occasional-Paper-Revisiting-the-economics-of-Inclusionary-Zoning-April-2015.pdf

Stein, Clarence S. 1939. *Toward New Towns for America.* Cambridge, MA: MIT Press.

Stiglitz, Joseph E. 1977. 'The Theory of Local Public Goods'. In *The Economics of Public Services,* edited by M. S. Feldstein and R. P. Inman, 274–333. London: McMillan.

———. 2012. *The Price of Inequality: How Today's Divided Society Endangers Our Future.* New York, NY: W. W. Norton.

Suzuki, Hiroaki, Jin Murakami, Yu-Hung Hong and Beth Tamayose. 2015. *Financing Transit Oriented Development with Land Value Capture.* Washington, DC: World Bank Group.

Suzuki, Hiroaki, Robert Cervero and Kanako Iuchi. 2013. *Transforming Cities with Transit: Transit and Land–Use Integration for Sustainable Urban Development.* Washington, DC: World Bank Group.

Tamaki, Keiichi and Narayanan Edadan. 2013. *Market-based Mass Housing Development Strategy for Sustainable Inclusiveness of Cities in India: Challenges and Opportunities.* Manila: Asian Development Bank.

Thoreau, Henry David. 1854. *Walden, or Life in the Woods.* Eldritch Press. www.eldritchpress.org

Tongia, Rahul and Earnest J. Willson III. 2011. 'The Flip Side of Metcalfe's Law: Multiple and Growing Costs of Network Exclusion'. *International Journal of Communication* 5: 665–681.

Town and Country Planning Organisation (TCPO), Government of India. 2007. *Model Guidelines for Urban Land Policy*. Accessed 4 July 2018, http://www.cmamp.com/CP/FDocument/GuidelinesULP.pdf

United Nations. 1976. 'The Vancouver Action Plan'. *United Nations Conference on Human Settlements*, Vancouver.

———. 2012. *World Urbanization Prospects: The 2011 Revision*. New York, NY: United Nations, Department of Economic and Social Affairs, Population Division.

———. 2015. *World Urbanization Prospects: The 2014 Revision*. New York, NY: United Nations, Department of Economic and Social Affairs, Population Division.

United Nations Environment Programme (UNEP). 2015. *Cities and Buildings*. UNEP-DTIE—Sustainable Production and Consumption Branch. Accessed 24 August 2018, http://energies2050.org/wp-content/uploads/2013/09/2013-06-UNEP-Cities-and-buildings-activities_16-pages-GB.pdf

United States Department of Commerce. 1926. *A Standard State Zoning Enabling Act*. Advisory Committee on Zoning. Washington, DC: United States Government Printing Office.

———. 1928. *A Standard City Planning Enabling Act*. Washington, DC: United States Government Printing Office.

United States Department of Housing and Urban Development. 1993. *Impact Fees and the Role of the State: Guidance for Drafting Legislation*. Washington, D.C.

United States Environmental Protection Agency (US EPA). 2004, 11 March. What is Smart Growth? *Smart Growth*. Accessed 4 March 2016, https://www.epa.gov/sites/production/files/2014-02/documents/smartgrowth

Unwin, Raymond. 1912. *Nothing Gained by Overcrowding! How the Garden City Type of Development May Benefit Both Owner and Occupier*. Westminster: P. S. King & Son.

UN-HABITAT. 2009. *Planning Sustainable Cities: Policy Directions*, Global Report on Human Settlements 2009.

———. 2016. *World Cities Report 2016—Urbanisation and Development: Emerging Futures*. Nairobi: United Nations Human Settlement Programme.

University of Hyderabad–HSMI (Human Settlements Management Institute). 2017. *Land-based Instruments for Financing Smart Cities in India*. HUDCO Chair Programme, Housing and Urban Development Corporation, New Delhi.

Venables, Anthony J. 1996. 'Equilibrium Locations of Vertically Linked Industries'. *International Economic Review* 37 (2): 341–359.

———. 2007. 'Evaluating Urban Transport Improvements: Cost–Benefit Analysis in the Presence of Agglomeration and Income Taxation'. *Journal of Transport Economics and Policy* 41 (2): 173–188.

Vickerman, R. 2008. 'Transit Investment and Economic Development'. *Research in Transportation Economics* 23 (1): 101–115.

Vickrey, William S. 1963. 'Pricing of Urban and Suburban Transport'. *American Economic Review* 53 (2): 452–465.

Von Thunen, Johan. 1826. *The Isolated State.* Hamburg: F. Perthes.

Walters, L. C. 2011. *Land and Property Tax: A Policy Guide.* Nairobi: UN-Habitat and the Global Land Tool Network.

Wang, Ying, Su Song, Shiyong Qui, Lu Lu, Yilin Ma, Xiaoyi Li and Ying Hu. 2017. 'Study on International Practices for Low Emission Zone and Congestion Charging' *Working Paper*, World Resources Institute: Ross Center. Accessed 27 September 2017, https://www.wri.org/

Weber, Adna. 1899. *The Growth of Cities in the Nineteenth Century: A Study in Statistics.* New York, NY: Macmillan.

Weber, Alfred. 1971 [1909]. *The Theory of the Location of Industries*, 2nd ed. Chicago, IL: University of Chicago Press.

Wellisch, Dietmar. 2004. *Theory of Public Finance in a Federal State.* Cambridge: Cambridge University Press.

Western Australian Government, Department of Housing. 2010. *Affordable Housing Strategy 2010–2020: Opening Doors to Affordable Housing.* Perth: Western Australian Government, Department of Housing.

Wicksell, Knut. 1964 [1896]. 'A New Principle of Just Taxation'. In *Classics in the Theory of Public Finance*, edited by R. Musgrave and A. Peacock, 72–118. London: Macmillan.

Williams, Stockton, Ian Carlton, Lorelei Juntunen, Emily Picha and Mike Wilkerson. 2016. *The Economics of Inclusionary Development.* Washington, DC: Urban Land Institute.

Williamson, Jeffrey. 1965. 'Regional Inequality and the Process of National Development: A Description of the Patterns'. *Economic Development and Cultural Change* 13 (4): 1–84.

———. 1974. *Late Nineteenth Century American Development: A General Equilibrium History.* New York, NY: Cambridge University Press.

World Bank. 1994. *World Development Report: Infrastructure for Development.* Washington, DC: World Bank.

———. 1997. *World Development Report 1997: The Role of the State in a Changing World.* Washington, DC: World Bank.

———. 2009. *World Development Report 2009: Reshaping Economic Geography.* Washington, DC: World Bank.

———. 2010. *Cities and Climate Change: An Urgent Agenda.* Washington, DC: World Bank.

———. 2013. *India: Urbanisation Beyond Municipalities.* Washington, DC: World Bank.

———. 2015. *Leveraging Urbanisation in South Asia: Managing Spatial Transformation for Prosperity and Liveability*, Conference Edition. Washington, DC: World Bank.

Wright, Frank Lloyd. 1958. *The Living City.* New York, NY: Horizon Press.

Wright, Henry. 1935. *Rehousing Urban America.* New York, NY: Columbia University Press.

Index

About the Author

Prasanna K. Mohanty is Chair Professor of Economics at the University of Hyderabad, teaching Urban Economics and Transport Economics. Dr Mohanty is Honorary Executive Chair of National Institute of Urban Management, Adviser to Centre for Good Governance, Hyderabad, and a Director in the Board of Reserve Bank of India.

An officer from the Indian Administrative Service, Dr Mohanty was Chief Secretary to the Government of Andhra Pradesh. He worked as the Mission Director, Jawaharlal Nehru National Urban Renewal Mission, Government of India; Director General, Centre for Good Governance, Hyderabad; Commissioner of metropolitan cities of Hyderabad and Visakhapatnam; and Vice-Chairman of Hyderabad Urban Development Authority.

Dr Mohanty earned his MA and PhD in Economics from Boston University. He was Rockefeller Foundation Post-doctoral Fellow at Harvard University. He has authored *Financing Cities in India: Municipal Reforms, Fiscal Accountability and Urban Infrastructure* (2016) and *Cities and Public Policy: An Urban Agenda for India* (2014) and co-edited *Urbanisation in India: Challenges, Opportunities and the Way Forward* (2014), published by SAGE.